CONTENTS

AF215386

M.LETSCHERT/SHUTTERSTOCK

Waag (p74)

KAVALENKAU/SHUTTERSTOCK

Joost van den Vondel statue, Vondelpark (p160)

AMSTERDAM

THE JOURNEY BEGINS HERE

It's incredible how little Amsterdam has changed since I first came here aged four. Its medieval core and canal ring are still entirely recognisable in the 17th-century paintings hanging in galleries like the stunning Rijksmuseum. And yet, over the past couple of decades I've been writing about the city for Lonely Planet, there have been radical changes – not only the regeneration of industrial areas like NDSM-werf's former shipyards, now home to artist studios, or even the construction of entire neighbourhoods on newly created islands, like IJburg and Houthaven. But above all, in Amsterdam's recent and momentous reckoning with its past, recognising the role of the slave trade and colonisation in the city's history and prosperity, and in its rapid uptake of sustainability strategies that include becoming a circular economy. In a sense, by drawing on its centuries of visionary ambition and determination, the city itself is coming full circle.

Catherine Le Nevez

lonelyplanet.com/authors/catherine-le-nevez

A Lonely Planet author since 2004, contributing to well over 100 guides, Catherine has a Doctorate in Creative Arts in Writing and insatiable wanderlust.

My favourite experience is the **Vondelpark** (p160). An urban oasis, it's beautiful in all seasons, from its scented summer rose gardens to blazing autumn foliage, frozen winter ponds and spring blossoms.

WHO GOES WHERE

Our writers and experts choose the places which, for them, define Amsterdam.

WUT_MOPPIE/SHUTTERSTOCK

As a regular visitor to the Netherlands, I find it almost miraculous that Amsterdam's Nieuwmarkt (pictured; p74), Plantage and the Eastern Islands (NPEI) still retain such a laid-back vibe, despite being super-central and packed with top-rate attractions. Within NPEI, my single favourite spot is cafe-restaurant **De Plantage** (p85). It's a delight, whether you're sipping wine, enjoying a refined yet good-value meal, or just walking past in the calming pre-dusk atmosphere.

Mark Elliott

Instagram@markbekaz

A UK-Belgian dual national, Mark has been writing about the Benelux countries for nearly 30 years. He has contributed to well over 70 guidebooks for numerous European and Asian countries.

DEBELL92/SHUTTERSTOCK

My favourite experience was getting off the downtown cobblestone to push my daughter's stroller around smoother, spacious pathways in Amsterdam Noord and around the green lungs of the Oost. In Oost, relaxing on park benches and encountering ducks and other birdlife in **Oosterpark** (pictured; p190) and **Park Frankendael** (p194) felt like a mini countryside escape (except with hot, tasty *frites* in hand).

Barbara Woolsey

Instagram@xo.babxi

Barbara is a travel writer who has been covering Amsterdam for Lonely Planet since 2019. She also frequently DJs at clubs and festivals in the Netherlands, Germany and beyond.

ALL THE ART

Masterpieces pack Amsterdam's world-class museums, where collections are founded on works by the Dutch Masters, including Rembrandt and later luminaries like Van Gogh. Fabulous museums are also dedicated to modern and contemporary art, along with art-in-the-makin-g at *broedplaatsen* ('breeding grounds') like Noord's massive warehouse NDSM Loods. Everywhere you go, you'll find original and unexpected public art, such as a Picasso sculpture in the Vondelpark.

Westergas

'Cultural village' **Westergas** (pictured; p110) brings together creative spaces across 19th-century former gasworks buildings. Among the highlights, **Museum Villa** presents playful and experiential contemporary art.

Culture Ferry

Museum-hop between 30 different locations aboard seasonally operating sloop boat **Cultuur Ferry** *(cultuurferry.nl)*, cruising the waterways in a figure-eight loop between Amsterdam Centraal and Museumplein.

Coming Soon

Amsterdam's next major contemporary art showcase will be the **Hartwig Museum** (p177), opening in 2028; in the run-up, get a preview at 'testing ground' **Hartwig Proxy**.

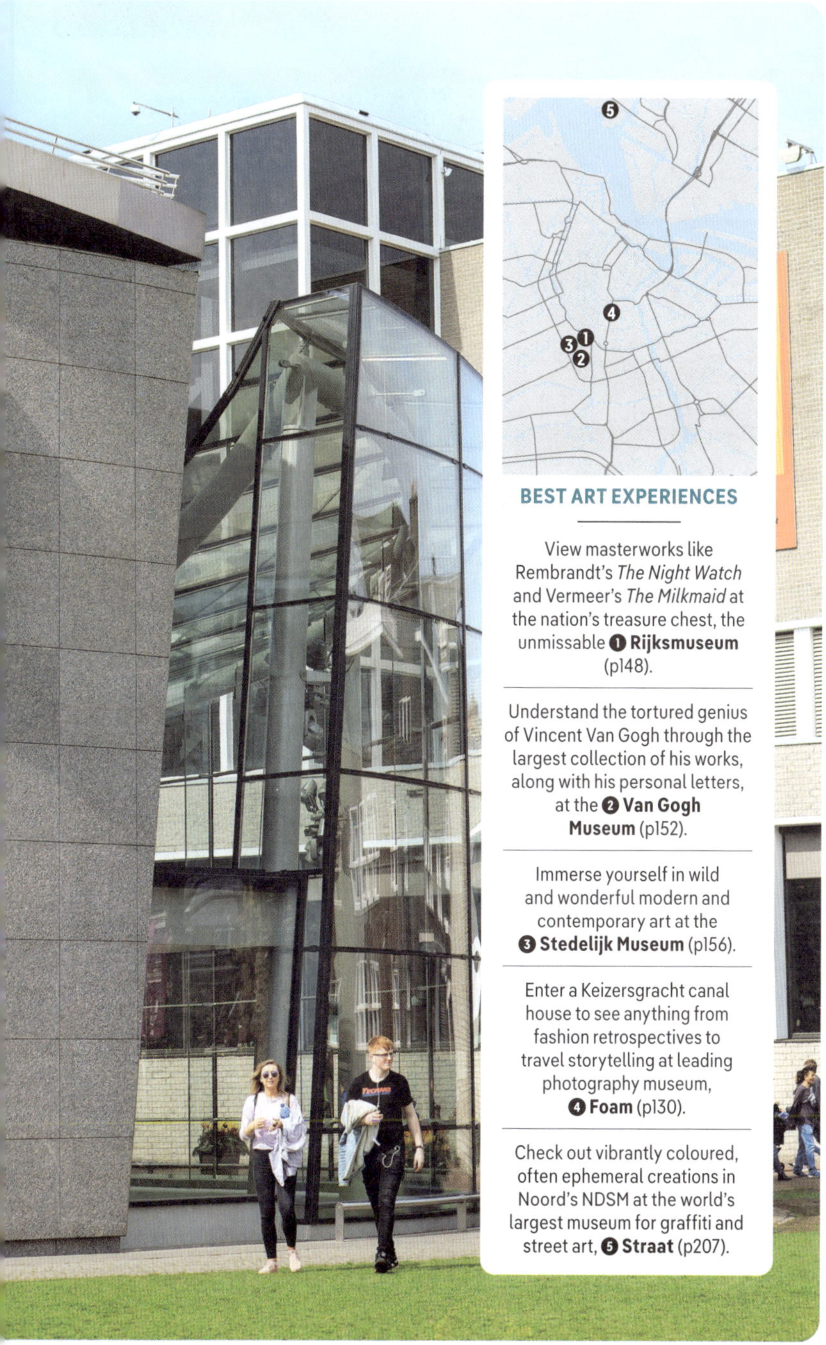

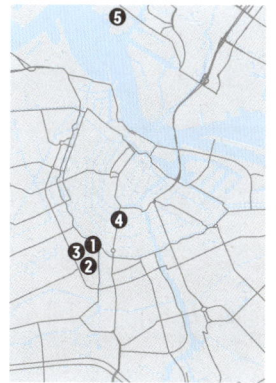

BEST ART EXPERIENCES

View masterworks like Rembrandt's *The Night Watch* and Vermeer's *The Milkmaid* at the nation's treasure chest, the unmissable ❶ **Rijksmuseum** (p148).

Understand the tortured genius of Vincent Van Gogh through the largest collection of his works, along with his personal letters, at the ❷ **Van Gogh Museum** (p152).

Immerse yourself in wild and wonderful modern and contemporary art at the ❸ **Stedelijk Museum** (p156).

Enter a Keizersgracht canal house to see anything from fashion retrospectives to travel storytelling at leading photography museum, ❹ **Foam** (p130).

Check out vibrantly coloured, often ephemeral creations in Noord's NDSM at the world's largest museum for graffiti and street art, ❺ **Straat** (p207).

COLORMAKER/SHUTTERSTOCK

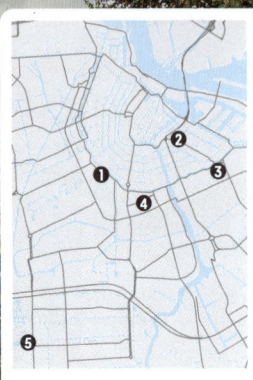

Hortus Botanicus (p82)

URBAN IDYLLS

Escaping Amsterdam's built environment is a breeze: the city is blessed with beautiful stretches of greenery. The varied parks and gardens are great places to picnic, spot birdlife, catch markets, attend concerts, find kids' playgrounds, and get active with sports.

Picnics

A picnic blanket is a good idea to guard against muddy ground. In most parks, barbecuing isn't permitted; in others, it's only allowed in designated areas.

Park Care

Amsterdam's parks and gardens have plentiful rubbish bins; use them to keep the environment pristine and protect local wildlife, or take rubbish with you.

BEST PARK & GARDEN EXPERIENCES

Unwind in Amsterdam's favourite green space, the ❶ **Vondelpark** (p160), a haven of manicured lawns, ponds with swans, sculptures, quaint cafes, footbridges and winding footpaths and cycleways.

Discover rare species at the 1638-established botanical garden ❷ **Hortus Botanicus** (p82), with a palm house, butterfly house and the world's first fully sustainable, climate-neutral greenhouse.

Experience Oost's green spaces at the almost-tropical ❸ **Oosterpark** (p190) and Park Frankendael's manicured gardens.

Trawl the Albert Cuypmarkt for picnic supplies and head to the undulating lawns and ponds of the ❹ **Sarphatipark** (p173) in the heart of De Pijp.

Climb through the treetops, meet goats and boat on the waterways in sprawling forest ❺ **Amsterdamse Bos** (p180).

VISIONARY ARCHITECTURE

Amsterdam's beauty was built on freedoms of trade, religion and aesthetics. Wealthy 17th-century merchants determined the city's look in essentially an early urban experiment. Its lovely canalscapes were spared from wartime destruction and the city has been careful to preserve its core from zealous developers. Today, contemporary additions continue taking shape beyond the historic centre.

Along the IJ River

Striking buildings include 21st-century icons like the glass-and-steel concert hall *Muziekgebouw aan 't IJ* (p91) and the gargantuan gateway-style **Pontsteiger** (pictured; p117) in pioneering climate-neutral neighbourhood Houthaven.

Rotterdam

A quick day trip from Amsterdam, Rotterdam rebuilt after it was flattened in WWII in adventurous, eye-popping styles. Among the latest additions is **FENIX** (p223), topped by a spiralling stainless-steel 'tornado'.

Arcam

The best place to glimpse the future of Amsterdam's urban landscape is **Arcam** (Amsterdam Architecture Foundation; p87), with exhibitions and runs guided tours.

BEST ARCHITECTURE EXPERIENCES

Stop by the ❶ **Oude Kerk** (p50), dating from 1306 in Gothic style and a testament of time as Amsterdam's oldest surviving building.

Admire the beautiful ❷ **Westerkerk** (p102), a Dutch Renaissance landmark on the Prinsengracht by city sculptor Hendrick de Keyser, who also designed the Noorderkerk and Zuiderkerk.

See the sumptuous interiors, rear coach house and hedged garden of a 1672 residence, now the ❸ **Museum Van Loon** (p132).

Witness the grandeur of Amsterdam's ❹ **Centraal Station** (p53), a turreted, 1889 red-brick neo-Renaissance/neo-Gothic marvel by Pierre Cuypers, who also designed the Rijksmuseum.

Be wowed by the Amsterdam School, Jugendstil and art-deco façade and spectacular interior of cinema ❺ **Koninklijk Theater Tuschinski** (p134).

TULIP TIME

Bursting into a rainbow of red, orange, yellow, pink, purple and white, tulips are a spectacular sight. The city has had a fervour for tulips ever since the heady days of 17th-century Tulipmania. Year-round you'll find everything from glass tulips to tulip-shaped artisan chocolates, and if you're here in season, opportunities to see the blooms abound.

BEST TULIP EXPERIENCES

Pre-empt the upcoming season on Nationale Tulpendag (National Tulip Day; third Saturday in January), when growers association Tulpen Promotie Nederland plants 200,000 tulips on ❶ **Museumplein** (p155).

Book for ❷ **Keukenhof's** (p235) mid-March to mid-May opening season to see seven million bulbs bloom.

Learn about the history of the tulip and speculative frenzy 'Tulipmania' at the Jordaan's delightful and illuminating ❸ **Amsterdam Tulip Museum** (p108).

Get up early to go behind the scenes of ❹ **Royal FloraHolland** (p183), where millions of blooms are sorted for shipping worldwide.

Shop for bulbs and kitschy souvenirs (wooden tulips, fluffy clogs) at the ❺ **Bloemenmarkt** (p129), Amsterdam's once-floating flower market (now perched on piles).

FROM LEFT: J. VANOVKINA/SHUTTERSTOCK, PAKIN SONGMOR/GETTY IMAGES

Amsterdam's Tulip Festival

Flower beds, floating flowers in ponds and waterways, and flower-lined routes through the city are part of the month-long **Tulp Festival** (Tulip Festival; tulpfestival.com) throughout April.

Bollenstreek Bike Rides

A quintessential Dutch experience in spring is cycling through tulip fields like those in the **Bollenstreek** (Bulb Region; p236). In summer, blooms here include dahlias.

High-Priced Horticulture

At the peak of the tulip boom in the 17th century, the best bulbs cost more than a canal house.

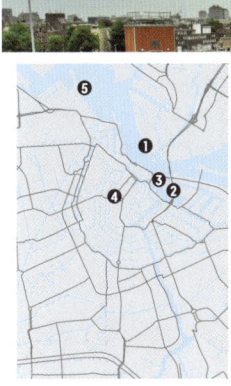

NEMO's rooftop (p89)

BEST VIEWING EXPERIENCES

Strap into a six-seater giant swing sailing over the 100m-high edge of 1970s office block turned attraction-packed skyscraper ❶ **A'DAM Tower** (p201).

Climb the external staircase (or enter from the museum) to reach boat-shaped NEMO's deck-like ❷ **roof terrace** (p89) for free city panoramas.

Sip sky- and light-themed cocktails at 11th-floor bar ❸ **LuminAir** (p92) or take in the 360-degree views out on its terrace.

Scale 376 spiralling steps to the top of the 109m-high tower at Delft's ❹ **Nieuwe Kerk** (p230) for views as far as Rotterdam and Den Haag.

Head to former pirate broadcasting station ❺ **REM** (p117), a red-metal rig that is now a one-of-a-kind bar-restaurant in the middle of the IJ River.

CITY VISTAS

Amsterdam's low-rise skyline means you don't have to head up to great heights to get elevated views looking down over its web of rivers and canals, charming gabled buildings, church bell towers and leafy stretches of greenery-filled parkland by day, and twinkling lights reflecting in the waterways by night.

Rooftop Bars

Sundowners on Amsterdam's rooftop bars are a fabulous way to take in the panoramas; check seasonal opening dates as many close outside the summer season.

Water-Level Views

For a completely different perspective, see the cityscapes below street level on a canal cruise (p27), with close-up views as you glide beneath fairy-lit humpbacked bridges.

11

Ice skating, Museumplein (p155)

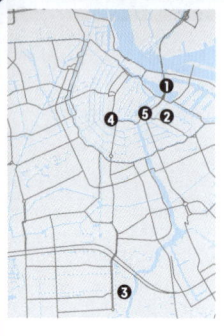

BEST EXPERIENCES FOR KIDS

Perform hands-on experiments and engage in activities like designing your own wind turbine at the fantastic interactive **❶ NEMO Science Museum** (p88).

Meet creatures great (like lions, elephants and giraffes) and small (such as arrow-dart frogs) at the historic and animal-friendly **❷ Artis Zoo** (p84).

Ride the miniature Amstel Trein, get lost in the yew-hedge maze, play minigolf and more in the **❸ Amstelpark** (p177).

Visit the enchanting 100-room mansion for adorable felt mice (and sets for the children's artist-author's later books, including a mouse roller-coaster) at **❹ Het Muizenhuis** (p66).

Descend to the large subterranean recreation site at **❺ Vrog** (p93) for streetwise activities from trick trampolining to parkour.

WITH KIDS

Amsterdam is one of Europe's most kid-friendly cities. Virtually all quarters of the city – except the Red Light District, of course – are fair game for the younger set, there are parks and playgrounds galore and sights and activities geared especially for kids.

Pancake Boat

From its dock in Amsterdam Noord, the **Pannenkoekenboot Amsterdam** (*Pancake Boat Amsterdam; amsterdam. pannenkoekenboot.nl*) runs 75-minute river cruises on the IJ accompanied by unlimited pancakes.

Seasonal Treats

Kids will love the skating rinks that spring up in public spaces, such as on **Museumplein** (p155). Don't miss treats such as *speculaas* (spiced biscuits), traditionally eaten around Sinterklaas (St Nicholas' Eve; 5 December).

TALES OF THE CITY

Having turned the grand old age of 750 in 2025 (and with origins stretching back further still), Amsterdam teems with history. As the nation rethinks, re-examines and reckons with dark aspects of its history, momentum is building across Amsterdam's wealth of outstanding museums to include a wider range of voices and tell richer, fuller stories.

'Golden Age'

Museums are addressing the 17th-century era of wealth accumulation, until recently referred to as the Gouden Eeuw ('Golden Age'), in light of its foundations on colonisation and slavery.

Jewish Cultural Quarter

Powerful **Joods Cultureel Kwartier** *(Jewish Cultural Quarter; jck.nl)* sights include the **Hollandsche Schouwburg** (p76) memorial, as well as the **Portuguese Synagogue** (p78), **Joods Museum** (p78) and **National Holocaust Museum** (p78).

Amsterdam Museum

Closed for renovations until 2028, the city's history museum – the **Amsterdam Museum** *(amsterdammuseum.nl)* – has satellite exhibitions, including projection mapping on a 200-sq-metre city model at **Amsterdam in Motion** (p114).

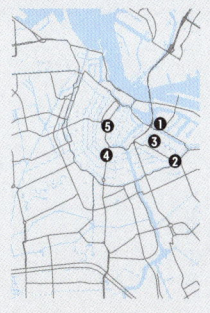

BEST EXHIBITION EXPERIENCES

Navigate seafaring in the 1656 Admiralty of Amsterdam storehouse and replica galleon in front of national maritime museum **❶ Het Scheepvaart-museum** (p85).

Ponder themes of race, ethnicity and identity at the reinvented **❷ Wereldmuseum** (World Museum; p188), particularly its profound *Our Colonial Inheritance* exhibition.

Reflect on the circumstances and actions undertaken in WWII Nazi-occupied Amsterdam at the moving **❸ Verzetsmuseum** (Dutch Resistance Museum; p78).

Dig into the **❹ Stadsarchief** (Amsterdam City Archives; p130), home to over 50km of shelves containing records of the history of its citizens.

Peer at objects spanning 115,000-year-old mollusc shells to 1980s mobile phones unearthed in the north–south metro line's construction at **❺ Below the Surface** (p48).

UNDER THE RADAR

Amsterdam's compact size means you don't have to venture far to get off the beaten track. Across this diverse city, you'll find fascinating local haunts and places to discover lesser-known sights like quirky and offbeat museums and galleries, beautiful outdoor spaces and unique ways to experience its waterways.

BEST UNDER-THE-RADAR EXPERIENCES

Distil your own rum during a 90-minute distilling workshop and tour at ❶ **Spirited Union Rum Company** (p165) in the trendy neighbourhood of Hoofddorppleinbuurt.

Paddle along Amsterdam's waterways by SUP from numerous locations, or take a kayaking tour through the Jordaan's charming canals with ❷ **Kayak in Amsterdam** (p107).

Windsurf, wingfoil, wakeboard, flyboard at sandy urban beach ❸ **Strand IJburg** (p95), or play beach volleyball or sand soccer, or hit the skate zone.

Browse makers markets, shop for Dutch design, see films and try cutting-edge food concepts at tram sheds turned cultural centre ❹ **De Hallen** (p167).

Escape Amsterdam's most crowded shopping high street, Kalverstraat, in shopping mall ❺ **Kalverpassage** (p67), containing unexpected works of art.

Ex-Squats

Longstanding counterculture history has given Amsterdam a stash of former squats that remain hotbeds of creativity, such as **OT301**, **OCCII**, and former fallout shelter **Vondelbunker** (pictured; p167).

Alternative Tours

Tours that Matter (toursthatmatter.com) dives into subjects like freedom, innovation, colonialism and fair trade, diverse society, urban agriculture and sustainability on walking and cycling tours.

Gig Guide

The best place to find out about live, often alternative gigs and concerts is gig guide **Hidden Agenda** (hidden agenda.nl); filter by venue or by genre.

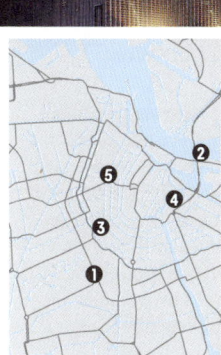

Melkweg (p134)

BEST FREE EXPERIENCES

Attend free lunchtime concerts from 12.30pm on Wednesdays lasting half an hour at Amsterdam's premier concert hall, the ❶ **Concertgebouw** (p155).

Catch at least one free event a week, such as evening concerts, jam sessions or workshops, at the Muziekgebouw's jazz stage, ❷ **Bimhuis** (p92).

Join hundreds of people stomping to high-BPM beats at ❸ **Melkweg's** (p134) long-running 'Techno Tuesday' – a rare free club event.

See uncut diamonds, watch diamond-polishing and be dazzled by sparkling jewels at fascinating diamond factory ❹ **Gassan** (p76) in Nieuwmarkt.

Listen to the organs being played during lunchtime concerts from 1pm to 1.30pm on Wednesdays at beautiful landmark church ❺ **Westerkerk** (p102).

FOR FREE

By any measure, Amsterdam is not a cheap destination and although the costs of accommodation and dining can quickly mount up, there is a bright side. Not only is the entire canal ring a UNESCO World Heritage Site (effectively a free living museum), but there are plenty of things to see and do for free.

Festivities

Amsterdam's festival calendar includes numerous free events, many held at outdoor locations such as Museumplein, Westerpark, Oosterpark, Noorderpark and Amsterdamse Bos during the summer months.

Markets

Browsing Amsterdam's multitude of open-air markets will give you a flavour of Amsterdam's local life, with food and drink stalls sometimes offering free tastings, too.

Perfect Days

Amsterdam's compact layout and superb cycling infrastructure and public transport makes it easy to pack a lot into your days. These itineraries are a starting point for exploring the city.

Van Gogh Museum (p152)

ALEXANDER TOLSTYKH/SHUTTERSTOCK

DAY 1

Vondelpark, Oud-West & Oud-Zuid

☼ Head to **Museumplein** (p155) to ogle the masterpieces at the **Van Gogh Museum** (p152) and **Rijksmuseum** (p148; book in advance). Modern-art buffs might want to swap the **Stedelijk Museum** (p156) for one of the others. They're lined up in a walkable row. For a nature-filled alternative, stroll in the green oasis of the **Vondelpark** (p160).

Lunch Slow-food favourite **Gartine** (p49) grows ingredients in its garden.

Medieval Centre

☼ Spend the afternoon in the Medieval Centre, the oldest part of the city. Explore the secret courtyard and gardens at the **Begijnhof** (p62). Walk up the street to the **Dam** (p54), where the **Royal Palace** (p46), **Nieuwe Kerk** (p54) and **Nationaal Monument** (p54) provide a dose of Dutch history. Bend over to sip your *jenever* (Dutch gin) like a local at atmospheric **Wynand Fockink** (p52).

Dinner Make a reservation at **D'Vijff Vlieghen** (p52), a jewel spread across five 17th-century canal houses.

Southern Canal Ring

☾ When the sun sets, it's time to par-tee at neon-lit **Leidseplein** (p135). **Paradiso** (p134) and **Melkweg** (p134) host the coolest agendas. Otherwise, head to the clubs and *cafés* (pubs) around the square or nearby **Rembrandtplein** (p131). For all-hours clubbing, head out of the centre to venues like **Radion** (p167).

DAY 2

De Pijp & Zuid

☼ Browse the **Albert Cuypmarkt** (p172), Amsterdam's largest street market, where stalls are piled high with cheeses, fish, *stroopwafels* (caramel-syrup-filled waffles) and bargain clothing. Then hit the high-tech **Heineken Experience** (p175) or discover Amsterdam School architecture at the **Museum De Dageraad** (p174).

Lunch Brunch is De Pijp's forte; **Bakers & Roasters** (p78) does it best (and all day).

Western Canal Ring, Jordaan & the West

☼ Immerse yourself in the **Negen Straatjes** (p103), a noughts-and-crosses board of speciality shops in the Western Canal Ring. The **Anne Frank Huis** (p100) is also in the neighbourhood, and it's a must (book well ahead). The claustrophobic rooms, their windows still covered with blackout screens, give an all-too-immediate feel for Anne's life in hiding.

Dinner Canal views rival the modern European cuisine at **De Belhamel** (p107).

Western Canal Ring, Jordaan & the West

☾ Spend the evening in the congenial Jordaan. Hoist a glass on a canal-side terrace at **'t Smalle** (p103), or quaff beers at heaps of other *gezellig* (cosy) haunts – some of the city's most charming *bruin cafés* are tucked in the Jordaan's narrow streets and alongside its canals.

DAY 3

Nieuwmarkt, Plantage & the Eastern Islands

☼ Wander through the **Waterlooplein Flea Market** (p75) in Nieuwmarkt. Nearby is Rembrandt's studio, where he lived and worked during his most prolific years; it's now the **Museum Rembrandthuis** (p72). Neighbouring **Gassan Diamonds** (p76) gives free tours, giving you the opportunity to see diamond cutters in action. Or check out the intriguing **Verzetsmuseum** (Dutch Resistance Museum; p78), or sea treasures at **Het Scheepvaartmuseum** (p85).

Lunch Try a hot-spiced Surinamese sandwich at **Tokoman** (p87).

Amsterdam Noord

☼ Hop on a free, five-minute ferry to **Noord** (p198), one of the city's coolest neighbourhoods. Check out the exhibits at the **Eye Film-museum** (p205), the artists' studios in the sprawling **NDSM Loods** (p202) and street-art museum **Straat** (p207). Ascend attraction-packed **A'DAM Tower** (p201) for views across the IJ River to the city centre.

Dinner Views peak at **Moon** (p201), the revolving restaurant atop A'DAM Tower.

Oosterpark & East of the Amstel

☾ There is fantastic nightlife in Noord; or, back on the city side of the IJ, spend the evening at **De Ysbreeker** (p197), looking out over the bustling Amstel River.

WHEN TO GO

Each season in Amsterdam has its own charms, from spring tulips to summer picnics, autumn festivals and winter *gezelligheid* (conviviality, cosiness).

Amsterdam is a year-round destination: there's no longer a real 'tourist season' at all. Crowds flock for tulip season, which officially starts on Nationale Tulpendag (National Tulip Day; p155), the third Saturday in January, when Museumplein is carpeted with 200,000 tulips, but really comes to life from around mid-March to mid-May. As the weather warms up, the city fills with visitors throughout the summer months, with plenty of opportunities to escape rising temperatures in the city's lush parks, gardens and forest, and out on its picturesque waterways. As autumn leaves start to fall from September/October, it's a fabulous time for photography as the gabled canal houses are revealed. The city is at its quietest in winter (outside of lively celebrations over Christmas and New Year), but sights stay open and museums and *bruin cafés* (traditional pubs) make wonderful refuges from the elements. No matter when you're here, festivals abound.

⊕ I LIVE HERE

SPRING COLOUR

Jurriaan Teulings is a Dutch travel photographer living in De Pijp. @jurrpix

My perfect spring day is catching 'tulip fever' in less touristic East Amsterdam. Enjoy breakfast/lunch in **Javastraat** (p192), stroll through blooming **Flevopark** (p187) and cross the bridge over the Amsterdam-Rijnkanaal railings adorned with tulips. End up at **Oranjesluizen**, a pretty set of sluices you can walk across. Opposite, **Schellingwoude** is an incredibly picturesque Dutch village, or walk west to Noord and ferry back.

THE NETHERLANDS' LARGEST BAROMETER

Each night the Hotel Okura Amsterdam's roof is illuminated by LED lights reflecting the barometer's reading for the following day. Blue lights forecast a bright, sunny day. Green means bad weather. White (the most common) means the weather will be changeable.

Hotel Okura Amsterdam (p242)

Weather Through the Year

JANUARY	FEBRUARY	MARCH	APRIL	MAY	JUNE
Avg. daytime max: **6°C**	Avg. daytime max: **7°C**	Avg. daytime max: **10°C**	Avg. daytime max: **13°C**	Avg. daytime max: **17°C**	Avg. daytime max: **19°C**
Days of rainfall: **17**	Days of rainfall: **13**	Days of rainfall: **14**	Days of rainfall: **13**	Days of rainfall: **13**	Days of rainfall: **12**

CLIMATE ADAPTATION

Lying at or below sea level, Amsterdam is vulnerable to rising sea levels and heavier downpours as a result of global warming. The city is adapting to the changing climate by increasing its greenery across rooftops and creating new open, nature-filled spaces.

Headline Festivals

Amsterdam's biggest event is **King's Day** (Koningsdag; p54), on King Willem-Alexander's birthday, 27 April (26 April if the 27th is a Sunday). Celebrations start the night before on King's Night (Koningsnacht); from 6am, the city becomes a sea of orange outfits and *vrijmarkt* (flea market) stalls. 🌸 **April**

One of the world's LGBTIQ+ capitals, Amsterdam has over 500 events in the 15-day-long **Pride Amsterdam** (p250); the highlight is its waterborne Canal Parade, with 80 spectacular floats sailing through the city. 🌸 **July/August**

Massive five-day (and night) electronic music festival/ industry conference **ADE** (Amsterdam Dance Event; p134) has more than 1000 events at over 200 venues across the city. 🍂 **October**

Light-art displays illuminate the waterways (with app-based routes and boat cruises) during the **Amsterdam Light Festival** (*amsterdamlightfestival.com*), part of the magical Amsterdam Winter Festival. ❄️ **Late November–mid-January**

Local Favourites

From Friday to Sunday over the Easter weekend, electronic music, art and sustainability festival **DGTL** (p203) at NDSM-werf in Amsterdam Noord runs on renewable energy and has plant-based food stalls. 🌸 **March/April**

On 1 July, **Keti Koti** (p155), meaning 'broken chains', has a parade from Waterlooplein to Oosterpark for the national commemoration of Dutch colonies' abolition of slavery, followed by a huge party on Museumplein with stalls sizzling up Surinamese BBQ and serving syrup-laced shaved ice. 🌸 **July**

Parks, squares, canal houses and floating stages on the picturesque *grachten* (city canals) host concerts by talented young classical and jazz musicians during the 10-day **Grachtenfestival** (*grachtenfestival.nl*). 🌸 **August**

Open-air deck-chair cinema **Pluk de Nacht** (*Seize the Night; plukdenacht.nl*) screens independent arthouse, documentary, animation and short films (in English or with subtitles) over 10 summer evenings overlooking the IJ River. 🌸 **August**

🛡️ I LIVE HERE

WINTER ILLUMINATIONS

Li Chiao is a UX designer from Los Angeles who's been working in Amsterdam's fast-paced tech scene for more than a decade.

In December and January, it's fun to see the Amsterdam Light Festival by boat. Different artists create light sculptures along the canals and some are interactive. You can walk or bike the route too, but the best way to see it is on the water.

Amsterdam Light Festival

AMOC

The Atlantic Meridional Overturning Circulation (AMOC) – part of global ocean circulation that includes the Gulf Stream, transporting warm water from the tropics to the North Atlantic and keeping temperatures mild – is weakening, which would cause dropping temperatures and sea ice off the Dutch coast.

JULY	AUGUST	SEPTEMBER	OCTOBER	NOVEMBER	DECEMBER
Avg. daytime max: **21°C**	Avg. daytime max: **21°C**	Avg. daytime max: **18°C**	Avg. daytime max: **14°C**	Avg. daytime max: **10°C**	Avg. daytime max: **7°C**
Days of rainfall: **13**	Days of rainfall: **14**	Days of rainfall: **13**	Days of rainfall: **15**	Days of rainfall: **17**	Days of rainfall: **17**

GET PREPARED
FOR AMSTERDAM

Useful things to load in your bag, your ears and your brain.

Clothes

Layers No matter the time of year, pack layers of clothing, bearing in mind that the Dutch weather is notoriously fickle and there can be chilly spells even in summer. In spring, summer and autumn, a light trench coat or jacket and a small travel umbrella will mean you're prepared for the weather. In winter, bring a proper heavy coat, woolly hat, scarf and gloves to ward off the often-freezing temperatures (and you'll still want that umbrella).

Bags A stylish slimline backpack will blend in anywhere. Other than small handbags/daypacks, bags typically have to be checked at museum cloakrooms.

Smart casual wear In all but the most upmarket restaurants, smart jeans, a nice shirt and proper shoes/boots are acceptable.

Cycle-friendly clothing Bring covered footwear and light, breathable clothing that won't get caught in spokes.

Manners

The Dutch are renowned for being straight talkers. Don't be offended if locals give you their frank, unvarnished opinion. It's not considered impolite; rather, it comes from the desire to be direct and honest, and communicate clearly.

Never walk in bike lanes (marked by white lines and bicycle symbols) and always look both ways before crossing them – for your safety and everyone else's.

📖 READ

The Diary of a Young Girl (*The Diary of Anne Frank*; Anne Frank; 1947) Moving account of a young girl's life hiding from the Nazis.

The House of Fortune (Jessie Burton; 2022) Sequel to *The Miniaturist* (2014), set in 1705 Amsterdam after the excesses of the 17th century.

The Floating Amsterdam Flower Shop (Annabel French; 2025) Romance on Amsterdam's canals and rivalry threatening a blossoming business.

Amsterdam: Urban Architecture & Living Environments (Sandra Hofmeister & Anneke Bokern; 2025) Contemporary architecture.

Words

Hallo (ha-*loh*) Hello
Groetjes (*khroot*-yes) Greetings
Dag (dakh) Hello, goodbye; used for everyday interactions.
Tot ziens (tot zeens) Formal way of saying goodbye.
Tjuus (choos) Informal, cute form of goodbye.
Excuseer mij (eks-kew-*zeyr* mey) Excuse me
Dank je wel (dahnk yuh vell) Thank you (often shortened to 'dank')
Graag gedaan (*khraakh* khuh-*daan*) You're welcome
Goedemorgen (hood-*mor*-khun) Good morning (formal)
Goedenavond (hood-un-*ah*-vohnd) Good evening (formal)
Hoe gaat het met u/jou? (hoo khaat het met ew/yaw) How are you? (polite/informal)
Ja (yaa) Yes
Nee (ney) No

Alstublieft/alsjeblieft (al-stew-*bleeft*/a-shuh-*bleeft*) Please (polite/informal)
Hoe gaat het met u/jou? (hoo khaat huht met ew/yaw) How are you? (polite/informal)
Goed, en met u/jou? (khoot en met ew/yaw) Fine, and you? (polite/informal)
Proost! (prohst) Cheers!
Kunt u alstublieft helpen? (kunt ew al-stew-*bleeft* hel-puhn) Could you please help me?
Spreekt u Engels? (spreykt ew *eng*-uhls) Do you speak English?
Ik begrijp het niet (ik buh-*khreyp* huht neet) I don't understand.
Ik kijk alleen maar (ik keyk a-*leyn* maar) I'm just looking.
Hoeveel kost het? (hoo-*veyl* kost huht) How much is it?
Wat kan u aanbevelen? (wat kan ew *aan*-buh-vey-luhn) What would you recommend?

📺 WATCH

Van der Valk (Channel 3 & ITV; 1972–77, 1991–92 & 2020–24) Cult-classic crime drama about a street-smart detective.

Nightwatching (Peter Greenaway; 2007; pictured above) Period film depicting civilian militiamen seeking to be immortalised in a group portrait.

Wild Amsterdam (Mark Verkerk; 2018) Offbeat documentary narrated by Abatutu, a tomcat.

Dirty Lines (Pieter Bart Korthuis; 2022) Comedy-drama set in 1980s Amsterdam based on real events.

A Small Light (Joan Rater; 2023) Award-winning biographical miniseries about Miep Gies, who helped the Frank family in WWII.

🎧 LISTEN

Geef Mij Maar Amsterdam (*I Prefer Amsterdam*; Sophie Straat; 2020) Contemporary cover of the 1955 classic.

Republic of Amsterdam Radio (republicof amsterdamradio.com) Online radio station with music, podcasts and interviews from Dutch and international artists.

Broadcast Amsterdam (broadcastamsterdam.nl) Live music, gig guides and local podcasts, including restaurant reviews, trends and seasonal tips.

The One About Haunted Amsterdam (stuffdutchpeoplelike .com/podcast) Podcast by Stuff Dutch People Like covering Amsterdam's dark past.

Schiphol International Airport

GETTING THERE

Amsterdam is exceptionally well connected. Major global hub Schiphol International Airport is located 18km southwest of the city centre, served by trains, buses and taxis, and trains link Amsterdam with the rest of the Netherlands and destinations across Europe, including direct Eurostar services to London.

Visitor Transport Tickets

An **Amsterdam Travel Ticket** *(gvb.nl; 1/2/3 days €18/24/30)* is a paper chip card that allows unlimited transport, including to and from Schiphol Airport; you can purchase it at ticket machines and GVB service desks at the airport and major train stations, or pre-order it online for collection at the same locations. The **Amsterdam & Region Travel Ticket** *(€21/31.50/40.50)* version includes day-trip destinations (such as Haarlem) in the surrounding area.

Wi-Fi

Schiphol has fast, free wi-fi throughout the airport: select Airport_Free_Wifi.

SIM Cards

SIM cards at the airport are expensive; you can find them at the Airport Telecom Shop or the Albert Heijn supermarket in Schiphol Plaza. Alternatively, consider buying an eSIM for the Netherlands before travelling.

Taxis & Ride-Hailing Services

Especially late at night, when trains and buses are less frequent (and road traffic is lightest), taking a taxi may be more convenient. It takes around 25 to 40 minutes to the city centre and costs from €40 to €80. Only take official taxis, departing from stand A1 in front of Schiphol Plaza. Ride-hailing services (Uber and Bolt are the main operators) may work out cheaper; meet drivers at app pick-up points E1 to E6 further northwest on Koepelstraat.

FROM THE AIRPORT TO THE CITY CENTRE

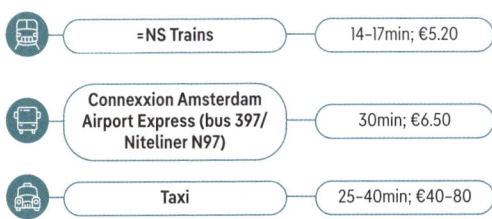

=NS Trains		14–17min; €5.20
Connexxion Amsterdam Airport Express (bus 397/ Niteliner N97)		30min; €6.50
Taxi		25–40min; €40–80

TIP

Travelators and lifts/ elevators located behind the ticket machines lead to Schiphol's train station beneath the terminal (platform 3). Frequent services include up to eight trains an hour (fewer at night) that make the trip to Amsterdam's Centraal Station (p53).

V. E/SHUTTERSTOCK

Centraal Station (p53)

OTHER POINTS OF ENTRY

Rail

In the heart of the city, Amsterdam Centraal Station has Eurostar services from London, Paris and Brussels; ICE services to Frankfurt; Nightjet services to Vienna; and European Sleeper services to Berlin. (DSB services to Copenhagen are expected to launch in 2026.) Amsterdam Zuid has international services from Brussels, with more destinations in the works.

Bus

FlixBus, serving destinations across Europe, has bus stops at Sloterdijk, to the west of the city centre, and Bijlmer ArenA, located in Amsterdam's southeast. Both are connected to Amsterdam Centraal Station by train and metro. Sloterdijk is also the terminus for European bus services by BlaBlaCar Bus, and Prague services by RegioJet.

Ferry

DFDS Seaways has overnight car and passenger ferry crossings, with cabins and onboard entertainment, sailing nightly between North Shields, near Newcastle, in the UK and the port of IJmuiden, 32km to the northwest of Amsterdam. IJmuiden is linked by a coach service from the ferry port to Amsterdam Centraal Station.

FROM LEFT: WOLF PHOTOGRAPHY/SHUTTERSTOCK, ERMAN GUNES/SHUTTERSTOCK

Negen Straatjes (Nine Streets; p103)

GETTING AROUND

Amsterdam's centre is easily walkable, while the surrounding neighbourhoods are perfect for cycling, and the city has a superb public transport network of trams, buses and metros, and free ferries.

Walking

Busy streets and narrow lanes mean the city's central neighbourhoods are easiest to explore on foot, which also allows for serendipitous discoveries of the cosy *bruin cafés* (traditional pubs), restaurants and charming shops that make Amsterdam so special.

When navigating the historic central canal ring, remember that the major canals all run in a horseshoe-shaped loop, in alphabetical order (the only exception is the Singel, once a fortification line, which forms the innermost ring). It will also help to familiarise yourself with the locations of the main squares Dam (800m south of Centraal Station), and Leidseplein and Rembrandtplein (both in the Southern Canal Ring).

TIP

If you're only planning to cycle short distances, an alternative to hiring a bicycle for a day is to use bike-hire apps with pay-per-minute plans such as **Donkey Republic** (donkey. bike).

Bicycle

Cycling is a way of life in the Netherlands. Bikes are more common than cars in Amsterdam, and 42% of all journeys are on *fietsen* (bikes). It's an ideal way to get around all but the busiest or narrowest streets, and especially good for accessing parks and neighbourhoods beyond the centre.

Rental shops are everywhere; you'll have to show a passport or European national ID card and leave a credit-card authorisation or pay a deposit (usually €75 to €100). Prices per 24-hour period for basic 'coaster-brake' bikes average €15. Bikes with gears and handbrakes cost more. Electric bikes start from €40 for 24 hours. Theft insurance (standard/electric bikes from €5/10 per day) is strongly advised.

Choose a rental company that doesn't have branding to blend in.

Take care to ride in the red-paved bike lanes, not on pedestrian footpaths, and to watch out for tram tracks, pedestrians and other cyclists.

Tram

Most public transport within the city is on its distinctive blue-and-white trams. Many of the 15 lines converge on Amsterdam Centraal Station. The vehicles are fast, frequent and ubiquitous.

Bus

In areas with fewer trams, the gaps are filled by buses (all will be electric by 2030).

Metro

Amsterdam has five metro lines extending to the outer suburbs. They're mostly used by commuters; line M52 is handy for visitors, running from Amsterdam Noord via Centraal Station and Rokin (near Dam), Vijzelgracht (in the Southern Canal Ring), De Pijp, and Europaplein (in Zuid).

TIP
Amsterdam's trams, buses and metros stop running for the night at around midnight to 12.30am, at which point the city's network of 11 night buses takes over. Regular services start up again around 6am.

PUBLIC TRANSPORT ESSENTIALS

GVB App
Amsterdam's public transport is run by **GVB** *(gvb.nl)*. Its excellent app incorporates the journey planner 9292.nl, which calculates your most efficient journey options and provides live transport updates including crowd estimates.

OVpay
For one-off journeys, if you don't have a travel card, by using OVpay you can check in and out with your contactless debit or credit card or phone. It's charged per kilometre plus a fixed base rate, and billed as a single transaction at the end of each day (no prior registration needed). You'll need to use the same card/payment method to both check in and out.

Day Tickets
GVB has day tickets and multiday ticket options (up to seven days), available as paper chip tickets or as barcode tickets within the GVB app.

Travel Cards
An Amsterdam Travel Ticket or Amsterdam & Region Travel Ticket can be a great money-saver.

The Amsterdam Travel Ticket is valid for unlimited travel by NS trains, the Connexxion Amsterdam Airport Express bus 397, and the Niteliner N97, and unlimited access to all GVB trams, buses, night buses and metros.

A wide-ranging option is the Amsterdam & Region Travel Ticket, which is valid for unlimited travel by bus, tram, metro and train in Amsterdam and the region with the operators GVB, NS trains, Connexxion buses, and regional EBS buses that go to towns such as Haarlem, Muiden and Zaanse Schans.

I amsterdam City Card
Amsterdam's tourist pass, the **I amsterdam City Card** *(iamsterdam.com),* includes GVB trams, metros, buses and ferries (but not transport to/from Schiphol Airport), 24 hours' bike rental and a canal cruise, along with admission to over 70 museums and attractions (though there are notable exceptions).

Durations range from one to five days. Buy a digital card on the website, or a physical card at the I amsterdam store at Amsterdam Centraal Station.

Checking In & Out
Check in on each ride by tapping your day ticket or travel card to the reader, and tap again on exiting to check out. Your card will be valid after checking in on your first journey.

Ferry

Free passenger and bicycle ferries cross the IJ River to Amsterdam Noord, making them a great way to explore lesser-visited areas. Most depart from the waterfront behind Centraal Station; line F3 to Buiksloterweg (the most popular for sightseeing in Amsterdam Noord) runs frequently during the day and more intermittently at night.

Taxi & Ride-Hailing Services

Taxis are not an efficient way to get around; Amsterdam's web of canals and traffic makes travel slow, and they are usually only available at stands and in busy areas. Locals generally prefer ride-hailing services; Uber and Bolt are the main operators.

Car

Avoid driving in central Amsterdam. The city presents numerous challenges, including its maze of narrow streets, often blocked by unloading trucks; unfenced canals; abundant bicycle lanes; and tram tracks (80% of inner-city streets have a speed limit of 30 km/h). Parking is scant and wildly expensive. Check the website amsterdam.nl/en/traffic-transport/low-emission-zone/cars for details of low-emission vehicle requirements within the A10 ring road and P+R (park and ride) locations.

All streets in the central canal ring are one-way, and you must drive on the right. When approaching intersections, some canal bridges might not have traffic signs. Watch out for pedestrians and bikes.

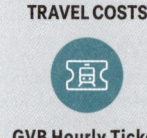

TRAVEL COSTS

CERI BREEZE/SHUTTERSTOCK

GVB Hourly Ticket
1 hour €3.40
1 night bus ride
€5.60

GVB Day Ticket
1 day €9.50
7 days €42.50

**I amsterdam
City Card**
1 day €65
5 days €135

 ACCESSIBILITY

Centuries-old buildings mean Amsterdam is only moderately equipped to meet the needs of travellers with reduced mobility, but improvements are helping improve its accessibility. Most canal cruises, buses and metro stations are wheelchair accessible. Some trams have wide-opening doors and levelled platforms; those that don't will not be easy for those in wheelchairs. Check **GVB** (gvb.nl/en/accessible-public-transport) for wheelchair-friendly stops, use the GVB journey planner's accessibility option, or configure virtual stop assistance in the app. **Accessible Travel Netherlands** (accessibletravel.nl) and **Able Amsterdam** (ableamsterdam.com) are good resources for further information.

Boat cruise on the Amstel River

HOW TO...

Navigate Amsterdam's Canals

Water makes up more than a third of Amsterdam's surface area. Threading through the city, upwards of 165 canals, including newly built and uncovered historic waterways, wind across 75km, spanned by some 2069 public road, cycle and pedestrian bridges – more than any other city in the world.

Strolling along the banks of its medieval canals and UNESCO-listed 17th-century *grachtengordel* (canal ring) is enchanting, but getting out on the water gives you a completely different perspective of the city.

Boat Cruises

Canal cruises are a delightful way to see the city. Several operators depart from moorings at Centraal Station, Damrak, Rokin and opposite the Rijksmuseum in the Southern Canal Ring. Prices are similar. To avoid the steamed-up glass window effect, look for a boat with an open seating area. On a night tour you'll see the bridges lit up (these tours usually cost a bit more).

The I amsterdam City Card includes a free cruise with a choice of several operators, including Blue Boat, Mokumboot, Stromma and Lovers.

A multitude of other options include brunch and dinner cruises.

DIY Boating

Hiring a boat for a few hours lets you glide past landmarks and explore out-of-the-way areas at your own pace. Numerous outfits hire boats typically accommodating six or more passengers; the electric boats are emission-free and quiet. You don't need a boat licence or experience (instruction is given at pick-up). The minimum rental age is 18.

Sports & Activities

Opportunities are also available to explore the canals on guided kayak or SUP tours, or to hire a kayak or SUP to paddle yourself.

Swimming is possible at designated areas like Marinehaven (p92).

Canals and ponds freeze over less often than they used to due to the warming climate, but in years they do, skaters take to the ice. Stay away from the ice unless you see large groups of people and be very careful at the edges and under bridges – areas with weak ice.

BOATING RULES

Stay on the waterways' right (starboard) side.

Commercial traffic has right of way, as do longer and/ or taller boats, and boats on your right.

Speed limits vary between 6km/h and 7.5km/h (the top speed for many electric rental boats).

Life jackets/ vests are only compulsory for children under eight but check rental companies have them on board for all passengers.

It's illegal to drink alcohol (or take drugs) while in control of a boat.

No shouting or amplified music.

Many bridges have low clearance (less than 2m).

Switch on your lights at dusk.

SERHII_TESLIUK_TESLA/SHUTTERSTOCK

OVERTOURISM

Amsterdam's wildly effective publicity has seen it become a victim of its own success. The city's population in 2024 of 933,680 people was dwarfed by a staggering 22.9 million overnight visitors – an increase of 472.5% this century – *and* 15.1 million day-trippers. Overtourism problems upending residents' lives and impacting visitors' enjoyment are now being rebalanced by city authorities. When travelling here, you can be part of the solution.

A Balancing Act

Today's numbers are all the more astonishing considering that Amsterdam's year-2000 population of 730,000 welcomed a then-record 4 million tourists. By 2019, overnight stays had skyrocketed to 21 million, prompting the city to take the extraordinary step of no longer actively promoting itself as a tourist destination.

Current figures could actually be higher (up to 25.4 million for 2024 and 24.9 million for 2025, based on 2019 projections) if not for a raft of measures since introduced as part of its 'City in Balance' objectives. These set out to discourage throngs disturbing residential neighbourhoods, short-term apartment rentals driving rents and property prices up, and local shops and community services being displaced by souvenir and snack vendors – all of which threaten to destroy the charm and free-spirited culture that attracted visitors here in the first place.

Quality & Quantity

Rebalancing has seen a fundamental shift in the city's tourism image – away from a place for hard-partying groups seeking a free-for-all of alcohol, sex and drugs. So far this decade, measures in the city centre have included banning Red Light District tours and cannabis smoking in the street, curbing bar opening hours,

Choose quieter times
Midweek is quieter than weekends and (except for Christmas and New Year), winter is quieter than spring to autumn.

Reduce your carbon footprint
Excellent rail connections include direct London services and European night trains.

Find local festivals
Scores of smaller, less inundated options take place throughout the year.

Take meaningful tours
Look for insightful tour alternatives such as refugee-guided cruises with Rederij Lampedusa (p91).

Reduce waste
Bring a reusable bottle and fill it at one of Amsterdam's 500 taps and fountains, mapped at waternet.nl.

Get involved
Rent a boat and equipment from Canal Motorboats (p109) and fish plastic out of the canals.

Respect the city
Don't block footpaths, walk in cycle lanes, overdo selfies, litter, make excessive noise or get messy. Treat Amsterdammers' home the way you'd want others to treat yours.

proposing relocating the Red Light District's brothels altogether, and launching a 'Stay Away' campaign deterring disruptive behaviour.

To claw numbers back to manageable levels, in 2021 the city set a target of 20 million overnight stays a year. It aims to achieve it over the coming years with a ban on new hotels (once the handful currently under construction are completed, a hotel will have to close before a new one can open) and a cap on the number of beds. Restrictions on increasingly regulated holiday rentals like Airbnb limit hosts to 15 days per year in the city centre and De Pijp, and 30 days elsewhere in Amsterdam. The city has also levied Europe's highest per-night, per-person tourist tax of 12.5%. From 2026, it will reduce river and ocean-going cruise ships, with plans to relocate its dock out of the city by 2035.

Combating overtourism's waste, pollution, litter and stress on resources is also crucial for Amsterdam to achieve its world-leading sustainability goals that include climate-proofing and adopting a circular economy by 2050.

VISITING RESPONSIBLY

Amsterdam's historic centre and 17th-century canal ring attract the lion's share of visitors. Many never even venture any further, but it's only a tiny facet of the city. By spreading out, not only will you help take pressure off this small, densely concentrated area, you'll discover a mosaic of local neighbourhoods home to all kinds of museums, sprawling parks and forest, unique shops, vibrant nightlife and rich and diverse local life.

Staying in one of Amsterdam's neighbourhoods will help alleviate strain on the city centre and can cost considerably less. Avoid private holiday rentals that contribute to the housing shortage (hotels can often work out cheaper). If you're self-catering, look for apartment hotels with kitchen facilities.

Superb cycling infrastructure and public transport also extend to the surrounding regions, filled with grand historic cities, classic Dutch landscapes, beaches and exhilarating activities. Day trips from the city are as little as 15 minutes away by train. It's also entirely viable to stay outside the city and day-trip into Amsterdam.

VERONIKA GALKINA/SHUTTERSTOCK

Magere Brug (p124)

KAJAHIIS/SHUTTERSTOCK

Poffertjes

DINING OUT

Amsterdam's sizzling food scene spans a rich and diverse smorgasbord, from classic and reinvented Dutch recipes to plant-based and global cuisine.

As part of Amsterdam's sustainability initiatives and commitment to a circular economy, there's a wave of environmentally aware, health-conscious establishments. Vegetarian and/or vegan options are proliferating across the city. Reducing food waste is a priority and homegrown produce is also ramping up; by 2030, at least 25% of its food will come from the region.

Across the dining landscape, you'll find an increasing focus on wine, cocktail and craft-beer pairings. And this multinational city, home to 174 nationalities, has a cornucopia of cuisines from countries all over the world.

Amsterdam is a major startup hub, which extends to its dining scene. All over the city you'll find expanding minichains of local eateries. Popular ones include Stach (gourmet sandwiches and deli items), SLA (design-your-own salads), De Bakkerswinkel (baked goods) and the Butcher (burgers); there are countless others. Foodhallen (p167), in De Hallen tram-depot turned cultural-complex, has a host of food stands under one roof surrounding a communal dining area. It's a fantastic place to take the city's dining temperature.

Dutch Specialities

Hearty, warming traditional Dutch cuisine revolves around meat, potatoes and vegetables. Typical comfort-food dishes include *stamppot* (potatoes mashed with vegetables and topped with sausages), *hutspot* ('hotchpotch' stew of potatoes, carrots,

Best Amsterdam Dishes	HARING	KIBBELING	STROOPWAFELS	POFFERTJES
	Herring; prized Hollandse Nieuwe is only caught from May to September.	Battered small pieces of whitefish (such as cod or hake).	Cookie-like wafers sandwiched together with sticky caramel syrup.	Puffy mini-pancakes dusted with icing sugar; a market-stall favourite.

onions and braised meat), *erwtensoep* (split pea soup with bacon or smoked sausage and thick rye bread) and *boerenkool met worst* (mashed potatoes with kale and smoked sausage).

Pannenkoeken are pancakes; the Dutch variety is thin and huge, served one to a plate and topped with savoury or sweet toppings, constituting a meal in itself.

Desserts include *appeltaart* (tall apple pie made from brown-sugar shortcrust pastry filled with cinnamon apples) accompanied by *slagroom* (whipped cream), *spekkoek* (layered spice cake) and *hangop* (thick, creamy strained yoghurt with fruit compote).

Fresh winds are blowing through the Dutch traditional kitchen, breathing new life into centuries-old recipes by giving them a contemporary twist. Creative chefs are also taking concepts from the rest of the world and melding them with locally sourced meats, seafood and vegetables.

Vegetarians & Vegans

The Netherlands is a plant-based dining pioneer. A quarter of main meals eaten here are vegetarian and Amsterdam surpasses national averages: 60% of residents follow flexitarian, pescatarian, vegetarian or vegan diets. It's on target for the municipality's goal of having 65% sustainable, plant-based choices available by 2030.

Vegetarians and vegans will find a multitude of options at all price points, from market-stall snacks through to high-end gourmet dining. Numerous cafes and restaurants are exclusively vegetarian or completely vegan, and those that aren't will usually have vegetarian (and often vegan) dishes or set menus available.

Snacks, Sweets & Quick Eats

Besides restaurants and *eetcafés* (pub-like places serving affordable meals), there are several quick options. At *broodjeszaken* (sandwich shops), simply stroll up to the counter and choose your fillings for a fluffy white or wheat roll. *Haringhuizen* (herring stands), *haringhandels* (herring carts) and *vishandels* (fishmongers) are the best places for a *broodje haring* (herring sandwich).

Locals love their *kaas* (cheese). Nearly two-thirds of all cheese sold is Gouda. The tastiest varieties have strong, complex flavours. Edam is similar to Gouda, but slightly drier and less creamy. Leidse (or Leyden) cheese is laced with cumin seeds and light in flavour.

The most famous confectionery is *drop*, sweet or salty liquorice sold in a bewildering variety of flavours.

MAREK MINOR/SHUTTERSTOCK

Rollende Keukens

FOOD & DRINK FESTIVALS

Bite of Amsterdam (p177) Held in May in Amstelpark.

Festival Trek (p177) Food-truck festival held in July in Amstelpark.

Amsterdam Wine Festival (p177) Held in September in Amstelpark.

Rollende Keukens (p115) Food-truck feast with over 100 'rolling kitchens', held in May at gasworks turned cultural village, Westergas.

Kwaku (p193) Massive food-and-football fair held on summer weekends; now the Netherlands' largest multicultural festival.

OLIEBOLLEN

Deep-fried dough balls popular around Christmastime from pop-up stalls.

FRIET/VLAAMSE FRITES/PATAT

Fries; thick-cut, twice-fried and slathered with sauces like mayo, peanut or sambal.

BITTERBALLEN

Small, round meat-ragout *kroketten* (croquettes), served as *borrelhapjes* (bar snacks).

OUD AMSTERDAMMER

Crumbly *oud* (aged) *kaas* (cheese), ideally accompanied by mustard.

Café Papeneiland (p103)

BAR OPEN

Centred on cosiness and charm, Amsterdam is a *café* (pub) society, with *jenever* (Dutch gin), beer, cocktails and more in the mix.

Amsterdam became famed for its alternative counterculture as Europe's *magisch centrum* ('magic centre') during the 1960s and '70s, and one of the world's most vibrant LGBTIQ+ capitals. As cheap flights opened mass tourism up from the 1980s, spurred on by marketing campaigns promoting a place where anything went, increasingly commercialised central areas like the Red Light District, Leidseplein and Rembrandtplein became magnets for hardcore partiers and hen-and-stag celebrations. In 2003, Amsterdam appointed the world's first *nachtburgemeester* ('night mayor'); a clean-up was introduced in 2007; and from 2013, Amsterdam's clubbing scene expanded with 24-hour-licensed city-fringe locations.

Then the pandemic forced a reset. Many outlying clubs closed their doors, but the clean-up accelerated (including 2023's anti-nuisance 'Stay Away' campaign). There are now plans for an official 'Institute for Night Culture' (INC) off Rembrandtplein to support up-and-coming young artists, musicians and performers, and a fantastic array of cutting-edge cocktail bars, wine bars, independent breweries and creative, sustainability-focused hybrid spaces.

All the while, *magisch centrum*–era venues thrive and Amsterdam's cosy *café* scene continues virtually unchanged.

Café Culture

When the Dutch say *café*, they mean a pub, and there are more than 1100 throughout Amsterdam. In a city that values socialising and conversation more than drinking itself, *cafés* aren't just about consuming

---

Lonely Planet's Top...

BRUIN CAFÉ
Café Papeneiland (p103) is a 1642 jewel with Delft Blue tiles and a central stove.

JENEVER
Try Western Canal Ring tasting house Proeflokaal A van Wees (p103) for Jordaan-distilled spirits.

BEACH BAR
All-day hangout Pllek (p204) opens onto the sand by the IJ River in Noord.

BEER GARDEN
Laid-back waterside cafe Hannekes Boom (p90) was built from recycled materials.

alcohol: they're places to hang out for hours of contemplation or camaraderie. Scores have outside seating on *terrassen* (terraces), which are glorious in summer and sometimes covered and heated in winter. Most serve food as well.

Amsterdam is famed for its historic *bruin cafés* (brown cafes; traditional drinking establishments). The name comes from the wood panelling and nicotine stains from centuries of use. Most importantly, the city's brown cafes provide an atmosphere conducive to conversation – and the nirvana of *gezelligheid* (conviviality, cosiness).

Beer, Wine & Spirits

The Dutch take beer very seriously. Lager is the staple, served cool and topped by a two-finger-thick head of froth to trap the flavour. *Een bier*, *een pils* or *een vaasje* will get you a normal glass of beer; *een kleintje pils* is a small glass and *een fluitje* is a small, thin, Cologne-style glass. Local brands include Heineken, Amstel, Grolsch, Oranjeboom, Dommelsch and Bavaria (which, despite its name, isn't German but Dutch).

Amsterdam's craft-beer scene has boomed in recent years. Alongside stalwarts like Brouwerij 't IJ (pictured right; p93) and Brouwerij De Prael (p64), whose beers you'll find around town as well as at the breweries, are innovative brewers such as Brouwerij Troost (p114) and Gebrouwen door Vrouwen (Brewed by Women; p166). You'll also find numerous craft-beer specialist bars and/or shops.

Jenever (ye-nay-ver; traditional Dutch gin; also spelt *genever*) is made from juniper berries and is drunk chilled. It arrives in a tulip-shaped shot glass filled to the brim – tradition dictates that you bend over the bar, with your hands behind your back, and take a deep sip. *Jonge* (young) *jenever* is smooth and relatively easy to drink; *oude* (old) *jenever* has a strong juniper flavour. A common combination, known as a *kopstoot* (head butt), is a glass of *jenever* with a beer chaser.

More Dutch people are drinking wine than ever before, and wine bars are popping up all over the city, although almost all wine here is imported from elsewhere in Europe and beyond.

NEED TO KNOW

Crucially, *café* culture should not be mistaken for coffeeshop (marijuana-smoking cafe) culture. There's a *big* difference between a *café* (pub) or *koffiehuis* (espresso bar) and a coffeeshop. A coffeeshop may serve coffee (never alcohol), but its focus is cannabis and hash.

Smoking (any substance) is banned by law in *cafés*.

Bar closing times vary; small establishments close at 1am/2am midweek/weekends; mid-sized establishments at 1am/3am and large establishments 4am/5am.

An exception is the Red Light District, with a clamp-down on establishments of all sizes: closing times are 1am/2am midweek/weekends, with no admittance after 1am.

Door policies typically require people to be well groomed, not intoxicated, and respectful

Tipping isn't mandatory but you're welcome to tip to show your appreciation, especially in cocktail bars.

COCKTAIL BAR
Inspired by Amsterdam's streetscapes, Bar Mokum (p183) uses local spirits and liqueurs.

INDEPENDENT BREWERY
Brouwerij 't IJ (p93) is in a tiled former bathhouse beneath a towering 1725-built windmill.

ROOFTOP BAR
A 360-degree panorama unfolds from LuminAir's (p92) 11th-floor bar and terrace.

LGBTIQ+ SCENE
Reguliersdwarsstraat (p136) is lined with popular venues flying the rainbow flag.

FROM LEFT: MILOS RUZICKA/SHUTTERSTOCK, IVO ANTONIE DE ROOIJ/SHUTTERSTOCK

Muziekgebouw aan 't IJ and Bimhuis (p92)

SHOWTIME

A wellspring of culture and creativity for centuries, Amsterdam teems with unique venues, performances and innovative artforms across the board.

Amsterdam supports a flourishing arts scene, with loads of big concert halls, theatres, wonderful arthouse and independent cinemas, comedy clubs and other performance venues filled on a regular basis. Music fans are superbly catered for here, and there is a fervent subculture for just about every genre, especially jazz, classical, rock and avant-garde beats.

Entertainment in the city can range from afternoon matinees to three-day-long raves, so opening hours are as sporadic and diverse as the cultural offerings are themselves. Check individual venues for full details and buy tickets well in advance where possible. To find options of all kinds, head to **Hidden Agenda** *(hiddenagenda.nl)*; you can filter by location, venue, dates and/or genres.

Amsterdam is a long-time global meeting point for nationalities from all over the world, so English is widely spoken throughout the city. As a result, many cinema screenings are in English or have English subtitles, and theatre performances are marked 'LNP' (language no problem) if understanding Dutch isn't vital.

Music, Performance & Cinema

Jazz, classical and rock are the most prevalent live-music genres. Jazz is extremely popular, from far-out, improvisational stylings to more traditional notes. The grand Bimhuis is the big game in town, drawing visiting musicians from around the globe, though its vibe is more that of a funky little club. Smaller jazz venues abound and it's easy to find a live combo.

Amsterdam's classical music scene, with top international orchestras, conductors and soloists crowding the agenda, is the envy of many European cities. Choose between the flawless, historic Concertgebouw (p155) or dramatic, newer Muziekgebouw aan 't IJ (p92) for the main shows.

Many of the city's clubs also host rock and pop bands. Huge touring names often play smallish venues such as the Melkweg (p134) and Paradiso (p134); it's a real treat to catch one of your favourites here.

English-language comedy thrives in Amsterdam, especially around the Jordaan. Local theatre tends towards the edgy and experimental.

Amsterdam is cinephile heaven, with oodles of arthouse cinemas.

Arts Festivals

The centrepiece of Amsterdam's cultural calendar is the **Holland Festival** *(holland festival.nl),* held over 18 days in June. Since it was established in 1947, it has been staging experimental theatre, music, opera and musical theatre, dance, film and visual arts at landmark venues like Leidseplein's neo-Renaissance Internationaal Theater Amsterdam (p137), the Concertgebouw and Muziekgebouw, as well as smaller, edgier venues like those at the former gasworks turned creative village, Westergas (p110).

For 10 days in September, the **Nederlands Theater Festival** *(Netherlands Theatre Festival; tf.nl)* takes place in 11 theatres across Amsterdam with cutting-edge dance, theatre and performance art. Running in parallel, the **Amsterdam Fringe Festival** *(amsterdamfringefestival.nl)* is a platform for emerging artists who perform in over 220 shows across 22 venues.

During the summer season, outdoor performances take place at open-air theatres in the Vondelpark (p161) and in Amsterdamse Bos (p180).

LONELY PLANET'S TOP...

Local Music Venues

Cinetol (p173) Small De Pijp venue for pop, rock, experimental, indie, hip-hop and more.

Maloe Melo (p115) Nightly blues, rock and jam sessions.

Concerto (p143) Watch live gigs at the Netherlands' biggest music store.

Cinemas

Koninklijk Theater Tuschinski (p134) Fantastical 1431-capacity cinema with sumptuous art-deco interior.

The Movies (p106) In the Haarlemmerbuurt, Amsterdam's oldest cinema dates to 1912.

Rialto (p173) De Pijp's 1920s art-deco theatre has international and arthouse films.

Filmhallen (p167) Mainstream, documentaries and live opera screenings.

Koninklijk Theater Tuschinski (p134)

ENTERTAINMENT BY NEIGHBOURHOOD	
Medieval Centre & the Red Light District	Home to some young rock/DJ clubs throughout the 'hood, and avant-garde theatres on Nes.
Nieuwmarkt, Plantage & the Eastern Islands	Classical venues include the Muziekgebouw aan 't IJ, Bimhuis and Conservatorium.
Southern Canal Ring	Clubs and live-music venues fan out around Leidseplein.
Western Canal Ring, Jordaan & the West	Venues for comedy, blues and cult films, plus the Westergas complex.
Vondelpark, Oud-West & Oud-Zuid	Home to the world-renowned Concertgebouw, free theatre in the park and squats turned culture-centres.
De Pijp & Zuid	Great cinemas, new openings in Zuid and theatre in the city's forest.
Oosterpark & East of the Amstel	Mega-venues (and Amsterdam's beloved football team Ajax) entertain here.
Amsterdam Noord	Live music plays regularly at IJ-side venues like Pllek.

KIEV.VICTOR/SHUTTERSTOCK

Albert Cuypmarkt (p172)

SHOP

The capital's shelves are stocked with all kinds of antiques and curios, along with cutting-edge Dutch design, food, drink and fashion.

Stumbling across offbeat little boutiques is one of the great joys of shopping in Amsterdam. The best areas for quirky finds are the Haarlemmerbuurt, along Haarlemmerstraat and Haarlemmerdijk. To the south, there's satisfying browsing among the pint-sized, one-of-a-kind shops in the Negen Straatjes (p103). Staalstraat in Nieuwmarkt is another bountiful vein.

The busiest mainstream shopping streets are Kalverstraat by the Dam and Leidsestraat, which leads into Leidseplein. Both are lined with clothing and department stores. De Bijenkorf is Amsterdam's famed department store, taking pride of place by the Royal Palace at Dam 1. A lovely array of clothing, toys, household accessories and books spreads over five floors. Thrifty Dutch chain Hema carries a bit of everything – wine, homewares, clothing – and is a great place for reasonably priced Dutch design goods.

Near the Vondelpark, stylish fashion boutiques line Cornelis Schuytstraat and Willemsparkweg. Close by, PC Hooftstraat queues up Chanel, Gucci and other luxury brands along its length.

Fashion

Dutch fashion is fabulous for browsing at Amsterdam's charming boutiques. Locals have mastered the art of casual style, and it streams right out of the no-nonsense side of the national character, resulting in cool, practical designs.

Dutch Design

Dutch designers have shown a singular knack for bringing a creative, stylish and sustainable touch to everyday objects. Items are colourful and sensible, with vintage and humorous twists mixed in. They solve problems you didn't know you had. Once you own a hand towel with a rivet in one corner for hanging, you'll wonder how you ever lived without it!

Antiques

Stores selling gorgeous antiques are all around the city. The Spiegelkwartier (Spiegel Quarter) offers a long line of shops along Spiegelgracht and Nieuwe Spiegelstraat that attract moneyed browsers.

Delftware

The Dutch have been firing up the iconic blue-and-white pottery since the 1600s. Authentic Delftware comes only from Royal Delft. A few Amsterdam shops sell the real deal.

Flower Bulbs

Exotic tulip bulbs are popular gifts to take home. The Bloemenmarkt (p129) in the Southern Canal Ring is ground zero for the colourful goods. Ask the vendors about customs regulations, since bringing bulbs into your home country can be prohibited.

Cheese & Jenever

Dutch *kaas* (cheese) is famous and makes a great souvenir if customs allows and if it's properly wrapped. *Jenever* (Dutch gin) is a distinctive souvenir. Bols is the main brand.

Markets

No visit to Amsterdam is complete if you haven't experienced one of its lively outdoor markets. In addition to regular street markets – such as De Pijp's Albert Cuypmarkt (p172), the Jordaan's wonderful markets like the Noordermarkt (p107), and Oost's multicultural Dappermarkt (p187) – check dates for the design-oriented Sunday Market and artisan Pure Markt, both at various locations, and the IJ Hallen (p203) flea market, in Amsterdam Noord.

LONELY PLANET'S TOP...

Fashion Shops

Rain Couture (p106) Multiseasonal, stylish wet-weather gear for the fickle Dutch weather.

Donsje (p165) Handmade, sustainable babies' and children's wear with adorable designs.

Love Stories Archive (p177) Amsterdam-designed lingerie and swimwear at this boutique stocking samples and end-of-line runs.

Denim City (p165) Emerging labels and recycled creations offer fresh, original styles.

Design Shops

Frozen Fountain (p114) Striking furniture, textiles and homewares from emerging and established Dutch designers.

POLSPOTTEN (p114) Showcase for innovative Dutch design furniture, objects and lighting.

WonderWood (p66) Moulded-plywood creations, including vintage furniture and smaller wooden decorations.

Moooi (p142) OTT Dutch design from spun fibreglass chandeliers to twists on the classic Delft vase.

SHOPPING BY NEIGHBOURHOOD

Medieval Centre & the Red Light District	Bookshops, design emporiums and more.
Nieuwmarkt, Plantage & the Eastern Islands	Home to the Waterlooplein Flea Market and eccentric local shops on Staalstraat.
Western Canal Ring, Jordaan & the West	The Negen Straatjes hold teensy speciality shops; Jordaan shops are artsy and eclectic; Haarlemmerbuurt has cool boutiques.
Southern Canal Ring	Hunt for art and antiques in the Spiegelkwartier (Spiegel Quarter), and fashion, music and homewares nearby.
Vondelpark, Oud-West & Oud-Zuid	Stylish boutiques on Cornelis Schuytstraat and Willemsparkweg and ultra-luxe labels on PC Hooftstraat.
De Pijp & Zuid	Beyond Albert Cuypmarkt are quirky shops, galleries, and vintage and designer fashion boutiques.
Oosterpark & East of the Amstel	Trawl the ethnically diverse Dappermarkt.
Amsterdam Noord	Vintage finds and cool homewares in industrial surrounds.

THE GUIDE

Chapters in this section are organised by neighbourhood. Neighbourhoods are delineated by a specific local character or identity, where you'll find unique specific experiences, local insights, insider tips and expert recommendations.

Prinsengracht canal (p104)
YASONYA/SHUTTERSTOCK

NEIGHBOURHOODS AT A GLANCE

Find the neighbourhoods that tick all your boxes.

Medieval Centre & the Red Light District (p42)

Centuries-old landmarks like the Oude Kerk rub shoulders with the infamous Red Light District, *jenever* (gin) tasting rooms, bars and restaurants galore.

Western Canal Ring, Jordaan & the West (p96)

Across from the boutique-filled Western Canal Ring's Anne Frank Huis, the Jordaan teems with cosy *cafés* (pubs), with sustainable developments further west.

Vondelpark, Oud-West & Oud-Zuid (p144)

South of the rambling Vondelpark, genteel Oud-Zuid harbours Amsterdam's grandest museums; north, lively Oud-West is one of Amsterdam's most up-and-coming areas.

Southern Canal Ring (p118)

By day, visit the city's grand canal houses and less-heralded museums. By night, hit the clubs around Leidseplein and Rembrandtplein.

De Pijp & Zuid (p168)

Home of the Heineken Experience and colourful Albert Cuypmarkt, trendy De Pijp stretches south to Zuid's parklands and sky-scraping developments.

NDSM

Klaprozenweg

Spaarndammerdijk

Basosweg   Transformatorweg

Haarlemmerweg

Van Hallstr

Frederick Hendrikstr

Marnixplein

Marnixstr

Nassaukade

Bilderdijkstr

Kinkerstr

A10

Jan Evertsenstr

Kostverlorenvaart

Jacob van Lennepkanaal

Overtoom

Overtoom

De Lairessestr

Schinkel

Van Baerlestr

De Boelelaan

A10

Europaboulevard

Amstelveenseweg

Het Nieuwe Meer

Amsterdamse Bos

✈ Schiphol International (2km)

Eye Filmmuseum

A'DAM Tower

Centraal Station

Dantrak

Anne Frank Huis

Westerkerk

Dam

Oude Kerk

Royal Palace

Rokin

Museum Rembrandthuis

Begijnhof

Rembrandtplein   Museum Willet-Holthuysen

Reguliersdwarsstraat

Golden Bend

Leidseplein

Regulier-sgracht

H'ART

Spiegelkwartier

Museum Van Loon

Vondelpark

Rijksmuseum

Stedelijk Museum

Heineken Experience

Van Gogh Museum

Albert Cuypmarkt

Ceintuur

40

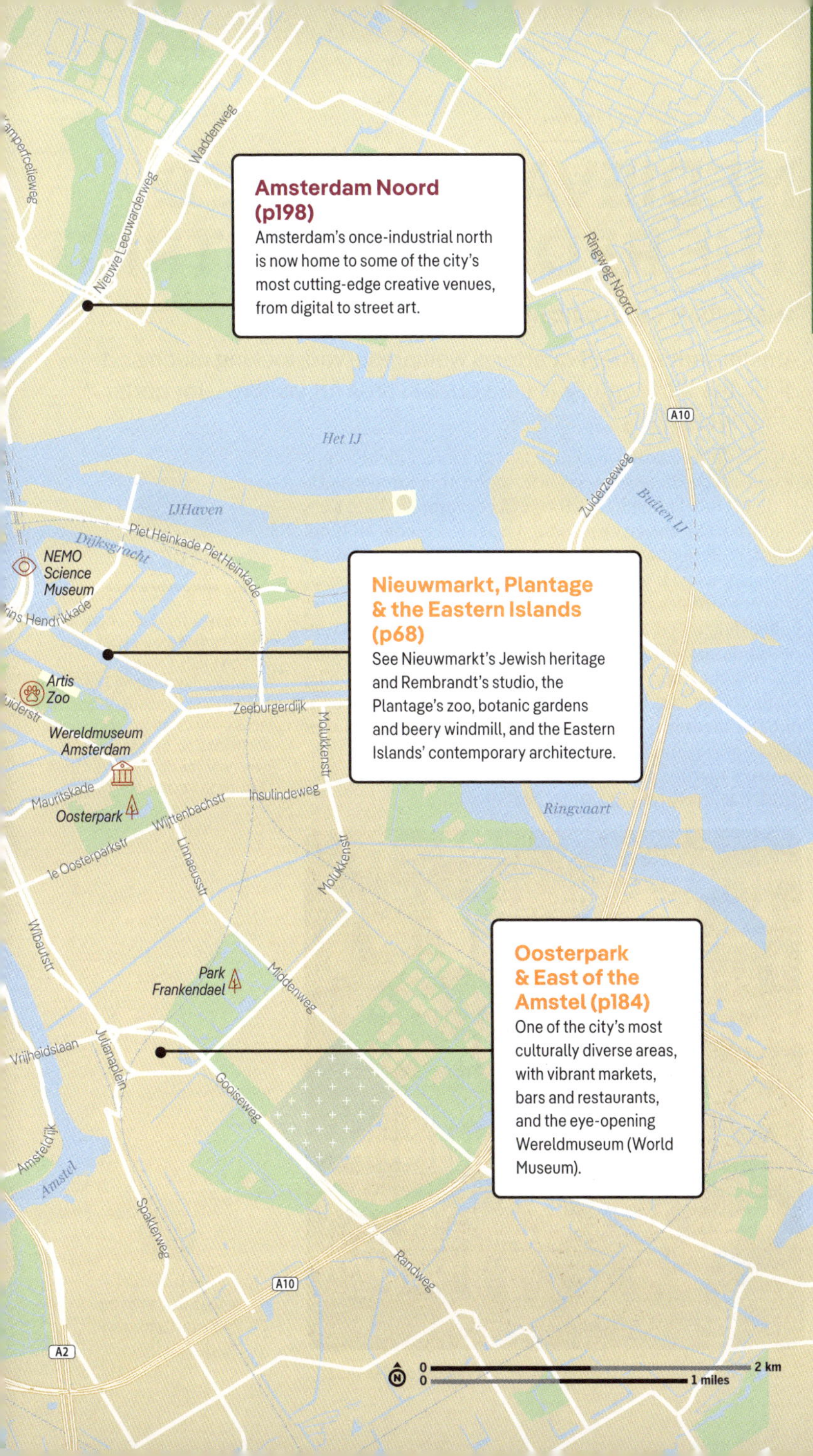

Amsterdam Noord (p198)

Amsterdam's once-industrial north is now home to some of the city's most cutting-edge creative venues, from digital to street art.

Nieuwmarkt, Plantage & the Eastern Islands (p68)

See Nieuwmarkt's Jewish heritage and Rembrandt's studio, the Plantage's zoo, botanic gardens and beery windmill, and the Eastern Islands' contemporary architecture.

Oosterpark & East of the Amstel (p184)

One of the city's most culturally diverse areas, with vibrant markets, bars and restaurants, and the eye-opening Wereldmuseum (World Museum).

NEMO Science Museum

Artis Zoo

Wereldmuseum Amsterdam

Oosterpark

Park Frankendael

Het IJ

IJHaven

Ringvaart

Buiten IJ

0   2 km
0   1 miles

Researched by Barbara Woolsey

MEDIEVAL CENTRE & THE RED LIGHT DISTRICT

AMSTERDAM'S HISTORIC HEART

Amsterdam's oldest quarter is well preserved, looking much as it did in the 17th century. It's the busiest area for visitors – for better or for worse.

Amsterdam's medieval centre is a glorious kaleidoscope of contrasts. On its eastern side, in the area known as De Wallen, Oudekerksplein is the perfect example. Oude Kerk (Old Church), the city's solemn, treasured medieval landmark, is circled by everything from Red Light windows to 5D porn, as well as ordinary scenes such as restaurants, business offices and a kindergarten. Steps away, more coffeeshops, Red Light windows and risqué bars and venues abound, while all upper floors are residential. Don't colour your impressions of this part of Amsterdam on its adult zones, and its many tourist traps, alone. Throughout the medieval centre, wander the atmospheric lanes and you'll stumble upon an array of surprises, from 17th-century tasting rooms to *bruin cafés* (traditional pubs), hidden courtyards and tiny speciality shops.

TOP TIP

If you're after somewhere to drink or dine around Centraal Station (p53), Chinatown is just 550m southeast along Zeedijk. There are also a couple of casual places on the station's revitalised northern side, alongside the IJ River near the docks for the free ferries to Amsterdam Noord.

Wynand Fockink (p52)

See p239 for places to stay in the Medieval Centre and Red Light District.

Map showing the Medieval Centre and Red Light District area of Amsterdam with locations marked: WESTERN CANAL RING, Torensluis, Gravenstr, Nieuwendijk, Beursplein, Warmoesstr, Korte Niezel, Gelderskade, RED LIGHT DISTRICT, **5** Oude Kerk, Oudezijds Voorburgwal, **1** Royal Palace, Jodenbreestr, Dam, Wynand Fockink **4**, Gasthuismolenst, Herengracht, Singel, Squist, Oude Spiegelstr, MEDIEVAL CENTRE, Kalverstr, Rokin, Nes, St Lucienst, Oudezijds Achterburgwal, NIEUWMARKT, Nieuwmarkt M, Oude Hoogstr, St Antoniesbreestr, Oude Schans, M Rokin, Rusland, Kloveniersburgwal, Heren, Heren, Wijde Heist, Begijnhof **2**, Rokin M, Grimburgwal, Spui, Vleminckx **3**, Heiligeweg, Nieuwe Doelenstr, Groenburgwal, Waterlooplein, Zwanenburgwal, Muntplein, Singel, Binnen Amstel, Amstel

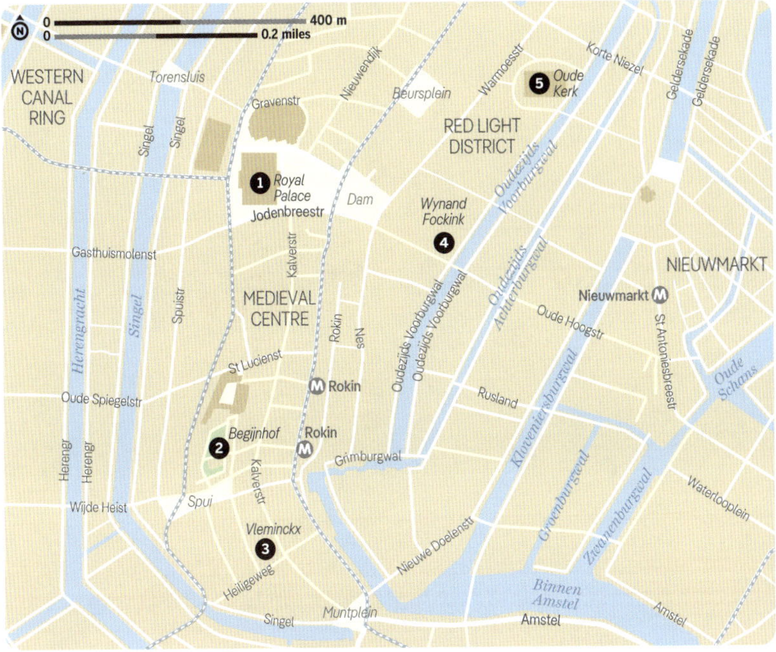

0 — 400 m / 0 — 0.2 miles

☆ Highlights

❶ Royal Palace
Marvel at opulent chandeliered interiors and take in a Dutch history lesson at the city's landmark palace. **p46**

❷ Begijnhof
Push open the door to find this tranquil courtyard's hidden gardens, churches and tiny historic houses still lived in today. **p62**

❸ Vleminckx ▼
Bite into crisp *frites* (fries) slathered in mayonnaise from Amsterdam's best stand. **p57**

❹ Wynand Fockink
Bowl up to this 17th-century tasting house for a *jenever* (Dutch gin). **p52**

❺ Oude Kerk
Visit Amsterdam's oldest surviving building in its Red Light District location. **p50**

🚶 Getting Around

Walking
You'll need to get around this area on foot; much of the area is pedestrianised. The Red Light District especially gets very crowded with large groups.

Rideshare services
Rideshare vehicles are not permitted to pick up guests in downtown Amsterdam; meet your driver at the designated spot at Muntplein.

Centraal Station
Multiple tram and metro lines, as well as ferry routes to Amsterdam Noord, all converge at Centraal Station. Find multiple tram lines at Dam. The main metro stop is Rokin.

MEDIEVAL CENTRE & THE RED LIGHT DISTRICT

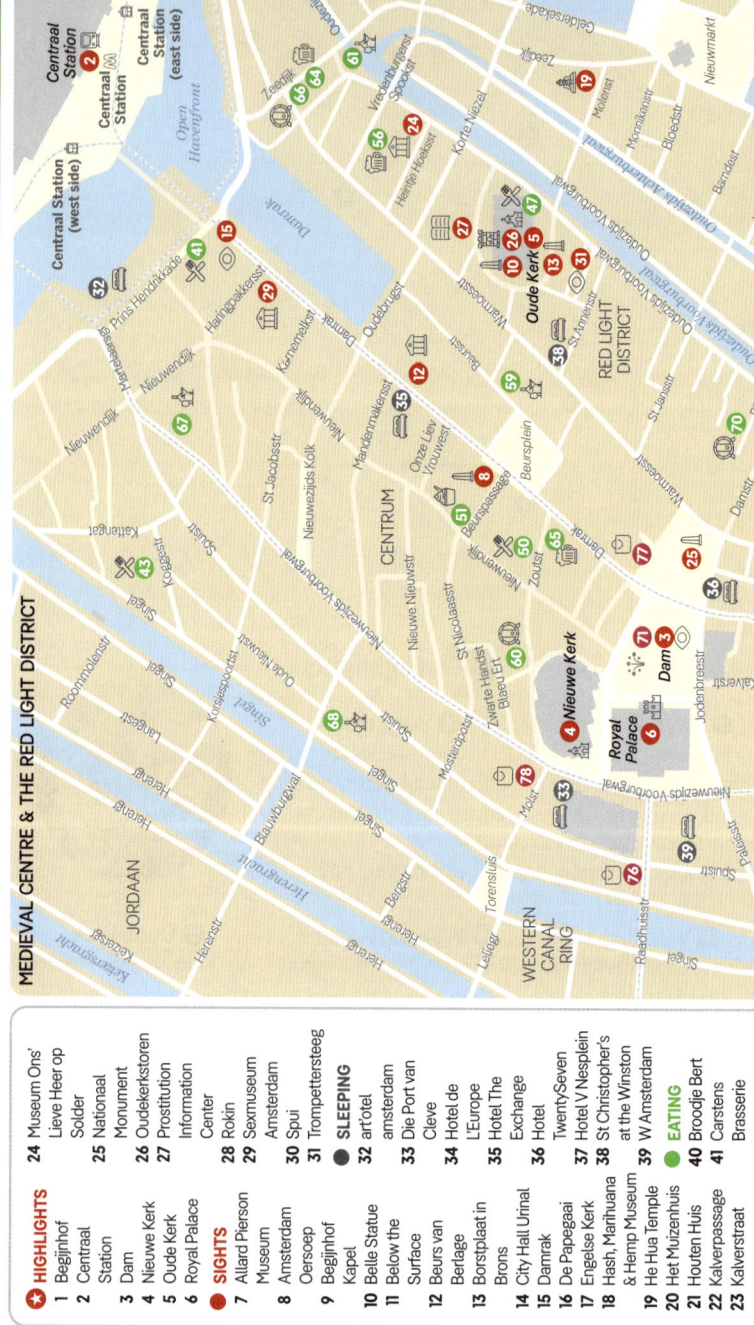

HIGHLIGHTS
1 Begijnhof
2 Centraal Station
3 Dam
4 Nieuwe Kerk
5 Oude Kerk
6 Royal Palace

SIGHTS
7 Allard Pierson Museum
8 Amsterdam Oersoep
9 Begijnhof Kapel
10 Belle Statue
11 Below the Surface
12 Beurs van Berlage
13 Borstplaat in Brons
14 City Hall Urinal
15 Damrak
16 De Papegaai
17 Engelse Kerk
18 Hash, Marihuana & Hemp Museum
19 He Hua Temple
20 Het Muizenhuis
21 Houten Huis
22 Kalverpassage
23 Kalverstraat
24 Museum Ons' Lieve Heer op Solder
25 Nationaal Monument
26 Oudekerkstoren
27 Prostitution Information Center
28 Rokin
29 Sexmuseum Amsterdam
30 Spui
31 Trompettersteeg

SLEEPING
32 art'otel amsterdam
33 Die Port van Cleve
34 Hotel de L'Europe
35 Hotel The Exchange
36 Hotel TwentySeven
37 Hotel V Nesplein
38 St Christopher's at the Winston
39 W Amsterdam

EATING
40 Broodje Bert
41 Carstens Brasserie

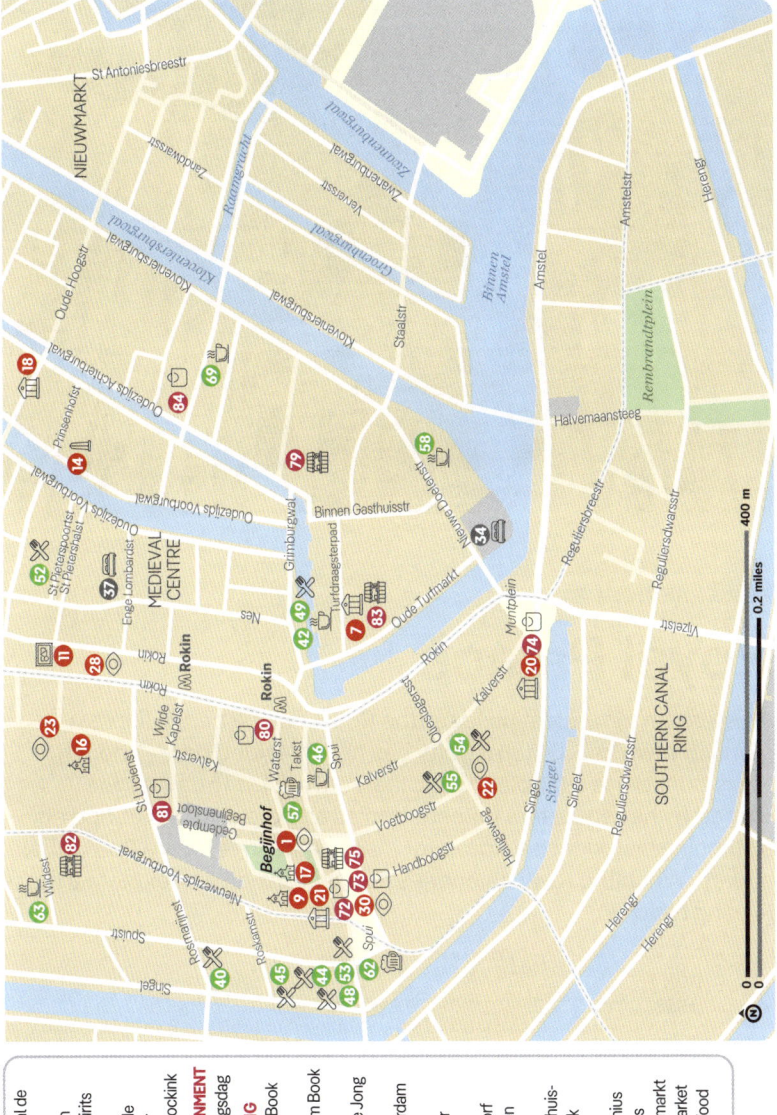

ANDRA PHOTOGRAPHY/SHUTTERSTOCK

TOP EXPERIENCE

Royal Palace

Amsterdam's grandest building, the Royal Palace began life as a glorified town hall. Dutch royalty has never resided here – though Louis Bonaparte (Napoleon's brother) did briefly. Today, it's the monarchy headquarters for ceremonies and dignified visits, and also a stunning historical backdrop for mass gatherings on the Dam (p54) square. When the royal calendar's free, pop inside and explore a most riveting history.

DON'T MISS

Dutch Baroque architecture

Citizens' hall

Art by Dutch Masters

Famous chandeliers (all 51 of them)

Napoleon's furniture

Façade bulletholes

Palace History

Today's Royal Palace (Koninklijk Paleis) began life as a glorified town hall and was completed in 1665. Its architect, Jacob van Campen, spared no expense to display Amsterdam's wealth in a way that rivalled the grandest European buildings of the day. The result is Dutch Baroque–designed opulence on a big scale. It's worth seeing the exterior at night, when the palace is dramatically floodlit.

Civic council played hard and fast here during the 'Golden Age', but only for about 150 years until the French Revolution. Without much resistance, Le Petit Caporal ('Little Corporal') took over and appointed his brother, Louis Bonaparte, King of

PRACTICALITIES
● paleisamsterdam.nl ● adult/child €13.50/free ● 10am-5pm

Holland in 1806. Enacting sovereign 'squatting rights', Louis eventually moved in, making 1 million guilders worth of renovations (about €11.5 million today) to transform the Stadhuis (city hall) into his royal abode.

The 'other Bonaparte' reigned and claimed residence here for only two years before abdicating. He allegedly found it damp and uncomfortable, and Dutch merchant nobility less than enchanting. In 1813, the Dutch served France a formal eviction notice coinciding with the Napoleonic Empire's collapse. Prince William Frederick of Orange-Nassau returned from exile, and the Kingdom of the Netherlands was established. Dutch royalty have never resided here, preferring their palace in Den Haag (p225), making the younger Napoleon the first and only occupant of the palace in Amsterdam.

King Willem-Alexander uses the palace only for ceremonies; when royal appointments aren't happening, you can go inside for a self-guided tour.

Inner Opulence

Marvel at how the interiors gleam, especially the marblework – at its best in the *burgerzaal* (citizens' hall) at the heart of the building. Sculptures and ceiling paintings depict 'Justice, Prudence, and Strength', harking back to the hall's civic origins. Floors are inlaid with world maps: envisioned as a world schematic, with Amsterdam positioned at the centre, they depict the eastern and western hemispheres and a 1654 celestial map.

Most rooms are spread over the 1st floor. Counting all 51 of its sparkling chandeliers, damasks and gilded clocks makes an excellent treasure hunt. Spectacular paintings by Dutch Masters, including Ferdinand Bol and Jacob de Wit, adorn the walls.

Empire-Style Decor

In 1808 the building became the palace of King Louis, Napoleon Bonaparte's brother. In a classic slip-up in the new lingo, French-born Louis told his subjects here that he was the 'rabbit' *(konijn)* of Holland, when he actually meant 'king' *(koning,* which had the old spelling variation *konink).* Napoleon dismissed him two years later. Louis left behind about 1000 pieces of Empire-style furniture and decorative artworks. As a result, the palace now holds one of the world's largest collections from the period.

Palatial Workplace

Officially, the Dutch king, King Willem-Alexander, lives in this landmark palace and pays a symbolic rent, though his actual residence is Palace Huis ten Bosch in Den Haag. Notably, in 2025 when Queen Máxima made a much-discussed facial expression while meeting US President Donald Trump, the headline-making moment took place in Den Haag and not Amsterdam's Royal Palace.

PUBLIC EXECUTIONS

While today the Royal Palace forms a backdrop for large public gatherings on Dam square, it once was potentially a final view for those executed here.

During the Spanish Inquisition, over a thousand 'witches and warlocks' were burned at the stake. The last known public execution on Dam was in 1806. Peer closely at the palace façade and you can see holes where wooden gallows were affixed.

TOP TIPS

● Pick up a free audio guide upon entering; it explains everything you'll see in vivid detail.

● Check the website calendar for closures – usually in April, May, November and December, but they can also be on short notice.

● Book tickets ahead to ensure entry. You must choose a designated time slot; you can come up to 45 minutes before this (arrive early).

● Exploring typically takes an hour; alloq for longer lingering at special exhibits.

● On King's Day (p54), thousands of orange-clad locals celebrate the House of Orange on the Dam. Drink and dance with locals and see the palace lit with a tangerine glow.

FREE EGGS!

Look closely behind the bar at many *bruin cafés* (brown cafes; traditional pubs) and you might see a rack of hard-boiled eggs. They're an age-old custom, a snack meant to provide energy to drinkers – except back in the day, the eggs were raw. One step further was the *bokking egg*, or a raw egg served alongside *jenever* (Dutch gin) – sometimes even mixed with the spirit. How's that for liquid courage? Meanwhile, *bokking* means 'smoked herring', which sometimes also made a starring appearance.

Minding modern food-safety regulations, old-world Dutch establishments carry on this stomach-lining tradition with a modern twist. The eggs are often free; in some cases, there's a small charge. Brouwerij de Prael (p64) and Proeflokaal de Ooievaar (p55) are two places that sometimes keep pub eggs on stock.

THOMAS NUEHNEN/SHUTTERSTOCK

Rokin metro station

Amsterdam's Underground Treasury

Archaeological finds in Rokin metro

During the construction of Amsterdam's 2018-opened Noord/Zuidlijn (north–south metro line), more than 700,000 archaeological finds were unearthed from beneath the streets and waterways. Now, **Below the Surface** *(belowthesurface. amsterdam)* displays around 10,000 of them, dating as far back as 5000 BCE, in **Rokin metro station** as a uniquely urban archaeology exhibition for passengers to see.

Pass the metro turnstiles (holding a valid ticket). Along the steep escalator down to the platforms, glass-encased artefacts line up for about 10m from top to bottom. The southern entrance (on Rokin near the intersection with Spuistraat) display cases hold objects that illustrate transport and trades work, architectural fragments and household interiors, as well as personal effects illustrating locals' life over centuries. Meanwhile, objects at the northern entrance (on Damrak) span items related to science, medicine and communications, as well as weapons, armour, recreation and personal style. A chronological layout, from the Early Bronze Age to the 20th

DRINKING IN THE MEDIEVAL CENTRE & RED LIGHT DISTRICT: BRUIN CAFÉS

Hoppe: Take in interiors and exteriors listed as historical monuments at Hoppe, filling glasses since 1670. *9am-1am Sun-Thu, to 2am Fri & Sat*

In 't Aepjen: In a 15th-century building, this former inn was once frequented by sailors bartering *aapjes* (monkeys) for lodging. *2pm-1am Sun-Thu, to 3am Fri & Sat*

Café de Dokter: Chandeliers, a birdcage and smooth jazz set the tone in this seventh-generation family-run bar. *4pm-1am Wed-Sat*

Oporto: Cool decor untouched in decades: woodwork zodiac signs, iron-framed parchment lighting. Play darts, down a glass. *11am-late*

century, descends into Amsterdam's history – right to the present-day underground.

Collection highlights include coins (from as early as 1371), ice-skating blades from the Middle Ages, 15th-century padlocks, 17th-century pottery, an 18th-century piggy bank, 19th-century pocket watches and military uniform buttons, a 1922 car radiator cap, a 1935 toy car replica of the Bluebird that broke the world land-speed record the same year, and block-like 1980s mobiles.

A virtual 'tour' on the exhibition's website offers background stories for the Rokin items and an interesting catalogue for scrolling through items – from ID cards to rogue dolls' legs – by origin year.

Meet the Mummies

Diverse Mediterranean and Near East wonders

Run by the University of Amsterdam and named for its first professor of archaeology, Allard Pierson (1831–96), the **Allard Pierson Museum** *(allardpierson.nl; adult/child €15.50/3.50; 10am-5pm Mon-Sat)* contains a rich collection of Mediterranean and Near Eastern archaeology. You'll find actual mummies (among them, a child, adult and animals), vases from ancient Greece and Mesopotamia, a very cool wagon from the royal tombs at Salamis (Cyprus), and galleries full of other items providing insight into daily life in ancient times. With an extensive range of maps, atlases and nautical charts, its cartography collection is one of the world's largest.

Once Upon a Stock Exchange

Commerce exchanged for creativity

In Amsterdam's vast former stock exchange **Beurs van Berlage** *(Berlage Stock Exchange; beursvanberlage.com; 10am-6pm Mon-Fri non-event days),* you won't find brokers and traders. Rather, it's a busy space for concertgoers, art lovers and tech gurus. Catch an event (prices vary) on the former trading floors of the Beurszaal (Exchange Hall). Built in 1903, it reflects the vision of master architect and ardent socialist HP Berlage, who filled the temple of capitalism with decorations that venerate labour, including tile murals of the well-muscled proletariat. Unless there's an event on, you can visit on weekdays (when it's free). Stroll around and take it all in; financial buildings aren't made like this anymore.

DIGGING UP THE PAST

Archaeological discoveries became a means of justifying the Dutch empire's colonial activities as scholarly rather than oppressive. Leiden and Amsterdam Universities became prestigious centres for ancient studies contributing to new knowledge's 'greater good'.

Since 2023, the Allard Pierson Museum has reviewed its collections with a decolonial focus; for example, looking at maps and archives on Suriname prior to its 1975 independence in the Surinamica Collection (now a core archive).

Amsterdam's Wereldmuseum (p188) also sheds light on reevaluating Dutch collections, including the nature of artefacts and restitution (returning artefacts back to where they may have been unrightfully taken from).

Come for high tea

DRINKING IN THE MEDIEVAL CENTRE: CHARMED CAFES

De Laatste Kruimel: Despite being busy, the 'Last Crumb' is homey with canal-side terrace. Pies, quiches, cakes and coffee. *8am-5pm Mon-Thu, to 6pm Fri-Sun*	**Hummingbird:** Speciality coffee and art are the draws of this simple yet stylish coffee bar. *8.30am-5pm Mon-Fri, 9am-5.30pm Sat & Sun*	**Café de Jaren:** Watch the Amstel float from the waterside terraces of this bright, spacious grand cafe. Coffee and light bites. *10am-10pm Sun-Wed, to 11pm Thu-Sat*	**Gartine:** Away from Kalverstraat's prying eyes, alley-tucked charm with mismatched antique tableware and organic egg breakfasts. *9.30am-4pm Wed-Sun*

Belle statue

TOP EXPERIENCE

Oude Kerk

Amsterdam's oldest building, Oude Kerk (Old Church) dates back to 1306. Originally Catholic and now Protestant, the Gothic-style structure has an interesting cache of treasures – and some oddities. Ascend Oudekerkstoren (Oude Kerk Tower) for divine vistas and Amsterdam's oldest church bell. And naughty art might seem unusual for a house of God, but with the Red Light District on your doorstep, it fits in here just fine.

DON'T MISS

Oude Kerk Tower

Floor tombstones

Choir-stall carvings

Golden torso

Red Light history on Oudekerksplein

Contemporary art exhibitions

Concerts

Floor of Tombstones

The 1306-erected Oude Kerk is Amsterdam's oldest surviving building. The church, which honours the city's patron saint, red-robed St Nicholas (the inspiration for St Nick), also offers an intriguing moral contradiction in a different shade of rouge: active Red Light District windows surrounding the church.

Inside, many famous Amsterdammers are buried under the worn tombstones set in the floor, including Rembrandt's wife, Saskia van Uylenburgh. Annually on 9 March at 8.39am,

PRACTICALITIES
● oudekerk.nl ● adult/child €13.50/3.50, incl tower tour €21/8.50
● 10am-6pm Mon-Sat, 1-5.30pm Sun

a beam of naturally occurring light (a phenomenon dubbed the 'sunbeam of Saskia') touches her grave through a church window. A special event, 'Saskia's Breakfast', commemorates the moment with church music and discussions highlighting the often-overlooked role of women in art history.

Some 60,000 citizens lie beneath the church, from sex workers to recognised figures such as diamond dealer Kiliaen van Rensselaer, naval hero Jacob van Heemskerck, organist Jan Pieterszoon Sweelinck, and the family tomb of Cornelis de Graeff.

Nave Rarities

Check out the stunning 18th-century Vater-Müller organ above the back and the naughty 15th-century carvings on the choir stalls up front. While sexual humour might seem misplaced in the sanctuary, such images were common in many medieval churches, blending moral lessons with a laugh.

Contemporary art exhibitions regularly take place here, along with concerts and services featuring the church's four organs. As well as the Vater-Müller organ, the Oude Kerk has a 1965 transept organ, an Italian organ and a cabinet organ, all of which can be heard during concerts and services.

Red Lights on Oudekerksplein

Oude Kerk has a full-frontal view of the Red Light District's so-called Spanish Corner/Latin Windows, where windows right on Oudekerksplein have been traditionally staffed by sex workers from Latin America.

The square also holds the **bronze statue of Belle**, erected in 2007, which commemorates Red Light District history as well as sex workers worldwide. Bearing the inscription 'Respect sex workers all over the world', the bronze monument stands on a granite pedestal, poised with reserved confidence. She is the only statue in the world dedicated specifically to sex workers.

Meanwhile, the cobblestones by the main entrance contain another bold statement: the **Borstplaat in Brons** (Golden Torso) of a naked woman held by a padlocked hand. The torso mysteriously appeared one day, was removed by police and then put back by popular demand.

Oudekerkstoren

Guides lead intriguing tours up into the 67m-high Oudekerkstoren (Oude Kerk Tower). Prepare for lots of narrow stairs rewarded by sweeping views of the low-rise city's gabled rooflines.

Also take in the carillon of bells: 47 of them date back to 1658 and are among the world's oldest surviving. Still ringing out several times a day, they're a testament to the Hemony brothers, the master bellmakers who crafted them.

SWEET SANCTUARY

The delightful cafe **Koffieschenkerij** (9am-6pm), occupying part of Oude Kerk, offers prime views into the church interiors with a heavenly slice of cake and coffee. The sublime menu also includes spiced carrot cake, apple pie and gluten-free almond cake, as well as tea and flavoured sodas. In spring, take a seat in the courtyard garden popping with tulip blooms.

TOP TIPS

● Cash isn't accepted here; you'll need to bring a debit or credit card with you to pay the entrance fee.

● Tickets for 'Saskia's Breakfast' are limited and sell out quickly. Buy them on the church's website as early as possible. Typically, the ticket sale is announced via Oude Kerk's official Instagram and Facebook accounts about a month prior to the event.

● Ask for a map when you enter.

● Outside visiting hours, the church holds religious services (in Dutch) at 11am and 6pm on Sunday, when worshippers are welcome.

● Guided tower tours last 30 minutes and depart every half-hour.

CHINATOWN HISTORY

Along Nieuwmarkt, Zeedijk and Geldersekade streets, Chinatown fits snugly against De Wallen and the Red Light District to form Amsterdam's historic centre. This area grew around the early 20th century, when Chinese immigrants, primarily from Guangdong province, settled here, opening cafes, restaurants and small businesses.

Over the years, the neighbourhood expanded, blending Chinese, Indonesian and other Asian cultural influences via accessible immigration policies and residency for former Dutch colonies.

Come to Chinatown to dine in traditional Chinese (Cantonese) restaurants, enjoying authentic dim sum, Peking duck and other dishes flying out of steamy shopfront kitchens. Hole-in-the-wall atmosphere, big dining groups and quick service is what you'll get here.

Before the Imperial Shrine
Sacred Chinese-Buddhist architecture

In Chinatown, the **He Hua Temple** *(ibps.nl; by donation; 1-3.30pm Tue-Sat)* is Europe's largest Buddhist temple built in Chinese Imperial style.

Stocky yet palatial and well decorated, the temple was built in 2000 and is dedicated to Kuan Yin, the Buddhist goddess of mercy. Enter through the side gates (as is customary; the main gates are reserved for monks and nuns) and make a donation towards its community (along with local Chinese Buddhists, He Hua is also part of the Fo Guang Shan monastic order).

Light an incense stick and take in the significant Kuan Yin Shrine. See how many of the Bodhisattva statue's thousand hands you can count and look into her third eye. These features symbolise her ability to understand and help all beings with their suffering. Other quiet areas, including a jade Buddha shrine and meditation hall, offer a tranquil escape from Amsterdam's downtown hustle. The ornate 'mountain gate' – an intriguing concept in the narrow confines of the Zeedijk – refers to the traditional setting of Buddhist monasteries.

The temple is a vibrant setting for Amsterdam's Chinese New Year celebrations. Every year, a parade departs from the Kuan Yin Shrine to Nieuwmarkt. More cultural festivities, including lion dances and fireworks, pop off on the Dam square.

Standing Tasting Room for Dutch Spirits
Tiny watering hole for jenevers and liqueurs

Dating from 1679, the small **Wynand Fockink** *(wynand-fockink.nl; 2-9pm)* tasting house is an intimate place to knock back a shot glass of *jenever* (Dutch gin) or two. Go as early as you can and accept a tipsy afternoon – it's the best way of escaping constant queues, which become impossibly long by early evening. Even then, the tiny space gets so packed that the antique wooden interiors rumble and ordering becomes challenging. There's no seating.

You'll find Wynand Fockink tucked into the Pijlsteeg ('Arrow Alley'), named after the archery grounds once nearby. During the 17th and 18th centuries, the short alley was also known as a brothel strip.

In an arcade building, scores of *jenevers* – a clear, malted grain-based spirit produced using juniper berries – are aged over years and in different casks. Dutch liqueurs in flavours

Continued on p55

DRINKING IN THE MEDIEVAL CENTRE: COCKTAIL HAVENS

Super Lyan: The Kimpton Hotel's classy bar blends mid-century design with neon, futuristic vibes. *5pm-midnight Wed & Sun, to 1am Thu-Sat*

Cut Throat: A men's barbershop, cocktail bar and brunch joint. Sun-kissed daytime drinking includes margs and other cocktails. *11pm-1am Sun-Thu, to 3am Fri & Sat*

Dutch Courage: The name comes from when Dutch soldiers took a swig of *jenever* pre-battle. *5pm-1am Sun-Thu, 3pm-3am Fri & Sat*

Tales & Spirits: Sip decadent creations made with house infusions, syrups and vinegar-based shrubs. Vintage and one-of-a-kind glasses. *5.30pm-1am Tue-Sat*

TOP EXPERIENCE

Centraal Station

Amsterdam's grand Centraal Station, beyond being the epicentre of local and regional travel, is a fascinating sight within itself – if you know where to look. Built on an artificial island, the station was designed as a neo-Renaissance 'curtain', a controversial plan that effectively cut off Amsterdam from the IJ River. Hidden features include Delft-tile walls and a royal waiting room.

Cuyperspassage

Controversial History

Amsterdam's turreted transportation marvel dates from 1889. One of the architects, Pierre Cuypers, also designed the Rijksmuseum, and you can see the similarities in the faux-Gothic towers, the fine red brick and the abundant reliefs (for sailing, trade and industry). Beneath its beauty, however, lies an impressive engineering feat: the entire station was built over 8600 wooden piles driven deep into Amsterdam's marshy landscape.

Built on three artificial islands in the IJ River, the station effectively separated the city from its waterfront. At the time, this sparked a heavy debate between merchants, worried about the port, and others who saw that Amsterdam needed a rail system to keep up with European capitals.

Passage Art

Cuyperspassage, a tunnel cutting through the middle of the station (enter directly between the bicycle parking lot and train station), is a shortcut covered in porcelain art. Some 80,000 Delft Blue tiles, handcrafted by Dutch artist Irma Boom, line the inside. If you gaze at the porcelain, the tiles tell the story of Amsterdam's maritime past.

TOP TIPS

● Cuyperspassage takes you directly to the piers behind Centraal Station where free ferries run to Noord every 10 to 20 minutes through the day (no rushing required).

● The IJ waterfront is a popular place to sit. There's a nice view of Noord including the Eye Filmmuseum (p205) and teeny swingers atop A'DAM Tower (p201).

PRACTICALITIES

● ns.nl/en/station -information/asd/ amsterdam-centraal
● free ● 24hr

Dam

Strolling the Dam square, you're tracing the footsteps of where Amsterdam was founded in 1270. Fishermen and traders settled along the Amstel; to protect their settlement against flooding, they built a dam here. If you catch the Dam on the right day, the square flourishes as a place for expressing solidarity.

VERVERIDIS VASILIS/SHUTTERSTOCK

Nationaal Monument

TOP TIPS

● On **Herdenkingsdag (Remembrance Day)** on 4 May, King Willem-Alexander lays a wreath on the Dam and the city observes two minutes' silence at 8pm.

● Don't let the 'New Church' name fool you – **Nieuwe Kerk** (located right on the Dam) dates from 1408. It's possible to walk in and take a free peek, but you'll have to pay the admission fee to get up close.

PRACTICALITIES

● 24hr ● Rokin metro station ● tram lines 4, 13, 14, 17, 24

Founding History

The square was split into two sections: Vissersdam, a fish market (where **De Bijenkorf** department store now stands) and Vijgendam (roughly south of the square today), probably named for the figs and other exotic fruits unloaded from ships. A lot of history has happened here, not all of it friendly – including one death by an angry lynch mob and many executions.

Amsterdam's historic heart is still a national gathering spot, especially if there's a national celebration or public demo. On the average day, it's full of pigeons, tourists and buskers.

Nationaal Monument

On the square's eastern side, the obelisk Nationaal Monument was built in 1956 to commemorate WWII's fallen. Fronted by two lions, its pedestal has a number of symbolic statues: four males (war), a woman with child (peace) and men with dogs (resistance). The 12 urns at the rear hold earth from war cemeteries of the 11 provinces and the Dutch East Indies. The war dead are still honoured here at a ceremony every 4 May.

Exploding Orange

King's Day (27 April), the Netherlands' most beloved holiday, sees every kind of Dutch person gather on the Dam square to celebrate the House of Orange – monarchists and non-monarchists alike. A tangerine dream of drinking and dancing makes the Dam one of Amsterdam's best spots to celebrate the public holiday. Join the partying, orange-clad crowd of thousands outside the Royal Palace.

Continued from p52

such as *boterbabbelaar* (butterscotch), *bitterkoekjes* (almond cookies) and *appeltaart* (apple pie) are much easier to kick back. Beware the *drop* liqueur; it's a salty liquorice bomb that's not for everyone. If you're deliberating over which *jenever* to go for, try the house speciality *boswandeling* (secret of the forest), a vivacious combination of young *jenever*, herb bitters and orange liqueur – the result tastes like cloves.

Reservations only for large groups; cash payment is preferred.

Amsterdam's Last Surviving Distillery
Timeworn tasting house

At the magnificent **Proeflokaal de Ooievaar** (*proeflokaal deooievaar.nl; noon-1am Sun-Thu, to 2am Fri & Sat*), sip *jenevers* (Dutch gins) and liqueurs from one of the tiniest tasting rooms left in the Netherlands. The historic interiors of this *proeflokaal* (tasting house) might not feel much bigger than a distilling vat, but you'll find all you need here from the Van Wees' family distillery, De Ooievaar, in Jordaan. Going strong since 1782, it's the only craft distillery still kicking in Amsterdam.

In charming *bruin café* (brown cafe) style, perch up at the antique bar and sample an array of old Dutch tipples hard to find today. Among them, 'Bride's Tears' (liqueur spiked with floating gold flakes inside – traditionally served at weddings) and 'Cock's Comb', a bright-red, intensely herbal liqueur. Try a traditional 'Half & Half' *jenever* – a balancing act between crisp young *jenever* and malty, rich old *jenever*. 'Young' and 'old' don't refer to ageing but rather a distilling method.

Drinking Up in a Sailor's Pub
Tiny bottles with big history

A treasure dating from 1650, **De Drie Fleschjes** (*Three Little Bottles; dedriefleschjes.nl; 2-8.30pm Mon-Sat, 3-7pm Sun*) is Amsterdam's oldest tasting room. Run by the distiller Bootz, the pub is an evocative reminder of earlier maritime days.

While the wall of lined-up barrels made by master shipbuilders might appear decorative, it's fully active in distilling *jenever* and liqueur served here. It's a pub feature known as a 'drinks organ' – the wall's rowed-up, pipe-like arrangement could allow a patron to freely choose from multiple barrels, much like tickling the ivories.

ARCHITECTURAL HEAVE-HO

When you leave Proeflokaal de Ooievaar, no, it's not that *jenever* (Dutch gin) making you woozy. The historic building is indeed leaning over. Known as *op de vlucht bouwen* (built on the fly), the design allowed goods to be hoisted into upper floors without risking façade damage.

Amsterdam's slumping landscape isn't solely by design. Many canal buildings lean due to age and shifting foundations. How to tell the difference? *Vlucht bouwen* houses are perfectly tipped forward and might still have a hoisting beam or hook at the gable top. Windows and door frames appear parallel to the ground rather than warped in ageing constructions.

One of Europe's smallest pancake restaurants; reserve ahead

EATING IN THE MEDIEVAL CENTRE: EXPERTLY MADE SWEETS

Van der Linde: Generations-old ice-cream shop; queue for a velvety cloud of one flavour: vanilla. *noon-5pm Wed, Thu & Sun, from 10am Fri & Sat* €

Van Stapele Koekmakerij: Sells one thing: gooey dark-chocolate cookies with white chocolate inside, made fresh almost hourly. Long queues. *10am-6pm* €

Van Wonderen: Instagram-approved *stroopwafels* with modern twists including *speculaas* (spiced biscuit), salted caramel, marshmallows, coconut. *8.30am-10pm* €

Pannenkoekenhuis Upstairs: Climb steep stairs to reach this Delft-tile-sized restaurant. Only four tables; expect unhurried service. *noon-6pm, to 5pm Sun* €

The Bootz tasting room specialises in liqueurs, including the signature almond-flavoured *bitterkoekje* (Dutch-style macaroon) liqueur, as well as lots of *jenever* (Dutch gin). Peek at the collection of little traditional bottles, which the pub's name plays on and are hand-painted with portraits of former mayors. In Dutch, the bottles are known as *kalkoentjes* ('little turkeys') because of their shape (full bodied with a skinny neck).

Fun Sex Ed for Adults

Questioning humans' sexuality

Visiting Amsterdam's **Sexmuseum** (*sexmuseumamsterdam. nl; €10; 10am-6pm*) is anything but a titillating experience. It's more like...if a 'sex ed' class for adults made love to a gay bar. Come and have a cheeky giggle at Ripley's-style oddities exploring the history of human sexuality. Think lewd Pompeian plates to chastity belts, the world's earliest nudes, Kama Sutra art and Andre the Giant–sized genitalia sculptures. And if there was any question, over-the-top theatrical lighting, red velvet and Renaissance murals affirm the camp of it all.

Overall, a much sillier and more fun experience than other erotic museums in the Red Light District. Watch out for the mannequin in a trench coat: he's a flasher automated to fart.

Minimum age for entry is 16.

Get Beyond the Stereotypes of Sex Work

Prostitution Information Center tours

Established by a former sex worker, the **Prostitution Information Center** (*PIC; pic-amsterdam.com; noon-5pm Wed-Sat*) provides frank information about the industry to those in the trade and curious tourists. Guided tours in English (*5pm Wed-Sat; €25/person*) are led by experienced sex workers or the organisation's advocates, and offer an insider perspective on the Red Light District, including on current challenges – particularly, increasing government rules and regulations affecting sex workers' conditions and the district overall.

The centre itself aims to raise awareness about the realities of sex work. Informal, often collage displays on themes – for example, the history of sex work in Amsterdam – make the space feel more like a living room than museum. It's also a casual hangout where sex workers might come in for a quick coffee or volunteering; they might not always be there for the purpose of engaging visitors, so keep this in mind. A small on-site shop sells sex-positive souvenirs.

RESPECTING THE WINDOWS

Claudia, a brothel owner, shares tips for mindfully visiting the Red Light District

● Photographing active windows is offensive. Avoid photography overall to prevent misunderstandings.

● Be aware that sex workers' quarters are equipped with a safety button that, when pressed, activates an alarm (sometimes, loudly) for assistance. Brothel staff have a direct line to police ensuring quick action.

● Smoking marijuana is illegal here as throughout Amsterdam.

● Remember people live and work above brothels. Don't litter, keep bike lanes free and watch your volume.

● Avoid staring excessively (it might send mixed signals).

● Don't engage sex workers' in conversation without intent. Screening clientele requires time and focus. Window regulations are increasingly limiting business hours.

 EATING IN THE MEDIEVAL CENTRE: BEST DUTCH RESTAURANTS

Van Kerkwijk: Low-key and easy to miss, but locals know: daily house specialities of fine Dutch fare. Always packed. No reservations or menu. *11am-midnight* €€

Carstens Brasserie: Skylit restaurant championing local suppliers within a 60km radius. Seasonal multi-course meals. *6-9.30pm Thu-Sun* €€€

D'Vijff Vlieghen: Across five 17th-century canal houses, a vision of Delft Blue tiles and Rembrandts. Smoked goose breast, Dutch-crab mayonnaise. *5.30-10pm* €€€

De Silveren Spiegel: Exquisite from interiors (17th-century townhouse) to regional dishes. Book ahead; dress to impress. *6.30-11.30pm Tue-Thu, 12.30-10pm Fri & Sat* €€€

Hash, Marihuana & Hemp Museum

Hash, Hemp & Herb Botany

Cultivating cannabis knowledge

Even abstainers might find a little fascination at the **Hash, Marihuana & Hemp Museum** *(hashmuseum.com; adult/child €11.45/free; noon-8pm)* – especially if parenting houseplants or fermenting fruits and veggies is your thing. Without a trace of stoner comedy, this museum offers science-y insights into dope botany. Wander through a live cannabis garden to take in plants in different developmental stages and learn a lot about horticulture and cultivation. Displays on soil types and watering strategies, as well as pruning and propagation can all technically be applied to a horticultural green thumb. If you've ever let a Monstera die, maybe you'll learn a few tricks.

Other parts of the museum might not be as interesting from a non-smoker's perspective. You'll find an impressive pipe collection and exhibits on the evolution of vaporisers and medicinal marijuana. Admission also includes the **Hemp Gallery**, filled with hemp art and historical items (a few of Rembrandt's 17th-century Dutch contemporaries!), in a separate building 30m north.

SHUTTING OFF THE RED LIGHT

In recent years, city officials have reduced the number of Red Light windows in an effort to clean up the District. They claim it's not about morals but about crime and, also, overtourism. The city has banned guided tours here except for those with special permits. Opponents point to a growing conservatism and say the government is using crime as an excuse.

In 2025, some 300 windows remained, down from 482. Scores of sex workers and their supporters are protesting the closures. Closing the windows simply forces sex workers to relocate to less safe environments. A buy-back project to replace windows with studios and local shops was largely unsuccessful, resulting in tourist traps filling the gaps.

 EATING IN THE MEDIEVAL CENTRE: BEST DUTCH SNACKS

Vleminckx: Hailed as Amsterdam's best *friterie*, this 1887-opened kiosk offers crispy fries in cones plus over 20 sauces. *11am-7pm, to 8pm Thu* €

Broodje Bert: Sandwich shop named after its twist on the *broodje* (sandwich): 'Broodje Bert' (lamb meatballs). *9am-5.30pm Tue-Sun* €

Dutch Delicacy: Dutch cheeses to savour on a cheese board or vacuum packed to-go. Gouda-starring sandwiches. *9am-7pm, from 10am Sun* €

Rob Wigboldus Vishandel: Hole-in-the-wall fish shop serving excellent sandwiches with herring, Dutch prawns, fried whitefish and more briny delicacies. *8am-5pm* €

Stroll Beyond the Neon Lights

In 2020, authorities banned guided tours in the Red Light District due to pub crawls and stag parties disturbing residential life. Strolling medieval alleyways is more pleasant with less noise and litter, but there's a downside: fewer opportunities for culture and context. Requiring special permits, guided tours have dramatically decreased – eliminating problematic tours, but some good ones, too. On this self-guided walk, explore the hidden histories and perspectives behind the entertainment.

❶ Oude Kerk

Start in front of Amsterdam's oldest surviving building, the Oude Kerk (p50). Dating back to 1306, the Old Church pre-dates organised sex work in the district; the Red Light District essentially grew around the sacred place. If anything, locals are proud of Oude Kerk's location: it truly symbolises a culture of tolerance. During opening hours, go inside to see the tombstone floor covering 12,000 burial sites – among them, sex workers.

The Walk: Just 180m from the front of Oude Kerk, you'll find the Prostitution Information Center.

❷ Prostitution Information Center

Circling the square Oude Kerk sits on, Oudekerksplein, you'll reach the modestly red-curtained shopfront of the Prostitution Information Center (p56). The sex worker-run organisation offers some of the last remaining guided tours of the Red Light District. Guided by sex workers or advocates, these tours are excellent.

NEDERLANDSE LEEUW · OWN WORK/WIKIMEDIA/CC BY 4.0

Prostitution Information Center (p56)

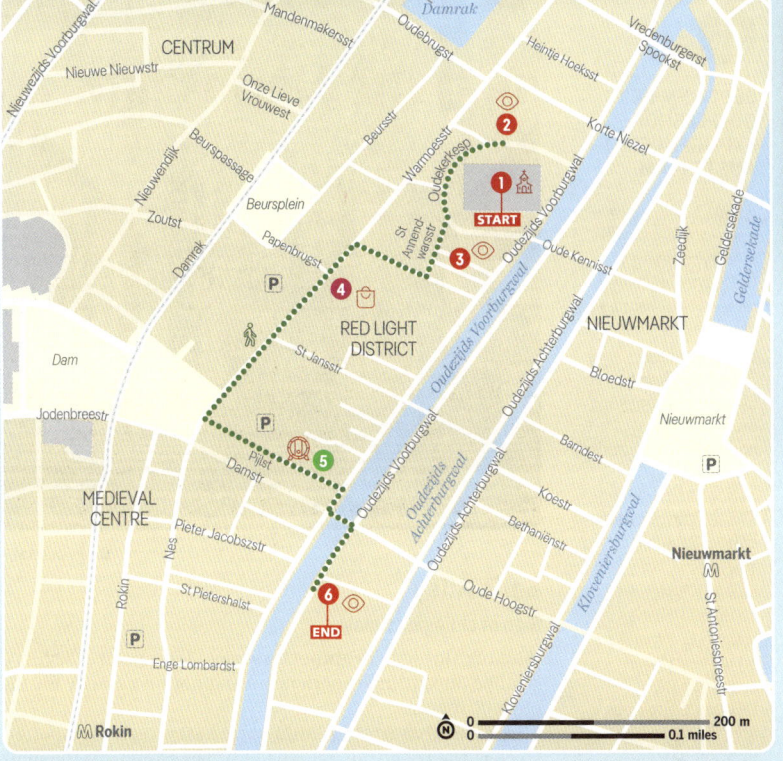

The Walk: Continuing further around Oudekerksplein, you'll reach the Belle Statue (p51) – a monument to sex workers – near the corner of Sint Annendwarsstraat. Then continue on to Amsterdam's narrowest alley.

❸ Trompettersteeg

Some years ago, visitors packed into the alley to get up close to red-light windows – among the most expensive in the area. All the red-light windows on Trompettersteeg (p60) were later ordered shut by the local government.

The Walk: The medieval alley is only 1m wide and creepy to walk through. Continue west and south to the Condomerie.

❹ Condomerie het Gulden Vlies

Cherry red, hypoallergenic and cartoon-character embodiments – the bright, cheerful Condomerie het Gulden Vlies is a shrine to condom art. The shop also has a history of raising awareness about sexual health, supporting HIV prevention charities and holding educational workshops.

The Walk: The constant crowd of ogling visitors makes for a rather jostling experience. Next, stroll south to Wynand Fockink.

❺ Wynand Fockink

Dating from 1679, Amsterdam's most famous tasting house, Wynand Fockink (p52), is tucked into an arcade behind the Anantara Grand Hotel Krasnapolsky. Its entrance is located on the medieval Pijlsteeg. The tiny tasting room is always overflowing; buy liqueur and *jenever* (Dutch gin) at the adjoining bottle shop instead.

The Walk: Head east across the canal and then south to the City Hall Urinal.

❻ City Hall Urinal

De Wallen has long had a problem with public urination. The City Hall Urinal was an early solution though Amsterdam-invented 'pee curls' have since perfected the idea. It's even a national monument, but the most bursting of bladders could never be worth the awful smell inside.

BEST LOW-KEY COFFEESHOP EXPERIENCES IN AMSTERDAM

If loud music, trippy decor and big crowds aren't your thing, these smaller, more relaxed coffeeshops offer mellow vibes.

Tweede Kamer
So-called 'Second Living Room' boasting *bruin café* vibes. Located in the historic centre, with local patrons and excellent Amsterdam-roasted coffee. *8am-1am*

The Hit
Low-key, historic-centre coffeeshop attracting a young crowd keen to get away from the raucous. Calm vibes and milkshakes. *9am-1am*

Boerejongens
(Map p121) Stylish, canal-side cannabis dispensary. Employees serve buds and style wearing suspenders and bowties. *7am-12.45am*

Katsu (Map p170)
Relaxed De Pijp coffeeshop brimming with diverse yet laid-back characters. All ages, all types. *10am-midnight, to 1am Fri & Sat*

La Tertulia (Map p98)
Mother-and-daughter-run coffeeshop with a Van Gogh–inspired mural and terrace. Crystals and plants adorn the interiors. *11am-7pm, closed Sun & Mon*

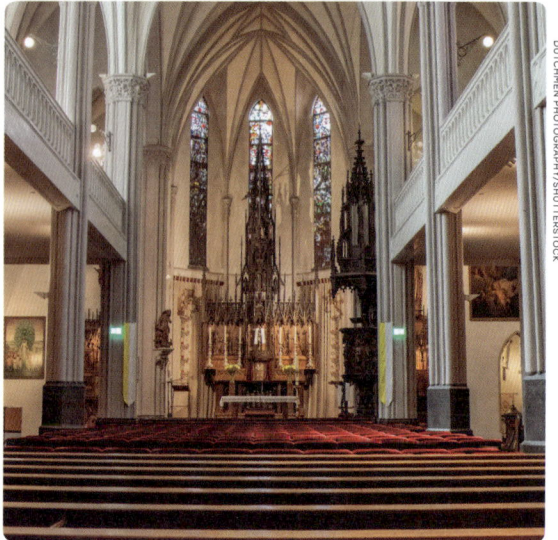

DUTCHMEN PHOTOGRAPHY/SHUTTERSTOCK

De Papegaai

Eerie Alley

Sign of changing times

Walking through **Trompettersteeg** (Trumpeter Alley) is a strange, unsettling experience – and not necessarily for the obvious reasons.

Trumpeted as Amsterdam's narrowest street, Trompettersteeg is where the busiest part of Amsterdam feels the most sombre and unalive. Blink and you might miss the alley's little opening in the block south of the Oude Kerk (p50). Claustrophobes shouldn't even attempt to bear its almost shoulder-hugging 1m width. Although the alley only goes for about 40m, the vibe gets weird rather quickly with broken glass, dusty shutters and thoroughly unartistic graffiti tags across concrete.

A couple of decades ago, walking through Amsterdam's narrowest alley was a nearly impossible feat – not claustrophobic because of width alone, but crowds packed in between. Once lined with windows, Trompettersteeg offered an opportunity to look into windows up-close (crowds would get hemmed in constantly). The sex workers here charged some of the area's highest prices.

On the left side, a couple of creative offices and a tattoo shop keep a faint pulse. Meanwhile, the right side is ramshackle with wooden boards and nails over closed windows. Nowhere else in the Red Light District does the government's 'clean-up' through window closures come more to life.

Enter the Hidden 'Parrot' Church

Little miracle

On Kalverstraat (p67), the curious Petrus en Pauluskerk, aka **De Papegaai** *(The Parrot; nicolaas-parochie.nl; 10am-4pm Mon-Sat, to 2pm Sun)* is not a bird of a feather for the surrounding shopping area.

The 17th-century Catholic church was a clandestine house of worship. The nickname Papegaai was a reference to its secret nest: behind a garden and a bird trader's home.

Once a site for the whispered prayers of Catholics who could not lawfully practice their religion, today this bird bellows during Sunday Masses in Latin with Gregorian chants. At most other times, this 'Parrot' inspires meditative calm. Sit in a pew and admire its stunning neo-Gothic design – dramatic arches reaching to the heavens, detailed stucco flourishes and stained-glass windows drawing in warm, natural light.

Shop for Amsterdam Swag at Mark Raven Grafiek

Special souvenirs

In a charming **gallery-boutique** *(markraven.nl; 10.30am-6pm)*, Amsterdam-born artist Mark Raven sells souvenirs made with love. The artist uses a technique called serigraphy (pushing ink through a fine mesh stencil to create layers of colour) to create detailed, moody Amsterdam cityscapes.

High-quality, screen-printed T-shirts and sweaters are sold exclusively in the shop (not online). You'll also find posters, coasters, fridge magnets – wonderful souvenirs in a destination where generic, tourist-shop trinkets abound. Prices are impressively reasonable (smaller prints go for as little as €30) and there's often a sale rack out front. Climb the shop's spiral staircase to find a small gallery of large prints also on display. Mark himself often works in the shop (both at the sales counter and upstairs painting) and is always happy to show customers around.

Savour Stroopwafels

Syrup waffles

The fourth-generation-run **Lanskroon** *(lanskroon.nl; 9am-5pm Mon-Thu, to 5.30pm Sat, from 10am Sun)* is famed for its signature take on *stroopwafel* (syrup waffles). Chewy, not crispy, and over-sized (big as a dessert plate), these rich treats could be the offspring of a *stroopwafel* and soft cookie. Luscious fillings such as caramel, coffee (caramel and espresso), honey (the most popular) and fig paste make for an even more indulgent bite. Come in the morning when they're at their most chewy, fresh out of the oven.

In winter, follow the locals inside for homemade spiced *speculaas* (spiced biscuits) and other Christmas treats. Summer's thick nut- and fruit-swirled ice creams are kid favourites.

LEGAL SEX WORK

In the Netherlands, the world's oldest profession is legal and highly regulated for modern times.

● Year prostitution officially legalised in the Netherlands: 2000

● Estimated number of registered sex workers in the Netherlands: 25,000–30,000

● Estimated number of registered sex workers in Amsterdam: 1700

● Minimum legal age to be a sex worker: 18 in the Netherlands; 21 in Amsterdam (also some select municipalities)

● Average age of registered sex workers in Amsterdam: 30

● Type of employment for sex workers: self-employed (an estimated 55% work full-time in the sector)

● Working from home is not allowed in the Netherlands except for in Utrecht as of January 2025

● Window opening hours vary; in Amsterdam, windows can only operate from 8am-6am (with a maximum 11-hour shift per worker)

WILL SALTER/LONELY PLANET

TOP EXPERIENCE

Begijnhof

It feels like something out of a storybook. You walk up to the unassuming door, push it open and *voilà:* a cloistered courtyard of tiny houses and gardens opens up before you. The 14th-century Begijnhof is no longer a secret, but manages to keep its aura of mystery – most impressively, in spite of big crowds and the inconspicuous staff who shush them.

Sacred Greenery

Dating from the early 14th century, the Begijnhof, an enclosed former convent, is an unusual place. These days, going in is like entering a nightclub: long queues form along the entrance on Gedempte Begijnensloot and staff 'bouncers' recite the rules before you even set foot through a turnstile.

Crowds mill in and around greenery and tiny houses; there's always at least one staffer in view watching everyone with an eagle eye and a ready walkie-talkie.

Still, the courtyard remains picturesque. Decorated windows, framing tiny houses and postage-stamp gardens, are a constant reminder of the Begijnhof's modern-day uniqueness as a residential community where sightseeing is commonplace.

DON'T MISS

Begijnhof Kapel

Engelse Kerk

Houten Huis

PRACTICALITIES

● begijnhofkapelamsterdam.nl ● free ● 10am-6pm

The well-kept *hof* (courtyard) holds venerable buildings: the charming 1671 Begijnhof Kapel; the Engelse Kerk, built around 1392; and the Houten Huis, the Netherlands' oldest preserved wooden house.

Begijnhof Kapel

One of the courtyard's pair of churches, Begijnhof Kapel is a 'clandestine' chapel where the Beguines were forced to worship after the Calvinists took away their Gothic church. Enter to find marble columns, stained-glass windows and murals commemorating the Miracle of Amsterdam. Wall paintings depict the story of a 1345 final sacrament administered to a dying man in Amsterdam. The next day, an undigested communion wafer was found in the ashes of the fire he vomited upon. This miracle turned medieval Amsterdam into a major pilgrimage site until the Reformation.

Engelse Kerk

The other church is known as the Engelse Kerk, built around 1392. It was eventually rented out to the local community of English and Scottish Presbyterian refugees – including the Pilgrim Fathers – and it still serves as the city's Presbyterian church. Look for pulpit panels by Piet Mondrian, in a figurative phase. Miraculously, the church has survived major fires and wars, and finds itself still in frequent use today. It's sometimes closed to visitors but you can attend an English-language Sunday service here (10.30am), or classical music and jazz concerts after the Begijnhof's daily 6pm public closing. Catch one of these evening events if you can; they offer unique 'after-hours access' to experience this spiritual place shrouded in darkness and at its most tranquil.

Current Residents

Today, 105 single women still live in the Begijnhof. You might see them through their windows, eating breakfast at a table or cooking in a kitchen, sometimes tending to front-yard gardens behind white-picket fences with gates. Sign-posted turnstiles indicate private entrances and walkways. This is perhaps the most fascinating part of strolling around: wondering what it's like to have a busy museum at your doorstep.

Hidden Treasures

Look out for the **Houten Huis** at No 34. It dates from around 1465, making it the oldest preserved wooden house in the Netherlands.

Keep your eyes peeled for likenesses of the Begijnhof's patron saints, Ursula and John, as well as biblical stones depicting Joseph with the donkey carrying mother and child.

Meanwhile, a statue in the **Kleine Hof** (Small Courtyard) depicts a Beguine woman; in the **Grote Hof** (Large Courtyard), the **Heilig Hartbeeld** (Sacred Heart Statue) depicts Jesus with a heart on his chest.

SISTERS WITHOUT COVENANT

The Beguines were a Catholic order of unmarried or widowed women who lived a religious life without taking monastic vows. The Begijnhof was their convent of sorts. They were not nuns, though their lifestyle was similar in devotion and communal living. The last true Beguine of Amsterdam, Sister Antonia, died in 1971, marking the end of a centuries-old sisterly tradition.

TOP TIPS

● As the courtyard is still a place of residence, visitors must be respectful (no open food or drinks are allowed and smoking is not permitted). Staff tell you these rules before entering.

● Photography of houses as well as flash photography is forbidden.

● Speak in whispered tones throughout the premises (in the open-air courtyard as in churches). It's surprisingly easy to forget. Staff diligently walk around reminding visitors; don't forget to turn your ringer off.

● Avoid the wooden door on the Spui's north side, which provides another entrance to the Begijnhof near the Houten Huis – only for church-goers and the women residents.

Savour Empowering Craft Beer

Conscience-led brews

Just a short veer out of the Red Light District, **Brouwerij de Prael** (*deprael.nl; noon-midnight Tue-Sun, from 2pm Mon*) is a warm-fuzzy brewpub with a compassionate, inclusive touch. Opened in 2002, De Prael's brewing excellence is driven by social employment and hiring individuals who face barriers to entering the traditional workforce. Most commonly, this has included the differently abled, but new hires could be anyone challenged by long-term unemployment, mental illness or other social and economic conditions.

The taproom boasts a superb selection of craft beers on tap. It's housed in a multilevel historic building (once an auction house and wagon workshop) and entertainment ranges from live music to comedy and quiz nights. On-site brewing was discontinued in 2024, so production tours are no longer available.

A Secretive Book Market

A rare find indeed

Thumbing through secondhand books doesn't get much better than in the secluded **Oudemanhuispoort Book Market** (*11.30am-6pm Mon-Sat*). In the atmospheric covered alleyway between Oudezijds Achterburgwal and Kloveniersburgwal, you'll find a few stands selling secondhand books, but also other printed curios from sheet music to maps and old posters (perhaps the perfect rare souvenir). Most tomes are in Dutch, but a little English section is separated out.

The used-book market, running since 1886, is mostly overseen by bespectacled older generation of fellows who are very friendly. As the building itself is now part of the University of Amsterdam, it's mostly frequented by students and professors (you'll know them by their tweed-patched elbows) who happen to be drifting through.

The ancient literary passage itself also has a storied past. One of the market's frequent patrons was said to be Van Gogh. Over the past 400-odd years, the red-brick, Dutch Renaissance–style Oudemanhuispoort building has been a convent, cholera hospital and arts academy. The complex is said to be overrun with ghosts...beware.

If you find a good book, take it into the courtyard lying opposite the market in the passage. Quiet and leafy green, it's a great hidden sit-down (if you don't mind a little haunting, that is).

English Books, Bits & Bobs

Amsterdam's ABC

Rambling over three storeys, the excellent **American Book Center** (*abc.nl; 11am-6pm Mon-Wed, 10am-7pm Thu-Sat, 11am-6.30pm Sun*) is the biggest source of English-language books in Amsterdam. The greatest strengths of 'ABC' – a fitting nickname – are in the artsy ground-floor department, but on

Museum Ons' Lieve Heer op Solder

LITERARY QUARTER

It's no coincidence that high-brow bookshops abound around the Spui square. The so-called 'Golden Age' saw Amsterdam become the 'book capital' of Europe – a major printing and publishing hub. Through busy port trade, paper was imported and distributed across borders on a dime. Soon, Amsterdam attracted experienced printers, typesetters and illustrators, creating a big literary scene.

Students, intellectuals and writers frequented the area, drawn by the University of Amsterdam nearby. Amsterdam gained a reputation for printing books that were banned elsewhere in Europe – works considered controversial in the Holy Roman Empire, France or Spain – perhaps scientific papers or political pamphlets.

the upper floors there's fiction and oodles of special-interest and travel titles. Wandering around here is a treat; good souvenirs, like an ABC tote bag or well-designed postcard, abound.

Scrunch Inside Our Dear Lord in the Attic

Hiding the man upstairs

Within what looks like an ordinary canal house is an entire Catholic church. **Museum Ons' Lieve Heer op Solder** *(Our Dear Lord in the Attic; opsolder.nl; adult/child €16.95/7.50; 10am-6pm)* was built in the mid-1600s for clandestine worship in defiance of the Calvinists. Head upstairs and squeeze inside: you'll see labyrinthine staircases, rich artworks, period decor and the soaring, two-storey church itself.

Peruse Handsome Wares on the Market Square

Art, stamps and more

Even centuries after the 'Golden Age', market trade is still a beloved activity in Amsterdam. Head to the **Spui** (pronounced 'spow', rhymes with 'now'), where inviting cafes and bookshops have long attracted Amsterdam's intellectual scene. The square hosts the **Amsterdam Book Market** *(10am-6pm)* every Friday (weather permitting). A couple of dozen stands gather to sell secondhand tomes ranging from lightly paged-through to rare. Most are Dutch titles, with some in English mixed in.

MOST UNUSUAL SHOPPING

Andries de Jong BV
Serving seafarers since 1787 with bells, bottled boats and other maritime gifts. Flags are quite affordable. *appointment only*

By Popular Demand
Nifty gifty wares and (mostly) easy to transport: windmill or bicycle lapel pins and rock 'n' roll–inspired Delftware. *10am-7pm Mon-Sat, from 11am Sun*

Posthumus
1865-established, preserved-timber shop. Sells everything stamp-related – lacquer and rubber stamps, wax and ink – in Dutch-themed designs. *10am-5.30pm Tue-Fri, from 11am Sat*

PGC Hajenius
The Dutch royal family frequents this tobacco emporium where Cuban cigars are sold in gilded-and-marbled interiors. *9.30am-6pm Tue-Sat, noon-5pm Sun, noon-6pm Mon*

WonderWood
As much a museum as a vintage furniture and decorations shop; look up to see the 1565-built timber ceiling. *noon-6pm Thu-Sat*

COLORMAKER/SHUTTERSTOCK

De Beurspassage

On Sunday, the displays on the Spui's cobblestone change to canvases and prints for the **Art Amsterdam Spui** *(artamsterdam-spui.com; 11am-6pm Sun)*. Save on gallery fees by buying directly from the artists here. Some 60 artists set up on the square weekly from March to December (note the book market goes all year).

Nearby, a triangular, square-like slice of Nieuwezijds Voorburgwal turns into the **Postzegelmarkt** *(Stamp Market; 10am-4pm Wed & Sat)* twice weekly. Stamp trading has been a tradition here for over a century. Find rare, highly collectable postage marks, but also coins, postcards, medals and other small antiques and ephemera.

The **Sunday Market** *(sundaymarket.nl; noon-6pm Mar-Dec)* for arts and antiques lines up along Rokin on the last Sunday of the month. Browse quality craft, fashion and design produced by talented locals. The same market travels around to other neighbourhoods on other Sundays; check the agenda online.

Explore the Mini Mouse Mansion

Mice have feelings too

While cats might be the folk saviours of Amsterdam's waterways, at least one cultural sight celebrates the anti-hero. **Het Muizenhuis** *(The Mouse Mansion; themousemansion.com; 10am-6pm)* is a museum-style dollhouse installation taking on the Dutch capital's long-running rat plague from a more light-hearted, loving perspective.

This enchanting world in miniature is the brainchild of artist and author Karina Schaapman, who crafted a 100-room home for adorable felt mice – Sam, Julia and friends – who could *never* be baddies. Schaapman has also produced a series of over a dozen children's books on their adventures. You can see the original mansion and sets for later books (even a mouse roller-coaster) at this two-floor 'mini museum' and buy toys, books and materials to build your own mouse mansion.

Take in the Aquatic Murals of Beurspassage

Captivating art arcade

In the beautiful, 19th-century shopping arcade **De Beurspassage** (open 24 hours), a captivating public-art exhibition is a love note to Amsterdam's canals. **Amsterdam Oersoep** is an immersive artwork by Dutch artists Arno Coenen, Iris Roskam and Hans van Bentem. In English 'Amsterdam Primordial Soup', as the city's canal waters are known, illustrates how water formed life in Amsterdam. Chandeliers crafted from bicycle parts illuminate its glass-mosaic-tiled ceiling; stained-glass lamps adorn its walls, where a shimmering fish fountain dispenses 'tolerance elixir' (water); and floor tiles depict ship wheels and anchors.

Take an Unexpected Art Tour at Kalverpassage

Escaping commercial Kalverstraat

You're sure to end up on crowded **Kalverstraat** at some point. Named after the livestock markets held here in the 17th century, Kalverstraat is now a place where shoppers stampede around high-street chain stores looking for sales. The Dutch Monopoly game has Kalverstraat as its most expensive street.

Duck into **Kalverpassage** *(kalverpassage.nl; 10am-7pm Mon-Wed, Fri & Sat, to 9pm Thu, 11am-6.30pm Sun)* to escape the crowds and check out some public art (also, one of few public bathrooms in the immediate area).

The shopping mall, unassumingly, doubles as a gallery with various statues and installations by international artists. Stroll around and discover the **Beetle Sphere** by Indonesian sculpturist Ichwan Noor. The bright-red 1953 Volkswagen beetle, compressed into a perfect aluminium sphere, can't be missed. Other installations, such as the **Covered Motorbike** by British artist Jonathan Monk, are less obvious. The basement-level **Our Generation – Oh Yeah!** by Chinese artist Gao Xiao Wu rises up through the atrium.

Scan QR codes beneath each artwork for an **Art Audio Tour** revealing more about the artist and inspiration. The mall's website provides a handy list of all artworks with images.

ALL PAWS ON DECK

Not with a howl but a purr, cats have quietly shaped Amsterdam's history. During the height of 17th-century maritime trade, felines were trusty crew members on cargo ships. Sprawling, labyrinthine vessels travelling the North Sea and beyond were highly prone to rodents, especially when carrying food supplies. At sea, a reverse cat-and-mouse game ensued: mice could hide, but they couldn't run.

Cats played an indispensable role in safeguarding expensive perishables like grains, sought-after spices, salted fish and meat (barrels were a squeaker's favourite), but also delicate textiles and paper. As shipping slowed down, many cats disembarked to continue service in canal houses and warehouses.

Look for cat cafes and feeding bowls along canals. Felines are also frequently depicted in Dutch art, folklore and literature.

NIEUWMARKT, PLANTAGE & THE EASTERN ISLANDS

STAY CENTRAL BUT DITCH THE HORDES

Contemporary architecture points at Amsterdam's current dynamism while great museums explain the complexities of its seafaring past, WWII travails and the fate of the once dynamic Jewish community.

This is the area that locals love to keep quiet. Central, with several great museums and plenty of architectural variety, Nieuwmarkt, Plantage and the Eastern Islands (NPEI) have barely a fraction of Amsterdam's tourists. Miraculously the crowds seem to fizzle out east of Nieuwmarkt. Areas of uninteresting modern architecture around Waterlooplein and Valkenburgstraat dissuade casual wanderers from discovering Entrepotdok, the eastern Oosterdok waterfront and the charmingly leafy Plantage area, where bars and restaurants are relatively widely spaced but tend to be more inspiring than average tourist spots.

Waterside views add interest to the rapidly redeveloping Eastern Islands: former docklands with a curious mixture of flashy contemporary architecture and areas of seemingly endless apartments. A long tram ride takes you to IJburg with its water sports and urban beach.

TOP TIP

Nieuwmarkt and the Eastern Islands have an eclectic mix of architecture, from the fantastical Scheepvaarthuis (a classic example of the Amsterdam School) to Renzo Piano's green-tinged NEMO Science Museum.

See p239 for places to stay in Nieuwmarkt, Plantage and the Eastern Islands.

Oosterdok

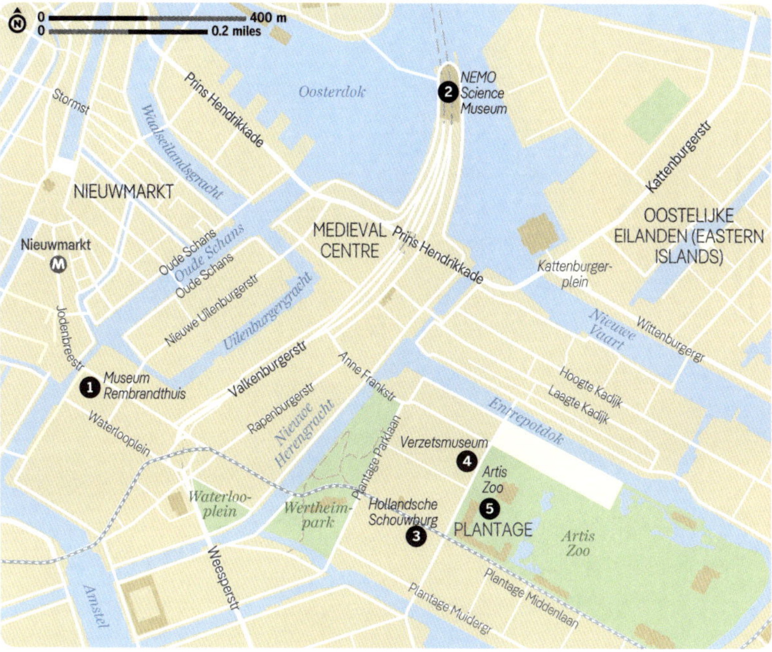
0 400 m
0 0.2 miles
Oosterdok
NEMO Science Museum
Stormst
Prins Hendrikkade
Waalseilandsgracht
NIEUWMARKT
Nieuwmarkt
Oude Schans
Nieuwe Uilenburgerstr
Uilenburgergracht
Jodenbreestr
Museum Rembrandthuis
Valkenburgerstr
Rapenburgerstr
Nieuwe Herengracht
Waterlooplein
MEDIEVAL CENTRE
Anne Frankstr
Plantage Parklaan
Verzetsmuseum
Artis Zoo
Hollandsche Schouwburg
PLANTAGE
Wertheimpark
Weesperstr
Amstel
Plantage Muiderg
Plantage Middenlaan
Entrepotdok
Hoogte Kadijk
Laagte Kadijk
Nieuwe Vaart
Wittenburgergr
Kattenburgerplein
Kattenburgerstr
OOSTELIJKE EILANDEN (EASTERN ISLANDS)

Highlights

1 Museum Rembrandthuis
Visit Rembrandt's former home and studio. **p72**

2 NEMO Science Museum ▶
Hands-on science and harbour views on the roof. **p88**

3 Hollandsche Schouwburg
Introduction to the Jewish community decimated during WWII. **p76**

4 Verzetsmuseum
Discover daring accounts of the Dutch Resistance during the WWII occupation. **p78**

5 Artis Zoo
The city's venerable zoo remains a forward-thinking, family-friendly oasis. **p84**

Getting Around

Walking & Cycling
It's often quicker to walk in the western half of this area. In the more distant islands and docklands, however, a bicycle or public transport makes sense.

Tram & Bus
IJburg-bound tram 26 starts behind Centraal Station following the IJ River waterfront and intersecting with tram 7 at Rietlandpark. Tram 14 goes via Waterlooplein and Plantage. Buses 22 and 43 are useful in Eastern Island areas.

Metro
Short hops on metro lines 51, 53 and 54 connect Centraal Station via Nieuwmarkt and Waterlooplein to Weesperplein, from which tram 7 heads to Azartplein via De Gooyer Windmill and Rietlandpark.

NIEUWMARKT

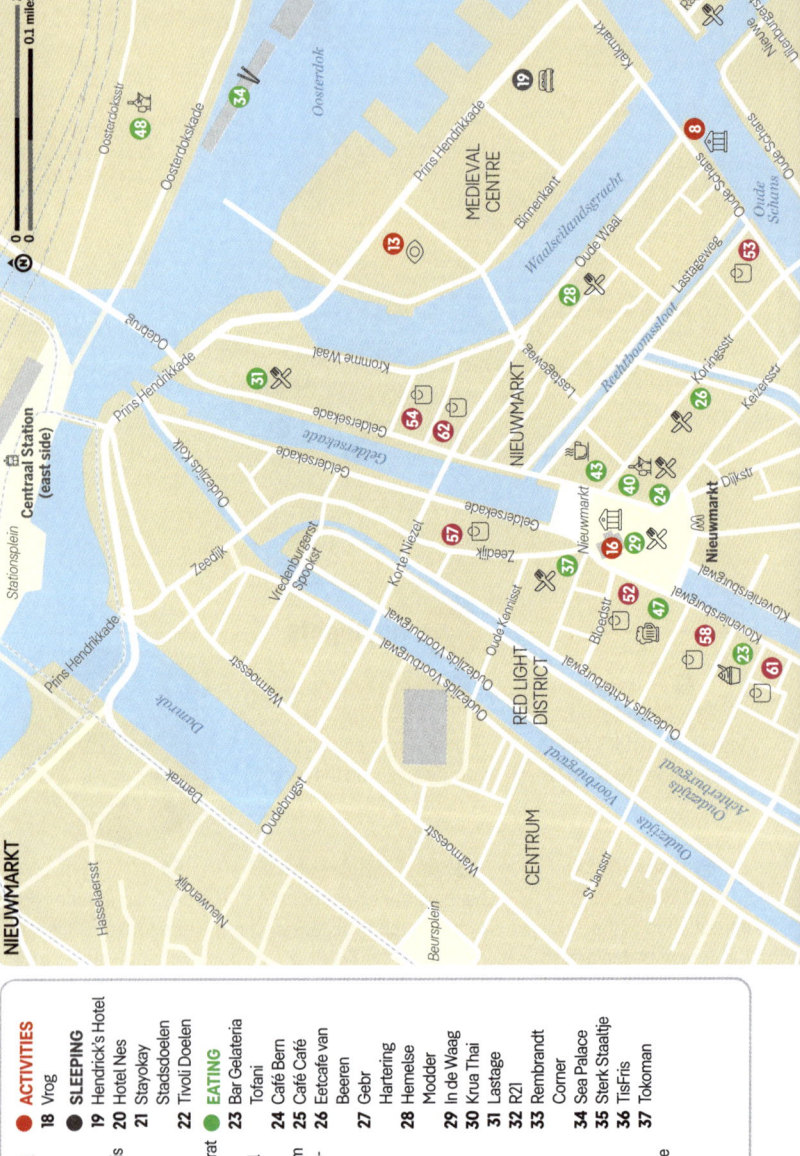

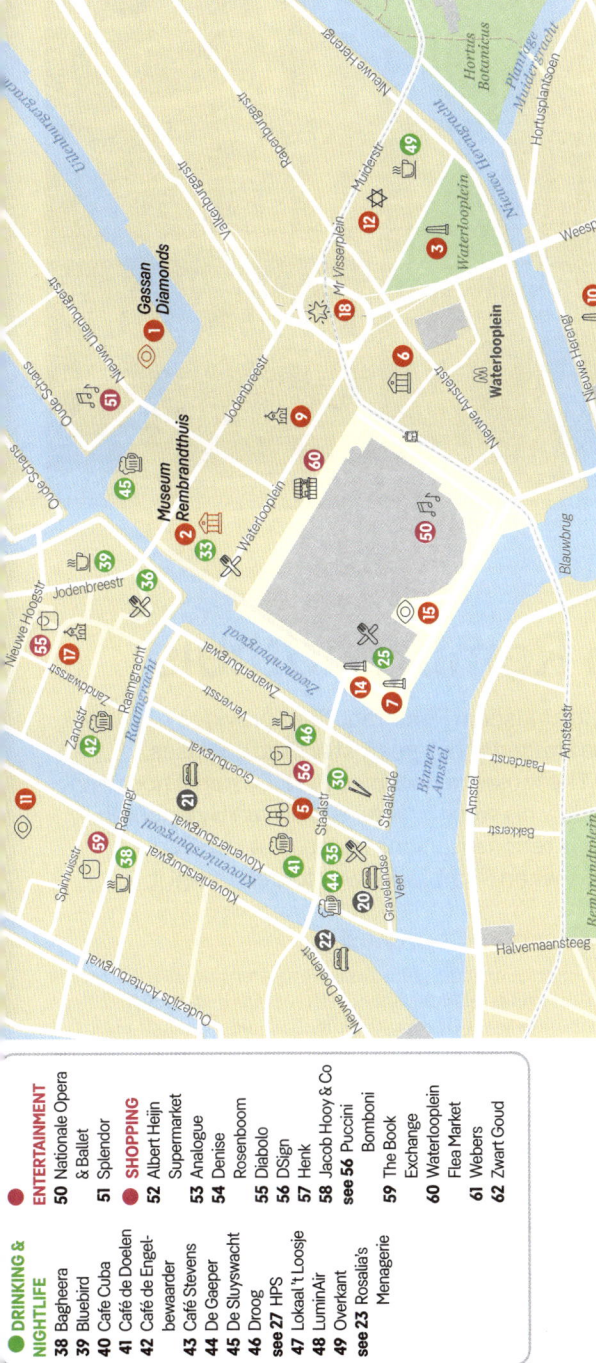

Gassan Diamonds

Museum Rembrandthuis

Waterlooplein

Hortus Botanicus

Plantage Middengracht

Waterlooplein

WOLF PHOTOGRAPHY/SHUTTERSTOCK

TOP EXPERIENCE

Museum Rembrandthuis

A couple of hours in the Museum Rembrandthuis provides a unique insight into one of the Netherlands' greatest artistic geniuses, Rembrandt van Rijn. The museum occupies the 1606 canal house he bought in 1639, helped by his wealthy wife, Saskia van Uylenburgh. Interiors are meticulous reconstructions based on a detailed inventory made in 1656 when Rembrandt was forced to sell it.

DON'T MISS

Etching or pigment demonstrations

Rembrandt's guild token (Sijdelcaemer)

Narwhal tusks (curio cabinet)

Pieter Lastman's *Crucifiction* (Voorhuys)

View over the salon (small oval window)

Kitchen & Courtyard

Collect your audio guide from the modern annexe then start on the lower level in the kitchen. Here is the bed-box where Rembrandt's maid Hendrickje Stoffels would sleep half-upright... at least before starting an affair with him after his first wife Saskia died. Most of the pots and crockery are from other sources but a glass box displays a few originals including a couple of tobacco pipes – objects that were broken and thrown in the cess pit, and only discovered long after in an archaeological excavation. The small open courtyard, home to a wooden toilet cubicle, is thought to be where Rembrandt painted *The Night Watch;* the studio wouldn't have been big enough.

PRACTICALITIES

● Map p70 ● rembrandthuis.nl ● adult/under-26/under-18 €21.50/15/8
● 10am-5pm

Voorhuys (Hall) & Sijdelcaemer (Antechamber)

The high ceilinged *voorhuys* entrance hallway doubled as a gallery and sales room displaying work to potential purchasers. Paintings displayed here now are mostly by artists who inspired Rembrandt's early work, notably including Pieter Lastman (1583–1633). The audiovisual guide does a great job of explaining various paintings' relevance in bite-sized chunks that you can skip if you're not interested. Clients interested in making a commission would be ushered through into the *sijdelcaemer* to discuss terms over a glass of wine. It now displays paintings by Rembrandt's apprentice students.

Salon

Tucked beneath the stairs, notice a tiny office, its desk strewn with papers and sealing wax. A darkened room gives a timeline of Rembrandt's life punctuated with mini portraits at different ages and small screens showing his art's development. Beyond is the salon, both living and sleeping room where you learn of Rembrandt's happy – then less happy – love life.

Etchings

Climb the narrow staircase. Part way up, a small side-room displays just a handful of Rembrandt's etchings from the museum's collection (which includes 285 of 310 known designs). To see the mostly tiny originals, lift the protective leather flaps. Other interesting displays show how etchings look on different papers and a sniff box lets you experience the perfume of the ink. You'll learn much more about etchings on the top floor.

Studio & Cabinet

Continue up the narrow staircase to the master's studio, whose four north-facing windows create daytime lighting conditions ideal for painting. Every second day there are fascinating demonstrations here on how Rembrandt selected and ground pigments with linseed oil to make paints. Across the landing is Rembrandt's 'Cabinet', a room crammed with curiosities similar to those he collected: giant clamshells, an Amazonian macaw-feather headdress, busts of Roman philosophers, stuffed alligators...all used at times as subjects for sketches.

Student Studio & Etching Studio

The next floor up houses the etching studio with demonstrations of technique and ink-making on those days that the pigment demonstration is not working. Otherwise, watch a video version on the large horizontal screen-table. Across the landing is the studio where apprentices worked in three separate booths. Here you can sit at an easel to have your photo taken as an artist. Exit upwards, hear an 'epilogue' about Rembrandt's bankruptcy, then exit via two large rooms of temporary exhibitions.

BANKRUPT!

Rembrandt had paid a fortune for the house. His style slowly fell out of fashion, his income declined and his wealthy wife was dead. Yet he continued to buy curios, borrowing extensively from moneylenders. Inevitably, in 1656 he had to sell up, moving to cheaper digs in the Jordaan. Ironically it's thanks to debt collectors' inventories that the museum could reproduce the interiors so authentically.

TOP TIPS

● Pre-booking a time slot is supposedly mandatory but when things are quiet (typically midweek afternoons), walk-ins are usually possible.

● The included audiovisual guide has 14 languages, including Ukrainian and Hebrew.

● To see and listen to absolutely everything could take four hours.

● Live demonstrations of either pigment making or etching demonstrations are included on alternate days *(10.30am-noon & 12.30-3pm)*. On 'off days' watch the video instead.

● No wheelchair access except to temporary exhibitions and gift shop.

● Ninety-minute etching workshops are available at 1pm on summer Thursdays, Saturday and Sunday (extra ticket).

● Free lockers hold small and mid-sized bags.

THE UNWANTED METRO

On a wall above the platform of **Nieuwmarkt metro station** there's a giant wrecking ball and patch of symbolically shattered brickwork. This recalls a period of civil unrest in 1975 when plans to create a metro line threatened to rip straight through the historic neighbourhood.

Citizens were horrified at losing heritage and homes, including many a hippy squat. At one point there were pitched battles with armoured cars, tear gas and volleys of paving stones. In the end the metro was built anyway, but the demonstrations did mean that demolitions were less severe than originally planned. It's an irony that the wrecking ball has become an anti-metro monument…in the metro.

Central Calm
MAP P70

Escaping the Red Light madness on Nieuwmarkt

Walk a block east from Ouderzijds Achterburgwal and the tourist-packed seediness of the Red Light District disappears, swapped for the low-key, cafe-ringed Nieuwmarkt. The transition is incredibly abrupt. Architecturally the square's centrepiece is the **Waag**, a multi-lobed brick mini castle, originally built in 1488 as a gate in the city walls. In 1601 those walls were demolished as the city expanded and the Waag was turned into Amsterdam's main weigh house. By the 17th century it was home to various guilds, including that of the surgeons who, after intoning suitable prayers, would perform human dissections in front of a paying crowd. One such scene is famously captured in Rembrandt's *The Anatomy Lesson of Dr Nicolaes Tulp* (displayed in the Mauritshuis museum in Den Haag; p225). Today, most of the ground floor is the eponymous cafe-restaurant, In de Waag.

Quietly Quirky
MAP P70

Strolling down Kloveniersburgwal

Assuming the wafting hash fumes from several coffeeshops haven't blurred your vision, a very imposing neo-Gothic façade should catch your eye as you wander south down Kloveniersburgwal from Nieuwmarkt. Behind the 1890s 'Bushuis' façade, this university structure incorporates **Oost-Indisch Huis**, the fine courtyard building that was once home to the Dutch East India Company (VOC). See p273 for why this causes controversy today. At Kloveniersburgwal's southern end, on the site now occupied by the grand **Tivoli Doelen** hotel, once stood the building for whose walls Rembrandt painted *The Night Watch*.

This whole area is dotted with quirky shops, including **Webers**, a bondage-gear vendor occupying one of Amsterdam's narrowest houses (built in 1696).

A defining landmark is the pretty, if partly hidden, clockspire of **Zuiderkerk** *(zuiderkerkamsterdam.nl)*, a 1611 church turned events venue. The classic view is from the **Groenburgwal Bridge** looking up the canal across a city map fashioned from old padlocks.

EATING & DRINKING ON & AROUND NIEUWMARKT: OUR PICKS
MAP P70

Café Stevens: *Bruin café* with lilting Latin music. Day-long menu of snacks (toasties, calamari rings), salads, spare ribs and even quinoa burgers. *9am-1am* €

Café Bern: Family-run bar, little changed since 1978. Curious 'sink' tables protect flames for fondue dishes and self-seared entrecote (€23). *bar 4-11pm, food 6-9.30pm* €€

In de Waag: Fairly priced drinks and light meals, considering the location in and around Nieuwmarkt's defining 'castle' of a building. Candlelit at night. *11.30am-10pm* €€

Lastage: Rogier van Dam's gastronomic oasis lost its Michelin star in 2023 but remains committed to sophisticated seasonal 'artisan' cuisine. *6.30-9pm Wed-Sun* €€€

Waterlooplein Flea Market

NIEUWMARKT, PLANTAGE & THE EASTERN ISLANDS

Come Rummage

MAP P70

Making sense of Waterlooplein Flea Market

From Monday to Saturday, **Waterlooplein Flea Market** *(water looplein.amsterdam)* softens the otherwise drearily non-aesthetic expanse of Waterlooplein with some 300 down-market stalls where you can browse through racks and stacks for vintage jeans, Dutch football shirts, retro leather jackets or endless selections of inexpensive jewellery.

South of the square is the combined city hall/opera-house complex, **Stopera**. Built in 1986, it fills the space created by total demolition of a run-down residential property that had been overwhelmingly Jewish before the WWII deportations (p77). The very few Jews who survived returned to find their houses ransacked; even the floorboards were removed to provide other Amsterdammers with scarce firewood to help them survive the desperate 'winter of hunger' in 1944–45.

As well as Jews, this area of Amsterdam had also been a refuge for Catholics in times when papist Christianity had been largely proscribed. The imposing 1841 church, **Mozes-en-Aäronkerk**, built on land where the family of Spinoza once lived, developed from what had once been a semi-clandestine prayer house.

OFFBEAT SHOPS AROUND NIEUWMARKT

Zwart Goud (Map p70) Sip super-strong coffee while perusing vinyl records.

Analogue (Map p70) Old-school cameras including Polaroids, plus photo development.

Denise Rosenboom (Map p70) Buy or learn to make Denise's signature 'Pussy Pendants'.

Jacob Hooy & Co (Map p70) A 1743 pharmacy retaining wooden drawers and containers.

Henk (Map p70) Vast selection of comics and a room of Funko Pop figurines.

The Book Exchange (Map p70) Mind-boggling selection of secondhand books in English.

DSign (Map p70) Colourful accoutrements, notably tulip bags and purses by by-Lin.

Diabolo (Map p70) Flamboyant carnival or clubbing gear in rainbow colours.

 EATING EAST OF NIEUWMARKT: COSY DINING — MAP P70

Eetcafe van Beeren: Between trad-French restaurant and Dutch *bruin café,* wafting tempting aromas. Meal of the day €15. *5-9.30pm Mon-Fri, 4-9.30pm Sat & Sun* €

Gebr Hartering: Founded by foodie brothers in a tiny wine-decor shophouse. Menus barely hint at the five- or seven-course adventure ahead. Canal views. *6-9pm* €€

Hemelse Modder: Neat, simple decor leaves little to distract you from the entrancing flavours created in the chef's inventive multicourse menus. *6-10pm* €€

R21: Refined yet completely unstuffy gastronomic dining across three connected antique buildings at a cosy canal-side location. *6-10pm Tue-Sat* €€€

PROCESSING DIAMONDS

Diamonds are the hardest material known on earth, so cutting and polishing them from raw stones into fabulous jewels is no small task. A key invention, the spinning grinder, helps create the facets, but until the 19th century these were turned by hand. Typically women did the turning while men did the cutting, stones being held in place by a form of temporary solder.

Steam-powered grinders later made grinding easier and faster while allowing improved options for gemstone design. However, the noise was appalling and inhaled dust meant that polishers' lungs were often destroyed and many had to retire in their 30s. Today, Perspex shields and vacuum pumps ensure that dust from new electric grinders is minimised.

Diamond Dazzle
MAP P70

Watching gem grinders at work

Once you get past quizzical security guards, **Gassan Diamonds** *(gassan.com/en/tours/diamond-experience-tour)* offers a fascinating and totally free opportunity to see diamond cutters in action. That's something you'd struggle to find even in Antwerp, the world's diamond capital. Gassan's website urges you to sign up for an arrival slot online, and that's wise, especially for non-English-speaking visitors. But it's often possible to join a tour at short notice by simply showing up at the restored 1879 factory building. The visit includes an engaging little museum section about the industry, the family company's history and the various gem-cutting possibilities: 'Gassan 121' is their own trademarked style.

Visitors are then ushered to sit around a viewing table and guess the value of real diamonds while perusing Gassan jewellery. While that's undoubtedly a sales technique, there's no pressure to buy and you can simply wander off and have a free coffee in the factory's former boilerhouse as you exit. Allow at least 40 minutes.

Shocking Deportations
MAP P80

Honouring the fate of a whole community

From the road, the **Hollandsche Schouwburg** *(jck.nl/en/location/hollandsche-schouwburg; free)* appears to be what it once was: an architecturally splendid 1892 theatre. However, behind the façade, the building is mostly a hollow shell: a powerful monument to the WWII deportations that virtually wiped out the Jewish community. An affecting 12-minute audiovisual presentation tells the story of how, from 20 July 1942, the playhouse became a holding place from which around 46,000 Jews were eventually sent to prison and death camps.

After liberation, the building's new owners tried to restart the theatre. The obscene insensitivity of suggesting 'a pleasant night out' in a place of such suffering meant this idea was quashed. However, by the time the city could decide how to use the building, its rear section was in ruins. Ironically, the state of semi-collapse now serves to underline the sense of tragedy. Use your audio guide to listen to heart-rending personal tales of deportees as you walk towards the stark memorial obelisk.

Try the chicken, mango and peanut salad

 EATING NEAR THE REMBRANDTHUIS: OUR PICKS MAP P70

Rembrandt Corner: Tourist-focused with salads, schnitzels and roast chicken. Offers classic Dutch *stamppot* (mashed veg/potato with meat). *10am-10pm* €

Krua Thai: Officially certified as being authentic in its Thai flavours, though heat is reduced for European palates. Rice and tap water cost extra. *5.15-10pm* €

Café Café: Lively music-bistro with imaginative fusion food like celeriac with hazelnut and *kombu dashi. kitchen 5.30-9.30pm, DJ/dancing from 10pm Fri & Sat* €€

TisFris: Contemporary cafe. Handy for light lunches: homemade soups, organic-based salads and open sandwiches. Vegan and veggie options. *9am-7pm* €

BACKGROUND

The Rise & Destruction of Jewish Amsterdam

In the 1580s, expulsions from Spain and Portugal brought large numbers of Sephardic Jewish refugees to rapidly expanding Amsterdam. Unlike elsewhere in Europe at the time, it was permitted for people of all faiths to buy property here. Tolerated more than truly accepted at first, Jews were barred from numerous professions by monopolistic guilds. However, some became diamond cutters (for which there was originally no guild) and others introduced unrestricted new trades like printing or finance.

17th- to Early 20th-Century Developments

Upon construction, the Portuguese synagogue here was Europe's biggest. It still houses the Ets Haim (Tree of Life), founded in 1616 and now the world's oldest Jewish library. In the 17th century, Ashkenazim (Jews from Europe outside of Iberia) arrived, fleeing pogroms in Central and Eastern Europe.

By Napoleonic times, Amsterdam was Europe's largest Jewish centre. During French rule, the guilds were abolished and with them any remaining restrictions on Jews. Amsterdam's Jewish community thrived in the 19th and early 20th centuries, though like all population groups there was a large spectrum: many of the wealthy spread out to the Plantage and other newer city suburbs, while the breadline poor remained concentrated in the original 'old Jewish Quarter' around Waterlooplein.

The Horrors of WWII

Before WWII, Jews constituted 13% of Amsterdam's population, a number swollen with Jewish refugees escaping Hitler's Germany. Then in May 1940, Nazi occupation began. Henceforth Jewish people were increasingly forced into a de facto ghetto in the Waterlooplein area, ostensibly administered by a Jewish Council ('Judenrat') from a neoclassical mansion

Portuguese Synagogue (p78)

at Nieuwe Keizersgracht 58 (p78). To what extent this council tried to help their fellow Jews, and to what extent they were unwitting or forced collaborators, is a matter of intense debate. However, the Judenrat was essentially complicit in helping manage a series of 'deportations' in which virtually the whole community was sent away – not to work in Germany as they were told, but to concentration and death camps in Poland. Barely 5000 survived the war: scarcely one in 16 people.

Learning about the City's Jewish Heritage

Visitors to Amsterdam often learn about this awful history through the Anne Frank Huis (p100) but for that you'll often need to book weeks ahead. Many other memorials to the city's Jewish heritage and tragedy make very compelling alternatives. Arguably the best place to start is the Hollandsche Schouwburg, which is moving, informative and free. To learn a whole lot more, there's a trio of paid sights administered by the Joods Cultureel Kwartier (Jewish Cultural Quarter; *jck.nl*); the combination ticket for the Portuguese Synagogue, Joods Museum and National Holocaust Museum (p78) saves 25% over buying separately.

MAP P70

OTHER MEMORIALS TO WWII & JEWISH SUFFERING

Auschwitz Memorial (Map p80) A panel of cracked sky-reflecting mirrors in Wertheimpark reading 'Nooit Meer' (Never Again).

National Holocaust Names Monument (Map p70) Dazzling mirror-work maze bearing the names of 102,000 Jewish (plus Sinti/Roma) victims of the Holocaust.

Former Judenrat HQ (Map p70) The 1725 mansion (Nieuwe Keizersgracht 58) that housed the Judenrat (Jewish Council), the Nazi-installed puppet organisation tasked with managing WWII ghettoisation.

Dockworker statue (Map p70) A 1952 figure commemorating a February 1941 strike that protested against the maltreatment of local Jews: the first deportation round-up had occurred here a few days earlier.

Joods Verzets- monument (Map p70) 1988 black slab commemorating WWII Jewish resistance.

For more about these horrors, you could cross over to the **National Holocaust Museum** (*adult/under-18/under-13 €20/8/6*), housed in a former school from which some Jewish children were spirited away to safety when passing trams masked the view of the guards. However, much of the same emotional, historical ground is covered by the more comprehensive and impressively nuanced Verzetsmuseum.

Surviving Synagogues

MAP P70

Celebrating the happier side of Jewish Amsterdam

Amsterdam's **Portuguese Synagogue** (*aka Esnoga; jck.nl; adult/under-18/under-13 €22/10/7, €2 online discount*) was the largest in Europe when completed in 1675. Surrounded by a quadrangle of low-rise administrative buildings, the impressively tall prayer house is still active and retains many of its 17th-century features, including sand-dusted floors to reduce noise, original pews with lockable seat-boxes and four towering stone pillars. It lacks electric light; candles are still lit in the vast chandeliers for services after dark, and during evening concerts (usually held one Thursday a month). A 'podcatcher' (point-to-activate audio guide) explains many features of Portuguese-Sephardic Jewish practice. Outer buildings include a 1930s *mikvah* (post-menstruation purification bath) and treasury basement with a 10-minute film about the community. To visit the 1616 **Ets Haim** (*jck.nl/ets-haim*), the world's oldest still-active Jewish library, email ahead for an appointment, though a small sample is displayed.

Esnoga tickets include entrance to the **Joods Museum** (Jewish Museum) across the road, whose main section occupies a disused but impressive Ashkenazi synagogue. It illustrates key religious and cultural customs of Judaism through objects, videos and film fragments, then goes on to tell the history of Amsterdam's Jewish community. The overall effect is a little scattergun and feels unfocused but there's an engaging 'Junior' section.

Historic Resistance

MAP P80

Life-or-death questions at the Verzetsmuseum

What would you have done if you'd lived in Amsterdam in WWII, a city suddenly occupied by Nazi Germans hell-bent on reorganising society to their warped ideology? Would you have had the courage to join the resistance? It's a question you can't help but ask yourself as you visit the sobering yet inspiring **Verzetsmuseum** (*Dutch Resistance Museum; verzetsmuseum.*

EATING & DRINKING IN NPEI: COFFEE & ICE CREAM

MAPS P70 & P80

Droog: Hidden within a prize-winning design studio is a super-quaint mini garden and an upstairs cafe that's ideal for coffee or a light lunch. *10am-5pm* €

Bakers & Roasters: Great barista coffee made using Brazilian and Kiwi know-how. Wide-ranging international brunch menus are ethically sourced. *8.30am-3pm* €

Bar Gelateria Tofani: Homemade Italian ice cream at €2.30 a scoop. The deliciously tart lemon sorbet is an ideal cool-down during a hot summer stroll. *10am-1am* €

IJscuypje Plantage: Handy for excellent ice cream as you exit the zoo. This growing chain uses fresh, sometimes novel ingredients and flavours. *noon-9pm* €

Verzetsmuseum

org; adult/student €14/7.50). Allow at least a couple of hours to learn the background and then discover the ways in which people did react – whether by taking arms or more subtly by helping those in hiding, forging documents or contributing to underground newspapers, radios and general strikes. Imagine you're seeking sanctuary, then choose from four doorbells to hear your neighbours' responses to your pleas. Learn how the Resistance press operated, how 300,000 people were kept in hiding and how all this was funded. What makes the museum particularly powerful are the highly nuanced personal stories, which illuminate people's complex predicaments rather than simply condemning those who failed to choose heroism.

An important side exhibit covers the WWII situation in the Dutch colonies, particularly the crushed early hopes amongst Indonesian independence activists.

Accessed very subtly through a 1930s door, the 'Junior' section is an absolute highlight of the whole museum for adults as much as youngsters. After a time tunnel of toys, you follow the stories of four Dutch children and how their backgrounds influenced their experience of the war and the fates of their families. It concludes with video interviews with the individuals in old age, in which you discover that their incredible stories were true.

A DARING ATTACK

One of the reasons that Nazi occupiers could so quickly institute a ghetto in WWII Amsterdam was orderly book-keeping. City population registers, which crucially included religious affiliations, were stored in the former Artis concert hall, a building that now contains Micropia (p82) and cafe-restaurant De Plantage (p85).

On 27 March 1943 the Dutch Resistance set out to destroy these records. The daring attack succeeded, but deportations continued and most of the heroes were executed. Some were celebrated after the war. Recognition for others took longer, notably Willem Arondéus and Frieda Belinfante whose homosexuality was probably a factor in their stories being less prominently told. That has reversed of late, notably with a 2023 Stephen Fry–presented TV documentary *Willem and Frieda: Defying the Nazis*.

EATING & DRINKING AROUND ENTREPOTDOK: OUR PICKS — MAP P80

Sotto: Scrumptious thin-crust pizza in the former 'People's Union' coffeehouse beside the Entrepotdok gateway arch. *5-10pm Mon-Thu, noon-10pm Fri-Sun* €

Gollem an het Water: Mini-chain of beer lovers' bars. Hard to beat for brew choice; try 'Precious' semi-cloudy IPA. Board games and TV sports upstairs. *4-11.30pm* €

Bloem: Tiny, community-oriented Bloem turns out impressive multicourse meals that are both vegan and gluten-free. Canal-side bar-terrace. *4-11pm, kitchen 5-9pm* €€

Éénvistwéévis: Locally famed for fresh seafood served slowly but with love. The interior was totally reworked in a 2025 makeover. *6-10pm Wed-Sat* €€

Sumatrakade

Java Eiland

IJHaven

Piet Heinkade

Veemkade

Piet Heinkade

Dijksgracht

Oosterdok

Naval Barracks

Kattenburg

NEMO Science Museum

Wittenburg

OOSTELIJKE EILANDEN (EASTERN ISLANDS)

MEDIEVAL CENTRE

Prins Hendrikkade

Kattenburgerplein

Nieuwevaart

Wittenburgergr

Oostenburgermiddenstr

Ezelsbrug

Oostenburgergracht

Kadijksgr

Nieuwe Vaart

Oostenburgergr

Hoogte Kadijk

Laagte Kadijk

Plantagekade

Entrepotdok

Verzets-museum

Artis Zoo
Micropia

Groote Museum

PLANTAGE

Hoogte Kadijk

Zeeburgerstr

Plantage Parklaan

Plantage Kerklaan

Artis Zoo

Nieuwe Herengr

Hollandsche Schouwburg

Plantage Middenlaan

Sarphatistr

Alexandekade

Mauritskade

Dapperstr

Plantage Muidergr

Singelgracht

Poeteststr

Plantage Middengracht

Nieuwe Achtergr

Alexanderplein

Commelinstr

DAPPERBUURT

Nieuwe Achtergr

Sarphatistr

1e Van Swindenstr

Mauritskade

Linnaeusstr

Weesper-plein

Roeteststr

Spinozastr

Sajetplein

Oosterpark

Ⓜ Weesperplein

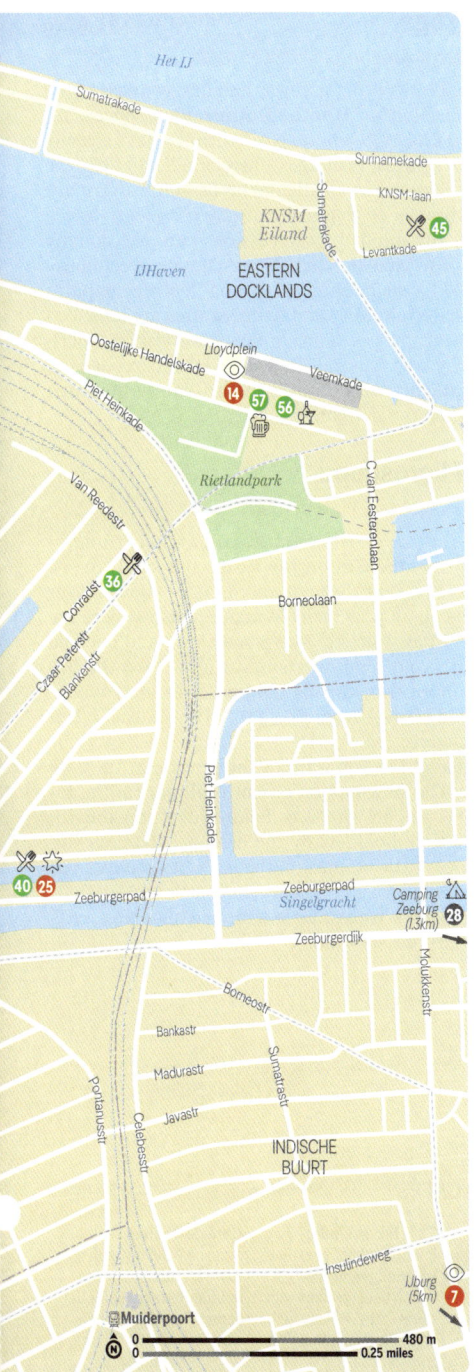

★ HIGHLIGHTS
1 Artis Zoo
2 Groote Museum
3 Hollandsche Schouwburg
4 Micropia
5 NEMO Science Museum
6 Verzetsmuseum

● SIGHTS
7 IJBurg
8 Arcam
9 Auschwitz Memorial
10 Booking.com HQ Building
11 De Gooyer Windmill
12 Het Scheepvaartmuseum
13 Hortus Botanicus
14 Lloyd Hotel
15 Museumhaven
16 National Holocaust Museum
17 OBA Oosterdok
18 Pelikaanbrug
19 WerfMuseum 't Kromhout
20 Wertheimpark

● ACTIVITIES
21 Aloha
22 Glow MiniGolf
23 Klimmuur Centraal
24 Marinehaven
25 Mooie Boules
26 Rederij Lampedusa
27 SUP to Go

● SLEEPING
28 Camping Zeeburg
29 Elephant Hostel
30 Hotel Jakarta
31 Hotel Park Plantage
32 Rooms25
see 14 Hoxton Lloyd Hotel

● EATING
33 A Beautiful Mess
34 Aguada
35 Ayo Makan
36 Barlotta
37 Bloem
38 Box Sociaal
39 Cantina Caliente
40 De Kop van Oost
41 De Plantage
42 Éénvistwéévis
43 Frank's Smoke House
44 IJscuypje Plantage
45 Kanis en Meiland
46 Scheepskameel
47 Sotto
48 TestTafel

● DRINKING & NIGHTLIFE
49 Bakers & Roasters
50 Brouwerij 't IJ
51 Café Eik en Linde
52 Café Scharrebier
53 Café Struis
54 De Druif
55 De Groene Olifant
56 De Nieuwe KHL
57 Fosco
58 Gollem an het Water
59 Hannekes Boom
60 Pension Homeland
61 Ruveggies Beach Bar Kiosk

●
ENTERTAINMENT
62 Conservatorium van Amsterdam (CvA)
see 2 Koningszaal
63 Kriterion
64 Mezrab
65 Muziekgebouw aan 't IJ

● TRANSPORT
66 Passenger Terminal Amsterdam

BUILDING THE PLANTAGE

The area that is today the Plantage was not originally planned to be the leafy city-centre oasis that it has become. It was developed from a former swamp area in the 17th century when the population inside the inner canal rings was growing rapidly. Rather than building houses, the authorities offered plots of land for sale, leading to the name, which means 'plantation'.

An economic crisis that followed led to many plots remaining unsold; some of these were developed into parks, resulting in a lovely place to stroll and laze. From the 1860s, however, the area finally became popular for housing, attracting wealthy merchants including a significant Jewish population up until the WWII deportations (p76).

Botanical Yoga

MAP P80

Unwind and learn in Amsterdam's green oasis

Step through a 17th-century gateway and find yourself in the compact but fascinating **Hortus Botanicus** *(dehortus.nl; adult/under-18 €13.50/7)*, a floral oasis within what's already Amsterdam's oasis area, Plantage. When founded in 1638, the gardens' predecessor grew medicinal herbs in the aftermath of terrible outbreaks of plague. Toady there's plenty to see for the botanically minded, yoga sessions run occasionally in the palm house, and the 2025 three-climate greenhouse is a poster child for sustainability: carbon-neutral computer technology tweaks humidity and temperatures are balanced using 'waste' heat sources. Some of the clever visitor experiences are glitchy, and frustratingly plant-label barcodes fail to link automatically with data in the brilliantly thorough app. The gift shop is a delight.

Under the Microscope

MAP P80

Life beyond the visible at Micropia

Micropia *(artis.nl/en/artis-micropia; adult/student/under-13 €17.50/8.75/free)* focuses on life forms too small to see with the naked eye. Peer through microscopes and discover unsettling facts about how many living organisms there are around us every day. Dare to take a body scan and become acquainted with your own microorganisms. Learn the un-romantic side of locking lips via the kiss-o-meter. Appreciate the beauty of viruses from Ebola to HIV – at least when they're glass models.

Don't get impatient as you wait for the elevator at the very start of a visit. The slow-motion ascent is all part of the introduction to set you on your way. Before you jump aboard, grab one of the free booklets by the entrance gate: as you go around, collect little stamps on the back. As you exit the stamps are counted by a slot reader.

Combination tickets are available with neighbouring Artis Zoo (p84) and Groote Museum.

Feel like you're in Antwerp with a Belgian Bolleke

 DRINKING IN NPEI: BEST BRUIN CAFÉS

MAPS P70 & P80

Café Scharrebier: Unreconstructed locals' *bruin café*, with 10 great-value Benelux beers on tap; a fine down-market alternative to nearby De Druif (p87). *11am-late*

Lokaal 't Loosje: Cult art-nouveau cafe retaining pictorial wall tiling from its days as a horse-tram waiting room. Excellent beers; heated terrace. *8am-1am*

Café Eik en Linde: Friendly locals' bar where knowledgeable staff match beer newbies with a brew they're likely to enjoy. *11am-late Mon-Fri, 2pm-2am Sat*

Café de Doelen: Textbook *bruin café* dating back to 1895. The most prized outdoor terrace tables lie across the street, canal-side. *11am-late*

Groote Museum

Big Questions

MAP P80

Mind-expanding moments in the Groote Museum

What is the meaning of life? Forty-two, per *The Hitchhiker's Guide to the Galaxy*? Reproduction? The highly enjoyable **Groote Museum** *(grootemuseum.nl; adult/student/under-18 €17.50/10/free)* is called *groote* (big) because it attempts to ask such big questions, particularly through examining natural cycles, connections across species and how our senses affect our perception and feelings. Walk through a scent tunnel. Drag yourself back through human evolution by tugging an umbilical cord. Try to beat a chimp at a number memory game. It's all housed in a grand historical building with random soundscapes adding an extra wacky dimension.

Start by picking one of three audio guides. Each takes you on a roughly hour-long amble, themed with seeing, doing or feeling – though in reality the routes overlap and you'll likely discover other fascinating distractions as you go, like the video of humans mimicking birds' mating dances, or a 2m-long dried whale's penis. If you come on a Thursday the museum stays open till 10pm and you'll often have it almost to yourself. Combo tickets with Artis Zoo (p84) save money.

WHY I LOVE THE PLANTAGE AREA

Mark Elliott, Lonely Planet writer

I've been visiting Amsterdam since 1982, observing the pressure of tourist numbers growing more oppressive year by year within the main canal rings. Remarkably, however, the lovely Plantage area seems to have retained its local vibe.

The few hotels and hostels here sit on attractive yet peaceful streets that are walking distance from the centre and very handy for several great museums. The low-key cafes of Kadijkplein and Rapenburgerplein are my go-to meeting places. Café Eik en Linde is a real gem of a community pub and De Plantage (p85) restaurant is hard to beat for high-quality food at great prices. They'll even let you order just a starter, and the site's atmosphere is enhanced after sunset as the tree-lamps start to glow.

DRINKING IN NPEI: BEST BRUIN CAFÉS

MAPS P70 & P80

De Sluyswacht: In a wonderfully wonky 1695 lock-keeper's house. Interiors are sparse and occasionally raucous. Canal-side terrace is a charmer. *noon-late*

De Groene Olifant: 19th-century elegance meets modern Bohemian with dark bentwood chairs and leaf-print wallpaper. Tram routes 7 and 14 meet outside. *3pm-1am*

Cafe de Engelbewaarder: Laid-back old cafe where people play chess and peruse photo exhibits. Live jazz on Sunday afternoons, September to June. *noon-1am*

De Gaeper: Cosy, student-oriented place that was converted into a cafe-bar from an old-time pharmacy in 1974. *10am-1am, typically closed Jul & Aug*

Artis Zoo

Delightful Artis is one of Europe's oldest zoos. Constantly evolving, conditions are exemplary and ever improving for the collection of over 750 animal species. The zoo's 14 hectares are shaded by mature trees and graced with monuments and historic buildings. You'll need several hours to see everything including aviaries, insectarium, reptile house, a tropical butterfly pavilion, big cats, elephants and howling white wolves.

EKATERINA KUPEEVA/SHUTTERSTOCK

TOP TIPS

● About six times daily, zookeeper talks focus on one specific animal. Check the online schedule.

● Enter near Micropia (p82). There are more exit gates: their push-mechanisms mean you can't get locked in.

● Combo tickets with Micropia (p82) and the Groote Museum (p83) save money.

PRACTICALITIES

● Map p80 ● artis.nl
● admission/student/ toddler €30.50/15.25/free
● discounts online
● 9am-6pm

Selected Curiosities

There are countless offbeat discoveries including Aldabra giant tortoises, brightly coloured poison dart frogs (that aren't poisonous) and sheep-sized capybara, the world's largest rodents. The macaque enclosure incorporates a thatched 1906 house in distinctive Minangkabau (Sumatra-Indonesian) style. There's even a small bird hatchery within a 1938 'old Holland' style former cookie bakery-shop.

Planetarium

An unexpected bonus is the zoo's comfortable planetarium, which puts on 30-minute projections (included in your ticket price) every hour on the hour. Note that the 11am and 1pm screenings are specifically for children. The other slots offer three possible show themes: 'interconnected earth', life on other planets, and a flight to the end of the universe. Headsets give English commentary. Don't arrive late: once it's started you can't get in, though you can exit any time.

Peeping in Without a Ticket

Don't have three hours to spare? Then get a free taster by drinking or eating at De Plantage, whose terrace tables survey a large aviary. Nearby, behind the Groote Museum (p83), admire the freely visible flamingo pool. Looking across the canal from Entrepotdoksluis you might spy giraffes.

Architectural Time Capsule

Snooping inside the Scheepvaarthuis

Housing Grand Hotel Amrâth, the **Scheepvaarthuis** building is a remarkable example of early art deco, considered the first and finest example of the expressionist Amsterdam School of architecture. Don't be shy to enter: staff are usually very obliging if you ask to wander around the public areas, which are a feast of 1920s design. Enter through heavy revolving wooden doors and climb wide marble stairs with extravagant wrought-iron detailing. On the second-floor landing there's a 1930s mahogany radiogram. But the interior highlight is the Great Hall on the 3rd floor, with its leaded glass ceiling panels designed by Willem Bogtman, featuring zodiac and nautical themes. That's suitably fitting for what was built (in two bursts between 1913 and 1926) as the collective office building for major shipping companies of the day.

The outwardly austere brickwork of the building's exterior is enlivened with plenty of neo-Gothic statuary and nautical detailing. Most memorable are gargoyle-like portrait bosses, jutting out of the walls with spooky, stylised faces of 17th-century explorers and mariners carved in the style of Anonymous masks.

Sailors' Tales

Ship ahoy at Het Scheepvaartmuseum

A full-scale replica of the 700-tonne galleon *Amsterdam* is the highlight of a visit to **Het Scheepvaartmuseum** *(National Maritime Museum; hetscheepvaartmuseum.com; adult/student/under-13 €18.50/8.50/free)*. The original, one of the VOC's largest tall-mast ships, was wrecked by storms during its maiden voyage to east Asia. (It only reached Hastings, England.) The tiny bunks, swinging hammocks, low beams and dangerous overhead ropes hint at how difficult life was for sailors in the Dutch 'Golden Age'. In the hold, you can try lifting heavy box-crates by pulley. In the prow, a 180-degree multiscreen projection takes you downriver on a virtual journey into the 18th-century port of Amsterdam. Meanwhile guilt-laden signboards reflect the realities that the VOC's trade was, by today's standards, worse than theft.

Inside the main museum, this theme (see p273) continues in excoriating detail with the powerful exhibition, *Shadows on*

EVER-EVOLVING ZOO

While preserving much of its protected historic architecture, Artis Zoo has gone to enormous pains to update and massively enlarge its enclosures to ensure that its animal 'guests' remain healthy and happy. Since 2023, for example, lions have a wider variety of habitat including a high rocky perch from which they can see (if not hunt) zebras: that's apparently psychologically important. The elephants have a canal-fed bath-pond of 1.5 million litres, deep enough for a proper swim, while their droppings are removed and used as an ingredient in a new synthetic building material.

The reworked 1910 bird building now has a spacious series of inside-outside forest houses. The wreathed hornbills waited less time for their cataract surgery than most humans would.

Divine roast aubergine with cashew cream and pomegranate

EATING IN NPEI: OUR PICKS NEAR THE ZOO

Box Sociaal: Moreish brunch options from loaded bagels to aubergine parmigiana served on crispy fries. Good coffee, insistent music. *9am-3.45pm €*

Aguada: Short, idiosyncratic menu of fondue, Indian, Indonesian and French creations served in a lovably cosy candlelit restaurant with relaxed vibes. *5-10pm €*

Cantina Caliente: School chairs and distressed walls, softened with cacti, make an informal spot for cocktails, Homeland beers and Mexican dishes. *noon-11pm €*

De Plantage: Fresh, creative cuisine in an impressive 1870s zoo building. Terrace seats enjoy evening tree-lights and the squawks of spoonbills. *10am-11pm €€*

This lovely waterside stroll takes you through central yet surprisingly peaceful areas, for lovely views that look best in post-sunset lighting.

START	END	LENGTH
Rembrandthuis	Kadijksplein	2.2km; 1hr

Cross Sint Antoniesluis, a former lock whose gates were once operated from the marvellously wonky little house that's now lively ❶ **De Sluyswacht** (p83) pub. Follow ❷ **Kromboomsloot** north; after an unpromising start, this is a gorgeous narrow curving canal.

Cut through to Oude Waal for a ❸ **viewpoint** looking northwest, a sunset glow colouring the sky behind floodlit Sint Nicolaaskerk. Cross the boat-flanked canal on ❹ **Waalseilandbrug**, a distinctive bridge with views east towards the octagonal bell-tower, Montelbaanstoren. Emerge on Prins Hendrikkade where a ❺ **road bridge** presents contrasting views: modernist glass of the Oosterdok developments to the north, poetic 17th-century charm of canal houses to the south.

Descend the ramp and stroll towards ❻ **NEMO Science Museum** (p88), eventually almost doubling back beside the ❼ **Museumhaven** (p89), a moored 'museum' of multiple houseboats. As you wander, there are many fascinating angles from which to enjoy the post-sunset lighting that gives added definition to the *Amsterdam* VOC galleon and the imposing white bulk of ❽ **Het Scheepvaartmuseum** (p85).

Climb another ramp past architecture studio-exhibition ❾ **Arcam** and finish with a drink on appealing squares Kadijksplein or Rapenburgerplein. You're spoilt for choices but ❿ **De Druif** is the classic.

The nearby Grand Hotel Amrâth occupies the **Scheepvaarthuis** (p85), a century-old classic of Amsterdam School architecture.

At No 33 a discreet **Armenian Church** has a carved 'khachkar' stone on its corner wall, a memorial to the 1915 massacres of Armenians in Anatolia.

The **Montelbaanstoren** is now a graceful clock tower with Baroque open steeple. However, it was originally built as part of Amsterdam's eastern defence wall (1512).

Het IJ

Piet Heinkade

Dijksgracht

Prins Hendrikkade

Centraal Station

CENTRUM

Nieuwezijds Voorburgwal

Warmoesstr

Hudnstr

Geldersekade

Binnen Bantammerstr

Binnenkant

Grand Hotel Amrâth

Oosterdok

Naval Barracks

Prins Hendrikkade

Prins Hendrikkade

Montelbaanstoren

MEDIEVAL CENTRE

Nieuwe Vaart

Prins Hendrikkade

Armenian Church

Oude Hoogstr

Nieuwmarkt

NIEUWMARKT

Jodenbreestr

Kadijkspl

Hoogte Kadijk

Nieuwe Herengr

END

Zwanenburgwal

START

Nieuwe Doelenstr

Binnen Amstel

Amstel

Waterlooplein

Wertheim-park

Hortus Botanicus

Entrepotdok

Artis Zoo

PLANTAGE

N

0   400 m

0   0.2 miles

NIEUWMARKT, PLANTAGE & THE EASTERN ISLANDS

THE GUIDE

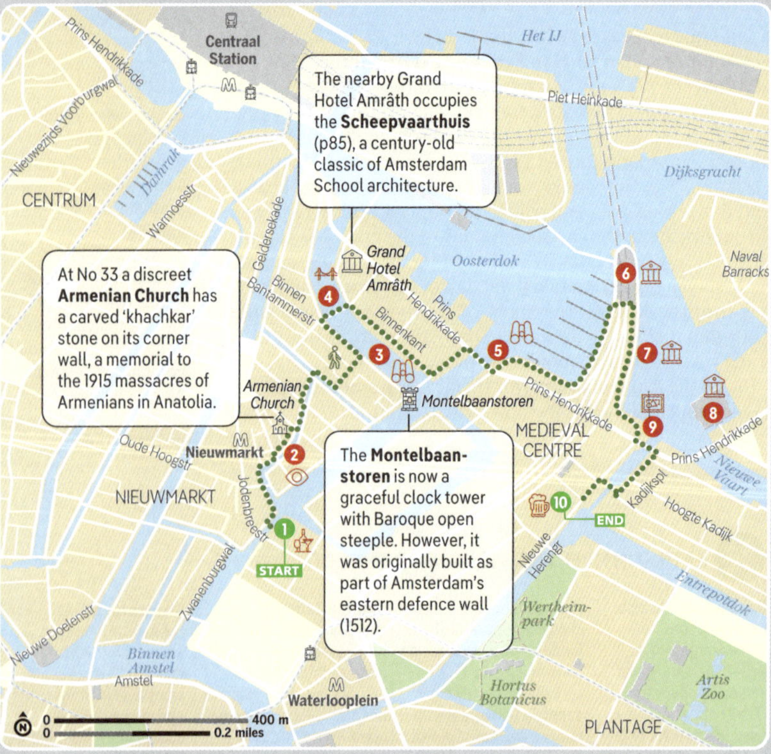

the Atlantic, examining colonial reverberations. Other rooms display historic ship figureheads, navigational instruments and priceless naval charts.

The imposing courtyard building is itself part of the attraction, a 1656 waterfront behemoth originally designed as a storehouse for the Admiralty of Amsterdam. Its sheer size can make the sub-exhibitions feel sparser than they are, but provides unwinding space in the large courtyard and waterside seating beyond the cafeteria. Even the toilets and automated baggage store are worth a look.

Tippling De Druif
MAP P80

Tasting jenever in a 16th-century hostelry

De Druif ('The Grape') is one of Amsterdam's oldest hostelries, a 1556 former *likeurstokerij* (distillery) and 'embarkation cafe' where sailors would register for work: the VOC warehouses were just across the canal in Entrepotdok. Piet Hein, a 17th-century naval hero, claimed De Druif was one of his favourite drinking holes 400 years ago. Today the timeless wooden interior remains dimly lit with old gas chandeliers and your eyes are inevitably drawn to a triple-layered stack of old gin barrels, though shots (€4.50) are now dispensed from Van Wees bottles rather than using the antique bronze-and-glass serving vessel.

Architecture of Tomorrow
MAP P80

A peep into Arcam

Generally abbreviated as **Arcam** (arcam.nl; adult/student/under-13 €5/2.50/free), the Amsterdam Architecture Foundation inhabits a small but suitably distinctive building with dinosaur-head metal curves and large glass walls, designed by Dutch architect René van Zuuk. Start a quick (say ¼ hour) visit in the dinky film booth for a six-minute *Future of Amsterdam* video looking at city-planning concepts from housing shortages to sustainability. Then peruse the one-wall timeline of architectural development since the Millennium. Open afternoons only. Check its online listings for informative guided architectural tours, usually in English on Sundays.

Bottled fresh juices too

CONVENIENT PICNIC SPOTS

Stock up with great-value bakery goods at the convenient Nieuwmarkt branch of **Albert Heijn supermarket** (Map p70). Or for a few more euros, order a beautifully crafted smoked beef, pesto and parmesan focaccia sandwich at gourmet deli **Sterk Staaltje** (Map p70). Supplement that with a delicious choc-ball from nearby Amsterdam institution, **Puccini Bomboni** (Map p70). To eat your picnic there are granite benches on Nieuwmarkt – which also has a water fountain – or seats facing the Amstel near the **Spinoza Statue** (Map p70). Alternatively walk a bit further and sit on the canal-side lawns in **Wertheimpark** (Map p80). Or climb to the open rooftop of NEMO (p88), where it's totally acceptable to consume your own food, possibly with a drink from the 5th-floor cafe.

EATING IN NPEI: TAKEAWAY OPTIONS
MAPS P70 & P80

Frank's Smoke House: Salmon, mackerel, eel, goose, cheeses and more. Smoked on-site; sold by weight or as sandwiches. *11am-6pm Tue-Sat, to 5pm Sun €*

Ayo Makan: Satisfying point-and-pick Indonesian meals served cold to take away or eat at four window-stools. Even the smallest €10 options are very filling. *3.30-8.30pm €*

Sterk Staaltje: Gorgeous, luxury deli with tantalising ready-to-eat treats and made-to-order sandwiches. *8.30am-7pm Mon-Sat, 10am-7pm Sun €*

Tokoman: Heavily automated takeaway for wok dishes, Surinamese sandwiches and snacks. Off Nieuwmarkt with a branch at Waterlooplein. *noon-9pm €*

CASTENOID/ GETTY IMAGES

TOP EXPERIENCE

NEMO Science Museum

Family-oriented and very much hands-on, this state-of-the-art science museum is truly interactive with four floors of investigative mayhem that kids of all ages will enjoy. You'll need several hours to see it all. The landmark green building is also worth visiting for its harbour setting and the free rooftop viewing terrace.

DON'T MISS

Chain Reaction show

Giant bubble maker

Invention 'comedy theatre'

Space bike

Willpower tests

Rooftop views

Events of the Day

Just beyond the ticket check on entry, there's a curved bench where you can sit and take note of the day's most interactive and performative events. Most run almost constantly but some have fixed start times. The central atrium's Heath Robinson series of contraptions is set up for one of these, the brilliant 'Chain Reaction' show. Almost everything is bilingual in Dutch and English.

1st Floor: Fenomena & Makerij

You could reverse the order to avoid initial crowds but most people start, logically enough, on the 1st floor, experimenting with an incredible array of fun, easy-to-use scientific

PRACTICALITIES

● Map p80 ● nemosciencemuseum.nl ● admission €21.50 ● 10am-5.30pm; book time slot (last entry 3.30pm) ● closed Mon Oct-Mar

experiences like using pulleys to hoist yourself up, making a tube-bubble as big as yourself, or playing with magnets and coloured light. Hidden downstairs behind the Makerij zone are more involved activities for children, such as drawing a 12-frame 'film' to play in a rotary spinner.

2nd Floor: Technium & Werkplaats

Marvel at the evolution of machines, build structures such as dams and test the forces acting on them, and learn more about water purification. Watch a pun-filled 10-minute Comedy Theatre where stand-up is 'performed' by an anthropomorphised series of familiar inventions (wheel, light bulb, hypodermic needle etc). Play cogwheel games, touch parts of a bicycle to learn how each works and design your own wind turbine. If you're with smaller children, make your way to the Werkplaats (Maker Space) where they can create their own spinning top or make AI pictures. There's seating and a cafe here, if you're already flagging.

3rd Floor: Elementa

Learn about atoms as the universe's building blocks, investigate the big bang and use microscopes to see what makes life possible. Observe the tracks of sub-atomic particles, ride a space-bike to the edge of the solar system and don a lab coat for a hands-on chemistry session in the laboratory.

4th Floor: Humania

Before examining what makes us human, a warning points out that this section is aimed at those over 12 and deals with subjects including death and sex that some might find uncomfortable. There are fascinating psychology games to test your free will. Hold an ice-cold tube to test willpower. Ponder the history of ideas on reproduction from the 17th-century discovery of 'moving beasties' in sperm to a video on CRISPR gene editing. Then sit with up to 12 people in the dome-shaped Forum room and vote via phone on your attitudes to possible climate crisis strategies followed by a discussion with fellow participants.

Up on the Roof

The huge, sloping rooftop space has some of the best views over Amsterdam and you don't need a ticket to visit, except during special events like the occasional outdoor cinema evening. There's a cafe and coffee kiosk, but you're welcome to use the many bench seats to eat your own picnic – there's even a water fountain. If you haven't come via the museum, the rooftop is accessed via a cinematically lit stairway from the southeast corner.

MUSEUMHAVEN

Though it's not officially part of NEMO, approaching the museum from Arcam you'll walk past **Museumhaven** (museumhaven amsterdam.nl); over 20 historic boats moored beside the promenade. Each is privately owned and maintained. Descriptive panels (in Dutch), repeated on the website, identify what makes each a listed 'monument' vessel. Dating from between 1890 and 1940, they cover a wide range of styles and Dutch regional origins.

TOP TIPS

● Booking a time slot is officially compulsory but on quiet days drop-ins might be possible.

● Don't lose your ticket. You'll need it to re-enter the paid section from the top floor's open-access cafe and rooftop.

● Rooftop closes 5.30pm, except Thursdays and Fridays in summer (9pm).

● Free rooftop concerts on summer Thursday evenings.

● Viewed from the west end of Niewe Vaart, the building looks like the prow of a sinking ship.

● Dutch website Nemo Kenislink (nemokennislink. nl) follows up 4th-floor climate change themes.

● Children can build their own mini chain reactions in the 1st-floor Workshop 1.

COFFEESHOP TIPS

Philosopher and coffeeshop connoisseur **Frederico Lafaire** has worked for 15 years at The Book Exchange (p75), a job requiring qualities of memory, special awareness and customer service. When smoking, he underlines the importance of not mixing weed with tobacco: 'It's tobacco and alcohol that mess up your body and your mind. Find a coffeeshop with a good "volcano", a vaporiser that's a little like a bong but without the water. You get the sensation without the impurities.'

Frederico's favourite NPEI coffeehouses:
Bagheera (Map p70) is friendly and has great strands [ie quality weed].
Bluebird (Map p70) feels like a public living room and attracts lots of locals.
Overkant (Map p70) doesn't do vaporisers but it's great value and has a lovely view to the botanical gardens.

CAVAN-IMAGES/SHUTTERSTOCK

OBA Oosterdok and Conservatorium van Amsterdam (CvA)

Machine Head

MAP P80

Catering to combustion engine fans

WerfMuseum 't Kromhout (*kromhoutmuseum.nl; adult/under-16/under-6 €10/5/free*) won't appeal to everyone and its opening times are very limited (Tuesdays plus the third Sunday of the month), but if historic engineering and the smell of industrial lubricants excites you, this might be heaven. The setting is an architecturally fine if busily chaotic 18th-century boatyard where vessels are still repaired. The eastern hall houses a 'working' museum devoted to the almost indestructible marine engines that were designed and built here. Volunteer guides set some of them in motion, including a 12HP petrol engine from 1904, for groups of suitably awed visitors. Most of the information panels are in Dutch but a few touchscreens have English-language videos on subjects as diverse as fuel injection processes, automatic lubrication and the Kromhout hot bulb engine mechanism.

 EATING & DRINKING AROUND OOSTERDOK WATERFRONT —— MAP P80

Pension Homeland: Embracing a 1970s interior, this bar and waterside terrace showcases its own Homeland craft beers. Weekend music. *noon-1am* €	**Hannekes Boom:** Waterside cafe built from recycled materials. Huge bench-tabled beer garden beneath colourful lights; winter fires inside. *11pm-late* €	**TestTafel:** Creative, experimental plant-based meals with many ingredients produced in Mediamatic's gardens and greenhouses. *4-11pm Wed-Sat, kitchen 6-8pm* €€	**Scheepskameel:** Cavernous, informal yet gastronomically excellent showcase for fresh ingredients matched with German wines. *6-9.30pm Tue-Sat* €€€

Library of Cool

MAPS P70 & P80

Admiring 21st-century architecture east of the station

If your idea of a library is a stuffy old place with an air of mildewed gentility, Amsterdam's 2007 central library **OBA Oosterdok** *(Central Library; oba.nl; 8am-10pm Mon-Fri, 10am-8pm Sat & Sun)* will make you think again. Multiple light, bright floors offer plenty of sitting space. Devoted to children, the airy basement has low shelves, low computer tables and eye-catching animal figures including a gigantic polar bear. A big attraction is the 7th floor with its 250-seat cinema, cafe-restaurant and outdoor summer viewing terrace with interpretation panel.

OBA is just one of many sparkling glass buildings in the redeveloped docklands east of Centraal Station. A sharp stilt-tipped glass 'nose' defines the DoubleTree Inn Hotel, an interesting counterpoint to the **Sea Palace** restaurant opposite. The latter is a triple-levelled floating pagoda of chinoiserie renowned for its dim sum lunches.

Seen from Annie Schmidstraat, the **Conservatorium van Amsterdam (CvA)** has glass wall-panels that create an iridescent rainbow of colour. Outside an alien blob creature appears to sit atop the parking lift and there's a 'manytree seat' – a wooden bench beneath a canopy of passionfruit vines.

The 2023 **Booking.com HQ Building** contains plenty of greenery to help it with sustainability goals. It's mostly closed to the public, but you can dine in the sparkly ground-floor Middle Eastern cafe-restaurant, **A Beautiful Mess**.

Cross the cycle-bridge and pass between the merrily colourful cafe **Hannekes Boom** and a rotated cube structure that houses **Klimmuur Centraal** climbing wall. Shimmy beneath the railway and cross a footbridge to admire two more dazzling contemporary glass masterpieces: the angular **Muziekgebouw aan 't IJ** concert hall and the contrastingly curvaceous **Passenger Terminal Amsterdam**.

Immigrants' Stories

MAP P80

Conscious cruising with Rederij Lampedusa

There are countless cheaper and more polished options for boat cruises along Amsterdam's pretty waterways. However, those of **Rederij Lampedusa** *(rederijlampedusa.nl; 90min cruise €35)* are very special in that your guide will tell you not just about Amsterdam but also of their personal experiences

---

GREAT VIEWPOINTS AROUND NPEI

Groenburgwal Bridge (Map p70) Lovely canal-framed views of Zuiderkerk.

LuminAir (Map p70) Top-floor cocktail bar with wide city views looking south across the water.

NEMO rooftop (Map p80) Climb the long stairway to a fabulous series of sloping viewpoints with seats from which to survey the Oosterdok area.

OBA Oosterdok (Map p80) There are fine views from each floor of the library. Those from the 7th-floor terrace are framed into a horizontal slot by concrete beams.

De Sluyswacht (Map p70) Four canals meet at this classic *bruin café* whose rear terrace views include a memorable angle on Montelbaanstoren clock tower.

Pelikaanbrug (Map p80) Canal views east to De Gooyer windmill and west towards Sint Nicolaaskerk.

 EATING & DRINKING IN THE EASTERN ISLANDS: OUR PICKS —— MAP P80

De Kop van Oost: Modern canal-side brasserie near De Gooyer (p93) with imaginative sharing-style menus. *4-9.30pm Tue-Wed, 11am-9.30pm Thu-Sun* €€

Barlotta: Causing a stir since 2024 for spot-on Mediterranean meals and top-of-the-range charcuterie. *sandwiches noon-4pm, restaurant 5pm-midnight Tue-Sat* €€

Fosco: Come for the building's century-old history, stay for beers, obliging service, upbeat music and street food. *5pm-midnight Mon-Thu, noon-1am Fri-Sun* €

Kanis en Meiland: Super popular bar-restaurant thanks to flavour-packed modern food and a waterside terrace with SUP access. *10am-11pm* €€

GREAT PERFORMANCE VENUES IN NPEI

Most of these operate September to June.

CvA (Map p80) Prestigious arts university venue with student concerts. *conservatorium vanamsterdam.nl*

Nationale Opera & Ballet (Map p70) Opera house and ballet. *operaballet.nl*

Muziekgebouw aan 't IJ (Map p80) Magnificent 2005 concert hall focussed on contemporary classical music. The attached Bimhuis is for jazz. *muziekgebouw.nl*

Splendor (Map p70) Behind a 1923 'Swiss' art-deco façade, two rooms host mostly folk music. *splen-doramsterdam.com*

Koningszaal (Map p80) Intimate chamber concerts in the Groote Museum (p83) building. *kamukoza.nl*

Kompaszaal (see p94) 1920s and '30s jazz-swing on Friday nights. *kompaszaal.nl*

De Nieuwe KHL (Map p80) Mostly Dutch folk and chanson. *dekhl.nl/podium*

getting here. It's fascinating and moving in equal part, as they are all former asylum seekers with eye-opening, heartfelt perspectives. One is an Egyptian former Arab Spring activist, another a Somali who stood up to Al-Shabaab. Some of the places your route passes have played a role in refugees' difficult process of regularising their legal status. Tales might also weave in how immigration has shaped Amsterdam and the city's history as a safe haven.

A further talking point is the pair of boats being used. Both the 12m-long *Alhadj Djumaa* ('Mr Friday') and 6m-long *Hedir* previously undertook perilous voyages bringing migrants across the Mediterranean to Lampedusa in Italy: how many people were squeezed aboard? You'll be asked to guess!

Booking ahead is essential as the 90-minute scheduled tours are relatively few and far between. There are also occasional performance cruises. Start beside the sustainability-arts centre Mediamatic.

Summer Splashdown

MAP P80

Getting wet at Marineterrein

When the summer heat is getting too much but you don't have the energy to head all the way to IJburg (p95) or Zandvoort, a handily central place for a quick dip is on **Marinehaven**. Just a beach-ball toss away from the Maritime Museum, you'll find delineated swimming lanes but the whole site is free. The only facilities are a pair of very basic changing booths (free) and toilet, for which you pay €1 to **Ruveggies Beach Bar kiosk** for all-day use. Across the inlet, **SUP to Go** *(supsupclub.com)* has half a dozen SUP boards to rent using a fully automated rental system in lockers that you open having pre-paid online.

Dockland Survivors

MAP P80

Discovering century-old maritime architecture

While most of the Eastern Islands' dockland infrastructure has been swept away and replaced by contemporary developments (p94), a trio of intriguing 1920s buildings remain, all linked to KHL (Koninklijke Hollandsche Lloyd), a passenger shipping company that served South American destinations from 1908 until the early 1980s. Most impressive is the **Lloyd Hotel**, originally designed in 1921 to host departing passengers bound for Brazil and Argentina. It was later a detention centre for WWII collaborators then a borstal, but is once again

DRINKING AROUND NPEI: BEST COCKTAIL BARS

MAP P70

Rosalia's Menagerie: Ring the doorbell to access this small, intimate but utterly exuberant drawing-room bar with its own bijou B&B. *6pm-1am*

HPS: A low-lit, party vibe with none of the stuffiness of many cocktail bars. Bar folks really know their mixes and create some special novelties. *6pm-late*

Cafe Cuba: Laid-back cocktail cavern that feels like you're on a Caribbean beach minus the sand... especially after sampling eight varieties of mojito. *noon-1am*

LuminAir: Contemporary glass-walled bar on the triangular rooftop of the DoubleTree Inn. Prize-winning mixologists create suave colours and flavours. *noon-late*

De Gooyer and Brouwerij 't IJ

a hotel today with interiors that have been beautifully conserved. Look inside to see an archaic photo-booth machine in the entrance hall, ball-lamp chandeliers and lashings of old tilework in public areas. If you book room 211 you'll find yourself in an original doctor's office.

In the 1920s, a significant proportion of departing passengers were refugees from Eastern Europe where millions had been uprooted by war, the Russian Revolution and the dire poverty that followed. So many of these folks were infested with lice and fleas that a special quarantine building was created next door to the hotel. It's now home to friendly, funky pub Fosco (p91), which has a couple of commemorative displays within. A few doors away to the east, **De Nieuwe KHL** was formerly the canteen for company captains and maritime staff and remains a low-key cafe and music venue to this day.

City Windmill

MAP P80

Beer tastings beneath the sails of De Gooyer

If Amsterdam is going to be your only experience of the Netherlands and you really want to snap a photo of a windmill, a great option is to jump on tram 7 to **De Gooyer**. Built in 1725 but moved here in 1814, it's huge and comes complete with creaking sails and pretty nighttime lighting. You can't go inside as it's now a private house, but the attached former bathhouse building is now one of Amsterdam's leading microbreweries, **Brouwerij 't IJ** (*brouwerijhetij.nl/proeflokaal-de-molen; 2-10pm*). They offer a dozen excellent draft beers to savour on the plane-tree-shaded terrace. Try Nijpa, a fruity full-flavoured IPA, or Zatte, a Belgian-style triple. Even the 9% Columbus costs less than €5. Once the main tasting room closes, you can keep drinking at the co-owned **Café Struis**.

FUN NIGHTS (OR AFTERNOONS) OUT

Mooie Boules (Map p80) Boisterously upbeat atmosphere for indoor petanque, drinks, food-court bites and traditional Dutch pub games. *mooieboules.nl/amsterdam*

Mezrab (Map p80) Super-friendly culture centre focused on story-telling, mostly English, some Persian. Wednesday night open mic: book your slot. *mezrab.nl*

Vrog (Map p70) Descend the graffitied rabbit hole to a large recreation site offering street-wise activities for children and young adults, from trick trampolining to parkour. *vrog.nl*

Kriterion (Map p80) Arthouse cinema. Films in English are marked 'Engels gesproken' on the website. *kriterion.nl*

Aloha (Map p80) Hawaiian-themed activities centre for bowling, minigolf, laser games and more. *aloha.nl*

Glow MiniGolf (Map p80) Glow-in-the-dark minigolf played wearing spurious 3D glasses. It's beneath bizarrely quirky Noah's Arq pub. *glowminigolf.amsterdam/en/prins-hendrikkade*

CONTEMPORARY ARCHITECTURE WALK AROUND THE EASTERN ISLANDS

This waterside walking route showcases residential architecture, transformed since 1980 from decrepit docklands into inner-city suburbs.

START	END	LENGTH
Pacman Building	Azartplein tram stop	2.2km; 1hr

Start at the **❶ Pacman Building**, right behind the RJH Fortuynplein stop on bus route 43 from Centraal Station (every half-hour). Dominating an area of otherwise low-rise housing, the building is a city planner's 'meteorite', ie disproportionately large construction. It contains **❷ Borneo Architectuur Centrum** (BAC), an architectural practice whose free exhibition room fascinatingly details the area's five decades of development.

Cross the 2001 red-metal, stepped footbridge, nicknamed **❸ Pythonbrug** for its reptilian undulations. Beyond the **❹ Zeeburg passenger ferry jetty** is a **❺ viewpoint** at the corner of Ertskade. It simultaneously surveys Venetiëhof, a giant circular housing block by architect Jo Coenen, and, looking west, **❻ The Wader**

(Steltloper), a tower block perched on distinctively in-pointing pillar 'legs'.

As greenery starts to hide houseboats, you'll spy a giant, angled grey building widely known as **❼ 'The Whale'** (De Walvis). Cross the causeway, pass a hippy garden area, and walk through the **❽ Piraeus Building**, considered a classic of 1990s Dutch architecture with its quirky fold-out windows.

Across KNSM-laan, look inside daytime cafe **❾ Kompaszaal**; interiors are little changed since 1956 when it was the waiting room for international passenger ships. Stretching west, the **❿ Loods 6** building contains galleries, a ceramics-makers space and more. Return to central Amsterdam from **⓫ Azartplein** (tram 7).

> A blue-and-grey 1957 crane that's visible from the **Kompaszaal's** upstairs terrace is nowadays repurposed as a boutique 'hotel' room called 'YAYS The Crane by Numa'.

> Community pressure to save this **small football field** led architects to scrap plans for 'Fountainhead', a building far bigger and more ambitious than The Wader.

> **The Whale** looks far more whale-like from the causeway leading to KNSM Island, which also affords good views of the classic Lloyd Hotel (p92) and 'dance boat' *Odessa*.

Sumatrakade

Het IJ

KNSM Eiland

Surinamekade

Veemkade

KNSM-laan

Levantkade

Lloydplein

IJHaven

Ertskade

Ertskade JFV Hengelstr

Eastern Docklands

Piet Hein Tunnel

Kees Brijdeplantsoen

Panamakade

Borneo Eiland

C van Eesterenlaan

Stuurmankade

Scheepstimmerstr

Stokerkade

Borneokade

Cruquiusweg

Zeeburgerkade

Cruquiusweg

Piet Heinkade

Cruquiusweg

H A J Baanderskade

0 — 400 m
0 — 0.2 miles

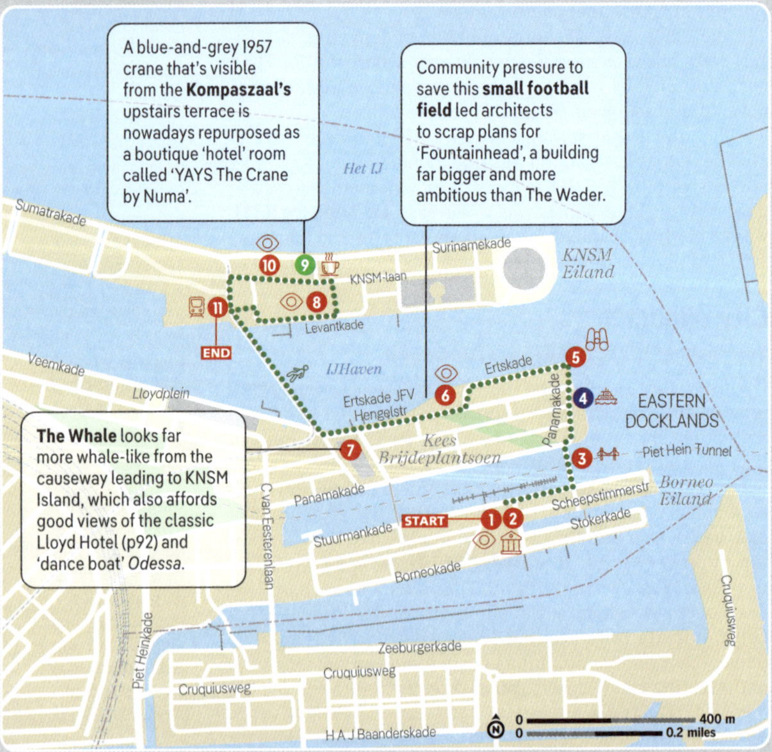

Hitting the Suburban Beach

MAP P80

Sand, sea and (wind)surf in IJburg

Need to cool down? You can jump on a sailboard or get a slice of beach life without leaving Amsterdam's city limits in the rapidly developing outer suburb of IJburg, an urban watersports getaway at the far eastern end of Zeeburg. **Strand IJburg** (*official season May-Sep; free*) is a wide, pale-sand artificial beach with buoy-differentiated swim zones including a shallow area aimed at smaller children. The beach area is pretty well equipped and though some of the facilities are starting to show signs of wear, it's a remarkable free resource for local families: no need to pay for the three beach volleyball courts, sand soccer, skate zone, hammocks, showers or (very basic) toilets. There's also a couple of drinking water fountains doubling as foot-washing facilities.

At the north end of the beach in cream-yellow container-boxes, **Surfcenter IJburg** (*surfcenterijburg.nl*) rents SUP boards, wingfoils and windsurfing gear. They run summer sports-training camps and weekends, and their website gives a good indication of wind strength and bathing temperature even if you aren't using their services. Nearby **King of Boardsports** (*kingofboardsports.com*) runs wingfoil lessons (€130 for two hours) and rents gear.

If you're more interested in boating, IJburg has that covered too, but you'll need to head back to the marina area where **Zeilschool IJburg** (*zeilschoolijburg.nl*) rents small skiffs and motorboats as well as offering sailing courses. It shares the same building as **Amsterdam Watersports** (*amsterdam watersports.com*), which offers a considerable menu of waterborne activities including wakeboarding and flyboarding – where powerful jets of water project you over a metre above the waves.

IJBURG ORIENTATION & TRANSPORT

Tram 26 from Centraal Station via Rietlandpark ejects passengers at the southeast end of IJburglaan. For the marina and its half-dozen terrace cafes, walk past a distinctive six-storey building with frilly balcony edges. For the beach, this is nicer than the marginally quicker route following Pampuslaan past ice-cream shop **IJscuypje**. There are free wooden cycle-racks at the back of the beach beside the lifeguard station.

Infrequent tour boats to Muidenslot/Pampus Island (p212) depart from the **jetty** almost opposite the Four Elements Hotel at the northern corner of the marina. The jetty is entirely without weather protection and there's no ticket office, not even a sign. Prebook on navigoamsterdam. nl/en/pampus.

 EATING & DRINKING IN IJBURG: OUR PICKS

Winkeltje: Very basic container-box shop turned beach cafe-bar with deck-chair seats and parasols. No fixed timings: opens when there's great weather. €

De Japanner Strandeiland: 'Okinawa-style' cafe with bento boxes, izakaya-style snacks and a bar. The only real beach dining. *noon-10pm Sat & Sun* €€

KOH/Barstow: Marina-side terrace combines full flavoured Thai food with a menu that covers TexMex, sushi, burgers and tataki-tuna bowls. *8.30am-9pm* €

Espressofabriek IJburg: Arrived early for your Pampus ferry? Wait it out with coffee from home-roasted single-origin beans. *8am-4pm Mon-Fri, 9am-5pm Sat & Sun* €

Researched by
Catherine Le Nevez

WESTERN CANAL RING, JORDAAN & THE WEST

CHARMING WATERWAYS, ENTICING SHOPPING AND CONTEMPORARY DEVELOPMENTS

Chart Amsterdam's urban evolution from the Western Canal Ring's grand legacies and Jordaan's snug streets to the West's industrial regeneration and striking sustainable architecture.

Like scenes straight out of 17th-century paintings, some of the city's loveliest canalscapes and gabled canal houses are just west of the Medieval Centre in the Western Canal Ring. By the Westerkerk, the Anne Frank Huis, where the young diarist hid with her family in World War II, is the area's main draw. Across the Prinsengracht, the Jordaan's tiny lanes, *bruin cafés* (traditional pubs) and markets evoke its heritage as a former *volksbuurt* (workers' quarter) and are wonderful to wander, as are the lesser-explored, peaceful Western Islands. Northwest of the Jordaan, the West is one of Amsterdam's most up-and-coming areas, with new developments continuing to spring up around the one-time lumber ports of Houthaven.

TOP TIP

After browsing the multitude of tiny shops in the jewel-box-like Negen Straatjes (Nine Streets; p103), stretch out on the spacious lawns of Westerpark (p115) or explore the galleries, restaurants, bars and awesome entertainment venues in the 19th-century former gasworks buildings at Westergas (p110).

See p240 for places to stay in Western Canal Ring, Jordaan and the West.

Jordaan

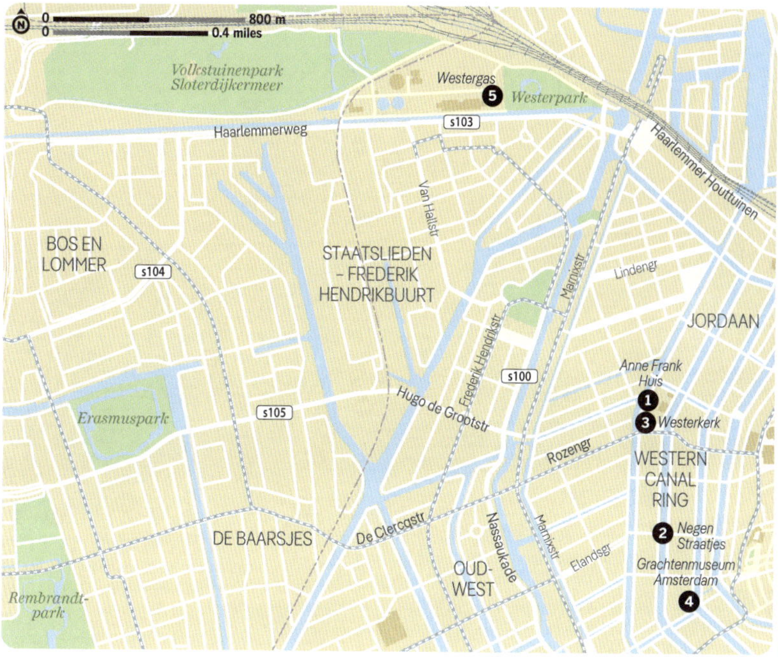

0 800 m
0 0.4 miles

Volkstuinenpark
Sloterdijkermeer

Westergas
5 Westerpark

Haarlemmer Houttuinen

Haarlemmerweg

s103

BOS EN
LOMMER
s104

Van Halstr

STAATSLIEDEN
– FREDERIK
HENDRIKBUURT

Lindengr

JORDAAN

Anne Frank
Huis
1

s100

Hugo de Grootstr

Frederik Hendrikstr

Marnixstr

Erasmuspark

s105

3 Westerkerk

Rozengr

WESTERN
CANAL
RING

De Clercqstr

Nassaukade

Marnixstr

2 Negen
Straatjes

DE BAARSJES

Grachtenmuseum
Amsterdam

OUD-
WEST

Elandsgr

4

Rembrandt-
park

⭐ Highlights

① Anne Frank Huis
Contemplate the brave
life and tragic death of the
young diarist where she hid
during WWII. **p100**

② Negen Straatjes ▶
Browse the speciality
shops along these 'nine
little streets' crisscrossed
by canals. **p103**

③ Westerkerk
Catch a carillon recital or
hear the organ in a lunchtime
concert at the landmark
church. **p102**

**④ Grachtenmuseum
Amsterdam**
Learn how the UNESCO-
listed Grachtengordel was
engineered. **p103**

⑤ Westergas
Explore the reedy
wilderness and old
gasworks buildings turned
into a cultural village. **p110**

🏃 Getting Around

Cycling & Walking
Cycling is ideal in the spread-
out northern Jordaan and West;
the Western Canal Ring and
southern Jordaan's narrow
streets are most easily explored
on foot.

Tram
Both the Western Canal Ring
and southern Jordaan can be
reached by tram (lines 2, 12 and
17) from Centraal Station; trams
travelling along the Jordaan's
western edge (5, 7 and 13) don't
go to Centraal.

Bus
Buses are handy for the
northern Jordaan and West.

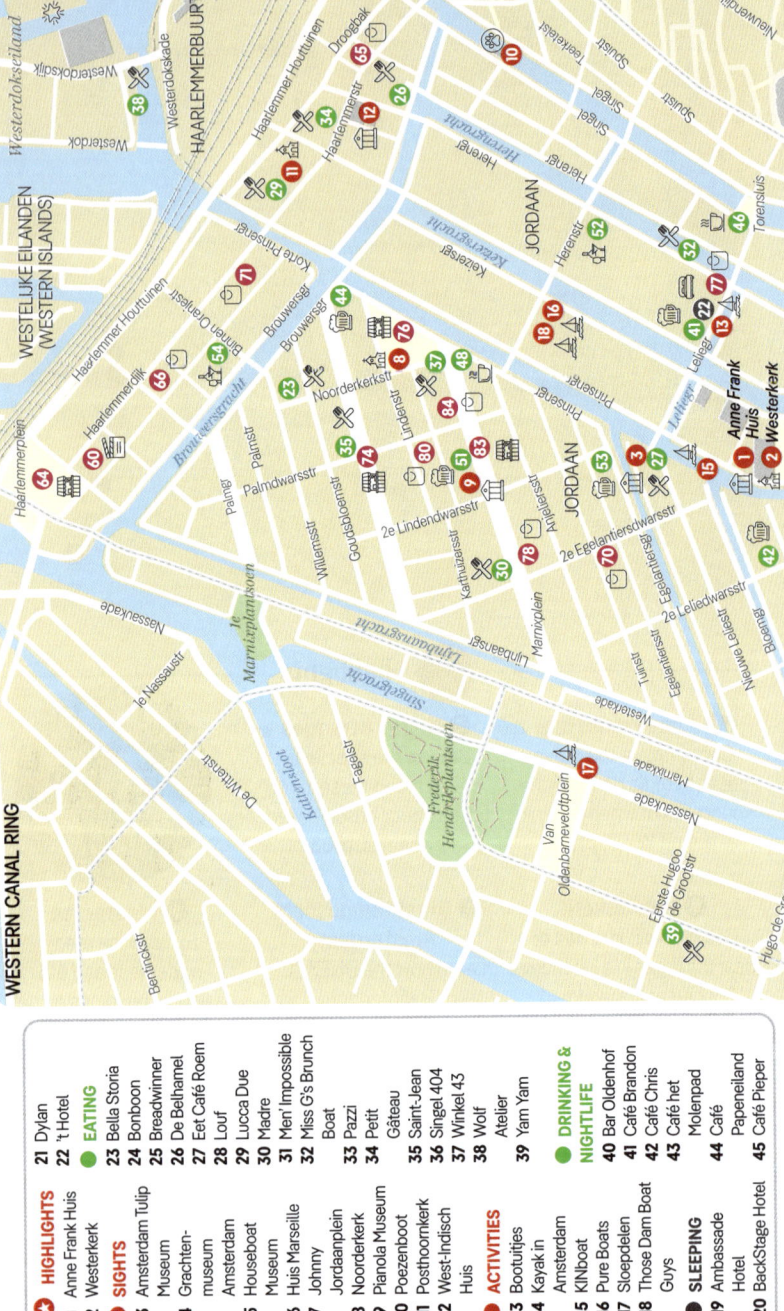

WESTERN CANAL RING

★ **HIGHLIGHTS**
1 Anne Frank Huis
2 Westerkerk

● **SIGHTS**
3 Amsterdam Tulip Museum
4 Grachten-museum
5 Amsterdam Houseboat Museum
6 Huis Marseille
7 Johnny Jordaanplein
8 Noorderkerk
9 Pianola Museum
10 Poezenboot
11 Posthoornkerk
12 West-Indisch Huis

● **ACTIVITIES**
13 Bootuitjes
14 Kayak in Amsterdam
15 Pure Boats
16 KINboat
17 Stoepdelen
18 Those Dam Boat Guys

● **SLEEPING**
19 Ambassade Hotel
20 BackStage Hotel

21 Dylan
22 't Hotel

● **EATING**
23 Bella Storia
24 Bonboon
25 Breadwinner
26 De Belhamel
27 Eet Café Roem
28 Louf
29 Lucca Due
30 Madre
31 Men' Impossible
32 Miss G's Brunch Boat
33 Pazzi
34 Petit Gâteau
35 Saint-Jean
36 Singel 404
37 Winkel 43
38 Wolf Atelier
39 Yam Yam

● **DRINKING & NIGHTLIFE**
40 Bar Oldenhof
41 Café Brandon
42 Café Chris
43 Café het Molenpad
44 Café Papeneiland
45 Café Pieper

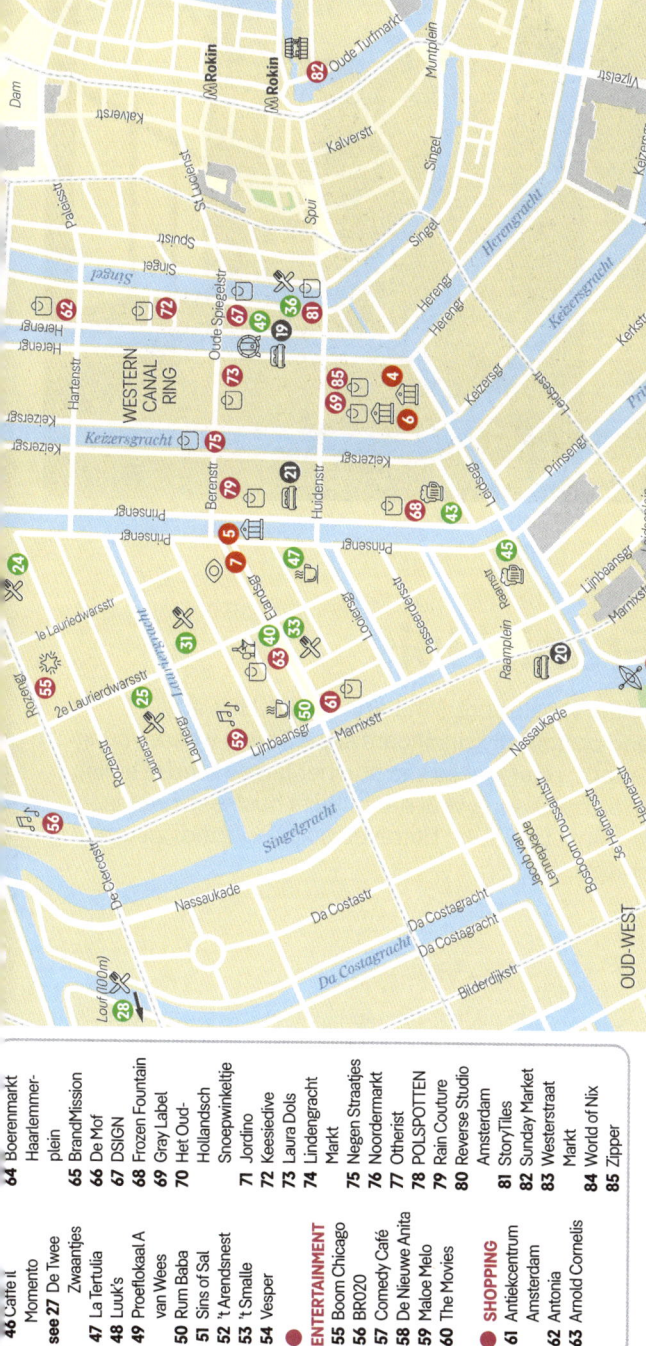

400 m

0.2 miles

46 Caffe Il Momento
see 27 De Twee Zwaantjes
47 La Tertulia
48 Luuk's
49 Proeflokaal A van Wees
50 Rum Baba
51 Sins of Sal
52 't Arendsnest
53 't Smalle
54 Vesper

ENTERTAINMENT
55 Boom Chicago
56 BRO2O
57 Comedy Café
58 De Nieuwe Anita
59 Maloe Melo
60 The Movies

SHOPPING
61 Antiekcentrum Amsterdam
62 Antonia
63 Arnold Cornelis

64 Boerenmarkt Haarlemmer-plein
65 BrandMission
66 De Mof
67 DSIGN
68 Frozen Fountain
69 Gray Label
70 Het Oud-Hollandsch Snoepwinkeltje
71 Jordino
72 Keesiedive
73 Laura Dols
74 Lindengracht Markt
75 Negen Straatjes
76 Noordermarkt
77 Otherist
78 POLSPOTTEN
79 Rain Couture
80 Reverse Studio Amsterdam
81 StoryTiles
82 Sunday Market
83 Westerstraat Markt
84 World of Nix
85 Zipper

RONALD WILFRED JANSEN/SHUTTERSTOCK

The bookcase to the hidden annexe

TOP EXPERIENCE

Anne Frank Huis

In the shadow of the Westertoren, the Anne Frank Huis is a heartbreaking and profoundly significant sight. This is where young Jewish girl Anne kept a diary while she and her family lived in hiding from the Nazis in a secret annexe of her father's business premises for over two years until they were betrayed and deported. Visiting will stay with you forever.

Diary of a Young Girl

Anne Frank was born in Frankfurt, Germany, in 1929. Together with her older sister Margot and parents Otto and Edith, the family fled when Hitler came to power in 1933, settling in Amsterdam, where Otto Frank founded companies selling foodstuffs in offices and warehouses on Amsterdam's Prinsengracht.

It took Hitler's forces a mere five days to occupy the Netherlands, Belgium and much of France in 1940. Anne's diary

DON'T MISS

Anne's red plaid diary

Secret annexe

Anne's bedroom

WWII newsreels

Peter van Pels' room

Former offices

PRACTICALITIES

● Map p98 ● annefrank.org ● adult/child €16/7, with introductory programme €23/14 ● 9am-10pm (exceptions are noted on the website)

describes how restrictions were gradually imposed on Dutch Jews: from being forbidden to ride streetcars to being forced to hand over their bicycles and not being allowed to visit Christian friends. Many Jews went into hiding. Otto and his colleague Hermann van Pels prepared a hidden 'secret annexe' of Otto's business in spring 1942.

In June 1942, Anne received her red plaid-covered diary for her 13th birthday. The following month, when 16-year-old Margot was summoned to Nazi Germany, the family took shelter in the hideout. Soon joining them were Hermann van Pels, his wife Auguste and their son Peter (called the Van Daans in Anne's diary), then dentist Fritz Pfeffer (called Mr Dussel in the diary). The household of eight lived with blacked-out windows in total daytime silence to avoid detection, and Anne's diary was the outlet for her fears and future ambitions. They were tragically cut short when the Gestapo arrived in August 1944 after the hiders were mysteriously betrayed. All eight were deported. Anne died in the Bergen-Belsen concentration camp in March 1945 just weeks before its liberation, aged only 15. Her diary was found in the deserted annexe, and published in 1947 by her father, Otto, the sole survivor. Millions of copies, translated in more than 70 languages, have since been sold worldwide.

Visiting the Anne Frank Huis

Accessed from Westermarkt, the Anne Frank Huis is contained within a modern, box-like shell that retains the building's original industrial character. Its museum shows multilingual news reels of WWII footage narrated using excerpts from Anne's diary. Temporary exhibitions also take place here.

You can see the former offices of Victor Kugler, Otto Frank's business partner, and office workers Miep Gies, Bep Voskuijl and Johannes Kleiman, who provided food, clothing, school supplies and other goods – often bought on the black market or with ration cards – for the hiders.

Above the office kitchen in the *achterhuis* (rear house), beyond the bookcase that ingeniously swings open on hinges, entering the annexe's stark former living quarters is to step back into 1942. At Otto's request, the annexe remains unfurnished, but Anne's pictures of Hollywood stars and Dutch royals remain where she glued them on the walls of her small bedroom, which she shared with Fritz Pfeffer. When the museum opened in 1960, Otto had models made of the house that preserve the cramped, concealed layout.

After visiting the annexe, view more poignant exhibits including Anne's original red-checked diary, alone in a glass case.

The museum shop stocks copies of Anne's diary and historic books. Also here is a cafe for quiet contemplation.

POWERFUL DETAILS

It's often the smallest details that are the most moving of all, for instance the film magazines Victor Kugler bought for Anne, displayed in his office; Anne's treasured children's tea set that she left with her next-door neighbour Toosje Kupers before going into hiding; and, in Anne's parents' bedroom, the markings charting their daughters' heights – Anne grew over 13cm while living in the secret annexe.

TOP TIPS

● Book early: time-slot-entry tickets are released on the museum's website at 10am on Tuesdays for visits six weeks later. No changes or refunds are possible. (Beware scam websites and scalpers.)

● Capacity is limited; arrive early for your pre-booked timeslot; afterwards, you can spend as long as needed; most visits last around an hour.

● Admission includes multilingual audio guides.

● Photography is not permitted.

● There are a number of steep stairs.

● Evenings tend to be the quietest time to visit.

Westerkerk

Gracing the Prinsengracht in the UNESCO-listed Grachtengordel (canal ring), the Westerkerk (Western Church) and its bell tower, the Westertoren (Western Tower) are beloved by Amsterdammers; Anne Frank recounts its chimes in her diary, former Queen Beatrix was married here, and it's immortalised in songs, paintings and photographs. As the tallest church tower in low-rise Amsterdam, it's a beacon across the city.

DENNIS VAN DE WATER/SHUTTERSTOCK

TOP TIPS

● The 50-bell carillon rings out across the neighbourhood; recitals typically take place from noon to 1pm on Tuesdays.

● Hear the organs being played during free lunchtime concerts from 1pm to 1.30pm on Wednesdays.

● See the online agenda for other performances, such as Bach night concertos by candlelight.

PRACTICALITIES

● Map p98 ● westerkerk. nl ● free; donations welcomed
● 11am-3pm Mon-Fri

The Church

Built in Dutch Renaissance style to designs by city architect Hendrick de Keyser (1565–1621), who died a year after construction began, and completed by his son, architect Pieter de Keyser and city mason Cornelis Dankers de Rij, the Netherlands' first Protestant church was consecrated in 1631 and is the focal point for Amsterdam's Dutch Reformed community. Its barrel-vaulted nave is the Netherlands' largest. The main organ, with panels decorated with instruments and biblical scenes, dates from 1686, and the choir organ from 1963.

After Rembrandt died bankrupt in 1669 at nearby Rozengracht, he was buried here in an unidentified pauper's grave. Look for the commemorative wall plaque in the north aisle. Among other Amsterdammers buried here are painter Govert Flinck and cartographer Joan Blaeu.

The Tower

The Westertoren was completed in 1638. Rising 85m high (87m including its rooster weathervane), it's topped by the blue imperial crown bestowed for the city's coat of arms by Habsburg emperor Maximilian I in 1489.

Climbing the tower to the first balcony for panoramic views was unavailable at the time of research due to multiyear restoration works – check for updates.

Browse the Negen Straatjes

MAP P98

Charming speciality shops

In a city filled with shopping opportunities, the **Negen Straatjes** *(de9straatjes.nl)* represent an especially dense concentration of consumer pleasures within the beautiful UNESCO World Heritage canal ring.

Between Raadhuisstraat and Leidsegracht, each of these 'nine little streets' is just a block long. The streets (from west to east, and north to south: Reestraat, Hartenstraat, Gasthuismolensteeg, Berenstraat, Wolvenstraat, Oude Spiegelstraat, Runstraat, Huidenstraat, Wijde Heisteeg) and four canals (west to east: Prinsengracht, Keizergracht, Herengracht and Singel) form a tight grid packed with some 250 shops.

Like the streets, the shops are tiny too, and many are highly specialised. You'll find boutiques with everything from pure silk fabrics to buttons, beads, ceramic tiles, rare watches, vintage bags and jewellery, leather goods, ceramics, art, antiques, candles, flowers and plants, board games, vinyl records and niche specialities, like flippers (and diving gear, at **Keesiedive**) and slippers (as well as slip-ons like clogs, at **Antonia**). Numerous fashion designers have flagship stores here; the area is a launchpad for many Dutch labels. Epicurean treats include cheese, chocolate and wine.

Most shops open daily; plan to spend at least a couple of hours wandering here. **Proeflokaal A van Wees** *(proeflokaal vanwees.nl)*, pouring its Jordaan-distilled house brands – 17-plus *jenevers* (Dutch gins) and 60-plus liqueurs – is a charming spot for a break.

Marvel at the Making of the Canal Ring

MAP P98

Secrets of the Grachtengordel

A 17th-century canal house on the Herengracht is a fitting place to discover the extraordinary engineering behind Amsterdam's canal ring. At the **Grachtenmuseum Amsterdam** *(grachten. museum; adult/child €17.50/9.50)*, audio-guided tours in

---

ORANJE LOPER

Rolling out across the neighbourhood, the Oranje Loper ('orange carpet') is a massive urban renovation project. Stretching 2.8km from the Raadhuisstraat to Mercatorplein, it's a multiyear undertaking that will create a cycling thoroughfare along Raadhuisstraat–Rozengracht, redevelop Westermarkt, redesign the Marnixstraat/Rozengracht intersection and see the planting of dozens of trees. Sections of tram tracks are being upgraded or extended and seven bridges are being restored. During the various stages of works, some tram stops will be closed and routes diverted (the closest stop to the Anne Frank Huis will be the Dam), so check transport updates at gvb.nl/en/oranje-loper. The entire project is due to wrap up in 2029.

 DRINKING IN WESTERN AMSTERDAM: BEST BRUIN CAFÉS   MAP P98

't Smalle: Dock your boat at this 1786 former *jenever* (Dutch gin) distillery with its convivial terrace. *2pm-midnight Mon-Thu, to 1am Fri & Sat, to 10pm Sun*	**Café Papeneiland:** With Delft Blue tiles and a central stove, this *bruin café* is a 1642 gem. *10am-1am Mon-Thu, 10am-3am Fri & Sat, noon-1am Sun*	**Café Pieper:** Antique beer mugs hang from the bar with a 1875 working Belgian beer pump at this stained-glass-windowed 1665 treasure. *noon-1am Sun-Thu, to 2am Fri & Sat*	**Café Chris:** Allegedly the Jordaan's oldest *bruin café*, dating from 1624: workers building the Westertoren collected their pay here. *noon-midnight Sun-Wed, to 1am Thu-Sat*
De Twee Zwaantjes: Opened in 1921, the 'Two Swans' is at its liveliest during Wednesday-night *levenslied* singalongs. *noon-1am Wed, Thu & Sun, to 3am Fri & Sat*	**Café Brandon:** Rare corner canal house from 1626, adorned with B&W pictures of Dutch royals and Ajax players. *3pm-1am Mon-Thu, noon-3am Fri & Sat, noon-1am Sun*	**'t Arendsnest:** Gorgeous *bruin café* with copper *jenever* boilers, serving only Dutch beer, *jenevers*, ciders, whiskies and liqueurs. *noon-midnight Sun-Thu, to 1am Fri & Sat*	**Café het Molenpad:** Quietly romantic, with low lamps and candlelight illuminating its small tables beneath pressed-tin ceilings. *noon-1am Sun-Thu, to 2am Fri & Sat*

WANDER THE HISTORIC WESTERN CANAL RING

Discover 17th-century bridges, buildings and waterways on this charming walk.

START	END	LENGTH
Singel	Felix Meritis	2.8km; 2½ hours

The **1 Singel** was originally a moat that defended Amsterdam's outer limits. The canal's 1648-built **2 Torensluis** (named for the tower that stood here until 1829) is Amsterdam's oldest bridge in its original state. On its northern side the **3 Multatuli statue** commemorates Dutch literary giant Eduard Douwes Dekker, pen name Multatuli; the nearby **4 Multatuli Museum** chronicles his life and work, with furniture and artefacts from his time in Indonesia.

Head north along the **5 Herengracht**, which intersects with **6 Brouwersgracht**. At the Herenmarkt is the 17th-century **7 West-Indisch Huis**, where the Dutch West India Company's governors authorised the establishment of Nieuw Amsterdam (now New York City).

Turning south, cross onto **8 Keizersgracht** (Emperor's Canal), where the red-shuttered **9 Greenland Warehouses** used to store whale oil that powered lamps and stoves pre-electricity. Continue south to the 1622 Dutch Renaissance **10 Huis Met de Hoofden** ('House with the Heads'), with carvings of Apollo, Ceres, Mercury, Minerva, Bacchus and Diana. Designed by architect Hendrick de Keyser and son Pieter, it now houses the Embassy of the Free Mind philosophical museum and library.

At Leliegracht, turn west then south onto **11 Prinsengracht**, home to the **12 Anne Frank Huis** (p100) and **13 Westerkerk** (p102). Back on Keizersgracht is the alternative theatre **14 Felix Meritis**; its colonnaded façade was a model for the renowned Concertgebouw.

The **Brouwersgracht** (Brewer's Canal) took its name from the many suds-makers located along it in the 16th and 17th centuries.

The **Herengracht** (Gentlemen's Canal) was named for the merchants and regents who built manors here; it remains some of the most sought-after real estate.

Multatuli worked in colonial administration in Batavia (now Jakarta); his novel *Max Havelaar* (1860) made him a social conscience for the Netherlands.

JORDAAN

WESTERN CANAL RING

NIEUWMARKT

Nieuwmarkt

Centraal Station (west side)

START

END

Rokin

Rokin

0   400 m
0   0.2 miles

small groups of up to 12 people depart every 10 minutes to avoid overcrowding and take in its permanent exhibition. Its high-tech holograms, videos, cartoons and scale models of the city and canal houses demonstrate how the canals and tilting houses lining them were constructed and the problem-solving that went into the city's expansion. There are thought-provoking temporary exhibitions (such as 'animals of Amsterdam's canals'). The history of the symmetrical Dutch Baroque house designed by Phillip Vingboons is conveyed in glorious period rooms. Kids love the interactive exhibits. Multiple lifts enable access for wheelchairs. Outside, the flower- and greenery-filled 'silent garden', a haven for birdlife, can be visited during special events.

Visiting typically takes around 1½ to two hours in all. It's possible to prepurchase tickets online but they don't give fast-track entry. Weekend afternoons are busiest, so try and come early midweek. The museum opens at noon on Mondays; 10am on other days. Last entry is at 4.30pm. Afterwards, you'll look at the surrounding canals in a whole different light.

Catch Contemporary Photographic Exhibitions

MAP P98

Influential photography museum

A pair of 17th-century canal houses are the showcase for photography that captures the zeitgeist in its artistic expression and spirited enquiry at **Huis Marseille** *(huismarseille.nl; adult/child €12.50/free)*. Its original building (Keizersgracht 401) was built around 1665 for French merchant Isaac Focquier (look for the map impression of Marseille's port on the façade's gable stone). Stuccowork and Jacob de Wit's ceiling painting were added the following century; the 18th-century garden house was reconstructed in 2003. Exhibition spaces and a depot fill the adjoining Keizersgracht 399.

In part to protect the light-sensitive photographs, there's no permanent display; instead, it mounts several major exhibitions each year, mainly curated from its own collection. Check the agenda to find out what's coming up: exhibitions typically last around three to four months, with the museum closed for a week between each one.

NIEUW AMSTERDAM TO NEW YORK

Enlisted by the Dutch East India Company (VOC; p273), English captain Henry Hudson changed course to explore the North American river now named for him. The Dutch established a fort on Manhattan, which grew into the settlement of Nieuw Amsterdam, and in 1626 an agent of the recently established Dutch West India Company (GWC) purchased the island from Native Americans for 60 guilders (then equivalent to US$24).

In 1653, they built a fortified wall (now Manhattan's Wall St) to keep out the British, but in 1664, its warships invaded and the GWC's local governor, Peter Stuyvesant, director-general of the colony of New Netherland, surrendered. The British swiftly renamed it New York. A fountain and bronze statue of Stuyvesant stands in the courtyard of the Herenmarkt's **West-Indisch Huis** (Map p98).

 EATING IN WESTERN AMSTERDAM: BEST BAKERIES ——— MAP P98

| **Breadwinner:** Organic plain or filled sourdough NYC-style bagels (poppyseed, onion, jalapeño, cheddar...). *11am-3pm Tue & Wed, 9.30am-3pm Thu-Sun* € | **Saint-Jean:** Flaky croissants, danishes, cruffins, brioche and cinnamon buns are among the 100% plant-based treats at this bright corner bakery. *8am-5pm* € | **Louf:** Sourdough loaves, focaccia, Viennese pastries and filled sandwiches; don't miss the *krentenbollen* (currant buns). *8am-3pm Mon-Sat, to noon Sun* € | **Petit Gâteau:** Exquisite pastries made on-site: tartlets topped with jewel-like fruits, glazed éclairs, macarons, shell-shaped madeleines and quiches. *10am-6pm* € |

BEST FASHION & VINTAGE SHOPS

BrandMission
(Map p98) High-end men's and women's sustainable fashion. *brandmission.nl*

Gray Label (Map p98) Organic cotton children's wear. *gray-label.com*

Rain Couture (Map p98) Multi-seasonal wet-weather trench coats, jackets and parkas. *rain-couture.nl*

De Mof (Map p98) Durable work- and casualwear since 1885; historical collections inspire its Waddenzee fishers' jumpers and coal workers' black jackets. *demofkleding.nl*

Zipper (Map p98) Vintage clothing from the 1950s to '90s, such as fleece-lined suede jackets. *zippervintageclothing.com*

Laura Dols (Map p98) Everything from 1920s beaded dresses to '40s hand-stitched leather gloves and shawls. *lauradols.nl*

Reverse Studio Amsterdam (Map p98) High-quality pieces by top fashion labels. *reverseamsterdam.com*

The Movies

Hang Out in the Haarlemmerbuurt   MAP P98

Food, film and sustainable fashion

Between Centraal Station and Westerpark, the hive of activity in the **Haarlemmerbuurt** (*haarlemmerbuurtamsterdam. nl*) is a legacy of the Brouwersgracht's former shipyards, breweries and warehouses. The neighbourhood's spine stretches along Haarlemmerstraat past the **Posthoornkerk**. Beyond the Prinsengracht, the street's western extension, the Haarlemmerdijk, continues to the neoclassical Haarlemmerpoort (p112) on the large square Haarlemmerplein. On Wednesdays, farmers market stalls set up here for its *boerenmarkt* (p107).

Today, this 1km-long thoroughfare is a buzzing commercial strip, lined with independent boutiques stocking fashion (vintage and new), cosmetics, books, music and homewares, with an increasingly sustainable focus, as well as food and drink specialists. Also here is Amsterdam's oldest cinema, 1912 art-deco gem **The Movies** (*themovies.nl*), showing indie and mainstream films (including films with English subtitles).

 EATING IN WESTERN AMSTERDAM: BEST CAFE DINING ——— MAPS P98 & P111

De Bakkerswinkel:
At Westergas, with mezzanine seating, sofas and sunny terrace. Geat-value cafe dishes. *9am-5pm Mon-Fri, 10am-5pm Sat & Sun* €

Eet Café Roem:
Sandwiches, toasties and giant Dutch pancakes looking down the Leliegracht from the Prinsengracht. *9am-9pm Mon-Fri, 10am-9pm Sun* €

Winkel 43: Popular from breakfast to evening drinks, and for the coveted *appeltaart* (apple pie). *7am-1am Mon, 8am-1am Tue-Fri, 7am-2am Sat, 9am-1am Sun* €€

Singel 404: Tucked-away canal-side spot (look for the red awning) for all-day breakfast, lunch and honey-mint lemonade at its handful of tables inside or out. *9am-6pm* €€

Treasure Hunt at the Jordaan's Markets

To market, to market...

Some of Amsterdam's most atmospheric markets set up in the Jordaan.

With the 1623-built Calvinist church the **Noorderkerk** *(noorder kerk.nl)*, home to classical concerts *(noorderkerkconcerten.nl)* and immersive projections of Van Gogh & Rembrandt In Amsterdam *(vangoghinamsterdam.com; adult/child €17/13)*, as its backdrop, the **Noordermarkt** *(noordermarkt-amsterdam. nl)* has been a marketplace since the early 17th century.

Saturdays see the Noordermarkt host a general market in front of the church, with everything from antiques and bric-a-brac to artisan arts, crafts, ceramics, prints, posters, vintage fashion, bags, hats and jewellery, as well as a *boerenmarkt* (farmers market) with organic produce. The *boerenmarkt* sets up from outside corner cafe **Winkel 43** – queuing for its towering slices of still-warm *appeltaart* (apple pie) is a local market-day ritual.

On Mondays, a general market takes over the Noordermarkt. Along the adjacent Westerstraat (once the Anjeliersgracht, meaning Carnation Canal, dug in 1650 and backfilled in 1861 to create a thoroughfare), the **Westerstraat Markt** (aka the Westermarkt) sells bolts of colourful fabrics.

Around the corner from the Noordermarkt, Saturday's lively **Lindengracht Markt** has been a neighbourhood tradition since 1894. Join locals browsing over 230 stalls selling fresh fruit, vegetables, seafood, fabulous cheeses, breads and Dutch delicacies like caramel-filled *stroopwafels*, colourful cut flowers, clothing and homewares.

At Haarlemmerplein, Wednesdays see producers sell fresh fruit, vegetables, breads, cheeses, flowers and other mostly organic produce at the **Boerenmarkt Haarlemmerplein**.

Wonderful food shops in the neighbourhood include **Het Oud-Hollandsch Snoepwinkeltje** *(snoepwinkeltje.com)*, with jar after apothecary jar of Dutch penny sweets, including the salty liquorice known as *zoute drop*. **Arnold Cornelis** *(cornelis.nl)* has beautiful cakes (eg fruitcake, cheesecake), biscuits, liqueur-filled chocolates and candies. Chocolates at **Jordino** *(jordino.nl)* include tulips and famous Dutch paintings. Just behind the Noordermarkt, **World of Nix** *(worldofnix.com)* specialises in non-alcoholic beers, wines and spirits, mocktails, cordials, mixers and infused sparkling waters.

BEST WESTERN AMSTERDAM CANAL CRUISES

Pure Boats (Map p98) Boutique operator with beautiful small boats; options include 90-minute daytime 'highlights' trips (with apple pie) or elegant evening trips (with cheese platters). *pureboats.com*

Those Dam Boat Guys (Map p98) Laid-back trips lasting 90 minutes with entertaining commentary. BYO refreshments. *those damboatguys.com*

Miss G's Brunch Boat (Map p98) Combines 90-minute weekend cruises with brunches, beats and Bloody Marys. *missgs.nl*

KINboat (Map p98) Solar-powered boats depart from KINboat's Prinsengracht dock, with drinks and snacks sold on board. *kinboat.com*

Kayak in Amsterdam (Map p98) Guided paddling excursions include a one-hour 'Around Jordaan' tour passing landmarks like the Westerkerk. *kayak inamsterdam.com*

 EATING IN WESTERN AMSTERDAM: BEST RESTAURANTS —— MAPS P98 & P111

De Belhamel: At the head of the Herengracht with canal-side tables, art-nouveau interior and French-influenced breakfast through to dinner. *9.30am-10pm* €€€

Wolf Atelier: Showcase for experimental chef Michael Wolf's tasting menus, with magical views at night. *6-10pm Tue-Fri, noon-5pm & 6-10pm Sat* €€€

BAK: Overlooking the IJ in a historic warehouse, crafting sustainable Dutch seafood, vegetables and wild game. *6-10pm Wed-Fri, 12.30-3pm & 6-10pm Sat & Sun* €€€

Lars: Michelin-starred address at Houthaven using produce from its rooftop garden. *6-10pm Tue & Wed, noon-5pm & 6-10pm Thu-Sat* €€€

TULIPMANIA

The Dutch tulip craze of 1636–37 ranks alongside the greatest economic booms and busts in history.

After success growing and cross-breeding tulips in the Netherlands' cool, damp climate, exotic frilly, flame-streaked specimens attracted the attention of wealthy merchants, and tulip growers arose to service the demand. A speculative frenzy ensued: bidding often took place in taverns, and people paid top florin (even more than an Amsterdam canal house) for the finest bulbs, many changing hands time and again before they sprouted.

When traders failed to fetch expected prices in February 1637, the market collapsed. Within weeks many of the country's wealthiest merchants went bankrupt and many more people lost everything. Enthusiasm for tulips endured, however, and the Netherlands remains the world leader of cultivation.

WOLF-PHOTOGRAPHY/SHUTTERSTOCK

Amsterdam Tulip Museum

Learn About the National Flower   MAP P98

The story of the tulip

Allow around half an hour or so at the charming Jordaan canal house containing the diminutive **Amsterdam Tulip Museum** (*amsterdamtulipmuseum.com; adult/child €7/4*), which offers an overview of the history of the country's favourite bloom. Through exhibits, timelines and two short films (in English), you'll learn how Ottoman merchants encountered the flowers in the Himalayan steppes and began commercial production in Türkiye, how fortunes were made and lost during Dutch 'Tulipmania' in the 17th century, and how bulbs were used as food during WWII. You'll also discover present-day growing and harvesting techniques. There's a great collection of tulip art and artefacts, such as vases designed to accommodate separate stems.

Even if you're not visiting the museum, you can stop by its gift shop overflowing with high-quality floral souvenirs (many artist commissions), including jewellery, bags, books, homewares like tea towels, aprons and tableware, and antique

Sake pairings too

EATING IN WESTERN AMSTERDAM: BEST VEGAN   MAPS P98 & P111

Koffie ende Koeck: Canal-side 'Coffee and Cookies' has an all-vegan menu spanning smoked-tofu sandwiches, frittata, quiches and cakes. *10am-5pm Wed-Sun €*

Madre: Skylit Mexican restaurant with artichoke tacos, sweet-potato quesadillas or charred pineapple and mango tostadas. *5.30-10pm Mon-Fri, 11am-10.30pm Sat €€*

Bonboon: Elegant four- and five-course vegan menus in bright Rozenstraat premises with beautiful tiles and big picture windows. *6-11pm Wed-Sun €€€*

Men' Impossible: Plant-based, zero-waste Japanese restaurant specialising in ramen with handmade noodles as part of five-course menus. *5-10pm Wed-Mon €€€*

and reproduction Delft tiles. It also stocks premium bulbs in season (spring-flowering varieties in autumn and summer-flowering bulbs in spring/early summer).

Discover Boat Life in the Jordaan   MAP P98

All about houseboats

The 23m-long *Hendrika Maria*, a former cargo ship from 1914, is now the **Houseboat Museum** (*houseboatmuseum. nl; adult/child €9.50/5*). It offers a good sense of how *gezellig* (cosy, convivial) life can be on the water. Restored in 2008, there's some fantastic vintage decor from 1967 to 1997 when it was a residence. An audio guide lets you navigate its surprisingly spacious 80-sq-metre interior; the actual displays are minimal, but you can watch a presentation on houseboats (some pretty and some ghastly) and inspect the sleeping, living, cooking and dining quarters with all the mod cons. Amsterdam's 2500 or so houseboats are connected to utilities including water, electricity, gas and the sewage system, thanks to the city's Project Schoonschip (Project Clean Ship), which saw every houseboat connected to the sewage system by 2017, dramatically improving the water quality of the canals. Museum tickets are cheaper before noon (online bookings only).

The houseboat museum is permanently moored on the Prinsengracht, across from **Johnny Jordaanplein**. This shady little square is named after Johnny Jordaan (the pseudonym of Johannes Hendricus van Musscher), a popular musician in the mid-1900s who sang the romantic music known as *levenslied* (tears-in-your-beer-style ballads). On the square, you'll find Johnny, and members of the Jordaan musical hall of fame, cast in bronze. On King's Day (p19), this is where many Jordaanians congregate for live music.

Meet Cats Aboard the Poezenboot   MAP P98

Kitty sanctuary

Feline fans may want to check out a different kind of 'houseboat', the **Poezenboot** (*depoezenboot.nl; by donation*) a floating animal sanctuary on the Singel. It was founded in 1966 by a local woman who became legendary for looking after several hundred stray cats at a time. The boat has since been taken over by a foundation and can hold some 50 kitties in proper pens. Some are permanent residents, and the rest are ready

BEST DIY BOATING

Eco Boats Amsterdam (Map p111) Hires electric boats for eight or 12 passengers from Zandhoek; skippered options also. *ecoboats amsterdam.com*

Sloepdelen (Map p98) Book 12-seater boats online; set sail from Nassaukade. *sloepdelen.nl*

Canal Motorboats (Map p111) Amsterdam's first and oldest operator has rentals from Westerdoksdijk, Zandhoek and Westerpark, including 'plastic fishing' equipment to clean up the canals. *canal motorboats.com*

Bootuitjes (Map p98) Hires saloon boats from its location on Leilliegracht in the Western Canal Ring. *bootuitjes.nl*

Canal SUP (Map p111 Get a unique perspective stand-up paddleboarding from this outfit's SUP shack in Den Brielstraat, near Westerpark; there's also an outlet in Houthaven at Canal SUP x Fuse. *canalsup.nl*

EATING IN WESTERN AMSTERDAM: BEST PIZZA   MAP P98

Lucca Due: In the Posthoornkerk's old rectory, with red-checked tables on its terrace, and premium pizza toppings. *3-11pm Sun-Wed, to 11.30pm Thu-Sat* €€

Bella Storia: Dough proved for 48 hours gives rise to pillowy bases topped with traditional ingredients and cooked in the wood-fired oven. *5.30-10pm Wed-Sun* €€

Yam Yam: Trattoria turning out thin-crust pizzas: salami and fennel seed; smoked ham, mascarpone and truffle and vegetarian varieties. *5.30-10pm Wed-Sat* €€

Pazzi: The original branch of the Amsterdam mini-chain where wood-fired pizzas are made with care and Italian beers are the ideal accompaniment. *5-10pm* €€

WHY I LOVE WESTERN AMSTERDAM

Catherine Le Nevez, Lonely Planet writer

Amsterdam's canals and complicated street names mean, even after a lifetime of exploring, getting lost is almost inevitable – but in this neighbourhood it's a joy. Meandering from the edge of the city's medieval heart along the former Roman border of the IJ River, passing the gabled buildings of the 17th-century canal ring, heading into the Jordaan's narrow lanes with tiny former workers' houses, stopping for a *fluitje* inside a candlelit *bruin café*, crossing the drawbridges of the Western Islands, cutting through Westerpark into the Spaarndammerbuurt and the high-tech construction at Houthaven, I'm struck that virtually the full sweep of Amsterdam's history is found in this small corner of the city.

to be adopted (after being desexed and implanted with an identifying computer chip, in line with Dutch law).

It's open from 1pm to 3pm on Tuesdays, Wednesdays and Saturdays; only six people are allowed onboard at a time and it doesn't take reservations, so arrive early and be prepared to wait if it's busy.

Travel Back a Century in Time   MAP P98

Player-piano museum

In the Jordaan, the **Pianola Museum** *(pianolamuseum. online; adult/child €9/5)* is a very special place, evoking the Art Nouveau to Art Deco eras of 1900 to 1935 and crammed with pianolas from the time. The museum has dozens, although fewer are on display at any given time, as well as more than 40,000 music rolls and a player pipe organ. It's open Friday, Saturday and Sunday afternoons for continuous tours, or by appointment. Intimate concerts are regularly held on the player pianos, featuring anything from Mozart to Fats Waller and rare classical or jazz tunes composed specially for the instrument – check dates and booking details on the website.

Ignite Your Creativity at Westergas   MAP P111

Gasworks turned cultural village

Exhibitions, installations, gigs, films, festivals and other events at vast post-industrial space **Westergas** *(westergas.nl)* tap into Amsterdam's sustainability-driven creative spirit. This late 19th-century Dutch Renaissance complex designed by Isaac Gosschalk, previously known as Westergasfabriek, was the city's western coal-fired gasworks until production ceased in 1967. From the 1990s, the heavily polluted site was decontaminated and industrial architecture preserved, as artists and entrepreneurs realised its potential. In 2003 it evolved into an urban 'cultural village', and in 2018, new ownership reenergised its cultural output.

Its historic, renovated buildings now house creative spaces like the grand former engineer's residence housing the artist-designed, 2025-opened contemporary art **Museum Villa** *(museumvilla.com; adult/child €17.50/9)*. The former purification hall, where sulphur was extracted, is home to the 2022-opened immersive digital art gallery **Fabrique des Lumières** *(fabrique-lumieres.com; adult/child €18/14)*, and

Continued on p114

 DRINKING IN WESTERN AMSTERDAM: BEST COCKTAIL BARS   MAPS P98 & P111

Vesper: Memorabilia-filled James Bond–inspired bar with twists like blue-corn foam, green-olive spherification and gold-dust-infused vodka. *6pm-1am Wed-Sat*	**Bar Oldenhof:** Speakeasy evoking the roaring 1920s with dimly lit dark-wood panelling, velvet armchairs and a jazz soundtrack. *6pm-1am Sun-Thu, to 2am Fri & Sat*	**Sins of Sal:** Dark, vampire-themed Latin cocktail den mixing mezcal and tequila with cactus leaf and fermented guava. *6pm-midnight Tue-Thu, to 2am Fri & Sat*	**Rum Barrel:** Caribbean-styled bar with over 300 different rums, fresh tropical juices and homemade infusions. *6pm-midnight Wed & Thu, to 2.30am Fri & Sat*

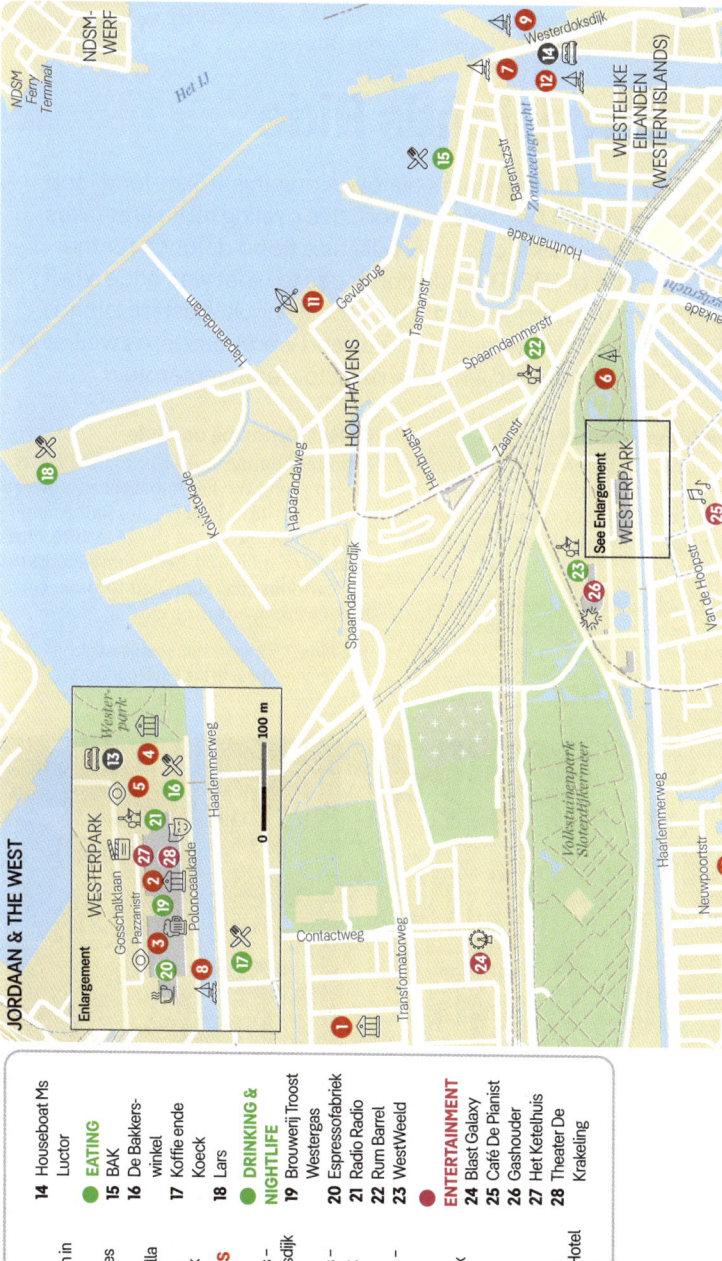

JORDAAN & THE WEST

Enlargement

WESTERPARK

Westerpark

Gosschalklaan

Pazzanistr

Poloncealaade

Haarlemmerweg

Contactweg

Transformatorweg

0   100 m

WESTERPARK

See Enlargement

NDSM-WERF

Westerdoksdijk

Het IJ

NDSM Ferry Terminal

WESTELIJKE EILANDEN (WESTERN ISLANDS)

Barentsztr

Zoutkeetsgracht

Houthankade

Nassaukade

Singelgracht

Haparandadam

Gevlebrug

HOUTHAVENS

Tasmanstr

Haparandaweg

Spaarndammerstr

Spaarndammerdijk

Hembrugstr

Zaanstr

Volkstuinenpark Sloterdijkermeer

Van de Hoopstr

Haarlemmerweg

Nieuwpoortstr

BOS EN LOMMER

Kostrostokade

0   500 m
0   0.25 miles

111

SIGHTS	14	Houseboat Ms Luctor
1 AMAZE		
2 Amsterdam in Motion	**EATING**	
3 Fabrique des Lumières	15	BAK
4 Museum Villa	16	De Bakkers-winkel
5 Westergas	17	Koffie ende Koeck
6 Westerpark	18	Lars
ACTIVITIES	**DRINKING & NIGHTLIFE**	
7 Canal Motorboats – Westerdoksdijk	19	Brouwerij Troost Westergas
8 Canal Motorboats – Westerpark	20	Espressofabriek
9 Canal Motorboats – Zandhoek	21	Radio Radio
10 Canal SUP	22	Rum Barrel
11 Canal SUP x Fuse	23	WestWeeld
12 Eco Boats Amsterdam	**ENTERTAINMENT**	
SLEEPING	24	Blast Galaxy
13 Conscious Hotel Westerpark	25	Café De Pianist
	26	Gashouder
	27	Het Ketelhuis
	28	Theater De Krakeling

Western Islands Ride

Uncover layers of Amsterdam's history along this 4.5km-long loop ride. Starting at the Haarlemmerpoort, this cycling route first takes in the Haarlemmerdijk – originally built as a flood defence for the city's expansion of 1612. The ride continues to what was once a busy early 17th-century harbour and is now the tranquil Western Islands, winding past historic bridges, wharves and warehouses, as well as an ingenious 'bubble barrier', en route back to Haarlemmerplein.

❶ Haarlemmerpoort

Once a defensive gateway to the city, the neoclassical Haarlemmerpoort, with Roman-temple-styled Corinthian pillars, marked the journey to Haarlem, a major trading route.

The Ride: Cycle south to Brouwersgracht and southeast along the waterfront to the Prinsengracht.

❷ Het Kanon bij de Sluis

The Haarlemmerdijk crosses the Prinsengracht along the Eenhoornsluis ('unicorn gate') – an 1878 lock connecting Amsterdam's inner canals to the IJ. A 1618 **cannon** later mounted here commemorates the cannons that signalled to ships when locks were opening or closing.

The Ride: It's a short spin southeast along Haarlemmerstraat to the Posthoornkerk.

IVO ANTONIE DE ROOIJ/SHUTTERSTOCK

Haarlemmerdijk

❸ Posthoornkerk

Set back from Haarlemmerstraat, the neo-Gothic Posthoornkerk was built in 1863 by Pierre Cuypers. In the 1970s, residents saved the triple-spired church from demolition; it's now an events venue.

The Ride: Return to the Prinsengracht and cycle north, under the road and railway bridge, and along Westerdokskade to Han Lammersbrug.

❹ Great Bubble Barrier

Just east of Han Lammersbrug, look for the diagonal **line of bubbles**. A pioneering green initiative, this 2019-installed 'bubble barrier' lifts plastic waste to the surface where it flows to a collection point without hindering the passage of fish or watercraft.

The Ride: Continue east along Westerdokskade, passing a 1920 railway swing bridge topped by a glass box housing gastronomic restaurant Wolf Atelier (p107). Turn north across Westerdoksbrug and follow the IJ north to Silodam.

❺ Silodam

Incorporating 1896 grain silos and a modern extension resembling stacked shipping containers, this 10-storey residential/commercial building has a wooden-decked viewing platform overlooking the IJ.

The Ride: Return to Westerdok and cycle west on Van Diemenstraat.

❻ Muurschildering Willem Barentsz

Covering four building façades on Van Diemenstraat's southern side are a series of Delft Blue **murals** (2008) by Klaartje Bruyn depicting the explorations of Dutch seafarer and scientist Willem Barentsz.

The Ride: Navigate south to Realengracht then west to the Drieharingenbrug.

❼ Drieharingenbrug

Linking the Western Islands of Realeneiland and Prinseneiland, double wooden drawbridge Drieharingenbrug ('Three Herrings Bridge') is named for the gable stone on the 18th-century house on its northern side.

BEST DESIGN & HOMEWARES SHOPS

Frozen Fountain (Map p98) Design platform showcasing striking furniture and interiors. *frozenfountain.com*

POLSPOTTEN (Map p98) Brand store of the 1986-founded Dutch design pioneer, with furniture, textiles, tableware and quirky decorative pieces. *polspotten.com*

Otherist (Map p98) Styled as a modern Wunderkammer (cabinet of curiosities), with entomological display cases. *otherist.com*

StoryTiles (Map p98) Hand-fired ceramic tiles: house numbers, Amsterdam streetscapes, windmills, bicycles, canals... *storytiles.com*

DSIGN (Map p98) Piet Design paper houses and glass tulips, Nijntje (Miffy) LED lamps and more. *dsign.amsterdam*

Antiekcentrum Amsterdam (Map p98) Cornucopia art, antiques, vintage and collectibles. *antiekcentrum amsterdam.nl*

Westergas (p110)

Continued from p110

2025 arrival **Amsterdam in Motion** *(amsterdaminmotion. nl; adult/child €18/free)*. Curated by the Amsterdam Museum, it incorporates a 15-minute journey through Amsterdam's past via projection mapping on a 200-sq-metre city model of 30,500 buildings at 1:1300 scale, and upper-floor interactive installations showcasing Amsterdam's present and future.

On-site brewery **Brouwerij Troost Westergas** *(brouwerij troost.nl; brewery tours per person €10)* has big silver tanks cooking up saison, blond ale and smoked porter varieties, distils its own *jenever* and gin, and makes sodas; brewery tours lasting 45 minutes take place on Saturdays. There's also a coffee roastery, **Espressofabriek**, and a slew of drinking and/ or dining offerings as diverse as, among others, mussels and gin, Algerian cuisine, and Japanese street food and retro arcade games, and a bakery-cafe, De Bakkerswinkel (p106), in the gasworks' old regulators house next to the drawbridge.

Entertainment options span a youth-oriented theatre, the **Theater De Krakeling** *(krakeling.nl),* to an arthouse cinema in the boiler house, **Het Ketelhuis** *(ketelhuis.nl),* while clubbing spaces include **Radio Radio** *(radioradio.radio),*

DRINKING IN WESTERN AMSTERDAM: BEST COFFEE

MAPS P98 & P111

Caffè il Momento: Exposed-brick space with a wall stencil of canal houses, quality espresso and great coffee art. *8am-6pm Mon-Fri, 9am-5pm Sat & Sun*

Espressofabriek: Aromas of roasting coffee waft from the monumental brick building housing this roastery at Westergas. *8am-4pm Mon-Fri, 9am-5pm Sat & Sun*

Luuk's: Espresso brews with pea-protein, oat, coconut or dairy, plus matcha and the best banana bread. *7.30am-4.30pm Mon-Fri, 8am-5pm Sat, 9am-5pm Sun*

Rum Baba: On Elandsgracht, selling its own-roasted beans, and brewing them to drink in or take with you to go. *8am-4.30pm Mon-Fri, 9am-5pm Sat & Sun*

with a DJ bar, club and radio station, and **WestWeeld** *(west weelde.nl)*, combining a huge nightclub, a bar-restaurant with a massive terrace, and an events space – events sometimes spill over to the adjacent industrial shell of the old transformer house, De Wester. Westergas' most iconic cultural stage is the giant, cylindrical former gas storage tank, the **Gashouder** (undergoing renovations until late 2026), with concerts, events and festivals.

The roaming **Sunday Market** *(sundaymarket.nl)*, with art, fashion and design, sets up here on the first Sunday of each month from March to October. Westergas' calendar also includes May's food-truck feast **Rollende Keukens** *(rollende keukens.amsterdam)*, with over 100 'rolling kitchens', as well as a multitude of music festivals, including July's open-minded electronic dance festival **Milkshake** *(milkshakefestival.com)* and pre-festival **Mini Milkshake** *(forallwholove.com)*. It is also the home base of the ADE Lab Village, growing the next generation of EDM artists and producers, as part of October's massive EDM extravaganza, the Amsterdam Dance Event (ADE; p134).

Linked to Westergas by a long wading pool and tree-shaded paths, expansive **Westerpark** has its roots in the city's earliest municipal park, originally established as the Westerplantsoen (Western Garden) in 1845 to provide workers with an escape from the industrial surrounds, and redeveloped after 1891 when the garden made way for the relocated western canal. Its lawns are a favourite hangout on sunny days.

Delve into Digital Worlds

MAP P111

Immersive attraction and arcade gallery

In a massive 3000-sq-metre industrial warehouse west of Houthaven, **AMAZE** *(amaze-amsterdam.com; adult/child €26.95/15.50)* is a multisensory maze of light and sound installations, smoke, mirrors, lasers and beats that recall its former life as a nightclub. In small groups, you move through its different spaces (of varying intensity) in around an hour. Prebook timeslots online and save time for the stunning cocktail bar. It's wheelchair accessible, but not suitable for anyone with conditions such as epilepsy or claustrophobia. Kids must be aged over 10 and accompanied by an adult. From Centraal, take bus 22 (direction Sloterdijk) to the Contactweg stop.

For a throwback to '90s digital nostalgia, the nearby **Blast Galaxy** *(blastgalaxy.nl; adult/child €15/10, Mario Kart room per person €10, karaoke from €80)* has over 100 retro arcade and console games like Donkey Kong, Double Dragon, Galaga, Mario Bros, Mortal Kombat, Pac-Man, Street Fighter, Tekken and Tetris. Admission includes unlimited games; you don't need additional coins or tokens. Mario Kart fiends can book the competition room (minimum four people). There are also Japanese-style karaoke rooms. It's typically open Wednesday to Sunday.

BEST ENTERTAINMENT

Boom Chicago (Map p98) Stages seriously funny improv-style comedy shows in English most nights, and runs two-hour improv taster classes on Saturdays. *boomchicago.nl*

Comedy Café (Map p98) Stand-up and open-mic nights in English and Dutch. *comedycafe.nl/ amsterdam*

De Nieuwe Anita (Map p98) Alternative living-room-like space with emerging musicians, comedy, cult films, spoken word performances and more. *denieuweanita.nl*

Maloe Melo (Map p98) Freewheeling altar of Amsterdam's blues scene, with nightly music from funk and soul to Texas blues and rockabilly. *maloemelo.com*

Café De Pianist (Map p111) Cosy poster-lined *café* (pub) with jazz concerts and jam sessions. *cafedepianist.nl*

BR020 (Map p98) Vinyl listening bar with album covers on the walls and regular live music. *br020 amsterdam.com*

Houthaven by Bike

Spin through a century of architectural advances on this 4.25km cycling tour. Between the 1920s-developed Spaarndammerbuurt and the IJ River is Amsterdam's first, 1876-dug harbour, Houthaven (aka Houthavens for its four lumber ports). Transformation of this industrial area began in 2010, with streets, bridges and seven artificial islands named for the Baltic cities from where timber was shipped. It's now Amsterdam's first climate-neutral neighbourhood.

❶ Museum Het Schip

Remarkable 1921-completed housing project Het Schip is a flagship of Amsterdam School architecture. Designed by Michel de Klerk for railway employees, the ship-like triangular block has a rocket-shaped tower linking the complex's wings.

The Ride: Cycle north along Oostzaanstraat to Spaarndammerdijk and cross over the top of the Spaarndammertunnel into Houthaven, then take the first left onto Houthavenweg.

❷ Het 4 Gymnasium

Secondary school Het 4 Gymnasium opened in 2016. Designed by Paul de Ruiter, the building has a vertical layered façade with wooden slats, triple-glazed translucent yellow, red and orange glass, solar panels and concrete core air conditioning that achieve year-round energy neutrality.

The Ride: Ride north along Archangelkade to Koivistokade, overlooking the working harbour Mercuriushaven, and turn east on Koivistokade to Danzigerkade.

YOURNEXTCONTENT/SHUTTERSTOCK

REM

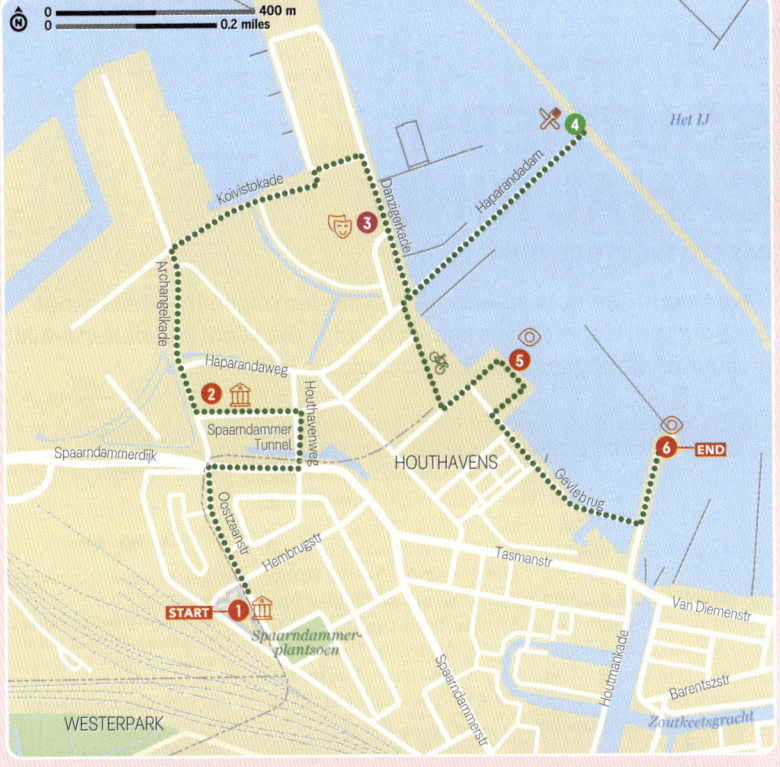

❸ Theater Amsterdam

Built in 2014 by Dutch architectural firm Dedato, this gleaming theatre has a 3800-sq-metre glass façade facing the IJ River. Its 4200-sq-metre main hall can accommodate huge sets for large-scale theatre and music productions.

The Ride: Ride northeast along the artificial peninsula Haparandadam, passing barges converted into houseboats and the vintage 1927 former vehicle and passenger ferry now containing bar-restaurant **Ferry**.

❹ REM

Rising 22m at the end of the peninsula, red-metal rig REM was a pirate radio and TV broadcasting station in the North Sea off the coast of Noordwijk in 1964 until being shut down. In 2011, the rig was towed here and now houses a fabulous restaurant with 360-degree views from its three platforms, including the former helipad rooftop terrace.

The Ride: Double back along Haparandadam and take the pedestrian and cycle bridge Wisbybrug across the islands Wiborgeiland and Stettineiland to Revaleiland. Ride northeast on Revaleiland to the IJ River.

❺ The July – Boat & Co

These islands' architecture is a contemporary interpretation of the Amsterdam School style. Apartment hotel The July – Boat & Co is a striking example.

The Ride: Take the Kolbergbrug southeast across Narva-eiland, Memeleiland, Libau-eiland and Karlskrona-eiland to Pontsteiger.

❻ Pontsteiger

Shaped like a gargantuan gateway, with a 48m-wide bridge spanning its two towers, the 90m-high Pontsteiger, built in 2017 by architects Arons & Gelauff, is one of Amsterdam's largest and highest residential buildings.

Researched by Barbara Woolsey

SOUTHERN CANAL RING

BACK TO THE 17TH CENTURY

Seventeenth-century splendour and modern nightlife – that's what the Southern Canal Ring is known for, plus excellent *kabinetten* (small museums), boutiques and Dutch nibbles in between.

The graceful arc of the Southern Canal Ring spans the area from the radial Leidsegracht in the west to the Amstel River in the east. The horseshoe-shaped loop of parallel canals are worth a day's exploring if only for the gorgeous scenery alone. Elegant canal houses and secret alleys boast quintessential Amsterdam experiences and surprises, too. Leidseplein and Rembrandtplein frame the neighbourhood: nightlife hubs where you'll also find important transport links. Around both squares, stroll some of Amsterdam's most charming streets, from canal houses to shopping streets for flowers, art and antiques. Energise on Dutch snacks, but feed your soul taking in canal and river landscapes.

TOP TIP

At first glance, Leidseplein and Rembrandtplein may look like nothing more than tourist traps for the stag and hen or travel-in-a-pack brigades. But they're serious (or not-so-serious) fun, with plenty of authentic bars and cafes just waiting to be discovered. To escape the hullabaloo and hang out with the locals, head to happening Utrechtsestraat.

Leidsegracht

See p241 for places to stay in the Southern Canal Ring.

Map labels:

N
0 — 400 m
0 — 0.2 miles

Heiligeweg · Nieuwe Doelenstr · Binnen Amstel · Amstel · Waterlooplein · M

Herengr · Herengr · Singel · Herengracht · H'ART ❶

Reguliersdwarsstr · Golden Bend ❷ · Reguliersgracht · Keizersgr

Ledsegracht · Keizersgracht · Reguliersgracht ❸ · Herengr · Keizersgr · Magere Brug

Langewe Leidsedwarsstr · Ledgsegr · Prinsengr · Kerkstr · Nieuwe Spiegelstr · Keizersgr · Keizersgr · Vijzelstr · Museum Van Loon ❹ · Reguliersgr · Utrechtsestr · Prinsengr · Amstel

SOUTHERN CANAL RING · Kerkstr · Amstelveld · Prinsengr

Max Euweplein · Zieseniskade · Prinsengracht · Prinsengr · Noorderstr

❺ Spiegelkwartier · Vijzelgr · Nieuwe Looiersstr · Frederiksplein · Frederiksplein

Stadhouderskade · Weteringschans · Lijnbaansgracht · Oosteinde · Sarphatistr

OUD-ZUID · Hobbemakade · Weteringcircuit · Den Texstr · Sarphatikade

Singelgracht · Stadhouderskade

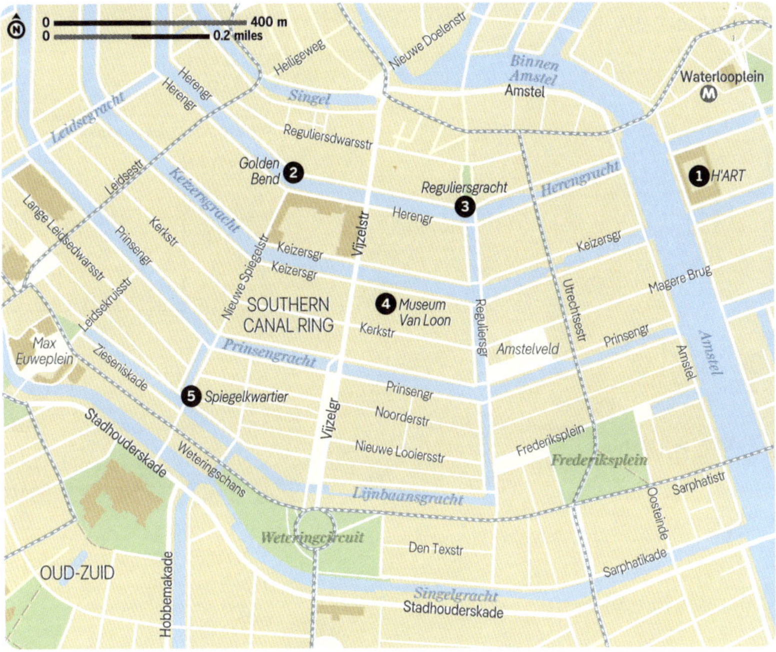

⭐ Highlights

❶ H'ART
Goggle blockbuster exhibitions at a world-renowned museum that, in 2023, changed its name and vision. **p122**

❷ Golden Bend
Amble along a stretch of canal-side property purring of 17th-century nobility. **p128**

❸ Reguliersgracht
Enjoy romantic 'ahhs' on the 'Canal of Seven Bridges'. Count as many in a single perspective. **p125**

❹ Museum Van Loon
Peek into the lavish lives of aristocrats in this extravagant canal-side home. **p132**

◀ ❺ Spiegelkwartier
Compile your own 'cabinet of curiosities' of Delft tiles, trinkets and prints. **p138**

🚶 Getting Around

Walking
This neighbourhood is all about slow, on-foot exploration; gaze up at magnificent architecture and be lured into interesting boutiques.

Cycling
Busy intersections and bumpy cobblestone make cycling rather impractical. There is free indoor, guarded bike parking outside of Vijzelgracht station.

Public Transport
This area is well served by trams. Trams run every few minutes between Leidseplein and Rembrandtplein to Centraal Station. There is also a metro station at Vijzelgracht.

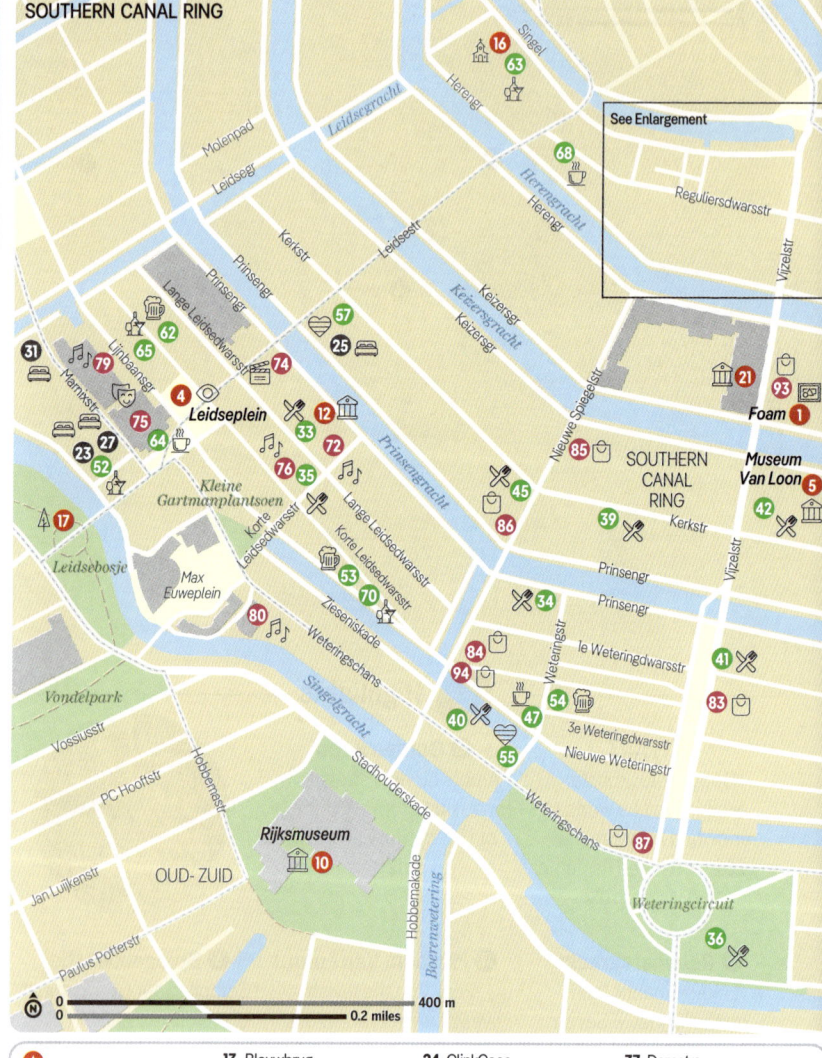

SOUTHERN CANAL RING

Singel
Herengr
Leidsegracht
Molenpad
Leidseg
Kerkstr
Leidsestr
Prinsengr
Lange Leidsedwarsstr
Prinsengr
Marnixstr
Lijnbaansgr
Leidseplein
Kleine Gartmanplantsoen
Korte Leidsedwarsstr
Lange Leidsedwarsstr
Korte Leidsedwarsstr
Leidsebosje
Max Euweplein
Zieseniskade
Weteringschans
Stadhouderskade
Singelgracht
Vondelpark
Vossiusstr
PC Hooftstr
Hobbemastr
Jan Luijkenstr
Paulus Potterstr
OUD-ZUID
Rijksmuseum
Hobbemakade
Boerenwetering
Keizersgracht
Keizersgr
Herengracht
Herengr
Reguliersdwarsstr
Nieuwe Spiegelstr
See Enlargement
Vijzelstr
Foam
SOUTHERN CANAL RING
Museum Van Loon
Kerkstr
Prinsengr
Prinsengr
Vijzelstr
Weteringstr
1e Weteringdwarsstr
3e Weteringdwarsstr
Nieuwe Weteringstr
Weteringschans
Weteringcircuit

0   400 m
0   0.2 miles

120

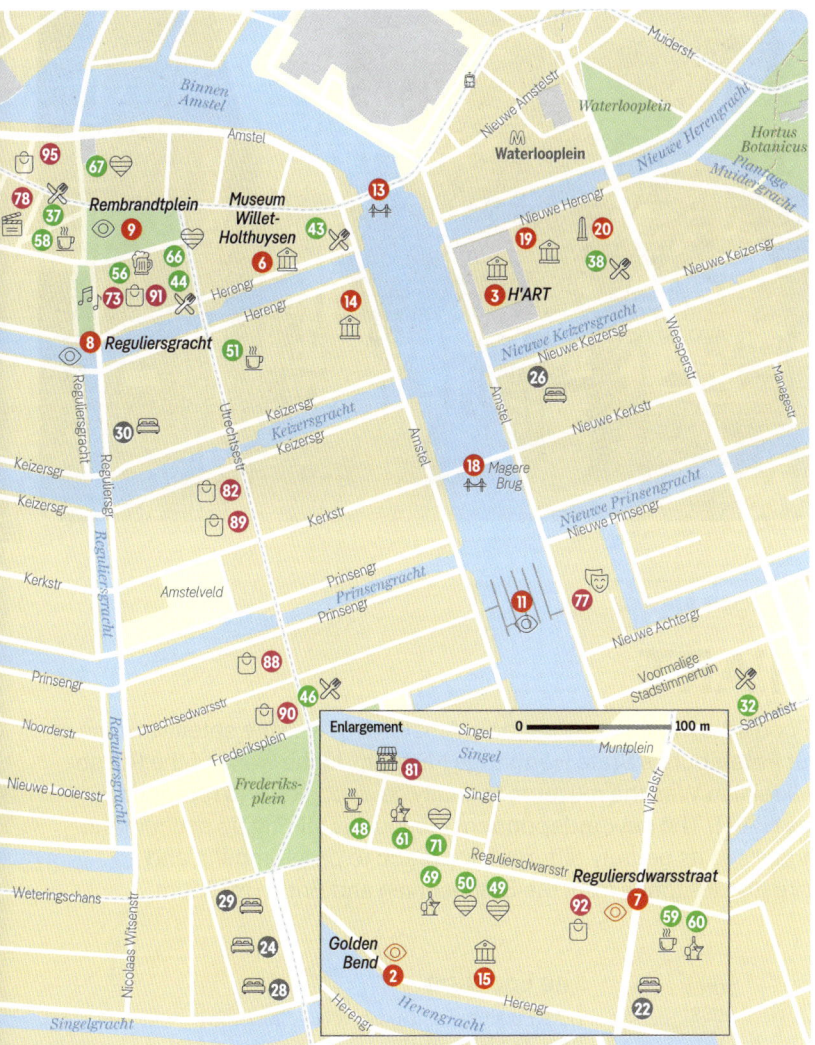

Rembrandtplein

Museum Willet-Holthuysen

Reguliersgracht

H'ART

Magere Brug

Enlargement

0   100 m

Golden Bend

Reguliersdwarsstraat

Binnen Amstel

Amstel

Muiderstr

Nieuwe Amstelstr

Waterlooplein

Nieuwe Herengracht

Hortus Botanicus

Plantage Muidergracht

Waterlooplein

Nieuwe Herenstr

Nieuwe Keizersgr

Nieuwe Keizersgracht

Nieuwe Keizersgr

Herengr

Herengr

Keizersgr

Keizersgr

Keizersgracht

Keizersgr

Amstel

Nieuwe Kerkstr

Nieuwe Prinsengracht

Nieuwe Prinsengr

Nieuwe Achtergr

Weesperstr

Magnesstr

Reguliersgracht

Reguliersgr

Reguliersgr

Kerkstr

Kerkstr

Prinsengr

Prinsengracht

Prinsengr

Amstelveld

Noorderstr

Utrechtsedwarsstr

Frederiksplein

Frederiks-plein

Nieuwe Looiersstr

Weteringschans

Nicolaas Witsenstr

Singelgracht

Utrechtsestr

Voormalige Stadstimmertuin

Sarphatistr

Vijzelstr

Singel

Singel

Singel

Muntplein

Reguliersdwarsstr

Herengr

Herengracht

Herengr

49 B'Femme	**63** Flying Dutchmen Cocktails	**73** De Heeren van Aemstel	**83** Hart's Wijnhandel
50 Blend XL	**64** ITA Brasserie	**74** De Uitkijk	**84** Hoogkamp Antiquariaat
51 Boerejongens	**65** Jimmy Woo	**75** Internationaal Theater Amsterdam	**85** Jaski
52 Café Americain	**66** Lellebel		**86** Kramer Kunst & Antiek
53 Café de Spuyt	**67** Montmartre	**76** Jazz Café Alto	**87** Mail & Female
54 Café de Wetering	**68** Otherside	**77** Koninklijk Theater Carré	**88** MaisonNL
55 Cafe Mankind	**69** Secret Garden	**78** Koninklijk Theater Tuschinski	**89** Mobilia
56 Café Schiller	**70** Shiraz Jardin des Vins		**90** Moooi
57 Church	**71** Taboo Bar	**79** Melkweg	**91** Property Of...
58 Coffee Tales		**80** Paradiso	**92** Shirt Shop
59 Coffeeshop Free	● **ENTERTAINMENT**		**93** Skateboards Amsterdam
60 Door 74	**72** Bourbon Street Jazz & Blues Club	● **SHOPPING**	**94** Spiegelkwartier
61 Duke of Tokyo		**81** Bloemenmarkt	**95** Vlieger
62 Eijlders		**82** Concerto	

121

ANP/ALAMY

H'ART

For a little more than a decade, Amsterdam was the satellite home of St Petersburg's State Hermitage Museum. In the wake of the Russo-Ukrainian War, the museum formally severed ties and rebranded as H'ART. The new, independent museum is stirring up excitement, thanks to its entirely different approach to programming and prestigious loans from the Smithsonian and British Museum.

DON'T MISS

Collaborative exhibitions

Museum van de Geest

Courtyard & outdoor cafe

Dignita Hoftuin

Outdoor greenery

Parks & monuments

The Location

H'ART is situated in a stately building known as the Amstelhof. Its palatial design, sprawled out across the Amstel riverbanks, makes it hard to believe that this was once a retirement home for elderly women from 1682 until 2007. Following extensive modernisations, Amsterdam's own Hermitage museum opened its doors to the public in 2009.

The museum, a result of long-standing ties between Russia and the Netherlands (Peter the Great learned shipbuilding here in 1697), kept long-running exhibits on loan from St

PRACTICALITIES
● amsterdammuseum.nl ● adult/child €15/free ● 10am-5pm

Petersburg. Those days ended with Amsterdam's formal notice of separation. Now, it's a whole new era of H'ART.

Collaborative Exhibitions

Gone are the days of the Portrait Gallery of the 'Golden Age', including Rembrandt works, and temporary exhibitions drawing from a Russian cache of art objects, covering themes such as the Romanovs or Dutch masterpieces.

H'ART is an entirely different animal. Previously, temporary exhibitions only changed about twice a year; now the museum promises three or four exhibitions per year and programming from diverse perspectives and cultures, and a new emphasis on contemporary art. Since the rebranding, H'ART has curated exhibitions of works by Dutch Masters, early modern sculptures by Constantin Brâncuși, and poignantly, a showcase of the renowned Russian abstract artist Wassily Kandinsky (he left the Soviet Union in 1921 due to political and creative reasons).

The Kandinsky works came on loan from the Centre Pompidou in Paris as per H'ART's new vision to be a 'museum for museums' showcasing exhibitions on loan from partner institutions. The Smithsonian American Art Museum, British Museum, Centre Pompidou and the Leiden Collection are among an impressive roster of archive and upcoming collabs.

Museum of the Mind

Tucked inside a cosy wing of H'ART's sprawling museum complex, the compelling **Museum van de Geest** (Museum of the Mind) is an art institution in collaboration with Het Dolhuys (The Madhouse), the Netherlands' national psychiatry museum in Haarlem. Single, changing exhibitions spotlight 'outsider art' produced by artists while in psychiatric institutions. Moving displays emphasise the power of art therapy in mental health.

Parks & Public Art

There are gardens and parks peppered with public art and monuments around the museum. H'ART's front **courtyard**, a loop of chestnut trees and young orange trees framing the museum's entrance, invites relaxation. The museum's **Grand Café** (outside the entrance in summer, on the indoor upper level in winter) has a surprisingly affordable menu – mostly *borrelhapjes* (deep-fried snacks) – for fuelling up.

Meanwhile, in the big, leafy garden behind H'ART, the glass-walled **Dignita Hoftuin** is one of Amsterdam's cosiest daytime dining experiences. The all-day brunch here focuses on veggie dishes, including Ottolenghi-style salads and eggs Benedict. Eat and lie on Hoftuin Park's soft grass in summer, or snuggle inside Dignita in colder weather.

Stroll around the park to see the black steel **Monument Vaz Diaz**, dedicated to a pioneering Dutch journalist, and the Daniel Libeskind–designed **National Holocaust Names Monument** inscribed with the names, birth and deceased dates of victims.

INTRODUCING... H'ART

Only a few days after the invasion of Ukraine, the museum announced it was 'freezing relations' with Russia. In a little over a year, the museum, formerly known as Hermitage Amsterdam, unveiled its new name, H'ART. A symbolic portmanteau, 'H' nods to 'Hermitage' and 'heritage', while 'ART' is meant to illustrate art as always at the 'heart' of changing exhibitions. The apostrophe reflects a new emphasis on connecting both ideas through collaboration.

TOP TIPS

● The Museum van de Geest is located in a separate wing from the main exhibition, where you likely won't be ticketed to enter. However, it is strongly recommended that you purchase a ticket (online or at H'ART's front desk) in support of a unique institution connecting art with mental health. In 2025, the museum was crowdfunding to avoid closure.

● Check the H'ART website for family art workshops.

● Buy your ticket online in advance as time slots for visits sell out.

● The ticket price always includes an audio guide.

● There is plentiful free public seating around the entrance and the museum offers free wi-fi.

LIFE ON THE AMSTEL RIVER

The Amstel has always been central to daily life in Amsterdam. Besides a transport and trading route, the river was also where residents sourced food (fish) and drinking water and washed clothes.

This intermingling of work and personal life brought major challenges for Amsterdam, a European city below sea level where water levels required active regulation – flooding had economic consequences, while stagnating, smelly canal waters posed risks to citizens' health and quality of life. While such locks were not new inventions (existing since medieval Europe), their unique integration into Amsterdam's urban centre was quite remarkable.

The Amstelsluizen ensured maritime business could keep booming and made city life more bearable.

Stand (and Kiss) on the Skinny Bridge

Romantic, cinematic setting

Dating from the 1670s (and rebuilt a few times since), the nine-arched, white-painted **Magere Brug** *(Skinny Bridge; free; 24hr)* is one of the last remaining wooden drawbridges left in central Amsterdam. Declared a national monument in 2003, the Grand Dame bridge elegantly swans over the Amstel and stays busy – throughout the day, a bridge-keeper raises her central section by a hand-operated machine so boats can pass through.

Magere Brug is also a movie star, having appeared in several films, including the 1971 James Bond thriller *Diamonds Are Forever* and *Deuce Bigalow: European Gigolo.*

The bridge is especially pretty at night, when it glows with 1200 tiny lights. Stand in the middle and feel it sway under the passing traffic. Local legend has it that if couples kiss on top of Magere Brug (or passing through by boat) their love will be eternal. If lucky, you might be privy to someone popping the question here; or, around sunset, watch photographers and landscape artists capturing the setting at its most cinematic and romantic in real time.

Admire the Amstel Locks

Waterworks innovation

One block south of Magere Brug along the Amstel River, spot a fine, historic example of hardworking waterworks.

This particular set of the **Amstelsluizen** (Amstel Locks) dates back to 1674 and they are still in use today. Impressively, they allow the canals to be flushed with fresh water from lakes north of the city, rather than salt water from the IJ River – an innovation that has made city life much more liveable over the centuries (especially before modern sewage systems). The locks (sluices) shut while fresh water flows in, and those on the western side of the city are left open as the stagnant water is pumped out to sea.

Throughout the day, you might hear the locks' mechanisms clank and creak to life, as exchanging water gushes and gurgles. Keep your eyes and ears open.

Like a tropical vacay in the gaybourhood

DRINKING IN THE SOUTHERN CANAL RING: COCKTAIL BARS

Door 74: Innovative cocktails in a classy, dark Prohibition era–inspired atmosphere. Themed cocktail lists change regularly. *8pm-3am Sun-Thu, to 4am Fri & Sat*

Duke of Tokyo: Trendy karaoke bar with a serious focus on Japanese-inspired cocktails, spiked with sake, plum liqueur and rum. *5pm-1am Sun-Thu, to 2am Fri & Sat*

Flying Dutchmen Cocktails: Amsterdam's best cocktail bar. Monthly changing mixology and the Netherlands' largest backbar: over 800 different spirits. *5pm-4am*

Secret Garden: Rainforest decor and an equatorial-inspired cocktail list packing mezcal and pisco punch. *6pm-1am, to 2am Fri & Sat*

Reguliersgracht

The prettiest of Amsterdam's canals, Reguliersgracht is most famous for the seven bridges it brings together in a perfect straight line. From its broadest perspective, though, you can count 15 bridges in all directions. Swing by for a quintessentially Amsterdam photo op, taking in houses along the canal. Lining up a wide mix of architectural styles, the total setting is a true feast for 'I spy'–ing eyes.

Seven Bridges

One of Amsterdam's most romantic canals flows through this neighbourhood. Though the best views are from aboard a boat, you can still get great vistas from land. Stand with your back to the Thorbeckeplein and with the Herengracht flowing directly in front of you to the left and right. Lean over the bridge and look straight ahead down the Reguliersgracht. It's one of the most photographed canal views in Amsterdam, sometimes nicknamed the 'necklace of bridges'.

At night, the seven bridges are lit with hundreds of tiny bulbs, creating rings of light that reflect on the water. This was added in the 20th century.

Innovative Engineering

Crossing Herengracht, Keizersgracht and Prinsengracht canals, the waterway was dug in 1658 to link the Herengracht with the canals further south. The builders placed the arches to line up perfectly: an unusual bit of showmanship. The name Reguliersgracht comes from the Reguliersklooster, a monastery of the Augustinian order ('Regulars') that once stood nearby. The monastery itself was demolished in the 16th century, but the name lived on.

Several houses were home to writers, merchants and Jewish families in the 17th and 18th centuries, though their stories aren't as widely told as those on the Golden Bend (p128). Architectural styles span neo-Renaissance flourishes to German medieval touches.

TOP TIPS

● Look for canal houses with stone plaques *(gevelstenen)* above doors, showing symbols (a rooster, sun, or tools) before house numbering became common.

● Where Keizersgracht and Reguliersgracht join up, count a whopping 15 bridges peering east-west and north-south.

PRACTICALITIES

● 24hr ● trams 4, 7, 10, 19, 24 (Rembrandtplein); metro 52 (Vijzelgracht)

Stroll the Southern Canal Ring

Puttin' on the Ritz is nothing new to the Southern Canal Ring. Most of the area was built at the end of the 17th century when Amsterdam was wallowing in the ill-gotten gains of the so-called 'Golden Age'. A wander through reveals grand mansions, swanky antique shops, an indulgent patisserie and a one-of-a-kind kitty museum. And while it's all stately, it's certainly not snobby – and an essential circuit for understanding Amsterdam's glittery past.

❶ Flower Market

Amsterdam's Bloemenmarkt (p129) has been a fixture along the Singel canal since 1860. Where it starts at the Singel, look to the north and see one of Amsterdam's most enduring emblems, the striking Munttoren (Munt Tower). Built in 1480, then rebuilt in 1620 after a fire, it's an evocative reminder of the city's long history.

The Walk: Keep a steady pace along the Flower Market; stands sell lame tourist knickknacks (yawn). Look up at the mansions as you walk across the Herengracht – many date from the 1660s.

❷ Golden Bend

During the so-called 'Golden Age', the Golden Bend was the 'it' spot, where the wealthiest Amsterdammers lived, loved and ruled their affairs. The gables (p129) here were allowed to be twice as wide as the standard Amsterdam model.

The Walk: Continue south, crossing Keizersgracht and Prinsengracht.

GONCHAROVAIA/SHUTTERSTOCK

View from the Museumbrug

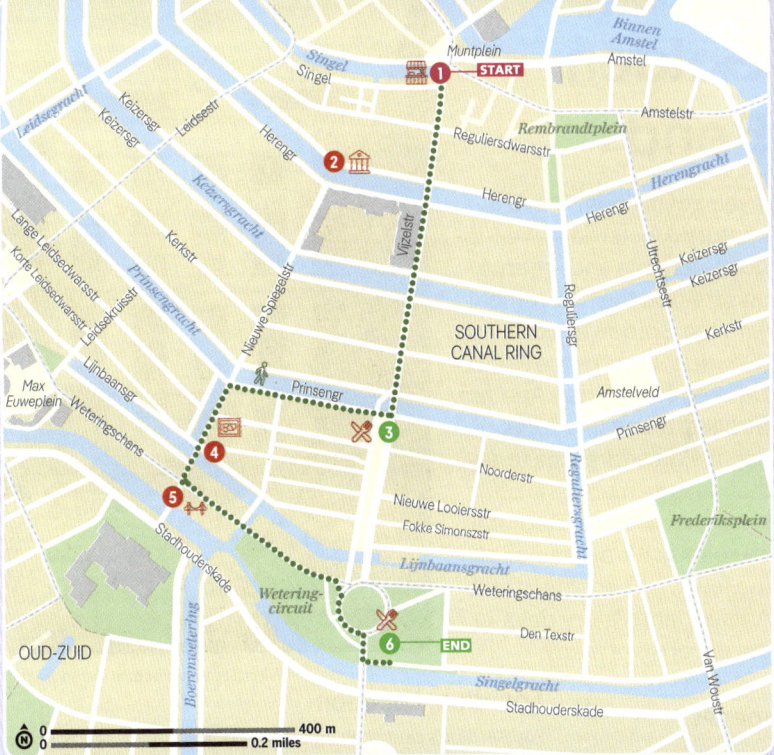

3 Patisserie Holtkamp

When you arrive at Patisserie Holtkamp (p139), take in the lush art-deco interiors (there's usually some kind of a queue, so you have time). Eat a meringue tart on the spot and take *kroketten* to go.

The Walk: Head west along Prinsengracht before following Spiegelgracht south.

4 Spiegelkwartier

Cruise along Spiegelgracht and Nieuwe Spiegelstraat, aka the Spiegel Quarter (p138), where antique shops and itty-bitty art galleries abound. Commercial art galleries here are good for window watching.

The Walk: Stroll all the way along Spiegelgracht, stopping just before the intersection with traffic-heavy Weiteringschans boulevard (across the street, you'll spot the gates of the Rijksmuseum packed with crowds).

5 Museumbrug

The eastern flank of the Museumbrug (Museum Bridge) offers a gorgeous, waterside perspective boasting all the scenic elements of a perfect canal photo: lush blooms upon railings and grandiose architecture. Here, the Singelgracht's waters seems to meander forever. You'll get the best composition of the scenery by taking the photo standing well into the cobblestoned street (watch out for whizzing cyclists).

The Walk: Work up an appetite strolling the length of Weteringschans. Where the boulevard becomes a cute, circular park, you've reached your next stop.

6 De Carrousel

De Carrousel (p133) is where you'll find some of Amsterdam's tastiest *pannenkoeken* (Dutch pancakes) served around the retired horsies of a merry-go-round. Usually, you can drop into this restaurant without a reservation. Put in a full order at once – staff disappear outside to serve tables on the wooden deck.

127

TOP EXPERIENCE

Golden Bend

If you got it, flaunt it. In 17th-century Amsterdam, well-to-do merchants and regents understood the assignment with the Golden Bend (Gouden Bocht) – the Rodeo Drive of the 'Golden Age' era. Strolling along this curve of canal-side addresses today, the heritage mansions offer more than just architectural eye candy. It's a glimmer of the few who benefited from Amsterdam's 'glory days' at the expense of many.

A heritage mansion on Herengracht

TOP TIPS

● Most buildings are only publicly visitable on the annual Open Monuments Day (second weekend of September).

● Canal-boat cruises (p27) offer a more sweeping perspective than street views.

● Look for Gerrit Berckheyde's *View of the Golden Bend in the Herengracht* in the Rijksmuseum (p148), which depicts the street mid-development.

Location, Location

Amsterdam's canal belt emerged through four phases of urban expansion during the 'Golden Age'; the Golden Bend arose as part of the last (around the 1660s and 1670s). The need to develop was simple, really – the city's elite suffered from a lack of luxury housing. Reclaimed land spanning the Herengracht to the Amstel River created new, deeper plots for rear gardens with unprecedented building permissions. With the city council's blessing, individuals could buy multiple plots, and build double- to triple-gabled, anything-but-humble abodes. Unlike earlier mixed-use canal houses, designed for middle-class work and living within a single house, Golden Bend mansions were purely residential and meant for only the wealthiest.

Retracing the Golden Bend's history starts at the corner of Herengracht and Vijzelstraat, among narrow, early canal homes. In a matter of steps, ornate mansions emerge, doubling and tripling their neighbours' width along the canal up to Leidsestraat.

Historic Houses

Today, the 500m stretch of prestigious, heritage buildings is a UNESCO-listed reminder of Amsterdam's era as Europe's de facto finance and trade capital. Buildings are mostly occupied by businesses now, keeping grand staircases, marble fireplaces and ceiling paintings only for imagination. The only Golden Bend house consistently open to the public is the eccentric Kattenkabinet art museum (p139).

PRACTICALITIES

● amsterdam.nl ● free
● 24hr

Stroll the Flower Market

Tulip turf

Flowers are not for special occasions, but an adornment of everyday life in Amsterdam. The Dutch are the world leaders in tulip cultivation since the 17th century; they also excel in bulbs such as daffodils, hyacinths and crocuses.

Founded in 1860, the famous **Bloemenmarkt** *(Flower Market; 9am-5.30pm, from 11am Sun)* was where nurserymen and -women sailed up the Amstel and sold their wares directly to customers. No longer floating (it's now perched on piles), the market is still a good place to buy real tulips in season and bulbs year-round, but it's become more of a high-kitsch, tourist affair than ever. Flower stands, from selection to price, don't change much from one to the other; miniature clogs, fridge magnets and wooden tulips abound.

Marvel at Smoking Antiques

Offbeat museum

The eccentric **Amsterdam Pipe Museum** *(pipemuseum. nl; adult/child €15/7.50, free with Museum Card; noon-6pm, closed Sun)*, an unexpectedly fascinating exhibition of tobacco and smoking pipes is – somewhat ironically – quite a breath of fresh air. Located in the grand 17th-century canal house, this unusual *kabinet* (small museum) holds one of the world's foremost collections of smoking-related paraphernalia. The collection spans more than 25,000 pipes dated from across two millennia and several continents (only about 2000 items are displayed at once).

Guided tours (book your ticket ahead with a time slot) show the earliest South American pipes, 15th-century Dutch pipes, Chinese opium pipes, African ceremonial pipes and much more. At the heart of the collection is Dutch collector Don Duco, who gathered the collection from around 60 countries over 40 years. During the 1960s, he became interested in clay pipes, which were often unearthed along Dutch riverbanks; his fascination with pipes grew as he began to see them as archaeological artefacts revealing much about cultures and craftsmanship – still the museum's legacy today.

GABLES GALORE

One of the most significant architectural features of canal houses are its gables, or roof-level façades. The gable hid the roof from public view, and helped to identify the house, until the French occupiers introduced house numbers in 1795. Gables later became a reflection of aesthetic rather than functionality.

There are four main types: simple spout gables, with diagonal outline and semi-circular windows or shutters (used mainly for warehouses from the 1580s to the early 1700s); step gables, a late-Gothic design favoured by Dutch Renaissance architects; neck gables, a durable design introduced in the 1640s; and bell gables, which appeared in the 1660s and were popularised in the 18th century.

Bookings are essential

 EATING IN THE SOUTHERN CANAL RING: BEST RESTAURANTS

Levant: Elegant Turkish eatery serving *meze* and grilled meats by candlelight. Reserve a spot on the back terrace right against the water. *5-11.30pm* €€€	**De Blauwe Hollander:** Comfort food at this red-lamp-lit place with Dutch staples like pea soup with bacon, and *stamppot* with pork sausage. *noon-10.30pm* €€	**Zoldering:** Michelin-starred bistro serving refined French-Dutch cuisine with seasonal and foraged ingredients. *5.30-10pm Mon-Fri, from 4pm Sat* €€€	**Buffet Van Odette:** Chef-restauranteur Odette serves decadent mains at her canal-side restaurant. *noon-3pm, 5.30-11pm Wed-Fri, from 11.30am Sat* €€

FREE WITH MUSEUM CARD

Museum Van Loon (p132) Get an insight into the lifestyle of Amsterdam's top rung from the 'Golden Age' to 19th century.

Museum Willet-Holthuysen (p141) Explore patrician canal-house life in this historic former family home.

Foam Amsterdam's renowned photography museum is generally free with a Museum Card; however, the 2024 Vivianne Sassen exhibition set a precedent for charging visitors a €2.50 surcharge.

Stadsarchief You never know what you might find in Amsterdam's archives – particularly the Schatkamer (Treasure Room) of old photos and maps showing the city's evolution.

Museum van de Geest (p123) Though you can walk in with a Museum Card, consider buying a ticket to support the museum's publicised financial struggles.

Inspect Blauwbrug's Intricate Features

Embellished bridge

Between Waterlooplein and Amstelstraat, **Blauwbrug** *(Blue Bridge; free; 24hr)* is Amsterdam's fanciest bridge. Street lamps dipped in bronze and iron, Amsterdam's imperial crown and coat of arms, as well as sculptures of fish and mythical sea creatures are just a few of Blauwburg's decorative elements. See how many you can 'I spy' here.

The stone bridge was built in 1884 to replace an older, blue-painted (hence the name) wooden crossing. This version was modelled after the Alexander III bridge in Paris, to impress visitors for the International Colonial and Export Exhibition. Who could imagine it would still be doing the same today?

Explore the Municipal Archives

Fascinating historical displays

A distinctive striped former bank dating from 1923 now houses over 50km of shelving at the **Stadsarchief** *(Amsterdam City Archives; amsterdam.nl/stadsarchief; free with Museum Card; 10am-5pm Tue-Fri, noon-5pm Sat & Sun)*. Stroll around fascinating displays of Amsterdam archival gems, such as the 1942 police report on the theft of Anne Frank's bike and a letter from Charles Darwin to Artis Zoo in 1868, can be viewed in the enormous tiled basement vault.

Take in Photography at Foam

Renowned photo museum

A visit to **Foam** *(foam.org; adult/child €16/11.75; 10am-6pm Sat-Wed, to 9pm Thu & Fri)* is always an eye-opening experience. One of the world's leading museums for international photographic exhibitions, the diverse programming spans fashion retrospectives to travel photography. From the outside, Foam (short for 'Fotografiemuseum') looks like a grand canal house, but these three buildings linked by staircases and passageways are the backdrop for spacious galleries, with an emphasis on experimental installations. The **Foam Editions** gallery *(included in regular admission; 10am-6pm Fri-Sun, 11am-6pm Wed, to 9pm Thu)*, featuring established and emerging photographers, supports the museum's educational projects. Some of Foam's rotating exhibitions do require an additional surcharge (even for Museum Card holders).

DRINKING IN THE SOUTHERN CANAL RING: BRUIN CAFÉS

Café de Spuyt: A mellow stop amid the hubbub off Leidseplein. Sip through the menu of more than 150 Dutch and Belgian beers. *4pm-3am Mon-Thu, 3pm-4am Fri & Sat*

Café de Wetering: Sip or snack in an interior that wouldn't look out of place in a Vermeer painting. *4pm-1am Mon-Thu, to 3am Fri, 3pm-2am Sat, to 1am Sun*

Café Schiller: Sit down among portraits of Dutch actors and cabaret artists, painted by the eponymous former owner. *3pm-1am Mon-Thu, 12.30pm-3am Fri & Sat, to 1am Sun*

Eijlders: During WWII, a meeting place for artists who resisted toeing the Nazis' cultural line. It gets noisier at night. *4.30pm-1am Mon-Thu, noon-2am Fri & Sat, to 1am Sun*

Rembrandtplein

First called Reguliersplein, then Botermarkt for the butter markets held here until the mid-19th century, this central square now takes its name from the cast-iron statue of the painter erected in 1876. By the early 20th century, Rembrandtplein evolved with cafes, restaurants and clubs opening their doors – though portrait of commercial nightlife, a few surprises are also painted in.

De Heeren van Aemstel

Rembrandt History

Rembrandtplein, of course, is named after the Dutch 'Golden Age' master Rembrandt van Rijn – he owned a house nearby from 1639 to 1656. You'll see a bronze sculpture of the *Night Watch* painter mounted on stone, a paint brush clutched in one hand. On the mid-July **Rembrandt Days** (Rembrandt Dagen) festival commemorating the artist on his birthday, you'll often find his Rembrantplein likeness draped in flower wreaths.

Rembrandt's statue shares the square with a modern companion: Dutch artist Joseph Klibansky's sculpture *The Thinker*, a life-sized astronaut figure, cast in bronze and reflective gold.

Worthy Hangouts

A couple of the square's cafes-bars are standouts. **De Heeren van Aemstel**, a student and expat favourite, bustles all nights of the week with live bands and themed nights. Cheap drinks promise packed seating outside in good weather. Meanwhile, **Café Schiller** has funky art-deco fittings for indoor relaxation.

Korte Reguliersdwarsstraat

Hidden in a small alleyway on the square's western side, Korte Reguliersdwarsstraat offers a calmer vibe and a little worthwhile gastronomy including Van Dobben (p140), Amsterdam's best wood-fired pizzas at **Demetra**, or a sandwich on homemade focaccia at **Coffee Tales**.

TOP TIPS

● A 10-minute stroll from Rembrandtplein, the Museum Rembrandthuis (p72) is in the artist's former home.

● A quick drink here is all you need. Head to nearby Reguliersdwarsstraat (p136) for livelier nightlife.

PRACTICALITIES

● 24hr ● tram lines 1, 4, 9, 14, 24

Museum Van Loon

At Museum Van Loon, an opulent canal-side mansion that has belonged to the Van Loon family since the late 1800s has been turned into a rich museum. 'Open house'–style exploring here is a time-warp to 19th-century Amsterdam from the viewpoint of aristocracy. Take in all the furnishings and art from the Van Loons' personal collection.

WOLF-PHOTOGRAPHY/SHUTTERSTOCK

Hedged gardens at Museum Van Loon

Mansion Museum

The beautiful mansion turned museum plunges you into the lavish lifestyle of the wealthy in 19th-century Amsterdam. Built in 1672, it was first home to acclaimed painter Ferdinand Bol. By the late 1800s, the Van Loons, a prominent patrician family, moved in.

The house is filled with grand furniture and family portraits that seem to whisper secrets as you pass from room to gorgeous room. Among the 150 portraits of the Van Loon family, you'll see important paintings such as *The Marriage of Willem van Loon and Margaretha Bas* by Jan Miense Molenaer.

Still, the main exhibit is the house itself. It's full of set-piece interior decoration, with intricate wedding-cake stucco on the ceilings, a garden room overlooking the formal hedges of the garden, and the glorious – but surely nightmare-inducing – decoration of the guest bedroom.

Hidden Spaces

Go downstairs to check out the mansion's old-fashioned basement kitchen, where cook Leida presided for almost 40 years. The wine cellar, pantry and storage are also open to visitors.

Meanwhile, the rear coach house once housed horse-drawn carriages. In the hedged courtyard garden, pop into the museum cafe after your visit for lemonade and apple pie.

Peer at a Blood-Stained House

Gruesome history

Gijsbert Dommer Huis, a handsome greystone gentleman, is known rather dramatically as the 'House with the Blood Stains'.

Six-time mayor and diplomat Coenraad van Beuningen lost his fortune, then his mind, and scribbled graffiti on the façade, allegedly in his own blood. His mysterious 17th-century writing – which includes Hebrew letters and obscure Kabbalah symbols – is still faintly visible. Going inside this private building isn't possible; pass by for a swift look, to respect the buildings' tenants.

Indulge in Pannenkoeken at De Carrousel

Traditional Dutch treat

For some of the best authentic *pannenkoeken* (Dutch pancakes) in Amsterdam, look no further than **De Carrousel** (*decarrouselpannenkoeken.nl; 10am-7pm Mon-Fri, to 8pm Sat & Sun*).

The restaurant serves some of Amsterdam's finest traditional large, thin Dutch pancakes (both sweet and savoury), as well as *poffertjes* (tiny pancakes topped with powdered sugar) and crispy, golden waffles, but its decor also takes the cake. In the middle of the neon-lit wooden building is an old carousel (merry-go-round).

Just put in your order quickly – De Carrousel is popular with big groups, especially those who've just smoked and might take time getting through a big order.

Savour a Mini Rijsttafel at Bojo

Indonesian cuisine

Bojo (*bojo.nl; 4-11pm*), started by two cousins who'd worked on a cruise ship together more than 40 years ago, is a good choice for some late-night, stomach-lining Indonesian food. Despite the little restaurant's close proximity to Leidseplein, the restaurant keeps an atmosphere that's surprisingly peaceful and *gezellig* (cosy). Cosied-up wooden tables embellished with colourful Indonesian decor even give off a little bit of a *bruin café* (brown cafe; traditional pub) vibe. Clubbers come for sizzling satay, filling fried rice and steaming bowls of noodle soup; the restaurant even does a mini *rijsttafel* (rice table). Make sure to book ahead.

FROM POSH TO PASSÉ

Built in the 17th century as part of exploding canal expansion, the Southern Canal Ring was laid out during the controversial 'Golden Age', when immense wealth was propelled by global trade and colonial exploitation. Wealthy merchants, bankers and regents built double-fronted canal houses, buying multiple adjoining plots, for example, along the Golden Bend (p128).

As Amsterdam industrialised and new neighbourhoods like the Plantage and Oud-Zuid developed, the upper class cut and run from the densely populated, busy canal belt. Suburban gardens became all the rage.

Canal houses were subdivided into apartments and boarding houses. By the early 20th century, many once-grand façades fell into disrepair – though today's revived appreciation for heritage buildings proves that trends truly are cyclical.

 EATING IN THE SOUTHERN CANAL RING: QUICK BUDGET LUNCHES

Lavinia Good Food: All-day healthy breakfasts, spelt mini-pizzas, smashed avocado, vegan brownies (no cash). *8.30am-4pm Mon-Fri, 9.30am-5pm Sat & Sun €*

Salsa Shop: Create your own burritos, bowls and taco salads. Good for an easy stop near Rembrandtplein. *11.30am-10pm Sun-Thu, to 11pm Fri & Sat €*

SLA: Quick, well-priced healthy lunches from an Amsterdam chain. Salads and bowls loaded with ingredients like zucchini noodles and curry hummus. *11am-9pm €*

Soup en Zo: Soups change daily in unusual flavours; spicy spinach and coconut or maybe potato with Roquefort. Takeaway only. *11am-8pm Mon-Fri, noon-7pm Sat & Sun €*

AMSTERDAM DANCE EVENT

Thanks to its historic, large-scale theatres and nightlife, the Southern Canal Ring plays a big role in **Amsterdam Dance Event** *(ADE; amster dam-dance-event. nl)*, one of Europe's biggest electronic-music festivals.

For five days every late October, more than 500,000 participants – DJs, labels and clubbers and everyone in between – come to dance to their favourite DJs and genres in massive club nights. During the day, though, ADE gets a little serious with a conference-like atmosphere and talks on sound production, trends and getting along in the industry.

The church turned nightclub Paradiso is one of the venues most associated with unforgettable ADE nights – tickets to events here sell out quickly. You'll also find big events in the former factory Melkweg.

Dance at Melkweg's Techno Tuesday
Cultural hot spot

In a former dairy factory, the nonprofit live-music venue and cultural centre **Melkweg** *(Milky Way; melkweg.nl; 10am-5am Mon, Tue, Fri & Sat, to midnight Wed, Thu & Sun)* hosts a galaxy of gigs. In the 1960s, the industrial building stood empty until it was squatted and repurposed as a multidisciplinary space by a theatre collective in 1970. Today, the 'Milky Way' is one of the Netherlands' most important concert venues, hosting up to 1500 people for DJs, club nights and live bands.

Its weekly 'Techno Tuesday' is a decade-long institution, seeing hundreds of people stomp to high-BPM beats – the best part is, admission is free.

Go to Paradiso for a Pop Concert
Worshipped concert hall

In 1968, a beautiful old church turned into the 'Cosmic Relaxation Center Paradiso'. Today, the Gothic architecture of the **Paradiso** *(paradiso.nl; showtimes & prices vary)* lends itself to neither religious nor hippy vibes, more so modern dance music: think indie rock and pop infused with electronic beats. The smaller hall hosts less boppy music, more up-and-coming, alternative bands and solo artists – but there's something special about the Main Hall, where it seems the stained-glass windows might shatter under the force of synthesiser beats paired with angelic acoustics. During the Amsterdam Dance Event, Paradiso gets packed to the rafters; it's the perfect time to catch a gig here.

Spend the Evening at Historic Cinemas
From arthouse to art deco

Opened in 1929 in a 17th-century warehouse on the Prinsengracht is **De Uitkijk** *(The Lookout; uitkijk.nl; ; adult/student €12.50/5; showtimes vary)*. Slip inside this arthouse stalwart and be surprised with a film you've likely never heard of. The programme mixes genres and countries, as well as classic oldies with more recent and foreign films, screening everything from *Clueless* to 1980s Japanese anime. Note that the films are often played in their original language (English, French, Spanish etc) with Dutch subtitles. Arrive early and linger a bit around the balcony and espresso bar – it's a truly European cinema-going experience. The theatre's doors open half an hour before the show; seating is first-come, first-serve.

A 10-minute walk into the heart of the canal belt, the fantastical 1921-completed **Koninklijk Theater Tuschinski** *(pathe.nl; showtimes & prices vary)* also offers a retro theatre evening with a lot more space (1431-seat capacity). A prime example of the Amsterdam School of architecture, the cinema is worth visiting for its sumptuous art-deco interior alone. The stunning *grote zaal* (main auditorium) screens blockbusters, while the smaller theatres play arthouse and indie films. Morning, 45-minute tours of the interiors take place before

Leidseplein

Historic architecture, bars, pubs, clubs, theatres and live-music venues – Leidseplein has a bit of everything. The square is always busy, especially since several tram lines converge here. After dark, Leidseplein is a major nightlife hub that gets thronged by a mainstream crowd of party lovers (more tourists than locals). Pavement cafes at the northern end are perfect for people-watching.

Leidseplein Nightlife

Choose from laid-back, if often heaving, theatre *cafés* (bars) and *bruin cafés* (brown cafes; traditional pubs), frenetic gay bars, smokey coffeeshops and pumping house clubs. The bars and clubs of Leidseplein feel more full of tourists than locals – but with a mix of options in the area, there's fun to be had and a well-connected tram station to whisk you away after.

Wander along Lijnbaansgracht and Korte Leidsedwarsstraat where you'll find diverse options for dinner and drinks, from live music at Jazz Café Alto (p140) to wine bars like **Shiraz Jardin des Vins** and clubbing with cocktails at **Jimmy Woo**.

Amsterdam's Living Room

Pull up a chair, order a cappuccino and watch the world spin by at the **Café Americain** (*cafeamericain.nl; 7am-11pm, to midnight Fri & Sat*). Nicknamed 'Amsterdam's living room', this splendid art-nouveau *grand café* (historic coffeehouse-bar), part of the Amsterdam American Hotel, is Leidseplein's most elegant highlight.

Opened in 1902 and a recognised *rijksmonument* (national heritage site), Café Americain was a *grand café* before the concept even existed. Huge stained-glass windows provide charming views. Within, it's all potted palms, whirring fans and dizzyingly high ceilings, plus a lovely, library-like reading table. There's also a terrace for sunny days. High teas are especially atmospheric; book 24 hours ahead.

TOP TIPS

● In the Southern Canal Ring, you're bound to end up at Leidseplein at some point to catch a tram – might as well explore and make the most of it!

● Across the water, head to **Leidsebosje** to escape the crowds.

PRACTICALITIES
● 24hr ● tram lines 1, 2, 5, 7, 10, 11, 12, 17, 19

Reguliersdwarsstraat

On Reguliersdwarsstraat, Amsterdam's major gay street, romp through the best nightlife across the canal belt – maybe even the city. The pedestrian strip is a potent cocktail of gay bars and nightclubs, cocktail joints and restaurants enjoyed by a young, diverse (gender, age and otherwise) crowd. Warm, summer evenings see everyone – party-goers to drag queens – melt outside into one big, street party.

SONIA.G/SHUTTERSTOCK

TOP TIPS

● Pedestrians only here; no parking bikes.

● Uber pickups are not allowed near here; there is a designated spot for drivers at Muntplein.

● For amazing men's fashion, Shirt Shop (p143), near the front of the strip, curates cool tops in geometric and abstract designs and funky sweaters.

Iconically LGBTIQ+

Reguliersdwarsstraat peacocked into a gay nightlife hot spot in the 1970s, when legendary clubs (since closed) shaped a vibrant LGBTIQ+ hub. Today, the street still has Amsterdam's highest concentration of gay clubs, but businesses have a high turnover – in recent years, everything from vegan fast food to Asian-French gastronomy has passed through. You might not even clock Reguliersdwarsstraat as a gay strip if not for a few rainbow flags and dragged-up bouncers. The gentrification of nightlife here has seen many LGBTIQ+ establishments close over the years. Predominantly partying twentysomethings, the crowd here is really no different than on any other Amsterdam nightlife street.

Gay nightlife institutions range from the twinkling disco-ball-lit dance floor at **Blend XL** to laid-back, chatty vibes at **Taboo Bar**.

Coffeeshops & Cocktail Bars

Coffeeshops (not specifically gay-oriented but very gay-friendly) include tiki-bar-inspired **Coffeeshop Free**, and the cosy corners of **Otherside** and **Betty Boop** – its now-closed sister branch was where Tarantino wrote some of *Pulp Fiction*.

Cocktails are taken seriously, spanning well-mixed classics (particularly at gay bars) and some inventive mixology. For craft cocktails, check out Secret Garden's (p124) tropical-influenced sips and Duke of Tokyo (p124), where sake- and umeshu-spiked drinks hype up some of the coolest karaoke rooms ever.

PRACTICALITIES

● reguliers.net ● bars close 3am weekdays, 4am weekends

the screenings – highlights include the restored Wurlitzer organ and historical insights about the performance stage (Marlene Dietrich and Judy Garland have both graced it).

The cinema was built by Polish Jewish immigrant Abraham Tuschinski who, along with most of his family, was murdered in Nazi concentration camps; the cinema was renamed 'Tivoli'. After the war it returned to its original name.

Attend a Performance at Carré
Circus institution

Circus, queer cabaret, musicals, literary readings and comedy shows – the **Koninklijk Theater Carré** *(carre.nl; showtimes & prices vary)* is a performance venue that truly does it all.

The Carré family started their career with a horse act at the annual fair, progressing to this circus theatre in 1887. The faces of jesters, dancers and theatre folk adorn the classical façade. With a capacity of 1700, it hosts a great programme of quality music and theatre; the Christmas circus is a seasonal highlight. There's a top-floor Dutch restaurant.

The first structure was of wood, but it was eventually rebuilt in concrete due to fire hazards (early performances were lit by gas lamps).

See a Play at the Internationaal Theater Amsterdam
Contemporary theatre

When the **Internationaal Theater Amsterdam** *(ita.nl; showtimes & prices vary)* was completed in 1894, it had a mixed reception. Public critics found the neo-Renaissance design to be too ornate and outdated, and as a result, the exterior decorations were never completed. The poor architect, Jan Springer, was so upset he retired – if only he could hear today's rave reviews appreciating its regal stature.

The horseshoe auditorium seats 1200 spectators and is used for large-scale plays, operettas and festivals such as the **Holland Festival** (the country's biggest music, drama and arts extravaganza). Don't miss the chandeliered splendour of its **ITA Brasserie** *(10am-midnight)* theatre cafe brimming with actors and theatre-goers deconstructing the avant-garde play they've just taken in.

QUEER LIFE ON THE CANALS

The LGBTIQ+ community is deeply interwoven across the downtown canal loop. In the 20th century, the Southern Canal Ring became a hub for queer individuals to gather in safety. While the district was laid out in the 17th and 18th centuries as an upscale residential district, later years – especially following WWII – saw wealthy residents move to newer suburbs and many buildings fell into disrepair. Vacant canal buildings were often subdivided, providing discreet spaces for activism to flourish. Queer-friendly establishments indicated themselves with hints such as little pink triangles in windows. The neighbourhood helped lay a strong groundwork for Amsterdam's reputation as a welcoming global LGBTIQ+ capital. Quaint, unpretentious gay bars along canal routes uphold this legacy.

 DRINKING IN THE SOUTHERN CANAL RING: LGBTIQ+ SPACES

Church: No sermons or psalms, this is a hardcore gay cruise club. Check website for dress code. *8pm-1am Wed, 10pm-4am Thu, to 5am Fri & Sat, 4-8pm Sun*	**Lellebel:** Dandy place with pink leopard-print walls, specialising in drag queen fabulousness, karaoke and bingo. *9pm-3am Mon-Thu, 3pm-5am Fri & Sat, to 3am Sun*	**Montmartre:** Crammed gay bar. Patrons sing along to Dutch ballads. Also karaoke, drag, and '80s and '90s hits. *5pm-1am Wed, Thu & Sun, to 4am Fri & Sat*	**Cafe Mankind:** Tucked-away gay-friendly cafe-bar with an appealing narrow terrace alongside the canal. Kitchen serves sandwiches and snacks. *noon-midnight Mon-Sat*

Spiegelkwartier

Set off at the Singelgracht and head north into the Spiegelkwartier (Spiegel Quarter), Amsterdam's canal-side art and antiques district. The heart of the action is along Spiegelgracht where cute, independently owned boutiques and galleries line some of the city's prettiest waterside scenery. The main stretch to focus on is Nieuwe Spiegelstraat where bric-a-brac, collectables and Dutch wares, old and new, abound.

WOLF-PHOTOGRAPHY/SHUTTERSTOCK

Spiegelgracht

TOP TIPS

● Grab coffee from **Back to Black**, the area's loveliest cafe, for the walk.

● The best time to come here is from mid- to late September when **Open Monuments Day**, followed by the **Spiegelkwartier Art & Antiques Week**, promise curated shows and extra gallery access.

PRACTICALITIES

● shop hours vary; typically 10am-6pm
● closest tram stop Rijksmuseum; closest metro station Vijzelgracht

Antique Shops

The main draw here is window shopping. Mostly, Spiegelkwartier antique shops keep up an air that's standoffish and museum-like – meaning only serious buyers should ogle here.

Kramer Kunst & Antiek is an exception where everyone's welcome and affordable items do pop up. Engrossing and crammed to the rafters, the third-generation family business is packed with fascinating antiques from silver candlesticks to crystal decanters and pocket watches (peek into the front window's eccentric items, including a human skull).

Kramer's speciality is antique blue-and-white Dutch tiles; near the back of the shop, rifle through a 'tile archive' – well-organised by motif (flora, fauna, landscapes etc). Some pieces date as far back as the 17th century, but some of the newer, 20th-century tiles go for as little as €100 or less.

The fine-art prints' dealer **Hoogkamp Antiquariaat** on Spiegelgracht has unique souvenirs. It sells old maps and landscapes of Amsterdam, its canals and more – shuffle through the display stacks out front.

Art Galleries & More

Small, private contemporary art galleries abound. Check out **Jaski**, a roomier commercial gallery selling paintings, prints, ceramics and sculptures by some of the most famous members of the CoBrA (Copenhagen, Brussels, Amsterdam) movement.

Attend Latin Mass at De Krijtberg

Neo-Gothic church

The spiky spires of the Catholic church **Krijtberg** *(krijtberg. nl; free; 2-5pm)* are an unmissable landmark amid rows of handsome homes along the Singel canal. Officially known as the St Franciscus Xaveriuskerk, Krijtberg (Chalk Hill) replaced a clandestine Jesuit chapel on the same site in 1883; it's remained Jesuit to this day. If you get the chance, have a peek inside the neo-Gothic church; the interior is typically, lavishly Jesuit, covered with paintings and statuary. English mass is held on Saturdays at 5.15pm, and on some religious holidays. On Sundays at 10.30am, the Latin Mass followed by Gregorian chanting at 12.30pm can be a moving spiritual experience.

Admire Feline Art at the Kattenkabinet

Eccentric art museum

When kitties go to the great sofa in the sky, most doting owners comfort themselves with a photo on the mantel; wealthy financier Bob Meijer founded an entire museum in memory of his late red tomcat John Pierpont Morgan III. Housed in one of the Golden Bend's (p128) famously double-wide canalside homes, the **Kattenkabinet** *(Cat Cabinet; adult/child €12.50/7.50; noon-5pm, closed Mon)* collection includes artworks by Tsuguharu Foujita, Théophile Alexandre Steinlen and Amsterdam's chief sculptor, Hildo Krop. A visit here also gives you the opportunity to explore one of the Golden Bend's grand houses; it's the only one open to the public.

Savour Royal Dutch Treats at Patisserie Holtkamp

Artisanal patisserie

Head to **Patisserie Holtkamp** *(patisserieholtkamp.nl; 8.30am-6pm Mon-Fri, to 5pm Sat)* to savour authentic Dutch treats fit for royalty. Check out the gilded royal coat of arms, topped by a crown, on the building's façade before entering; the historic patisserie is where the Dutch royals stock up on baked goods. Founded in 1886, the gorgeous art-deco interior (added in 1928 by architect Piet Kramer) is a feast for the eyes; sweet aromas of baking pastries greet you upon walking in.

The lavish spread displayed across the patisserie's shop-wrapping glass counters are fit for a queen. Delicacies include

SOMETHING OLD, SOMETHING NEW

What the shopfronts of Spiegelkwartier have in common is a unique cultural history. In the early 20th century, antique dealers began settling around Spiegelstraat, attracted by close proximity to the Rijksmuseum, which ensured a steady flow of collectors. Stately canal houses offered elegant spaces for antiques wheeling and dealing; from there, its reputation as an authority on beautiful, Dutch curios grew.

After WWII, parts of the canal ring declined; artists and squatters moved into the area, too. Their presence introduced an experimental, countercultural side to the area's artistic identity. By the 1970s and '80s, this mix of stalwart tradition with avant-garde creativity defined the area.

EATING & DRINKING IN THE SOUTHERN CANAL RING: BEST BAKERIES

Bakhuys Amsterdam:	**Patisserie Holtkamp:**	**Petit by Sam:** Patisserie	**Back to Black:** Ultra-cool
Watch as bakers knead sourdough and work the wood-fired oven. Toast, pastries, pizzas and sandwiches. *7am-5pm, from 8am Sat & Sun* €	Chocolate truffles are most beloved. Also fluffy Bavarian cream-topped cakes, *koekjes* (cookies) and tarts. *8.30am-6pm, to 5pm Fri & Sat* €	using natural ingredients (date puree, honey and almond flour). Vegan, dairy- and gluten-free options. *9am-5pm Mon-Fri, 9.30am-5.30pm Sat & Sun* €	neighbourhood cafe with teal walls and cakes, pies and powerballs baked in-house. Also roasts its own beans. *9am-6pm* €

AMSTERDAM SCHOOL

The Amsterdam School ushered in a new philosophy of city planning, given a boost by the 1928 Olympic Games held in Amsterdam. Humble housing blocks became brick sculptures with curved corners, odd windows and rocket-shaped towers, to the marvel (or disgust) of traditionalists.

The father of modern Dutch architecture, Hendrik Petrus Berlage (1856–1934), criticised the lavish neo-styles, instead favouring simplicity and rationalistic material use. He influenced what became known as the Amsterdamse School (Amsterdam School). The Koninklijk Theater Tuschinski (p134), De Dageraad (p174) and Scheepvaarthuis (p85; the first building in the style) are all icons you can enter.

---

pie and cookies, creamy cakes, meringue-topped tarts and Dutch pastries such as 'almond curls' *(amandelkrullen)*. Holtkamp is most famous for the monarchy's longstanding ordering of *kroketten* (croquettes) from here. They come in fillings ranging from veal to prawns or cheese, as well as chocolate truffles in endless flavours. The *kroketten* are on the menus of some of the city's top restaurants.

Take in Live Jazz Around the Ring

Jazz clubs

The neighbourhood's postwar exodus of wealthy residents, moving to bigger, greener suburbs, was a boon for inner-city Amsterdam's underground culture. Small, canal-side buildings and basements became intimate spaces for live-music venues and cultural spaces – most notably, jazz clubs.

The historic **Jazz Café Alto** *(jazz-cafe-alto.nl; admission Sun-Thu €5, Fri & Sat €10; 8pm-3am Sun-Thu, to 4am Fri & Sat)* has been staging jams and performances in the area since 1953. This is an intimate, atmospheric *bruin café*–style venue for serious jazz and (occasionally) blues. Find live gigs nightly – it doesn't take reservations so arrive as close to opening as possible to snag a seat. Jam sessions are free.

Meanwhile, **Bourbon Street Jazz & Blues Club** *(bourbon street.nl; 10pm-4am Sun-Thu, to 5am Fri & Sat)* is an intimate venue with a full and eclectic music programme. Check the website for a list of open jam sessions and performances ranging from jazz, blues and soul to rock, Latin and pop.

Try Dutch Sammies at Van Dobben

Dutch diner

Open since 1945, the *eetsalon* (casual lunchroom) **Van Dobben** *(eetsalonvandobben.nl; 10am-8pm Sun-Thu, to 9pm Fri & Sat)* stays true to its history. The restaurant keeps up a cool diner feel, with white tiles, a marble countertop, black stools and a siren-red ceiling. Take a spot up at the bar and enjoy a spread of Dutch snacks for low prices that are definitely not a sign of Amsterdam in current times.

Dine on *bitterballen* (meat croquettes) and finely sliced, open-face roast-beef sandwiches, among Van Dobben's best old-fashioned joys. White-coated staff who've worked here for decades specialise in snappy banter; let them turn you onto other sandwich variations. There's sliced pork with satay sauce (an unexpected yet usually well-received favourite), *pekelvlees* (akin to corned beef) or *halfom* (*pekelvlees* mixed with liver). The meat *kroketten* (croquettes) are up there with the best in the city.

Shop for Sexy Stuff at Mail & Female

Feminist sex shop

Spotting **Mail & Female** *(mailfemale.com; 11am-7pm, closed Sun)* on the corner of Nieuwe Vijzelstraat and Weteringschans is easy; its long wraparound windows, adorned with vibrators,

Museum Willet-Holthuysen

Built in 1687 for Amsterdam mayor Jacob Hop and redesigned in 1739, this house turned museum offers insight into the 19th-century lives of the merchant class' super-rich. Now managed by the Amsterdam Museum, it's named after Louisa Willet-Holthuysen, who lived a lavish, bohemian life here with husband Abraham from 1861. She bequeathed the property to the city in 1895.

Meet the Willet-Holthuysens

Stroll through the patrician house, taking in the lifestyle and interests of Abraham and Louisa with an audio guide. The pair were keen art collectors, and the rich selection of furniture and art includes notable paintings by Jacob de Wit. Look for the *place de milieu* (centrepiece) that was part of the family's 275-piece Meissen table service in the Louis XVI–style ground-floor dining room, and the 17th-century stained-glass windows upstairs. Downstairs, the preserved kitchen and scullery provide a glimpse of the work required to keep the house running.

Garden Greenery

The intimate garden (pictured) with a sundial is a reconstruction dating from 1972, created in the French classical style, as was fashionable in the 19th century. It was originally smaller than it is today, as a coach house occupied some of the space. Peek at the garden through the iron fence at the Amstelstraat end.

Amsterdam Museum

The Willet-Holthuysen House operates as a branch of the Amsterdam Museum (closed for renovations until 2028). The city's history museum regularly hosts excellent temporary exhibitions (sometimes mini-exhibitions) curated from its collection. Themes are wide-ranging but always linked to Amsterdam, from a peek into Dutch queer ballroom culture, to archival Dutch fashion worn by Rihanna.

TOP TIPS

● The museum is free with the I amsterdam or Museum cards.

● Pre-book your ticket online to secure your desired time slot (some do sell out).

● Audio guides are included with admission.

● Crowds tend to bottleneck near the entrance – consider exploring the museum back to front instead.

PRACTICALITIES

● museumvanloon.nl
● adult/child €16/9
● 10am-5pm

THRIFTING IN AMSTERDAM 101

Photographer **Nichon Glerum** works for Europe's largest flea market IJ Hallen (p203). She has not bought any new clothing for the past 16 years. Here is her best advice for secondhand treasure hunting like a pro. *@ijhallen*

Wear comfortable clothing. Many flea markets don't have changing rooms so dress for trying outfits on quickly and easily. My 'Thrift Ninja' outfit usually consists of loose-fits, leggings and easy-to-remove shoes.

It's OK to negotiate. It never hurts to ask for a discount. In my experiences selling and buying, smiling never hurts.

Carry the essentials. Cash (for fast transactions), a bag (not all vendors have them) and sunscreen (IJ Hallen, and many other markets, go outdoors in spring and summer).

Georgia O'Keeffe–reminiscent artworks and 'educational' posters of the female anatomy are made for stopping and staring.

What sets Mail & Female apart from other sex shops in Amsterdam is simple: it's not in the Red Light District and it has a clear focus on erotic toys and other paraphernalia not produced purely for the male gaze. Open since 1988, the boutique has long prided itself on catering to all genders and sexualities, but especially on giving women more options (hence the 'Female' in its name – the 'Mail' part comes from the boutique's early days as a postal-only service).

Peruse Enticing Designs Along Utrechtstraat

Shopping for homewares

The little concept store **MaisonNL** *(maisonnl.com; 1-6pm Mon, 10am-6pm Tue-Sat, 1-5pm Sun)* sells all sorts of beautiful things you didn't realise you needed, such as Christian Lacroix notebooks and cute-as-a-button mouse toys in matchboxes by Maileg. There's a clothing rack down the back.

On the corner of Utrechtstraat and Kerkstraat, **Mobilia** *(mobilia.nl; 10am-6pm Tue-Sat)* Dutch and international design is stunningly showcased at this three-storey 'lifestyle studio', with sofas, workstations, bookshelves, lighting, cushions, rugs and much more.

Founded by Dutch designers Marcel Wanders and Casper Vissers, the gallery-shop **Moooi** *(moooi.nl; 10am-6pm Thu-Sun)* features Dutch design at its most over-the-top, for instance a spun fibreglass chandelier, carbon-fibre chair, modular 'BFF sofa', life-size black horse lamp, or 'blow away vase' (a whimsical twist on the classic Delft vase).

Concerto

Go Record-Digging at Concerto

Major music emporium

The Netherlands' largest music shop **Concerto** *(concerto.nl; 10am-6pm, from noon Sun & Mon)* is a rare audiophiles' paradise. From the outside, the time-worn, dark-red façade looks like it hasn't been repainted since the shop opened in 1955. That lack of pretentiousness (just look at the chaotic stuff in its window displays) is what makes Concerto such a gem.

Dig around new and secondhand vinyl and CDs encompassing every imaginable genre, spanning rock to classical and jazz. Impressively, there's even an excellent selection of electronic music across genres (ask your DJ friends, it is quite rare to find this eclectic mix in any one vinyl shop).

Shop for Picnic Wine at Hart's

Classy liquor shop

Browsing French and Italian wines at the genteel, galleried **Hart's Wijnhandel** *(Hart's Wine Shop; hartswijn.nl; noon-6.30pm Mon, 10am-6.30pm Tue-Fri, to 5pm Sat)* is a sophisticated Amsterdam experience. Step inside past the charming, old-world shopfront and you'll instantly feel transported back to 1880 when Hart's first opened its doors. Staff are friendly and not snobby; though classical music playing in the background is an enchanting touch. Check the website to join a wine tasting.

BEST BOUTIQUES IN THE AREA

Property Of... This Amsterdam-based label produces dapper travel gear using chrome-free leather and recycled materials.

Shirt Shop Shop a kaleidoscopic array of tops made for men: cool designs and funky motifs all from European collections. Sex toys, too.

Vlieger Since 1869, this two-storey shop has been supplying Egyptian papyrus, handmade papers from Asia and Central America, and more.

Concerto The Netherlands' largest music shop is audiophiles' heaven – snuggle into vinyl listening facilities or catch regular live sessions.

Skateboards Amsterdam Everything required for the freewheeling lifestyle: cruisers, longboards, shortboards, electric and off-road boards, along with clothing (and endless band T-shirts).

Researched by
Catherine Le Nevez

VONDELPARK, OUD-WEST & OUD-ZUID

MONUMENTAL MUSEUMS AND SPRAWLING PARKS

At this neighbourhood's heart, the Vondelpark's rambling English-style gardens are strolling distance from the mega-museums of elegant Oud-Zuid and vibrant street life in and beyond Oud-West.

The Vondelpark's 47 hectares of lawns, roses, sculptures, fountains, ponds and winding paths are where Amsterdammers and visitors flock on sunny days. Footsteps to the southeast, vast, grassy square Museumplein is ringed by Amsterdam's biggest-hitting museums: the Netherlands' monumental national museum, the Rijksmuseum; the Van Gogh Museum, with the world's largest collection of Vincent Van Gogh's works; and the Stedelijk Museum, with modern and contemporary masterpieces.

On the Vondelpark's northern side, cafes, restaurants, shops and bars line Overtoom and surrounding streets, which blend into the up-and-coming Oud-West; converted tram sheds here now house cultural and food hub De Hallen. Luxury boutiques and eateries grace the leafy streets to the Vondelpark's south.

TOP TIP

Getting peckish after an afternoon in the Vondelpark? Amstelveenseweg, running along the western edge of the park, is a fabulous place to eat, with restaurants ranging from vegan to Chinese, Indonesian, Indian, Dutch and Italian, interspersed with stylish wine bars and cosy *cafés* (pubs). Wander along and see what you find.

Vondelpark (p160)

See p241 for places to stay in Vondelpark, Oud-West and Oud-Zuid

OUD-WEST

De Hallen
5

Bellamystr

Ten Katestr

Kinkerstr

Nicolas Beetstr

Borgerstr

J v Lennepstr

Passeerdersstr

Reamplein

Leidsegracht

Prinsengr

Jacob van
Lennepkanaal

2e Constantijn Huygensstr

Bosboom Toussaintstr

Nassaukade

Jan Pieter Heijestr

Nicolas Beetstr

1e Helmersstr

2e Helmersstr

Leidsekade

Leidseplein

Prinsengr

Prinsengr

Gerard Brandtstr

Vondelstr

Vondelstr

Van Baerlestr

Leidsebosje

Max
Euweplein

Leidsekruisstr

Singelgracht

Stadhouderskade

Vondelpark
4

Vossiusstr

PC Hooftstr

OUD-ZUID

Rijksmuseum
1

Johannes Vermeerstr

Vondelpark

Hobbemastr

3
Stedelijk
Museum

2 Van Gogh
Museum

Willemsparkweg

Van Eeghenstr

Museumplein

N
0 — 400 m
0 — 0.2 miles

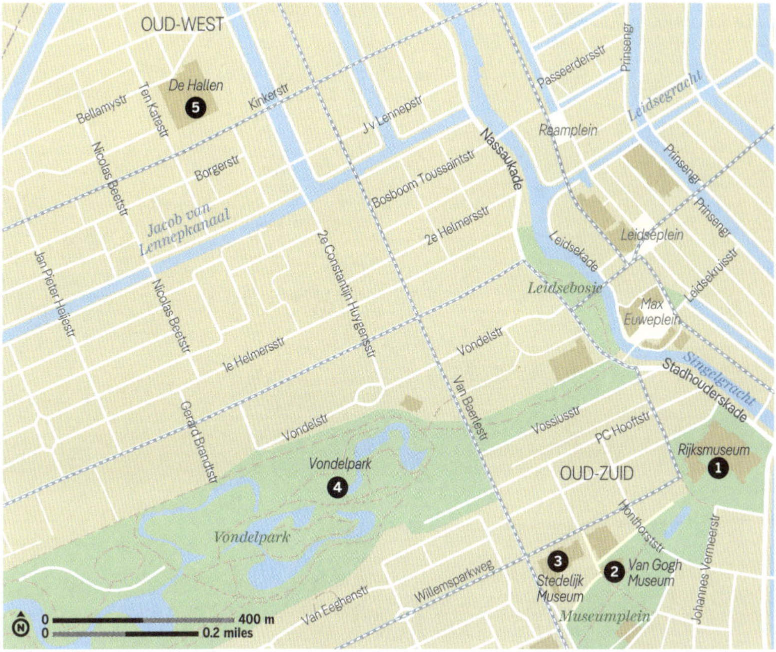

 Highlights

❶ Rijksmuseum
Lose yourself amid the riches in one of the world's finest museums. **p148**

❷ Van Gogh Museum
View the world's best collection of Van Gogh's work up close. **p152**

❸ Stedelijk Museum
Discover works by Mondrian, Matisse, Warhol, Appel, De Kooning, Yayoi Kusama and more. **p156**

❹ Vondelpark
Freewheel through the city's green heart, pack a picnic, spot a Picasso sculpture and attend its open-air theatre. **p160**

◄ ❺ De Hallen
Catch a film, browse Dutch design and fashion, and dine on street-food dishes at these converted tram sheds. **p167**

 Getting Around

Cycling
Riding a bicycle is ideal for getting around this neighbourhood; it's especially handy for the more spread out streets of Oud-West and for exploring within the Vondelpark itself.

Tram
Tram 1 traverses Overtoom; 3 serves Concertgebouw; and 2, 3, 5 and 12 stop at Museumplein. Tram 5 continues to Amsterdam Zuid, which is linked by metro 52 to Centraal, and train to Centraal and the airport.

Bus
Connexxion's Amsterdam Airport Express (bus 397; Niteliner N97) directly connects the airport with Museumplein, which can be convenient if you're staying in this area.

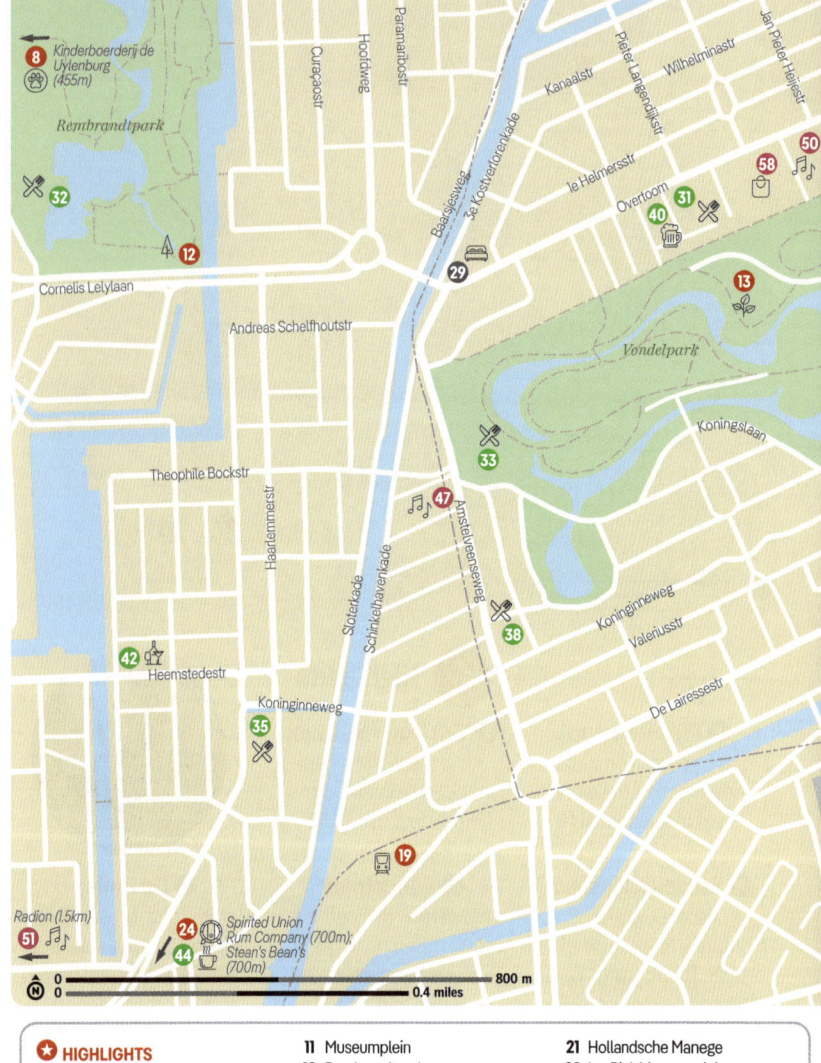

VONDELPARK & OUD-ZUID

Kinderboerderij de Uylenburg (455m)

Rembrandtpark

Kinderboerderij de Uylenburg (455m)

Curaçaostr

Hoofdweg

Paramaribostr

Baarsjesweg

1e Kostverlorenkade

Kanaalstr

Pieter Langendijkstr

Wilhelminastr

Jan Pieter Heijestr

1e Helmersstr

Overtoom

Cornelis Lelylaan

Andreas Schelfhoutstr

Vondelpark

Koningslaan

Theophile Bockstr

Haarlemmerstr

Sloterkade

Schinkelhavenkade

Amstelveenseweg

Koninginneweg

Valeriusstr

De Lairessestr

Heemstedestr

Koninginneweg

Radion (1.5km)

Spirited Union Rum Company (700m); Stean's Bean's (700m)

0   800 m
0   0.4 miles

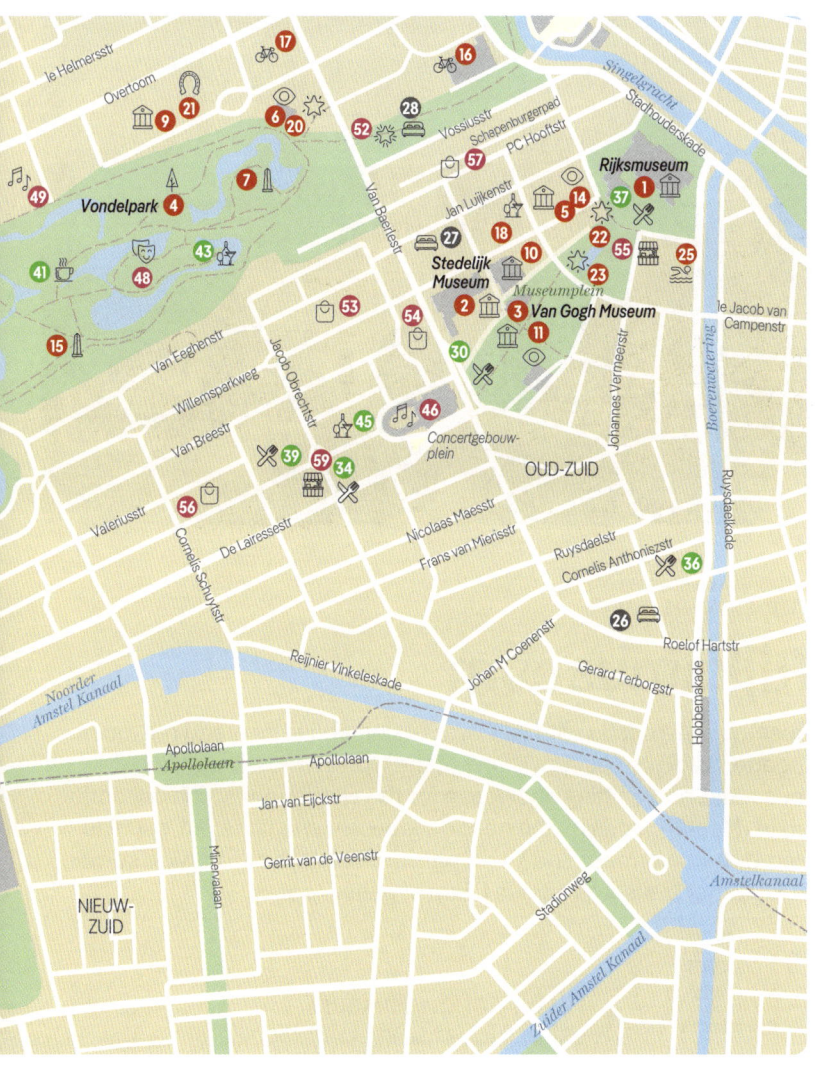

TOP EXPERIENCE

Rijksmuseum

Resembling a castle with its towers rising above its grand red-brick façade, the Rijksmuseum is one of the world's most magnificent museums, and a fitting showcase for the Netherlands' rich collection of art. Masterpieces by the nation's greatest artistic talent, such as Rembrandt, Vermeer and Van Gogh, are displayed alongside some 8000 other treasures across 1.5km of gallery space.

DON'T MISS

- Rembrandt's *The Night Watch*
- Vermeer's *Milkmaid*
- Jan Asselijn's *The Threatened Swan*
- Delftware pottery
- Dollhouses
- Gardens
- Rijks Michelin-starred restaurant

History of the Museum

Today's Rijksmuseum (pronounced 'Rikes') was more than two centuries in the making: the first museum conceived to hold national and royal collections opened in Den Haag's Huis Ten Bosch in 1800 (Jan Asselijn's *The Threatened Swan*, c 1650, was its first acquisition). During French rule, the collections moved to the new capital, opening on the top floor of Amsterdam's Royal Palace in 1809, where they were joined by paintings including Rembrandt's *The Night Watch*.

PRACTICALITIES

● Map p146 ● rijksmuseum.nl ● adult/child €25/free, guided tour per person €7.50 ● 9am-5pm

Following King Willem I's ascension to the throne, the collections shifted locations until architect PJH (Petrus Josephus Hubertus; 'Pierre') Cuypers was chosen to design a purpose-built permanent home for the national museum. Construction of the building, incorporating neo-Gothic and Renaissance styles, began in 1876 and it opened in 1885.

Building Layout

Subsequent renovations have retained Cuypers' interior layout over four levels, from Floor 0, with its skylit main atrium, to Floor 3. Pick up a floor plan from the information desk by the entrance. Galleries are well marked; each room displays the gallery's number and theme, which are easy to match to the floor plan. You can also navigate using the free Rijksmuseum app (p151). Book hour-long 'Best of the Rijksmuseum' guided tours in English for an insider's view.

Floor 2 Highlights

On the 2nd floor, the Gallery of Honour, with masterpieces spanning 1600 to 1700, is the best place to begin your visit. Among the masters here are Frans Hals; *The Merry Drinker* (1628–30) shows his broad, fluid brushstrokes. Beautiful works by Johannes (Jan) Vermeer featuring intimate, almost photographic-like domestic details include *The Milkmaid* (1660; also called *The Kitchen Maid*) and *Woman in Blue Reading a Letter* (1663). Jan Steen depicted chaotic households to convey moral teachings, as in *The Merry Family* (1668).

Works by Rembrandt include his self-portrait as the Apostle Paul, and a couple's intimate caress in *The Jewish Bride* (1665). The Rijksmuseum's star is Rembrandt's colossal *The Night Watch* (1642). Originally titled *Archers under the Command of Captain Frans Banning Cocq*, it was later renamed due to a layer of grime that gave the mistaken impression it was set at night. It has since been restored to its original colours. The extensive research and conservation project Operation Night Watch has provided visitors the unique opportunity to witness it undergoing studies and repairs surrounded by a glass chamber; no completion date for the multiyear project is yet known but it remains in full public view.

Splendid 17th-century treasures are displayed in rooms either side of the Gallery of Honour. On one side is delicate blue-and-white Delftware pottery from the late 1600s. The other features extraordinary dollhouses; merchant's wife Petronella Oortman employed carpenters, glassblowers and silversmiths to make items using the same materials as for full-scale versions.

Cuypers Library

From the 2nd-floor balcony, you can see the towering book-lined space of the Cuypers Library, one of the world's finest art libraries. Reservations are required for its reading room.

REFRESHMENTS AT THE RIJKSMUSEUM

When you need a break, there are options to dine and drink at the Rijksmuseum at all price points: the museum has two espresso bars (plus another in the garden pavilion in summer); a cafe in the atrium (with breakfasts, pastries, soups, salads and sandwiches); and a Michelin-starred restaurant, Rijks (p158), which can be accessed without a museum ticket.

TOP TIPS

● Buy tickets and choose entry times on the museum's website; you need to reserve a time slot in advance even if you already have a ticket or museum pass.

● The museum is busiest on weekends year-round and during school holidays, as well as from April to October. Mornings before noon and afternoons from 3pm on weekdays are usually the quietest times to visit.

● While you can see the highlights in a couple of hours, the collection is huge so consider allowing much longer here.

● There's a free *garderobe* (cloakroom) and free lockers in the main entrance hall.

RIJKSMUSEUM

Floor 3: 1900–2000

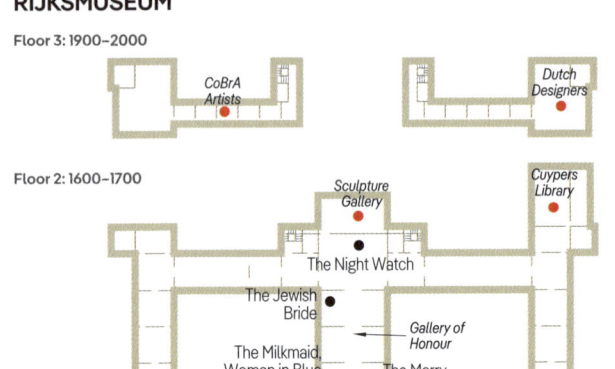

CoBrA Artists

Dutch Designers

Floor 2: 1600–1700

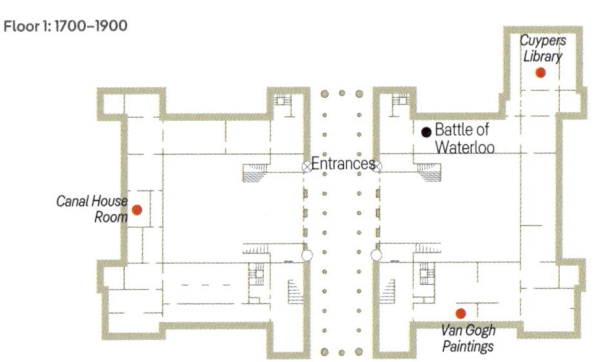

Cuypers Library

Sculpture Gallery

The Night Watch

The Jewish Bride

Gallery of Honour

The Milkmaid, Woman in Blue Reading a Letter

The Merry Family

Dollhouses

Delftware

View of Ambon

Great Hall

Floor 1: 1700–1900

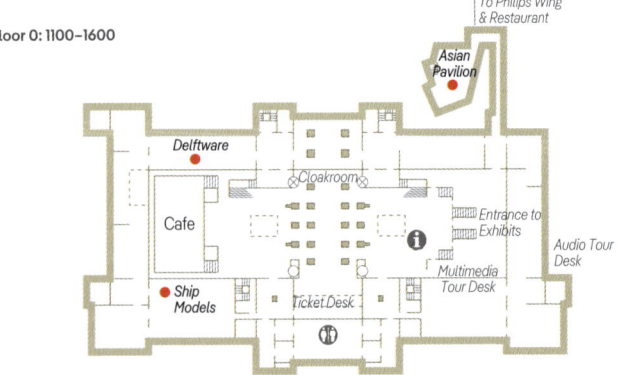

Cuypers Library

Battle of Waterloo

Entrances

Canal House Room

Van Gogh Paintings

Floor 0: 1100–1600

To Philips Wing & Restaurant

Asian Pavilion

Delftware

Cloakroom

Cafe

Entrance to Exhibits

Audio Tour Desk

Multimedia Tour Desk

Ship Models

Ticket Desk

Floor 1 Highlights

Highlights on the 1st floor, spanning 1700 to 1900, include the Rijksmuseum's largest painting, Jan Willem Pieneman's *The Battle of Waterloo* (1824), Van Gogh's famous 1887 *Self-portrait*, and a gilded, recreated 18th-century canal-house room.

Floor 0 Highlights

Covering the years 1100 to 1600, the ground floor's Special Collections span magic lanterns, armoury, ship models and Dutch status symbols from previous eras, such as musical instruments and silver miniatures. Early gems include works by Dürer, and Charles V's cutlery.

The serene Asian Pavilion, a separate sandstone-and-glass structure that's often devoid of crowds, holds first-rate artworks from China, Indonesia, Japan, India, Thailand and Vietnam.

Floor 3 Highlights

The museum's top floor encompasses 1900 to the year 2000. Works here include paintings by Karel Appel, Constant Nieuwenhuys and fellow CoBrA members of the post-WWII movement, and Dutch design furniture.

Outside the Rijksmuseum

The building was envisaged as a city gateway, linking Amsterdam's historic core with the new residential areas to the south. Part of Cuypers' brief was the bicycle-path passage that runs through the centre of the building, offering a close-up look at its architecture.

It's free to stroll the museum's gardens amid the roses, hedges, fountains and a greenhouse. Major sculpture exhibitions take place here.

Family Activities

With free entry for visitors 18 and under (time-slot bookings are still required), the Rijksmuseum is a great place to explore as a family. Guided family tours are available; check for hands-on workshops and other events for kids that are on during your visit.

A fun way to engage and intrigue seven to 12-year-olds is the Family Game (extra €2.50 per person; pick up devices at the multimedia tour desk), where two or more players using handheld devices sleuth out museum secrets in around an hour. Along the way, the quest reveals unexpected treasures of the museum you might otherwise miss.

Accessible Visits

The entire Rijksmuseum is accessible for wheelchairs, with lifts on every floor; the museum also has wheelchairs, mobility aids and folding stools for loan. Guided tours for people with visual impairment, sensory sensitivities and international sign language tours are detailed on the website.

RIJKSMUSEUM APP

Before visiting, it's worth downloading the museum's excellent free app. It features self-guided tours, including a highlights tour and various themed tours (eg women, architectural highlights of the building, or Dutch colonial history). You can also select works by number to locate them, or create your own personalised route. Remember to bring your own headphones. If you don't want to use your own phone, you can hire a device (€5) at the multimedia tours desk.

TOP EXPERIENCE

Van Gogh Museum

Opened on Museumplein in 1973 to house the collection of Vincent van Gogh's younger brother Theo, his benefactor and confidante, the Van Gogh Museum manages to feel personal and intimate, while containing the world's largest collection of the complex artist's work. It's home to some 200 paintings and 500 drawings by Vincent and his contemporaries, including Gauguin and Monet.

DON'T MISS

The Potato Eaters

The Yellow House

Wheatfield with Crows

Sunflowers

Congregation Leaving the Reformed Church at Nuenen

Self-portraits

Museum Backstory & Layout

Vincent van Gogh died in 1890, aged 37, having only sold a single painting in his lifetime, leaving his prolific collection to his brother, Theo, who died the following year. Theo's widow, Jo van Gogh-Bonger, then left it on her death in 1925 to her son, Vincent Willem van Gogh, who loaned it to the Stedelijk Museum until the Dutch government commissioned this dedicated museum.

The 1973 building was designed by De Stijl architect Gerrit Rietveld. Kisho Kurokawa's glass exhibition wing (nicknamed 'the Mussel') was completed in 1999, and in 2015, an extension

PRACTICALITIES

● Map p146 ● vangoghmuseum.nl ● adult/child €24/free, audio guide €3.75/2 ● 9am-6pm (to 9pm most Fridays) May-Sep, shorter hours Oct-Apr

Van Gogh Museum

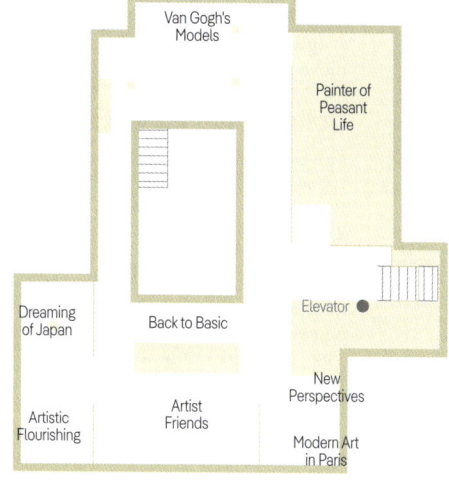

Floor 1

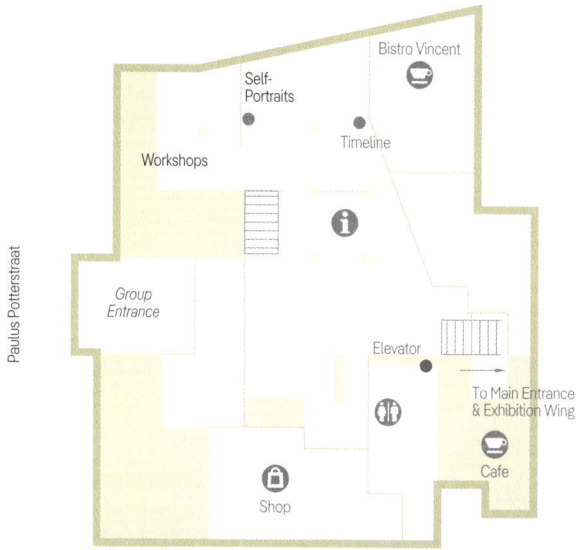

Floor 0

TOP TIPS

● Prepurchase timed-entry tickets online; it gets booked out days in advance.

● Time slots also need to be reserved even if you have a museum pass (note the I amsterdam City Card isn't valid here).

● Plan around two hours to visit (longer if you're a serious fan).

● Before 11am, after 3pm and Friday evenings are quietest.

● Check dates for 'Vincent on Friday' evening events (€11) with live performances and more.

● Ask at the information desk about treasure hunts for kids.

● Along with ground-floor cafes (in the atrium and next to the shop), **Bistro Vincent** has cuisine inspired by Van Gogh's paintings.

VAN GOGH'S LETTERS

What makes the museum so special is the intimate connection with the artist – in addition to his paintings and drawings, it holds over 800 handwritten letters, mainly between Vincent and his brother Theo, as well as artists such as Gauguin and Émile Bernard. You can also hear recordings. The museum has categorised all of Van Gogh's letters online at vangoghletters.org.

providing an additional 800 sq metres of space incorporated the striking entrance hall.

Spread over four levels, from the ground-level Floor 0 to Floor 3, the museum's chronological layout allows you to see Van Gogh's work evolve from his early depictions of sombre countryfolk in the Netherlands to his vivid, swirling landscapes in southern France. The individual paintings often move around depending on the current exhibition theme.

Collection Highlights

Van Gogh's earliest works are from his time in the Dutch countryside and studying at Antwerp's Royal Academy of Fine Arts. Peasant life is celebrated in many of his early works, such as *The Potato Eaters* (1885).

After his father became pastor of the Dutch Reformed Church in Nuenen in 1882, Van Gogh stayed at the vicarage, and painted *Congregation Leaving the Reformed Church at Nuenen* (1884–85) in early 1884, which he modified in late 1885, painting out a peasant with a spade in the foreground and adding mourning clothes to the congregation, after his father's death earlier that year. The painting, along with *View of the Sea at Scheveningen* (1882), was stolen in 2002 and recovered in 2016.

In 1886, Van Gogh moved to Paris, where his brother Theo was working as an art dealer. Unable to pay for models, Vincent started painting multiple self-portraits to improve his portraiture techniques. He met some of the Impressionists, and his palette began to brighten.

Van Gogh headed south to Provence in 1888 to paint its colourful landscapes and intense Mediterranean light. *Sunflowers* (1889) dates from this period, as does *The Yellow House* (1888), a rendering of the property Van Gogh rented in Arles; *The Bedroom* (1888) depicts Van Gogh's sleeping quarters at the house. Paul Gauguin came to stay, but their artistic differences led to fierce arguments. It was here, in 1888, during a bout of psychosis, that Van Gogh sliced off part of his ear.

Van Gogh had himself committed to an asylum in Saint-Rémy in 1889, where he continued to paint with a wild, expressive fervour. The countryside's olive and cypress trees feature in his works, as do his famous *Irises*. In 1890 he returned north in France to Auvers-sur-Oise to be closer to Theo. The ominous *Wheatfield with Crows* (1890) was among his last works before his suicide.

Other Artists

The museum also holds works by Vincent's peers, including Gauguin, Monet and Toulouse-Lautrec. There are also paintings by Van Gogh's precursors as well as later artists Van Gogh influenced.

Hang Out at Museumplein

MAP P146

Amsterdam's cultural heart

Amsterdam's most famous museums – the Rijksmuseum (p148), Van Gogh Museum (p152) and Stedelijk Museum (p156) – cluster around **Museumplein**, a vast public square that was laid out to host the World Exhibition in 1883, which gained its lasting title when the Rijksmuseum opened two years later. It's now a hub where locals and visitors mill around and everyone picnics on the lawns when the weather warms up. One of many facelifts over the years raised a triangle of turf at the western edge, which is a popular spot for sun worshippers. There's a large **Albert Heijn** supermarket concealed below.

Major renovations and upgrades in recent years have incorporated a renewal of its pond, planting numerous trees, and additional recreational facilities including a new basketball court and playground. In 2025, a state-of-the-art **skatepark** replaced earlier incarnations and is now an awesome spot for skateboarders, BMXers and in-line skaters, and is open 24 hours (with lighting until 10pm). Ice skating has taken place here since 1864; a picturesque **ice rink** sets up each winter.

Markets, concerts, festivals and some of Amsterdam's biggest celebrations take place here throughout the year.

Appreciate Exceptional Acoustics

MAP P146

Celebrated concert hall

One of Museumplein's trio of late 19th-century architectural beauties, Amsterdam's magnificent concert hall the **Concertgebouw** *(concertgebouw.nl; ticket prices vary)* was built for its 1888 debut by AL (Adolf Leonard; 'Dolf') van Gendt, who engineered its near-perfect acoustics. Former Royal Concertgebouw Orchestra conductor Bernard Haitink remarked that the world-famous hall was the orchestra's best instrument.

The Concertgebouw was designated a protected monument in 1972, and renovated between 1985 and 1988 to prevent the building from sinking. The home of the Netherlands Philharmonic and the Netherlands Chamber Orchestra, it presents a wide-ranging programme. In addition to the 1974-capacity Grote Zaal (main hall) and 437-seat Kleine Zaal (recital hall), the 150-capacity Koor Zaal (choir hall) is often used as a jazz club.

From September to June, free half-hour concerts take place at 12.30pm on Wednesdays (arrive early), with substantially discounted concerts from 11am to noon on Sundays.

BEST MUSEUMPLEIN FESTIVITIES

Nationale Tulpendag National Tulip Day (the third Saturday in January) sees Museumplein carpeted with 200,000 tulips, with a viewing platform, *dweilorkest* (traditional Dutch brass band) and a free pick-your-own bouquet. *tulpentijd.nl*

Bevrijdingsdag Dancing takes place on Liberation Day (5 May) as it did after WWII liberation. *bevrijdingsdans festival.nl*

Keti Koti Following the commemoration in Oosterpark, the 1863 abolition of slavery in Suriname and the Netherlands Antilles is celebrated at Museumplein on 1 July. *ketikotiamsterdam.nl*

Christmas Markets Museumplein turns into a magical village with craft stalls and mulled wine from mid-to late December. *icevillage.nl*

New Year's Eve Family-friendly electric fireworks at 6.45pm then celebrations from 10.30pm to the countdown and more fireworks.

 EATING IN VONDELPARK & AROUND: CLASSIC DUTCH

MAPS P146 & P164

Visque Winkel: Fishmonger with *kibbeling* (small fried fish pieces), sandwiches, smoked eel and herring. *noon-6pm Mon, 8am-6pm Tue-Fri, 9am-5pm Sat €*

Friet Boutique: Deep-fried goodness: crispy fries (with sauces), *frikandellen* (sausage), *bitterballen* (meat croquettes) and cheese-filled *kroketten*. *noon-10pm €*

Lunchroom Grannies: Breakfast favourites, eg *chocoladebroodje* (chocolate sprinkles on bread), and lunch, like *zuurvlees* (vinegar-stewed beef). *9am-5pm Wed-Sun €*

Hap Hmm: Comfort food since 1935, from grandmother's recipe meatballs to chicken casserole, schnitzel and pancakes. *5-9.15pm Mon-Fri €€*

RICHIE CHAN/SHUTTERSTOCK

TOP EXPERIENCE

Stedelijk Museum

The Stedelijk is an impressive, light, bright modern art museum, displaying artworks from its 90,000-strong collection dating from 1870 to the present day. The permanent collection rotates, but you're likely to see works by Monet, Picasso, Kandinsky, Matisse, Chagall, Warhol, Rothko, De Kooning and more. Temporary installations of the latest in contemporary art show in its newer wing.

Museum History & Architecture

DON'T MISS

Modern art masterpieces

De Stijl exhibits

Temporary exhibitions

Stedelijk Library

Don Quixote Sculpture Hall

This fabulous museum traces its history back to 1874 when collectors and benefactors came together to establish a modern-art museum. The collection was initially displayed in the Rijksmuseum before moving into its own nearby building, a gabled, red-brick, Dutch Renaissance–style masterpiece designed by Amsterdam city architect AM (Adriaan Willem) Weissman, in 1895. From 1920, it narrowed its focus on modern and contemporary art, including design and photography of the time, and held the Van Gogh collection (largely moved when the neighbouring Van Gogh Museum was built). During WWII the collection was safeguarded by curator Willem Sandberg, who became director in 1945, establishing the groundbreaking exhibition format that the museum is famed for today.

PRACTICALITIES

● Map p146 ● stedelijk.nl ● adult/child €22.50/free ● 10am-6pm

The adjoining newer wing is a radical architectural departure, designed by Dutch architectural firm Benthem Crouwel Architects and opened in 2012. Known as 'the Bathtub' (for reasons that are immediately apparent when you see it), its smooth white 'tub' is made from Twaron, a synthetic fibre five times as strong as steel, which is typically used in yacht hulls.

Collection & Exhibitions

Of the Stedelijk's vast repository, some 500 works from 1870 to today are displayed in the permanent collection presentation at any one time. While they are regularly rotated, major Dutch and international artists always feature alongside lesser-known creators.

On the ground floor, you're likely to see all sorts of modern masterpieces: Henri Matisse cut-outs, Picasso abstracts, De Stijl art and design by Piet Mondrian and Willem de Kooning, vivid paintings by Karel Appel, and other world-renowned works. Temporary exhibitions also take place here. Children will find inventive hands-on installations and other activities themed around current exhibitions in the ground-floor family lab.

Head up the grand staircase (look out for the installation at the top of the stairs) and the works become more modern, ranging from 1950 to 1980 (featuring the likes of pop art by Roy Lichtenstein and Andy Warhol, and soft sculptures by Yayoi Kusama), and from 1980 to the present. Exhibits and temporary exhibitions on this level change regularly too, so you never know what will be on hand, but count on it being offbeat and provocative.

Library & Shop

Below the entrance hall, the Stedelijk's library (open by appointment 11am to 4pm Tuesday and Thursday, closed mid-July to late August) is a great resource, with catalogues, books, archive material, art magazines, and art and design documentaries, as well as wi-fi. Admission is free.

Art, design and photography books, prints, stationery, jewellery and unique gifts are sold at the museum shop in the entrance hall.

Drinking & Dining

The Stedelijk is home to three dining venues: the **Fonda Bar** in the entrance hall, with specialist coffee, Japanese tea and pastries; the **Fonda Café** (open Wednesday to Sunday) at the centre of the museum, serving soups, salads and sourdough sandwiches and toasties; and in the 'bathtub', opening out to a terrace, **Café Restaurant Sandberg** (open for breakfast and lunch daily, and dinner until late Tuesday to Saturday) with seasonal twists on Dutch classics.

SCULPTURE HALL

In the 21st-century wing, the museum's entrance hall was previously home to a locally loved sculpture garden. To commemorate Amsterdam's 750th anniversary in 2025, the entrance was renovated to incorporate the Don Quixote Sculpture Hall, showcasing works by sculptors such as Henry Moore, Anne Imhof and Damien Hirst. There's free access (no ticket required) when the museum's open, and after-hours views of the illuminated sculptures.

TOP TIPS

● Tickets must be booked on the website. Some major temporary exhibitions attract an additional surcharge.

● You usually only need to choose the day of your visit, with your ticket valid all day. For some temporary exhibitions, you also need to reserve a start time; you can visit the rest of the exhibition outside that time slot.

● Free audio tours (in English and Dutch) provide in-depth and entertaining insights for both the main and temporary exhibitions. You can also use your own phone (bring headphones) by scanning the QR code at the museum. There's also a special kids audio tour and map.

WHY I LOVE VONDELPARK, OUD-WEST & OUD-ZUID

Catherine Le Nevez,
Lonely Planet writer

What's really special about this neighbourhood is that while it's home to Amsterdam's biggest and busiest sights and the nature-filled haven of the Vondelpark, heading only a few footsteps away in any direction, you're immersed in local life.

The neighbourhood is filled with small localities like the international restaurants along Amstelveenseweg; buzzing shops, cafes and bars on and around Jan Pieter Heijestraat; vegan restaurants and Amsterdam's best coffee around Bilderdijkstraat; elegant boutiques and cafes around Cornelis Schuytstraat; ritzy window shopping along PC Hooftstraat; and up-and-coming areas like the post-industrial spaces in Hoofddorppleinbuurt.

IVO ANTONIE DE ROOIJ/SHUTTERSTOCK

Moco Museum

Go Moco

MAP P146

Villa-housed modern and contemporary art

Overlooking Museumplein's northwestern corner from Honthorststraat, the Villa Alsberg, a beautiful 1904 villa designed by architect Eduard Cuypers, cousin of Rijksmuseum architect Pierre Cuypers, has been converted into the **Moco Museum** *(mocomuseum.com; adult/child from €17.95/15.95, with canal cruise from €35, with Heineken Experience from €40)* for 'Modern Contemporary', an independent museum founded by couple Lionel and Kim Logchies – private collectors and curators, who opened it in 2016. Its collection includes modern, contemporary, digital, immersive and street art by artists such as Andy Warhol, Keith Haring, Damien Hirst, Jeff Koons and Banksy. Sculptures displayed in the garden include a giant red gummy bear by artist WhIsBe (for 'What is Beauty') and outsized rocking horse by Dutch designer Marcel Wanders. Temporary exhibitions run in parallel throughout the year.

 EATING IN VONDELPARK & AROUND: OUR PICKS ———— MAPS P146 & P164

Ron Gastrobar: Casual fine-dining (and Michelin-starred) 'gastrobar', with tapas-style dishes, dry-aged steaks and stellar seafood. *noon-10.30pm* €€€

Daalder: Menus (set and à la carte) are as artistic as the neon-lit, street-art-style dining room décor. *6.30-10.30pm Mon, Thu & Sun, 12.30-4.30pm & 6.30-10.10pm Fri & Sat* €€€

Rijks: Michelin-starred dining in the Rijksmuseum, highlighting Dutch produce and reflecting international influences. *11.30am-2pm & 6-10pm Tue-Sun* €€€

Bolenius: Waterside restaurant with Michelin red and green stars, and produce harvested from on-site greenhouse. *noon-3pm & 6-10pm Tue-Fri, 6.30-10.30pm Sat* €€€

Smaller than the mega-museums nearby, Go Moco takes around 90 minutes to visit. Tickets are cheapest early morning and late afternoon; there are higher-priced 'priority' and 'flex' tickets that mean you don't have to book a time slot, giving you more give in your schedule. The option for a ticket that also includes a one-hour canal-boat tour on its open-topped, lipstick-pink 'Moco Boat' is a great deal; over 18s can get a combined ticket with the Heineken Experience (p175).

Discover Diamonds & Liqueurs

MAP P146

Amsterdam icons

Just off Museumplein at Paulus Potterstraat 2, 1840-founded **Royal Coster Diamonds** (*royalcoster.com; guided tour free, private tour/Royal Experience tour/masterclass €5/22.50/475*) is the oldest working diamond factory in the world. On free 30-minute guided tours, you can watch craftspeople cut and polish rough stones into sparkling gems, while learning about the origins of diamonds and assessing their quality and value. Also here is the world's largest collection of unset diamonds and the Royal 201 diamond, glittering with 201 facets. Afterwards you get to browse the wares. There are also private 45-minute tours; hour-long Royal Experience tours that reveal rooms and pieces not otherwise on display; and hands-on four-hour masterclasses where master polishers guide you in polishing a certified diamond (which you get to keep). All tours need to be booked ahead online.

The neighbouring **Diamond Museum** (*diamondmuseum. com*) delves deeper into the history of diamonds in Amsterdam; it was closed for renovations at the time of writing and reopens in its new adjacent location at Paulus Potterstraat 6 in 2026.

On the same street at Paulus Potterstraat 12–16 is another local institution, Bols, the world's oldest distilled spirit brand, which has been distilling liqueurs in Amsterdam since 1575. You can taste them during an hour-long audio-guided tour of the **Bols Cocktail Experience** (*bols.com; tour €19.50, with 30/60min cocktail workshop €34.50/46.50*), getting to grips with the tools, glass shapes, ice and different aromas (atomisers cover an entire wall) to construct and shake your own cocktail, finishing with a Bols concoction of your choice in the glitzy Mirror Bar. If you're a keen mixologist, head behind the bar on a cocktail-making workshop. Minimum age is 18.

FRIDAY NIGHT SKATE

Every Friday night year-round (except in rain and snow), the Vondelpark is the departure point of a two-hour-long mass in-line skate through the streets of Amsterdam. Accompanied by volunteers, the **Friday Night Skate** (Map p146; *fridaynightskate. com*) follows various routes each week of around 20km in all.

It's open to anyone with sufficient skills (most crucially, braking!); wearing a helmet as well as wrist, elbow and knee guards is strongly recommended. You'll also want to bring water and lights for when it becomes dark.

Arrive at the meeting point, adjacent to Het Documentaire Paviljoen, by 8.15pm for the 8.30pm departure. If you're not an experienced street skater, check the website for details of 'entry-level skates' covering 12 to 15km (four to five circuits of the Vondelpark).

EATING IN VONDELPARK & AROUND: BEST VEGAN ———— MAPS P146 & P164

Alchemist Garden: This bright cafe has dishes like almond-cheese and courgette quiche, and semolina and spinach lasagne. *9am-9pm Mon-Sat, noon-9pm Sun* €

Soil: Fermentation, curing and smoking are used in mushroom *bitterballen*, tempeh burgers and other innovations, alongside natural wines. *noon-10pm Mon-Sat, to 9pm Sun* €€

Meatless District: Industrial-style space with classy dishes like braised artichoke with lemon aioli, Korean fried cauliflower and watermelon sashimi. *5.30-10pm Wed-Mon* €€

Old Soul: Daily changing Surinamese vegan dishes, such as yam and fried plantains and stuffed bitter melon and jackfruit stew. *5-10pm Wed-Sun* €€

MELANIE LEMAHIEU/SHUTTERSTOCK

Openluchttheater

Vondelpark

Shaped somewhat like a cricket bat lying on its side, with the 'handle' pointing towards Leidseplein and the base on Amstelveenseweg, this elongated green space is an urban idyll and the city's favourite place to unwind. Even when it's filled with picnickers, joggers, skaters and a constantly whizzing parade of bikes, its spacious layout means it never feels uncomfortably crowded.

DON'T MISS

Joost van den Vondel statue

Rose garden

Picasso's *The Fish*

Proeflokaal 't Blauwe Theehuis

Openluchttheater

Het Documentaire Paviljoen

Park History

Originally a private park for the wealthy only, these sprawling, English-style gardens were laid out on marshland and opened in 1865, and expanded between 1875 and 1877 to the current size. Although known as Nieuwe Park (New Park), in 1867 a statue of poet and playwright **Joost van den Vondel** (1587–1679) was created by sculptor Louis Royer. Locals began referring to the park as 'Vondel's Park', and it was formally renamed. The fragrant **rose garden**, with some 70 different species, was added in 1936. Bought by the city council in 1953, the park finally opened to the public.

During the 1960s and '70s, Amsterdam became the *magisch centrum* (magic centre) of Europe. As hippies flocked here a housing shortage saw speculators leaving buildings empty

PRACTICALITIES
● Map p146 ● amsterdam.nl ● free ● 24hr

and squatting (illegal since 2010) became widespread, and Dutch authorities turned the park into a temporary open-air dormitory. Although the sleeping bags are long gone today, an indie spirit persists.

After the Vondelpark was listed as a national monument in 1996, renovations incorporated an extensive drainage system to counteract it sinking, while conserving its historic appearance.

Sculptures

Sculptures dotted throughout the park include many ephemeral installations and artworks. Among the permanent pieces is Picasso's 6m-high abstract work *Figure découpée l'Oiseau* (The Bird; 1965), commonly known as **The Fish**, which he donated for the park's centenary on the condition it remain here.

Drinking & Dining

Refreshments inside the park gates include the blue-and-white, flying-saucer-shaped **Proeflokaal 't Blauwe Theehuis**, a Brouwerij 't IJ taproom; garden cafe **De Vondeltuin**; and Hansel-and-Gretel-like chalet **Groot Melkhuis**.

Entertainment & Festivals

Open-air theatre the **Openluchttheater** *(openluchttheater.nl)* hosts free performances (world music, dance, plays and more) from Friday evenings to Sunday afternoons May to September.

Het Documentaire Paviljoen *(idfa.nl)*, in the colonnaded, Italian-Renaissance-style Vondelparkpaviljoen, which has film screenings and events, is the home base of the citywide IDFA (International Documentary Film Festival Amsterdam), the world's largest documentary film festival, held over two weeks in November.

The park is a stage for numerous events, including during Pride Amsterdam (p250). Traditionally, the Vondelpark closes the night before King's Day (p19), opening at 9am on the national day for a children's *vrijmarkt* (street market).

Sports & Activities

One of the joys of the Vondelpark's meandering layout is an unstructured stroll, but there are opportunities to get more active. Football games regularly take place on designated fields, and the park is perfect for cycling away from road traffic – rent wheels nearby at **Black Bikes** *(black-bikes.com)* or **A-Bike** *(a-bike.nl)*. It's also a great place to run; the longest lap of the park is 3.2km along the outer paved roads.

In-line skating is popular – follow the outer roads in an anti-clockwise direction and watch out for kids, dogs and bikes. On neighbouring Overtoom, the Netherlands' biggest skate shop **This Is Soul** *(thisissoul.com; day/overnight skate rental from €10/5)* rents skates (bring ID to leave behind) and offers lessons in the park for beginners to advanced skaters (learning how to handle different surfaces, and braking, stopping and falling techniques). Amsterdam's Friday Night Skate (p159) sets off from the park.

BIRDLIFE

The oasis-like Vondelpark is a haven for birdlife. Species such as coots, great spotted woodpeckers, herons, jackdaws, kingfishers, mallards, moorhens, mute swans, oystercatchers, parakeets, reed warblers, robins, sparrowhawks, tawny owls and wood-pigeons are commonly spotted, as well as white storks – a new stork pole was erected in the Schapenweide (Sheep Meadow) in 2025, with a total of four poles with nests.

TOP TIPS

● Bring a blanket for a picnic. There are delis and shops in the surrounding streets perfect for picking up bread, cheese, ready-to-eat dishes and drinks.

● Rubbish bins are plentiful; use them to keep the park pristine and protect its wildlife.

● Barbecues are not permitted in the park.

● Cafes within the park have toilets for customers.

● Public toilets are available throughout the park, with wheelchair-accessible toilets also available – check the city's municipal interactive map *(maps.amsterdam. nl/openbare_toiletten)* and navigate to the Vondelpark.

● The park is generally safe at all hours but be mindful after dark and stick to well-lit areas.

BEST MARKETS

Museum Market
(Map p146) Art, craft, design and food stalls on Museumplein on the third Sunday of the month. *museummarket.nl*

Ten Katemarkt
(Map p164) Fresh produce, nuts, cheeses and flowers fill this street market Monday to Saturday. *tenkatemarkt.nl*

Zuidermarkt (Map p146) Co-op–run market selling mostly organic fruit, vegetables, olives, breads, cheeses and wines every Saturday. *zuidermrkt.nl*

Maker Market
(Map p164) Browse sustainable, handcrafted designs and meet the artisans on Saturdays and Sundays. *dehallen -amsterdam.nl*

Art, Design & Vintage Market
(Map p164) Ceramics and jewellery are among the pre-loved treasures at this market on the second Sunday of the month. *facebook.com/an afternoonwiththe collectorsamsterdam*

Be Whisked Back in Time at the Hollandsche Manege
MAP P146

Neoclassical riding school

Bordering the Vondelpark's northern side, the grandiose indoor riding school **Hollandsche Manege** *(Dutch Riding School; dehollandschemanege.nl; museum adult/child €12.50/8.50, high tea €34.95, 30-minute riding/side-saddle lesson €49/55, one-hour riding lesson €77.50)* was inspired by Vienna's famous Spanish Riding School.

Built in 1882 by architect AL van Gendt, the neoclassical building retains its charming horsehead façade and is a national monument. Its **Levend Paarden Museum** (Living Horse Museum), closed Mondays, details the building's history alongside the 'world of the horse' through equine art and displays including historic riding equipment. In November, it hosts the niche four-day contemporary Dutch Equine Art Fair.

A highlight is watching a balletic carousel display with women riding side-saddle (seated with both legs to the horse's left side) and men riding to the right, which has Dutch Intangible Cultural Heritage designation. Check dates for packages that combine a demonstration with a museum tour and sumptuous high tea of pastries, sandwiches and tea served on beautiful Delftware, and in some cases a lesson – the Hollandsche Manege is the only riding school in the Netherlands where ladies' side-saddle riding is still taught today.

It's possible for visitors to book ahead for one-off 30-minute or hour-long standard private riding lessons at its arena.

Listen to Organ Music
MAP P146

Former church turned concert venue

Originally known as the Parkkerk for its position on the edge of the Vondelpark, the **Orgelpark** *(orgelpark.nl; adult/child from €20/12.50)* occupies a 1918 late neo-Renaissance brick church designed by Dutch architect EAC (Ernst Adolph Christiaan) Roest. It continued as a church until 1994. Since 2007, it has been a one-of-a-kind performance space for organ music, with its beautifully restored pneumatic Sauer organ (a national monument dating from 1922) and seven additional organs. The art-deco interior is a lovely setting for concerts. Around 80 events take place each year, including classical and jazz, along with combined performances with other artistic forms like film or dance – check the agenda online.

DRINKING IN VONDELPARK & AROUND: BEST COFFEE
MAPS P146 & P164

Monks Coffee Roasters: Sources and roasts outstanding coffee, with a phenomenal house blend; brilliant for brunch. *8am-4pm Mon-Fri, 9am-4pm Sat & Sun*

LOT61: See (and smell) beans being roasted on the Probat in the open cellar. Coffees are double shots (unless you say otherwise). *8am-6pm Mon-Fri, 9am-6pm Sat & Sun*

Trakteren: Preparation methods of single-origin beans include Aeropress, V60 pour-over, Chemex, syphon and cold press. *8am-5pm Mon-Fri, 9am-5pm Sat*

Stean's Beans: Only a glass window separates the roastery from the cafe at this fabulous Hoofddorppleinbuurt space. *10.30am-4pm Mon, 9am-4pm Tue-Fri*

AMBLE PAST OUD-ZUID'S ARCHITECTURE

South of the Vondelpark, stroll past grand villas and landmark Amsterdam School buildings in one of Amsterdam's most elegant neighbourhoods.

START	END	LENGTH
Haarlemmermeerstation	Café Wildschut	3.2km; 2 hours

Start at the Amsterdam School-style-❶ **Haarlemmermeerstation**, built in 1915 by H van Emmerik as the Amsterdam–Aalsmeer line's terminus. Passenger services ceased in 1950; today the Electrische Museumtramlijn Amsterdam's (p165) vintage trams depart here.

Northeast is neo-Romanesque Catholic church ❷ **Sint Agneskerk**, designed by Jan Stuyt and completed in 1932, with a glass mosaic of Sint Agnes and large Star of David above the entrance. Heading east, the 1917-opened ❸ **Amsterdams Lyceum**, the Netherlands' oldest selective secondary school, was designed by HAJ Baanders like a 'gatehouse' between Amsterdam's Oud-Zuid (Old South) and Nieuw-Zuid (New South). In WWII, it was used by the Nazis as a barracks and officers' mess.

Head north to the Vondelpark's southern edge. Turn east on Koningslaan and continue on Van Eeghenstraat, both lined with monumental late 19th- and early 20th-century villas. South on Jacob Oberchtstraat, the neo-Romanesque Catholic ❹ **Obrechtkerk** was built in 1911 by Jan Stuyt and Jos Cuypers (Pierre Cuypers' son).

Southeast, past the ❺ **Zuidermarkt**, the ❻ **Huize Loma** was a pioneering apartment block when it was built in 1913 by FA Warners. Finish at grand ❼ **Café Wildschut**. Built in 1923 by prolific Amsterdam School architect Gerrit Jan Rutgers, it features a striking curved façade, an interior of marble, brass and studded leather banquettes, and a sun-drenched terrace.

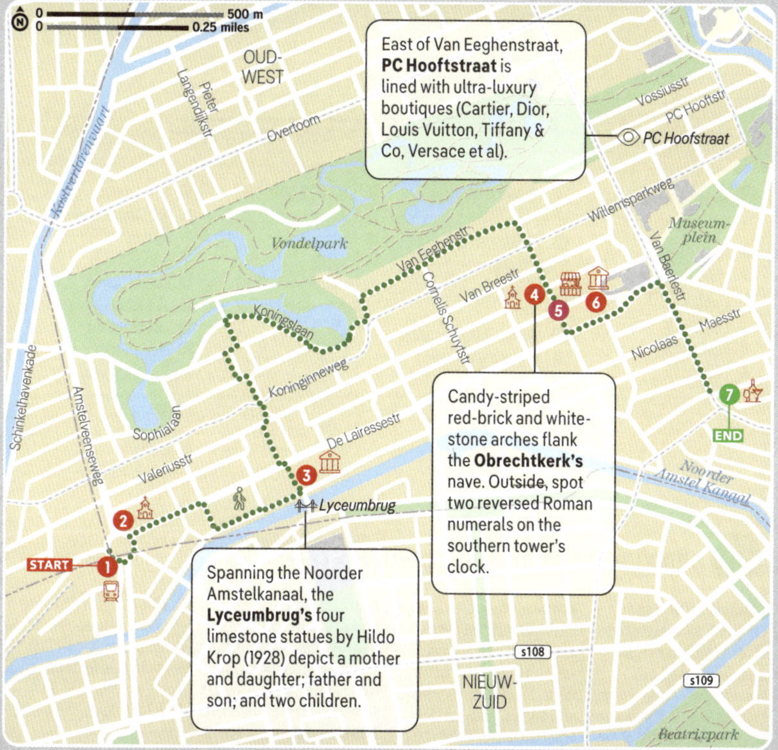
0 500 m
0 0.25 miles
OUD-WEST
Pieter Langendijkstr
Overtoom
Kostverlorenvaart
Vondelpark
East of Van Eeghenstraat, **PC Hooftstraat** is lined with ultra-luxury boutiques (Cartier, Dior, Louis Vuitton, Tiffany & Co, Versace et al).
Vossiusstr
PC Hooftstr
PC Hoofstraat
Willemsparkweg
Museum-plein
Van Eeghenstr
Cornelis Schuytstr
Van Breestr
Van Baerlestr
Maesstr
Nicolaas
Koningslaan
Koninginneweg
De Lairessestr
Schinkelhavenkade
Amstelveenseweg
Sophialaan
Valeriusstr
Lyceumbrug
START
END
Candy-striped red-brick and white-stone arches flank the **Obrechtkerk's** nave. Outside, spot two reversed Roman numerals on the southern tower's clock.
Noorder Amstel Kanaal
Spanning the Noorder Amstelkanaal, the **Lyceumbrug's** four limestone statues by Hildo Krop (1928) depict a mother and daughter; father and son; and two children.
s108
s109
NIEUW-ZUID
Beatrixpark

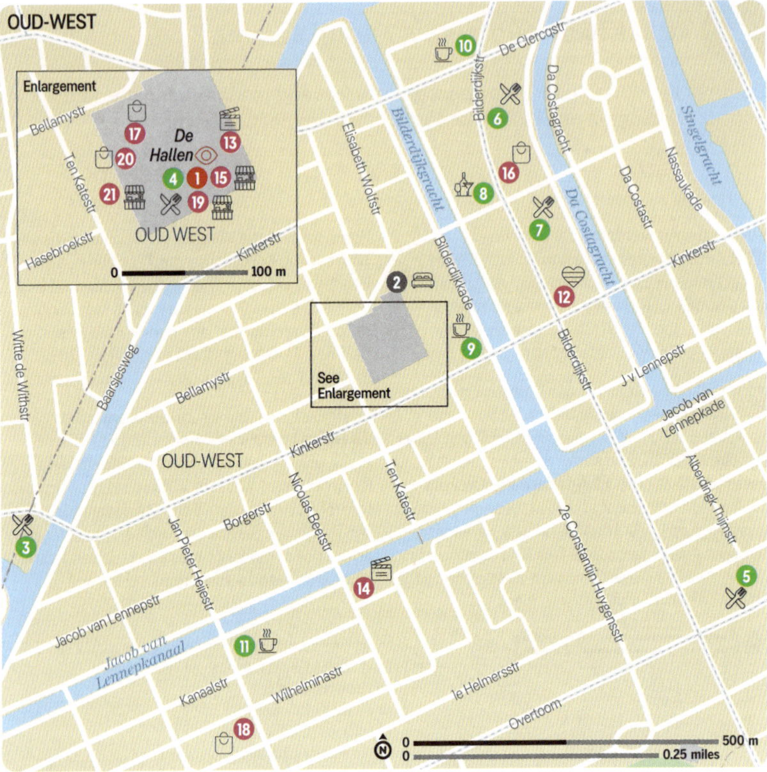

OUD-WEST

Enlargement

De Hallen

OUD WEST

0 ——— 100 m

OUD-WEST

See
Enlargement

OUD-WEST

0
0   0.25 miles
500 m

⭐ **HIGHLIGHTS**
1 De Hallen

⚫ **SLEEPING**
2 Hotel De Hallen

🟢 **EATING**
3 Daalder
4 Foodhallen
5 Hap Hmm

6 Meatless District
7 Soil

🟢 **DRINKING & NIGHTLIFE**
8 Karavan
9 LOT61
10 Monks Coffee Roasters
11 Trakteren

🔴 **ENTERTAINMENT**
12 De Trut
13 Filmhallen
14 Lab 111

🔴 **SHOPPING**
15 Art, Design & Vintage Market
16 Cane & Grain
17 Denim City
18 J&B Craft Drinks
19 Maker Market
20 Maker Store
21 Ten Katemarkt

Charming wood-panelled bruin café

🍸 **DRINKING IN VONDELPARK & AROUND: OUR PICKS**

MAPS P146 & P164

Lokaal van de Stad: Opening to an awesome Hoofddorppleinbuurt canal-side terrace, serving only Amsterdam craft brews. *8.30am-1am Sun-Thu, to 2am Fri & Sat*

Karavan: Opens to a huge beer garden that gets packed on sunny days, serving beers, natural wines, cocktails, mocktails and sodas. *9am-1am Sun-Thu, to 3am Fri & Sat*

Craft & Draft: Over 40 beers rotating on the taps and 100 more by the bottle. Try house collaborations with Netherlands' brewers. *4pm-midnight Sun-Thu, to 2am Fri & Sat*

Welling: Tucked behind the Concertgebouw; often hosts live music by jazz musicians after their gigs. *4pm-1am Mon-Fri, 3pm-1am Sat & Sun*

Splash in the Zuiderbad

MAP P146

Exquisite swimming pool

Originally the Velox cycling school, dating from 1897, this building behind the Rijksmuseum on Hobbemastraat was converted in 1912 into a beguilingly splendid public pool, the **Zuiderbad** *(amsterdam.nl/zuiderbad; swimming €5.50, wellness facilities €3.30)*. It's a grand edifice restored to its original glory, full of tiles (including the beautiful fountain with Amsterdam's city symbol 'XXX'), original wooden change-rooms and underwater lighting. There are steam cabins and herbal baths. The schedule for swimming *(recreatiezwemmen in diep water)* varies daily; check it online.

Ride Aboard a Historic Tram

MAP P146

Tram museum on the move

Not a museum in a static sense, the **Electrische Museum-tramlijn Amsterdam** *(museumtramlijn.org; adult/child Heritage Line return €7.50/5, City Tour €10/5)* gives you the opportunity to travel on historic trams from the Netherlands, Austria and Poland collected between the 1950s and '70s – the earliest date back to the 1890s. On Sundays from April to October, the Heritage Line (line 30) departs from red-brick Haarlemmermeer Station near the Vondelpark to Amstelveen via Amsterdamse Bos (p180). A return trip takes about 1¼ hours; you can hop off at scheduled stops en route. Check the timetable for rail-replacement buses and stops that are temporarily out of service.

Also in the summer months, a City Tour (line 20) runs every Saturday and on the second and fourth Sunday of the month, departing from the Dam and taking a circular route around the city, passing landmarks like Leidseplein and Rembrandtplein. The loop takes two hours.

Tickets for both the Heritage Line and City Tour are sold by the onboard conductor in keeping with tradition.

Atmospheric tram rides through Amsterdam's illuminated streets run on scheduled days from late November to early January; book these early online as they quickly sell out.

Distil Rum

MAP P146

High-spirited workshops

In the trendy neighbourhood of Hoofddorppleinbuurt, bordered by canals and filled with cafes, bakeries, a great coffee roastery (Stean's Beans; p162), restaurants and bars, you can distil your own rum.

During a 90-minute distilling workshop and tour at **Spirited Union Rum Company** *(spirited-union.com; distilling workshop & tour €70)*, you get to check out the production facility and create your own 70cL bottle using one of four rums as bases, then choose your botanicals (pineapple, grapefruit, cacao, cinnamon, coconut or coffee) in your own copper still. Workshops and tours include a tasting.

BEST SHOPPING

Maker Store (Map p164) Showcases 80+ Amsterdam artisans. *themakerstore.nl*

Donsje (Map p146) Adorable handmade booties, jumpsuits, trousers, cardigans, jackets and backpacks with nature themes. *donsje.com*

Floris van Bommel (Map p146) Brogues, loafers, sneakers, moccasins and boots by 9th-generation-run shoemaker established in 1718. *florisvanbommel.com*

Denim City (Map p164) Stocks startup labels' latest collections, recycles denim into original pieces and does repairs. *denimcity.org*

J&B Craft Drinks (Map p164) Choose from a huge range of craft beers, ciders and sodas from around the globe, available cold from the fridge. *jbcraftdrinks.com*

Nixx (Map p146) Has a superb range of Dutch cheeses, roasts nuts in store, and sells dried fruit and natural wines. *nixx-noten -kaas-amsterdam.nl*

Cane & Grain (Map p164) Specialises in *jenevers* and Caribbean rums, and organises tastings and workshops. *caneandgrain.nl*

Unearth quirky art, architecture and street life by strolling through Amsterdam's eclectic Oud-West (Old West), one of the city's most happening areas.

START	END	LENGTH
Vondelkerk	Gebrouwen door Vrouwen	3.5km; 2½ hours

West along the Vondelpark's northern edge, the neo-Gothic cross-basilica ❶ **Vondelkerk** was designed by Pierre Cuypers in 1872. Cross shop- and cafe-lined Overtoom, then cross ❷ **Jakob van Lennepkanaal**, one of Amster- dam's few canals named for a person, writer Jakob van Lennep (1802–68). Just north from lively commercial strip Kinkerstraat, via the ❸ **Ten Katemarkt** (p162), are the red-brick tram sheds now sheltering cultural centre ❹ **De Hallen**. Continue east on Kinkerstraat to buzzing Bilderdijkstraat; on Da Costakade is ❺ **Outsider Art Gallery**, featuring works by local artists with disabilities.

Along De Clercqstraat on the Wiebrug, at the entrance to multicultural neighbourhood De

Baarsjes, with streets named for Dutch naval figures, look down to see Leonie Mijnlieff's 2004 aluminium sculpture ❻ **Boegbeeld**, symbolising the figureheads that adorned ships' bows. Southwest along Kostverlorenvaart, the ❼ **Westermoskee** was built in 2015 in an Ottoman style, with a 25m-high dome and 42m-high minaret, and traditional Dutch architectural features.

Cross the Kinkerbrug to the east and turn south on backstreet Jan Pieter Heijestraat, named for poet and physician Jan Pieter Heije (1809–76). Once home to cheap worker accommodation, it's now busy with boutiques, restaurants and bars. Finish with a beer from ❽ **Gebrouwen door Vrouwen** (Brewed by Women).

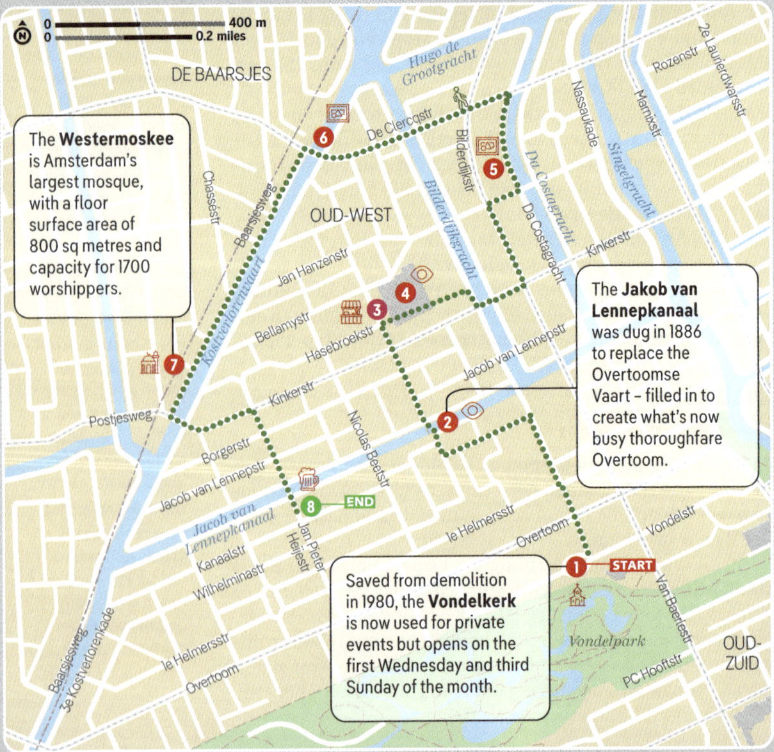

The **Westermoskee** is Amsterdam's largest mosque, with a floor surface area of 800 sq metres and capacity for 1700 worshippers.

The **Jakob van Lennepkanaal** was dug in 1886 to replace the Overtoomse Vaart – filled in to create what's now busy thoroughfare Overtoom.

Saved from demolition in 1980, the **Vondelkerk** is now used for private events but opens on the first Wednesday and third Sunday of the month.

Head to De Hallen

MAP P164

Food and cultural hub

Cavernous red-brick sheds built to service Amsterdam's trams from 1901 were converted a century later into a food hall and cultural complex, electrifying the surrounding Oud-West area north of the Vondelpark.

De Hallen *(dehallen-amsterdam.nl)* incorporates sustainable Dutch design and fashion boutiques, an antiques shop, a bike seller-repairer, a hairdressing academy-salon, a library, galleries, a nine-screen cinema, **Filmhallen**, and a hotel (p242).

At De Hallen's heart, its skylit food hall, **Foodhallen**, is an airy, open-plan communal dining area surrounded by 21 stands cooking everything from Mumbai street food to Dutch-speciality meatballs. 'Beats & Bites' on Fridays and Saturdays, with DJs, and 'Bands & Bites' when live musicians play on the first Thursday of the month, add to the party atmosphere. There's also a reading cafe with cultural events and an all-day bar-restaurant.

Regular events include markets, sustainability workshops and pop-up exhibitions.

Directly outside De Hallen you'll find the street market Ten Katemarkt (p162).

Ramble in the Rembrandtpark

MAP P146

Green escape

Northwest of the Vondelpark, surrounded by residential buildings in Amsterdam Nieuw-West, the bucolic **Rembrandtpark** spreads over 45 leafy (and watery) hectares and is criss-crossed by walking and cycling paths. Unlike the similarly named Southern Canal Ring party square, Rembrandtplein (p131), the Rembrandtpark is little visited by tourists. Barbecuing is permitted in some areas.

Home to abundant wildlife and birdlife, the park is a favourite with families for its water-play area and climbing pyramid adventure playground. In the northwestern corner there's a petting zoo, the **Kinderboerderij de Uylenburg**, where children can interact with donkeys, geese, goats, pigs, sheep, ponies and other friendly critters. It's being incorporated into the Stadsboerderij Rembrandtpark (Rembrandtpark City Farm); renovations are due to wrap up at the end of 2026.

BEST CULTURAL & NIGHTLIFE SPACES

Vondelbunker (Map p146) A 1947 fallout shelter beneath the 1e Constantijn Huygensstraat bridge contains this underground venue for music, film, poetry and more. *vondelbunker.nl*

Radion (Map p146) Former dental centre home to Amsterdam's techno scene with 24-hour clubbing, and cultural events. *radion.amsterdam*

Lab 111 (Map p164) Once a university science laboratory, now a cinema screening cult films with an in-house bar, Strangelove. *lab111.nl*

OCCII (Map p146) Legalised squat in former stables and tram sheds with an alternative scene from folk to punk. *occii.org*

OT301 (Map p146) Street-art-covered ex-squat in the former Netherlands Film Academy, hosting an eclectic roster of bands, DJs, theatre and workshops. *ot301.nl*

De Trut (Map p164) Once-squatted printing-machine-factory that's a decades-strong volunteer-run LGBTIQ+ club famed for its Sunday parties. *trutfonds.nl*

Researched by
Catherine Le Nevez

DE PIJP & ZUID

BUZZING MARKETS, LIVELY DINING AND EXPANSIVE GREENERY

Vibrant De Pijp has a distinct village-like character. To its south are peaceful residential areas, glitzy new developments and glorious parks, including Amsterdam's sprawling forest.

An island linked to surrounding districts by 16 bridges, De Pijp's straight, narrow streets reflect the stems of old clay pipes, hence its name, 'the Pipe'. The city expanded here in the 19th century, when tenement blocks were rapidly constructed to relieve pressure on the densely populated Jordaan and provide cheap housing for workers. In the 1960s and '70s, when many residents relocated for more space, the government refurbished the properties for immigrants. Artists, creatives, university students and entrepreneurs all flocked here, and gentrification took off, but it retains a village atmosphere, and is the gateway to a host of lesser-visited areas and under-the-radar sights across Amsterdam Zuid (Amsterdam South).

TOP TIP

Many successful Amsterdam businesses put down their first roots in De Pijp, and this innovative neighbourhood has a constant turnover of pop-ups, startups and new openings. Backstreets to watch include Frans Halsstraat, 1e Van der Helststraat, 2e Van der Helststraat, Cornelis Troostplein and Ruysdaelkade.

De Pijp

See p242 for places to stay in De Pijp and Zuid.

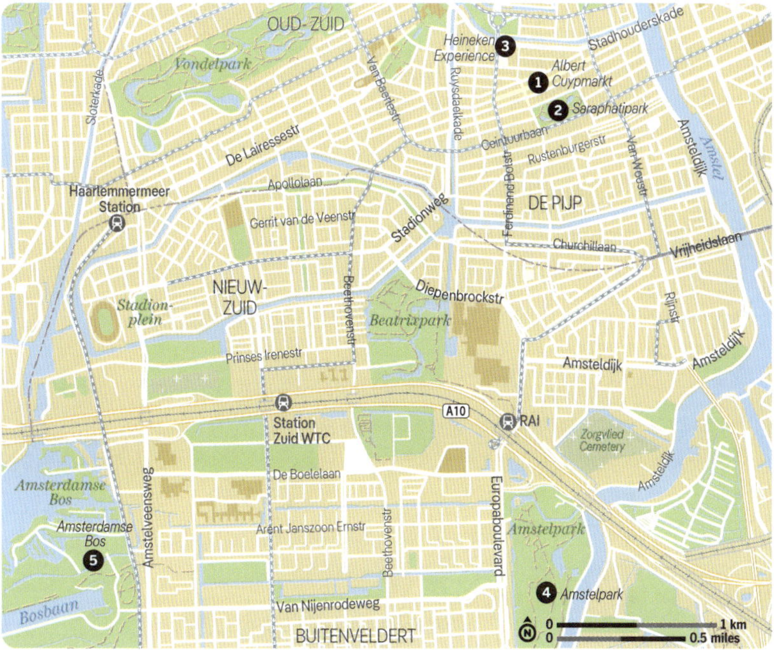
OUD-ZUID
Vondelpark
Heineken Experience
3
Albert Cuypmarkt
1
Saraphatipark
2
Stadhouderskade
Van Baerlestr
Ruysdaelkade
Sloterkade
De Lairessestr
Ceintuurbaan
Rustenburgerstr
Van Woustr
Amsteldijk
Amstel
Haarlemmermeer Station
Apollolaan
Gerrit van de Veenstr
Stadionweg
Ferdinand Bolstr
DE PIJP
Churchillaan
Vrijheidslaan
NIEUW-ZUID
Stadion-plein
Beethovenstr
Diepenbrockstr
Beatrixpark
Rijnstr
Prinses Irenestr
Amsteldijk
Amsteldijk
Station Zuid WTC
A10
RAI
Zorgvlied Cemetery
De Boelelaan
Amsteldijk
Amsterdamse Bos
Amsterdamse Bos
5
Amstelveensweg
Arent Janszoon Ernstr
Beethovenstr
Europaboulevard
Amstelpark
4
Amstelpark
Bosbaan
Van Nijenrodeweg
BUITENVELDERT
N
0
1 km
0
0.5 miles

Highlights

❶ Albert Cuypmarkt
Soak up De Pijp's spirit at the colourful stalls of the large six-days-per-week street market. **p172**

❷ Sarphatipark
Pack a picnic and head to the lush sanctuary of lawns, statues, ponds and fountains in De Pijp's central park. **p173**

❸ Heineken Experience
Tour the boisterously fun multimedia exhibits in the former brewery. **p175**

❹ Amstelpark
Savour a food festival, ride the Amstel Trein and see flowers bloom. **p177**

❺ Amsterdamse Bos
Cycle, boat or visit a goat farm in the vast expanse of Amsterdam's forest. **p180**

Getting Around

Metro
The Noord/Zuidlijn (north–south metro line; M52) has stations at De Pijp, Europaplein and its southern terminus, Amsterdam Zuid.

Tram
Tram 24 rolls north–south from Centraal Station along Ferdinand Bolstraat. Tram 4 travels from Centraal via Rembrandtplein to De Pijp. Tram 3 traverses De Pijp between the Vondelpark and Oost. Tram 12 from Centraal via Leidseplein cuts through De Pijp and Rivierenbuurt.

Bus
Some further-flung sights are served by Connexxion *(connexxion.nl)* buses (I amsterdam City Cards and GVB transport tickets aren't valid; you'll need separate tickets).

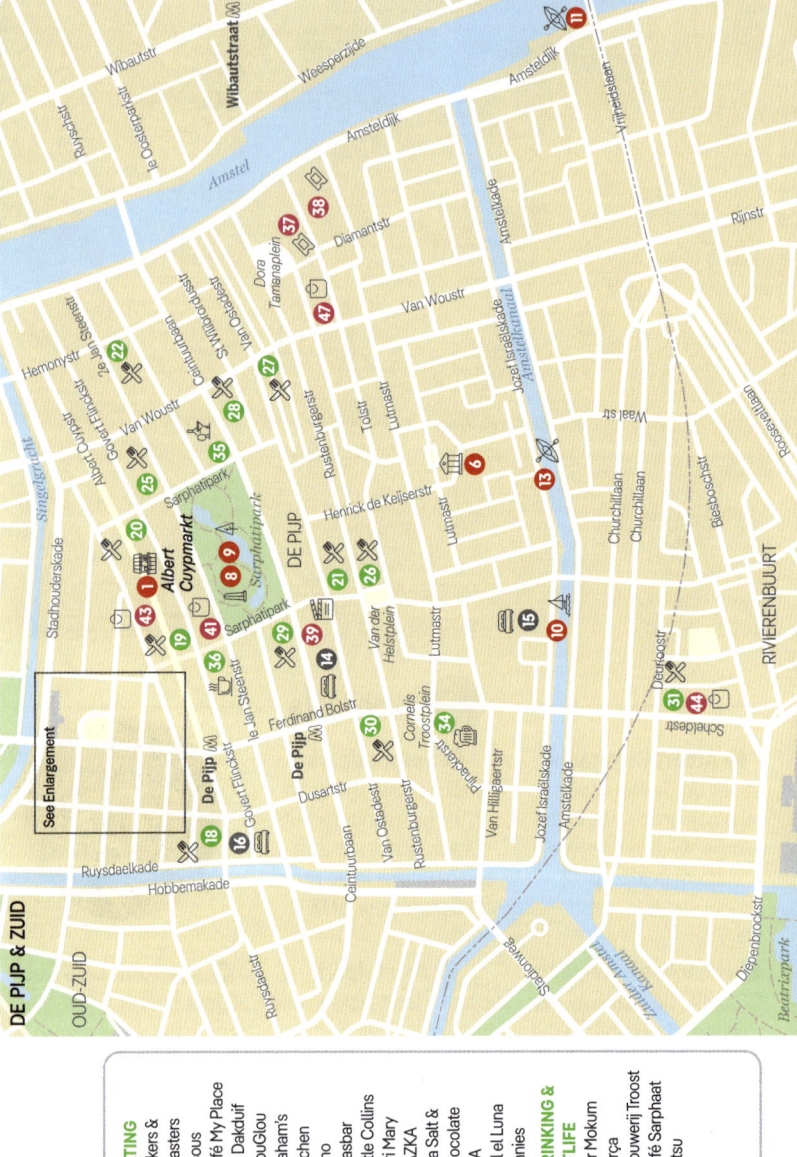

DE PIJP & ZUID

OUD-ZUID

RIVIERENBUURT

See Enlargement

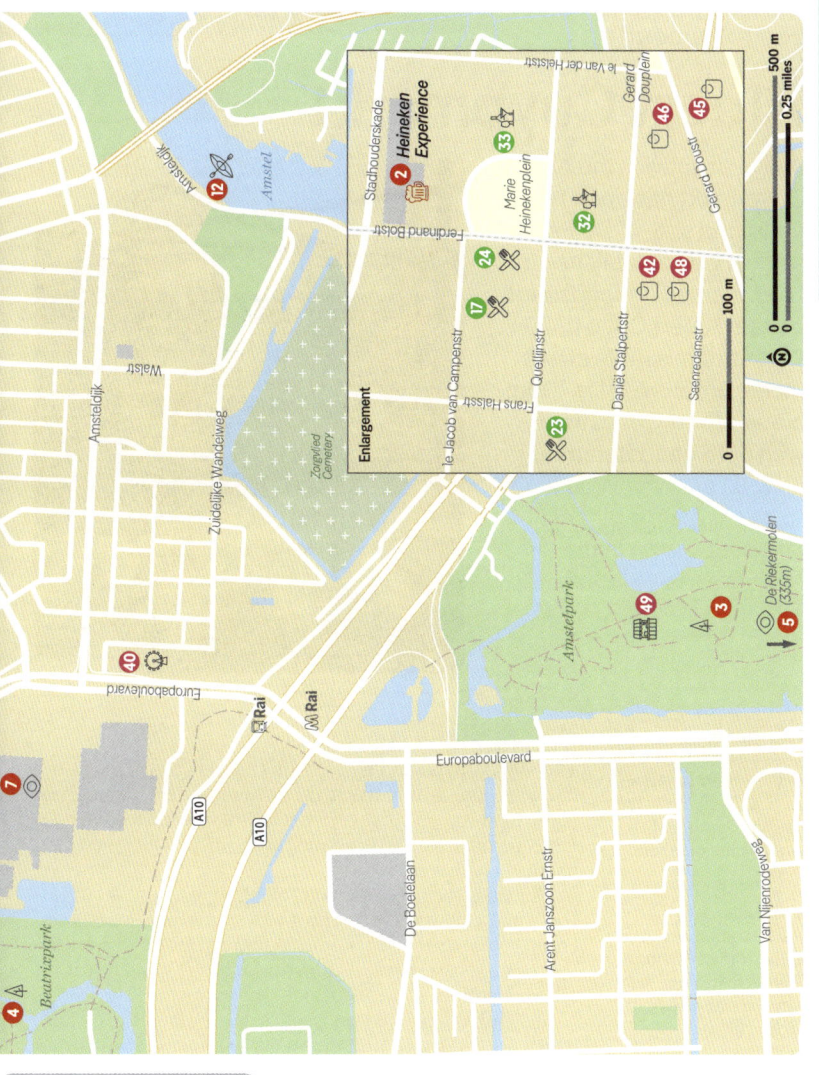

Enlargement

Heineken Experience

Marie Heinekenplein

ENTERTAINMENT
37 CC Amstel
38 Cinetol
39 Rialto
40 Upside Down

SHOPPING
41 Bier Baum
42 Blond Amsterdam
43 De Kleine Parade
44 De Winkel van Nijntje
45 Elcie
46 Love Stories Archive
47 Matts
48 Mercer
49 Pure Markt – Amstelpark

TOP EXPERIENCE

Albert Cuypmarkt

A hive of activity, the Albert Cuypmarkt has been the heart and soul of De Pijp since it was established in 1905. Named for landscape painter Albert Cuyp (1620–91), this unmissable street market stretching for 700m along Albert Cuypstraat, with Ferdinand Bolstraat to its west and Van Woustraat to its east, is the biggest and best known in the Netherlands.

RICHARD I'ANSON/GETTY IMAGES

TOP TIPS

● Crowds are fewest and pickings best early in the morning, which is when most locals come here to shop.

● Saturday sees the market at its most bustling. Early in the week and/or in adverse weather, there may be fewer stalls and earlier closures.

PRACTICALITIES

● Map p170
● albertcuyp-markt. amsterdam ● free
● 9.30am-5pm Mon-Sat

Market Stalls

The Albert Cuypmarkt buzzes with shoppers and market traders, with some 260 stalls setting up here six days a week. Aromatic food stands burst with fresh fruit, vegetables, cheeses, meat, poultry, fish, crustaceans, nuts, olives, oils, spices and bouquets of flowers.

Alongside them, browse bolts of fabric in a rainbow of patterns and colours, along with racks of inexpensive clothes, cheap socks, leather bags, glazed pottery, bike locks, phone covers, cut-price soaps, shampoos, cosmetics and all sorts of other essentials.

Don't miss the shops lining both sides of Albert Cuypstraat, which are hidden behind the stalls, selling everything from kitchen gadgets to luggage and much more.

Market Snacks

Ready-to-eat bites abound. Classic Dutch street-food snacks to eat as you wander range from raw, brine-cured delicacy *haring* (herring), served with *uitjes* (diced onions) and *zuur* (sweet pickles) to eat using a toothpick, or in a fluffy white roll as a *broodje haring* (herring sandwich); *kibbeling* (battered small pieces of whitefish); cones of *Vlaamse frites* ('Flemish fries', aka *friet*, *frieten* or *patat*), *poffertjes* (puffy mini pancakes dusted with icing sugar) and piping-hot *stroopwafels* (caramel-syrup-filled wafers).

Picnic in Sarphatipark

MAP P170

Urban oasis

De Pijp's favourite hangout on sunny days is the **Sarphatipark**. Created in 1885, this English-style park takes in 4.5 hectares of ponds, meadows and wooded fringes. At its centre is the 1886 temple-style **Sarphati Memorial**, with a fountain, gargoyles and a bust of doctor, businessman and urban innovator Samuel Sarphati (1813–66), for whom the park is named.

The gently sloping lawns here are idyllic for picnics – pick up provisions at the Albert Cuypmarkt and chilled craft brews at **Bier Baum**. There's a playground for littlies and a nature play area for older kids.

Take a Street-Food Tour

De Pijp bites

Dive into De Pijp's global food scene on a small-group insiders' tour (maximum eight people) with **Hungry Birds** (*hungry birds.nl; short flight/original tour €79/110*). Guides take you 'off the eaten track' to chow on Dutch and world specialities, visiting local hotspots from street vendors to family-run premises on 2½- to three-hour 'short flight' tours or 4½-hour original tours that have been running in De Pijp for over a decade. Prices include all food; the meet-up location is given after you make reservations. It also runs tours in Amsterdam's multicultural Oost.

Catch Emerging Musicians, Performing Arts & Films

MAP P170

Music, stage and screen

With a capacity of just 150, **Cinetol** (*cinetol.nl*) is an intimate place to catch established and emerging local acts across all genres: indie, folk, jazz, R&B, soul, rock, pop, punk, post-punk, garage, psychedelic, hip-hop, Afrobeat, EDM... Around 250 concerts take place each year; it also hosts exhibitions, screenings and album launches. On-site Tolbar cafe opens to a sunny terrace.

'Cultural clubhouse' **CC Amstel** (*ccamstel.nl*) presents performing arts events from circus to dance and visual theatre and art exhibitions.

Opened in 1921, art-deco cinema **Rialto** (*rialtofilm.nl*) shows eclectic arthouse fare from around the world (many in English or with English subtitles). Buy tickets online or at the box office.

**WHY I LOVE
DE PIJP & ZUID**

Catherine Le Nevez,
Lonely Planet writer

With its close sense of community and convivial hangouts, De Pijp is one of my favourite corners of the world. There have been changes – it wasn't that long ago that travelling here from Centraal was a long, meandering tram ride winding through the backstreets; since the metro opened in 2018, the three-minute, teleportation-like trip is virtually instantaneous – but De Pijp's character is still intact. It's the kind of place where there are always familiar faces at the shops, markets, cafes, bars and cinema, and on a summer's evening, Sarphatipark feels like a local festival. What I love most is its proximity to so many green spaces like Beatrixpark (p177), vast Amstelpark (p177), and even more vast Amsterdamse Bos (p180).

 EATING IN DE PIJP & ZUID: BEST BRUNCHES MAP P170

Bakers & Roasters:	Little Collins:	Vinnies:	Miri Mary:
Brazilian–Kiwi favourite for banana-nut-bread French toast, Navajo eggs and caipirinhas. *8.30am-3pm Mon-Fri, to 4pm Sat & Sun* €€	Creative dishes include oat-milk panna cotta with rhubarb, or poached eggs with smoked labneh and dukka. Walk-ins only. *9am-4pm* €€	Fabulous all-day brunches spanning blueberry spelt pancakes, coconut granola, spicy shakshuka and mimosas. *7.30am-5pm Mon-Fri, 9am-5pm Sat & Sun* €€	Weekend brunches with an Indian twist like butter chicken eggs Benny or masala cheese omelettes. *5.30-10pm Mon-Thu, 10.30am-3pm & 5.30-10pm Fri-Sun* €€

BEST WATER ACTIVITIES

Beyond Amsterdamse Bos (p180) you'll also find opportunities to hit the water.

Boaty (Map p170) Electric boats carry up to six people; rental includes a map outlining routes (no boat licence needed). Its Amstelkanaal floating jetty is an ideal launching pad before approaching busy city-centre canals. *boaty.nl*

SUP Tropisch (Map p170) By the Amstelkanaal, SUP Tropical hires SUPs, has route options for all levels and organises nighttime trips under the stars. *suptropisch.nl*

SUP Rental Amsterdam (Map p170) Rent stable Red Paddle SUPs (with instruction for beginners) by the Berlagebrug on the Amstel. *amsterdamboothuur.nl*

SUP SUP CLUB (Map p170) Book online to open SUP 2 GO lockers in locations including the Amstel Boathouse. *supsupclub.com*

Study Up on Amsterdam School Architecture

MAP P170

Architectural dawn

Designed by two of the Amsterdam School's founding members, Piet Kramer and Michel de Klerk, social housing complex De Dageraad (meaning 'the dawn') was a game-changer when it was completed in 1922. The architects devised buildings that were not only functional but also artistic, as evident in the wave-like brick façades' rounded edges, flowing balconies, integrated sculptures and wrought-ironwork.

Plans of De Pijp, floor plans, stained glass, sculptures and photos are displayed at its **Museum De Dageraad** (*hetschip. nl; museum adult/child €16.50/5, architectural walks €13.50*), accessed from Burgemeester Tellegenstraat. Museum tickets include a tour of the complex (the 3.30pm tour is in English). Check the agenda for two-hour walking tours of Amsterdam School architecture in the surrounding area.

The organisation also runs the Museum Het Schip (p116) in the 1921 Amsterdam School housing complex in Amsterdam West.

Admire Amsterdam's Century-Old Olympic Stadium

MAP P178

Sporting glory

Built for the 1928 Olympic Games, the elegant **Olympisch Stadion Amsterdam** (*olympischstadion.nl; tour from €12.50*) is a triumph of Amsterdam School architecture, designed by Jan Wils, a protégé of HP Berlage. It has a soaring tower from which the Olympic flame burned for the first time during competition. Other firsts included the world's first-ever parking signs on the inaugural day of Olympics competition, and first evening football match played under lights the following year. The stadium was the home ground of AFC Ajax until the Amsterdam Arena (now the Johan Cruijff ArenA) was built in 1996, when it was restored to again host track-and-field events. Concerts, festivals and other events also take place here; on King's Day, it hosts massive music festival **Kingsland** (*kingslandfestival.nl*). Arrange guided one-hour tours (minimum of five people) in advance.

On Saturdays, the small, friendly neighbourhood market **Stadionpleinmarkt** (*facebook.com/stadionpleinmarkt*) sets up on Stadionplein.

 EATING IN DE PIJP & ZUID: BEST CAFES ———————— MAP P170

SLA: Stylish salad bar with a zero-waste, organic kitchen for 'create-your-own' salads, wraps, bowls, smoothies and kombucha. *11.30am-9pm €*

De Dakduif: Filled baguettes, soups, savoury pies and De Pijp's best cinnamon-crusted apple pie. *hours vary €*

Café My Place: Plant-filled cafe with a sunny terrace, which morphs into an evening cocktail bar. *11am-8pm Wed, Thu & Sun, to 1am Fri & Sat €*

Sea Salt & Chocolate: Backstreet cafe with braided babka, *speculaas*-spiced cheesecake and sea-salt chocolate cake. *10am-10pm Mon-Fri, 11am-10pm Sat & Sun €*

Heineken Experience

Since it began brewing in Amsterdam in 1864, Heineken has become a global juggernaut: upwards of 25 million serves of its pilsner are drunk every day worldwide. Production at its old De Pijp brewery – the company's first built brewery – ceased in 1988 but this grand building along the Singelgracht on Stadhouderskade has been repurposed as the whizz-bang, multisensory Heineken Experience.

Heineken Tours

High-spirited 90-minute self-guided tours start with the company's heritage and the evolution of its distinctive translucent green bottles and red star logo. You'll then see the original gleaming copper vats, and experience brewing from the inside out as you're immersed in the production process via some 360-degree multimedia wizardry. Tours include two tastings.

Upgraded options include the highly worthwhile two-hour Rooftop experience, discovering the former malt attic, checking out innovations like foam infusions and testing experimental brews at the Heineken Studio, and sipping an additional beer overlooking an incredible view of Amsterdam from the terrace.

True Heineken devotees can book a 2½-hour VIP tour with a personal guide, five beers and food pairings.

Canal Cruises

It's also possible to combine a tour with a cruise on the city's waterways. Rock the City tours include a 45-minute canal cruise in a Heineken-bedecked covered boat departing from the canal directly out front. Alternatively, you can book an hour-long Flagship Cruise on a smaller open-topped sloop boat departing near the Rijksmuseum, a 15-minute walk away. Both include an extra two beers, with more sold onboard.

TOP TIPS

● Book tickets with time-slot entry online.

● Check for combination tickets with various other Amsterdam attractions.

● The world's only official brand store, the on-site Heineken Flagship Store, filled with bar gadgets, coasters, T-shirts and more, is accessible even if you don't have a Heineken Experience ticket.

PRACTICALITIES

● Map p170 ● heineken experience.com
● tours from €24.95, with cruise from €39.50, VIP €65 ● 10.30am-7.30pm Sun-Thu, to 9pm Fri & Sat

DISCOVER DE PIJP'S ART & ARTISTRY

Stroll along streets named for painters and precious stones past colourful public artworks in this vibrant and creative neighbourhood.

START	END	LENGTH
Royal Asscher HQ	Wake Me Up When I'm Famous	2km; one hour

Start in De Pijp's Diamantbuurt ('Diamond neighbourhood'), where the 1854-established diamond company retains its 1907-built **1 Royal Asscher HQ** in the castle-like main tower; its former factory now houses luxury apartments. On the residential façades around Dora Tamanaplein and Cullinanplein, look for nine small glass sculptures collectively known as **2 Revisiting the Cullinans** by Sanja Medic (2023).

Trace the Amstel north to Ceintuurbaan 251's 1884 neo-Gothic mansion **3 Huis met de Kabouters**: look up to the elaborately carved wooden gables to see two cheeky lime-green goblin sculptures dressed in red hats and shorts, one holding a red ball and the other reaching to catch it. Further north, short, narrow tree-lined street **4 Hemonylaan** has works of blue-and-white Delftware-style street art by stencil artist Hugo Kaagman covering several walls and an electricity building. Head along Albert Cuypstraat, home to the **5 Albert Cuypmarkt** (p172); on the corner of 1e Sweelinckstraat is a bronze **6 statue of André Hazes**, De Pijp–born *levenslied* (sentimental Dutch-language folk music) singer. Nearby on Gerard Douplein, you'll see **7 Drie Zuilen**, Henk Duijn's 1993 sculpture of three twisted ceramic 'pipes'.

On Frans Halsstraat, **8 Wake Me Up When I'm Famous**, by Jurriaan and Rinus van Hall, is a 2013 street-art mural with the words stencilled in white on a black background and selfie-favourite bench in front.

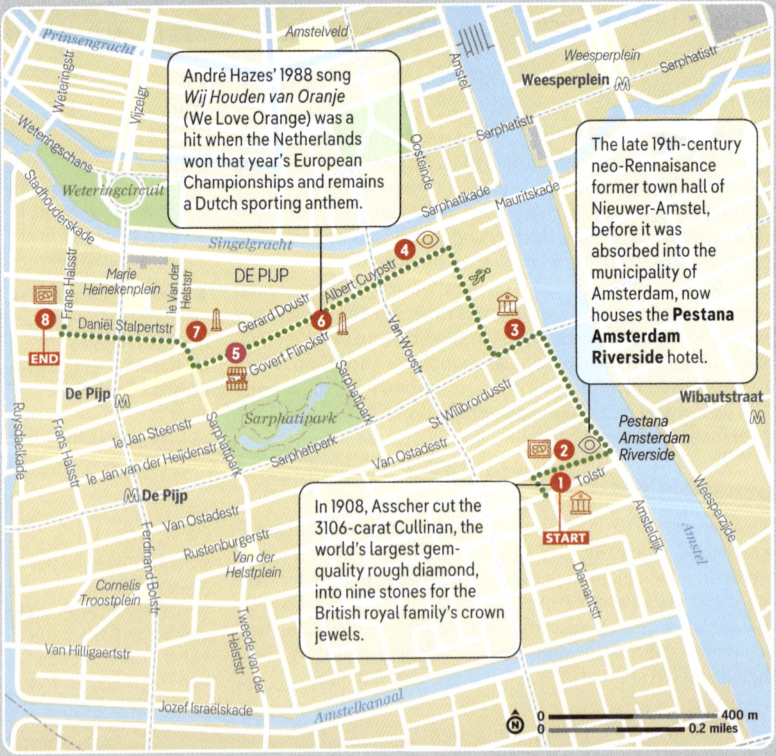

André Hazes' 1988 song *Wij Houden van Oranje* (We Love Orange) was a hit when the Netherlands won that year's European Championships and remains a Dutch sporting anthem.

The late 19th-century neo-Rennaisance former town hall of Nieuwer-Amstel, before it was absorbed into the municipality of Amsterdam, now houses the **Pestana Amsterdam Riverside** hotel.

In 1908, Asscher cut the 3106-carat Cullinan, the world's largest gem-quality rough diamond, into nine stones for the British royal family's crown jewels.

Anticipate the Hartwig Museum

MAP P178

Art in the making

Amsterdam will gain a major contemporary art museum when the **Hartwig Museum** (*hartwigartfoundation.nl*) opens in 2028. Construction is underway at Parnassusweg 220, a site that incorporates one of Zuidas' first buildings – a Brutalist former courthouse designed by architect Ben Loerakker and built between 1972 and 1975 that's now a protected monument. Established by the Hartwig Art Foundation, which presents works in locations citywide, the new museum will present exhibitions that especially spotlight emerging young artists and create art in working artist studios. It will also have an auditorium, a garden, food lab and bistro.

Ahead of its opening, temporary public space **Hartwig Proxy**, nearby at Parnassusweg 213, provides a preview of what's in store, acting as a 'testing ground' for the upcoming museum and an artistic gathering space.

Explore More Parks & Gardens

MAPS P170 & P178

Greenery galore

South of Sarphatipark are extensive parks, gardens and woods. Rose and rhododendron gardens, a glasshouse and orangery grace the **Amstelpark** (*amstelpark.info*), open 7am to 10pm April to September, until 6pm October to March, created for the 1972 flower show Floriade. At its southern edge near 1636 polder-drainage windmill **De Riekermolen** is a statue of Rembrandt sketching it. Amstelpark hosts the travelling artisan food, drink and design-filled **Pure Markt** (*puremarkt. nl*) on the second Sunday of the month from April to October. Festivals include epicurean highlights **Bite of Amsterdam** (*biteofamsterdam.com*) in May; food-truck **Festival Trek** (*festival-trek.nl*) in July; and the **Amsterdam Wine Festival** (*amsterdamwinefestival.nl*) in September.

Amstelpark activities include playgrounds, a city farm, a yew-hedge maze, mini golf (*minigolfamstelpark.nl; from €9*) and the delightful miniature **Amstel Trein** (*Amstel Train; amstel trein.nl; €3.50*), as well as rides for tots such as bumper boats at the **Speeltuin Amstelpark** (*speeltuin-amstelpark.nl; 1/10 tokens €1.30/12*); check individual seasonal opening times online.

Bordered by canals, the 1938-opened **Beatrixpark** (*amster dam.nl; free*), open 24 hours, has meandering paths, flowerbeds, forested areas and a chestnut alley over 17 hectares. Two stone lions guard the Artsenijhof medicinal herb garden.

BEST SHOPS

Elcie (Map p170) Elsbeth Schiphorst makes dresses, tops, jackets and leggings from leftover fabrics at her studio. *elcie.nl*

Mercer (Map p170) Sustainable streetwear and vegan sneakers. *themercerbrand.com*

Maats (Map p170) Cycling clothing and accessories; also organises bike rides. *maats.cc*

De Winkel van Nijntje (Map p170) Dedicated Miffy (Dutch: Nijntje) emporium. *dewinkel vannijntje.nl*

De Kleine Parade (Map p170) Kids and babies clothing, shoes, accessories and toys. *dekleineparade.com*

Love Stories Archive (Map p170) Samples, stock sales and discounted lingerie and swimwear by Marloes Hoedeman. *lovestories intimates.com*

Blond Amsterdam (Map p170) Barbie-pink shop with plates, bowls and mugs featuring whimsical illustrations, with a cafe. *blond-amster dam.com*

 EATING IN DE PIJP & ZUID: BEST TAPAS-STYLE DINING ———— MAP P170

Kaasbar: Classy space with a conveyor belt of 20-plus cloche-covered Dutch cheeses to pair with 40-plus by-the-glass wines. *5-11pm Mon-Thu, 1pm-1am Fri-Sun* €€

GlouGlou: Convivial neighbourhood wine bar with organic wines, and cheese, charcuterie and escargot platters. *3pm-midnight Mon-Fri, 2pm-midnight Sat & Sun* €€

Juno: Open-flame-grilled dishes complement natural wines in the dark-timber interior or under the fairy-light-strung trees. *5pm-midnight Tue-Fri, 1pm-midnight Sat & Sun* €€

Sol el Luna: Tapas and cocktail bar with sharing dishes like *pimientos de padrón,* grilled octopus and jamon iberico. *5-11pm Tue-Fri, noon-11pm Sat & Sun* €€

Henk Sneevlietweg

NIEUW-ZUID

Stadionplein

A10

Sportpark

A4

Amstelveenseweg

A10

Station Zuid WTC

Oude Haagseweg

Het Nieuwe Meer

De Boeletaan

VU

A J Ernststr

Van Boshuizenstr

Amsterdamse Bos

Van Nijenrodeweg

Bosbaan
Bosbaanweg

Amsterdamse Bos

Bos en Vaartlaan

Uilenstede

AMSTELVEEN

Grote Vijver

s108

Royal FloraHolland (6.5km)

Museum JAN (1.3km)

Cobra Museum (1km)

N

0 ——— 1 km
0 ——— 0.5 miles

⭐ HIGHLIGHTS
1 Amsterdamse Bos

● SIGHTS
2 Botanische Tuin Zuidas
3 Cobra Museum
4 De Boswinkel
5 De Ridammerhoeve
6 Hartwig Museum (opening 2028)
7 Hartwig Proxy
8 Information Centre Zuidas-Zuidasdok
9 Museum JAN
10 Olympisch Stadion Amsterdam
11 Royal FloraHolland

● ACTIVITIES
12 De Amsterdamse Manege
13 Kanoverhuur Amsterdamse Bos
14 Klimpark Fun Forest
15 Manege Nieuw Amstelland
16 SUP&Meer

● SLEEPING
17 Hotel & Wellness Zuiver

● EATING
18 Boerderij Meerzicht
19 Het Bosch

● ENTERTAINMENT
20 Bostheater
21 Cinema The Pulse

● SHOPPING
22 Pure Markt – Amsterdamse Bos
23 Stadionpleinmarkt
24 Zuidas Markt

🍴 EATING IN DE PIJP & ZUID: BEST CONTEMPORARY DINING   MAPS P170 & P178

Bisous: French/Zeeland cuisine (eg sole meunière) in a dramatic interior that feels like dining inside a Mondrian painting. *5.30-10pm Mon-Wed, noon-10pm Thu-Sat* €€€

Graham's Kitchen: Chef Graham Mee's menus (no à la carte) feature dishes like waffles with black-pearl caviar or amberjack with tofu brûlée. *6-10.30pm Tue-Sat* €€€

Het Bosch: On the banks of the Nieuwe Meer with a waterside terrace; local vegetables and line-caught seafood. *noon-3pm & 6-9pm Mon-Fri, 6-9pm Sat* €€€

NAZKA: Modern Peruvian fine dining (sea bream and strawberry ceviche or smoked eel with Andes potatoes and paired wines or cocktails). *6-8.30pm Tue-Sat* €€€

THE GUIDE

DE PIJP & ZUID

There's a kids' playground inside a mirrored sculpture, and a paddling pool.

The **Botanische Tuin Zuidas** (*Botanical Garden Zuidas; botanischetuinzuidas.nl; free; daily Apr-Oct, Mon-Fri Nov-Mar*), was created in 1967 for the biology faculty of research university Vrije Universiteit Amsterdam (VU). Some 8000 species and hybrids are planted over the 1-hectare site, including asters, bonsai, shrubs, bamboos and ferns, and the Netherlands' largest collection of cacti and succulents. Don't miss the cafe opening to a serene terrace.

Along this leafy neighbourhood's avenues, the Netherlands' leading sculpture biennale – and largest free art event – **ART ZUID** (*artzuid.nl*) exhibits dozens of works by celebrated sculptors and rising stars between mid-May and mid-September of odd-numbered years, with app-based audio tours and guided tours. Definitely catch it if it's on while you're here.

View Art in Amstelveen

MAP P178

Modern and contemporary masterpieces

Art aficionados will want to venture south to Amstelveen, home to a couple of impressive museums (both closed on Monday; combination tickets for the two cost €25).

The **Cobra Museum** (*cobra-museum.nl; adult/child €20/5*) sits alongside a canal. Dutch architect Wim Quist's light-filled two-storey building is the setting for work from the post-WWII highly expressionist CoBrA movement (named from the city initials where the group's founders lived: Copenhagen, Brussels and Amsterdam). Rotating displays from its 2000-strong collection's boldly coloured, avant-garde paintings, ceramics and statues include many by Karel Appel, the style's most famous practitioner; his 5m-high bronze-cast work *The Fountain* stands outside the main entrance. Temporary exhibitions of modern and contemporary art regularly take place; there's an airy cafe and excellent shop stocking CoBrA graphic arts and books. Connexxion bus 357 runs to the Amstelveen bus station, a two-minute walk from the museum.

Located 1.5km west, **Museum JAN** (*museumjan.nl; adult/child €13.50/7*) has a stunning collection of 20th- and 21st-century sculptural glass art collected by Jan van der Togt under the direction of artist Jan Verschoor, whose bronze and marble sculptures are also on display – the museum is built around Verschoor's house on Amstelveen's Dorpsplein (village square). Beautiful glass is sold at its museum shop.

ZUIDAS

Glinting office blocks tower above Zuidas ('South Axis'), but it's rapidly transforming beyond a business district. Massive infrastructure project Zuidasdok is seeing the A10 Zuid ring-road motorway widened and diverted underground, and train station **Amsterdam Zuid** becoming a major transport hub, with international rail services to Brussels since 2024, and more to destinations including London in the works. Over 1 million sq metres of space is being constructed by 2030. Around half is residential (an additional 7000 homes: 40% social housing, 40% mid-market and 20% high-end), spurring on amenities and recreational facilities, such as the Thursday **Zuidas Markt** (Map p178; *zuidasmarkt.nl*) and the 2025-opening cult, arthouse and mainstream **Cinema The Pulse** (Map p178; *cinemathepulse. eu*). In the World Trade Center Tower 5 central foyer, the **Information Centre Zuidas-Zuidasdok** (Map p178; *zuidas.nl*) has scale models.

FOKKE BAARSSEN/SHUTTERSTOCK

Bloesempark

TOP EXPERIENCE

Amsterdamse Bos

On the city's southwestern edge, this expansive and enchanting English-style forest offers an accessible escape to the countryside. First planted from 1934 to provide employment during the Great Depression, Amsterdamse Bos (Amsterdam Forest) sprawls over 1000 hectares of polder (drained land) now alive with woodland, meadows, lakes and waterways, abundant wildlife and birdlife, activities spanning boating to ziplining, and entertainment venues.

Visitor Facilities

One of Europe's largest city parks (triple the size of New York's Central Park), the forest is vast: stop first by the main entrance on Bosbaanweg (near the intersection of Van Nijenrodeweg and Amstelveenseweg) at the striking curvilinear timber building housing visitor centre **De Boswinkel**. Along with free exhibitions about the forest, it has maps that are helpful for getting your bearings, and sells tickets for 90-minute boat cruises (€10) on Wednesdays and Saturdays from May to September.

Across from De Boswinkel, bike-hire outlet **De Boshalte** (*deboshalte.com; bicycle hire per hour/day from €6/10*), closed

DON'T MISS

De Boswinkel

Boerderij Meerzicht

Klimpark Fun Forest

De Ridammerhoeve

Bostheater

PRACTICALITIES
● Map p178 ● amsterdamsebos.nl ● free ● forest 24 hours; De Boswinkel visitor centre 10am-5pm Wed-Sun

Tuesdays, rents a huge range of wheels for adults and kids; bring ID to leave as a deposit.

Restaurants, cafes and kiosks are dotted throughout the forest. On the northwest side of the Bosbaan (the long lake used for sculling), storybook farmhouse **Boerderij Meerzicht** (*boerderijmeerzicht.nl*), open Wednesday to Sunday, is a favourite for its animals (deer, peacocks and ponies), diggers and climbing frames in its playgrounds, and huge Dutch pancakes.

It's even possible to stay here at rejuvenating spa hotel **Hotel & Wellness Zuiver** (*zuiveramsterdam.nl*) or sleep amid nature at campsites and cabins at **Europarcs Amsterdamse Bos** (*europarcs.com/holiday-parks/het-amsterdamse-bos*).

Forest Adventures

Over 50km of cycling trails thread through the forest, which is also laced with walking trails (routes range from 4km to 9km), and 21.5km of bridleways. There are two horse-riding schools, **De Amsterdamse Manege** (*deamsterdamsemanege.nl*) and **Manege Nieuw Amstelland** (*manegenieuwamstelland.nl*).

The **Klimpark Fun Forest** (*funforest.nl/amsterdam; adult/ child from €32/23*) has 10 different ropes courses and ziplining through the trees.

Water activities include swimming areas at the Grote Vijver ('great pond'), where you'll also find kids' paddling pools and canoe and pedal-boat rental at **Kanoverhuur Amsterdamse Bos** (*kanoverhuur-adam.nl; canoe/pedal boat per hour from €9/15*). On the Nieuwe Meer ('new lake'), **SUP&Meer** (*supen meer.nl; SUP per 90min from €18*) rents SUPs and has lessons. Sports facilities span hockey, tennis, football and cricket.

Amsterdamse Bos' most delightful attraction is working organic goat farm **De Ridammerhoeve** (*geitenboerderij.nl; farm breakfast adult/child €16.80/12.85, cheese-making workshop €69.50, goat yoga €25.95*), closed on Tuesdays year-round, plus Mondays from October to March, where children can feed baby goats with bottles of milk. Its farm shop sells goat's-milk ice cream and other products; there are also regular cheese-making workshops and weekend goat yoga sessions. Next to the farm, there's a diamond-shaped beech-hedge maze and picnic area.

From around mid- to late March, the **Bloesempark** is another idyllic picnic spot when 400 Japanese cherry trees burst into blossom.

Entertainment

During the July to September summer season, the open-air **Bostheater** (*bostheater.nl*) stages everything from concerts and film screenings to Shakespeare and other plays (actors pause for planes to and from nearby Schiphol Airport as they fly overhead). Check the programme and buy tickets online (arrive early for the best seats). Hundreds of events are held in the forest, from artisanal **Pure Markt** (*puremarkt.nl*) to festivals for food, wine, film, EDM, techno, country, folk, blues and roots rock, dragon boat races, canoe sprints and much more; check the calendar at amsterdamsebos.nl/boskalender.

FLORA & FAUNA

Across diverse habitats of this urban wilderness, keep your eyes (and camera) primed to spot rare plants such as wild orchids and meadow flowers; animals from squirrels to frogs, salamanders, grass snakes, and grazing Exmoor ponies and Scottish Highlander cattle that roam freely; and birdlife including marsh harriers, hawks, buntings, buzzards, kingfishers, woodpeckers, reed and Savi's warblers, redshanks and black-tailed godwits.

TOP TIPS

● Cycling is a great way to get to Amsterdamse Bos and then explore the forest once you arrive.

● From 2026, the renewed **Sportas** (*amsterdam. nl/projecten/sportas*) cycling and walking paths directly link Amsterdam's Olympisch Stadion with Amsterdamse Bos and Amstelveen.

● On Sundays from April to October, travel here is aboard a vintage tram run by the Electrische Museumtramlijn Amsterdam (p165).

● Amsterdamse Bos is served by Connexxion buses. Line 357 runs from Elandsgracht via Leidseplein, Museumplein and the Olympisch Stadion; line 257 runs from Haarlemmermeerstation via the Olympisch Stadion; and line 178 runs from Amsterdam Zuid.

UNDERSTAND THE RIVIERENBUURT'S HISTORY

Directly south of De Pijp, discover the historic Rivierenbuurt ('Rivers neighbourhood') on an illuminating stroll through its leafy streets.

START	END	LENGTH
Statue of Anne Frank	Sonora Bar	4km; 2 hours

Begin where Anne Frank lived before the family were forced into hiding; on Merwedeplein, a bronze ❶ **statue of Anne Frank** by Jet Scheep (2005) depicts her holding her packed belongings, looking towards her apartment to which she would never return. Just south, her father Otto bought Anne's diary for her 13th birthday at ❷ **Jimmink**, which still sells books and journals.

Eastwards, a trio of corner-façade sculptures, ❸ **Oogstende boer en Meeuw** *(Harvesting Farmer and Seagulls)* by Willem Coenraad Brouwer (1929), illustrate the Rivierenbuurt before its development from farmland. On the Amstel, Martin Luther Kingpark has a 1.2m-high bronze ❹ **statue of Martin Luther King** by artist Airco Caravan (2020). Southwest, the charming 1887-built ❺ **Mirandapaviljoen** houses the Amstel Boathouse bar-cafe.

On Amsteldijk, the 1929-built Amsterdam School–style polder pumping station ❻ **Gemaalgebouw Stadwijck** was constructed to drain the land for development, and still pumps water up 1.6m into the Amstel today.

Head west along President Kennedylaan; at Europaplein is Femke Schaap's ❼ **Virtual Fountains** (2022): representing the reservoir below Rivierenbuurt where excess rainwater is collected, the blocks are projected with flowing water on dimly lit days and after dark. Finish at the 24th-floor ❽ **Sonora Bar**, with views over the Rivierenbuurt, RAI convention centre and Zuidas.

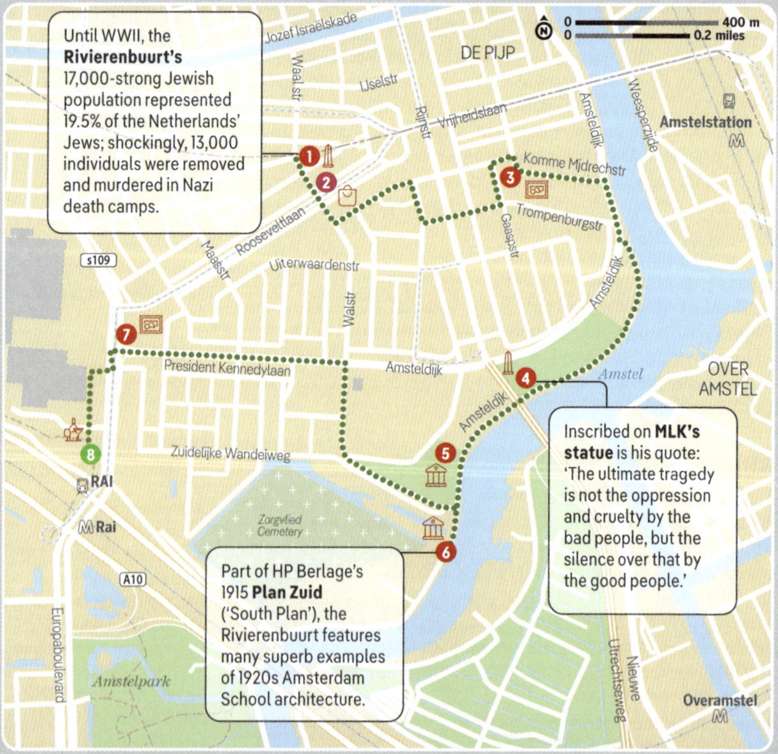
Until WWII, the **Rivierenbuurt's** 17,000-strong Jewish population represented 19.5% of the Netherlands' Jews; shockingly, 13,000 individuals were removed and murdered in Nazi death camps.
Inscribed on **MLK's statue** is his quote: 'The ultimate tragedy is not the oppression and cruelty by the bad people, but the silence over that by the good people.'
Part of HP Berlage's 1915 **Plan Zuid** ('South Plan'), the Rivierenbuurt features many superb examples of 1920s Amsterdam School architecture.
0 400 m
0 0.2 miles
DE PIJP
Jozef Israëlskade
Waalstr
IJselstr
Rijnstr
Vrijheidslaan
Amsteldijk
Weesperzijde
Amstelstation
Komme Mjdrechstr
Trompenburgstr
Gaasstr
Roosveltlaan
Maasstr
Uiterwaardenstr
Walstr
s109
President Kennedylaan
Amstel
OVER AMSTEL
Zuidelijke Wandelweg
RAI
Rai
Zorgvlied Cemetery
A10
Europaboulevard
Amstelpark
Utrechtseweg
Nieuwe
Overamstel

Marvel at the World's Largest Floriculture Marketplace

MAP P178

Waltz of the flowers

Southwest of Amsterdamse Bos near Schiphol Airport in Aalsmeer, international growers' cooperative **Royal FloraHolland** *(royalfloraholland.com; adult/child €12/9.50)* handles more than 100,000 transactions of plants and flowers on its digital platform (5.3 billion euros in sales in 2024), accounting for 90% of domestic and 60% of global trade. At this massive facility the size of 250 football fields, millions of colourful blooms on thousands of flower carts are sorted by barcode and travel via monorail to be shipped across the world.

Early risers can check out the extraordinary choreography on self-guided tours that give you a bird's-eye view of the warehouse floor from an elevated walkway, an insight into Royal FloraHolland's history spanning more than a century (including a peek at the former auction room) and sustainability (from optimised logistics to eco-friendly packaging), and the opportunity to pick up floral-themed souvenirs at its shop. It's open from 7am to 11am Monday, Tuesday, Wednesday and Friday, to 9am on Thursday; the earlier you arrive the more action you'll see. Take Connexxion bus 357 to Aalsmeer's Royal FloraHolland stop.

Create Content in an Immersive Social Media Setting

MAP P170

Instagram fantasyland

Across Europaplein from the **RAI** *(rai.nl)* convention centre, the **Upside Down** *(the-upsidedown.com; adult/child from €20.95/14.95)* is a whirl of optical illusions (upside-down rooms, larger-than-life art) and vivid immersive experiences (a walk-in dress-up closet, silent disco and LED-light ball pit), with over 25 photogenic spaces all designed to light up your IG or TikTok. Book a time-slot online, charge your phone and plan on around 90 minutes here (scan your ticket's QR code to download in-room camera photos for free). There are various combination tickets with other attractions.

MOKUM MOTIFS

Amsterdam's Jewish inhabitants gave Amsterdam its enduring nickname, Mokum – the Yiddish word for 'town' or 'safe haven' (derived from the Hebrew *makom*, meaning 'place'). Amsterdam natives are known as Mokummers.

The city's motto, *Heldhaftig, Vastberaden, Barmhartig* (Valiant, Steadfast, Compassionate), presented by Queen Wilhelmina in 1947, commemorates its citizens' protests against the persecution of Jews in WWII. It's emblazoned on the coat of arms, whose escutcheon (heraldic shield) is the basis of Amsterdam's flag: two horizontal red stripes and a central black stripe with three diagonal white St Andrew's crosses. Appearing on municipal buildings and merchandising all over the city, this symbol 'XXX' is believed to have originated back in 1505 when Amsterdam was a fishing town (St Andrew is the patron saint of fishers).

DRINKING IN DE PIJP & ZUID: BEST BARS

MAP P170

Bar Mokum: Ode to Mokum (Amsterdam's nickname), mixing cocktails made with local spirits and liqueurs. *5pm-1am Mon-Thu, to 2am Fri & Sat*	**Brouwerij Troost:** Watch beer being brewed at this original location of the organic craft brewery. *4pm-1am Mon-Thu, 4pm-2am Fri, noon-2am Sat, noon-11pm Sun*	**Café Sarphaat:** Perennial local favourite opposite Sarphatipark with a lovely old bar and outdoor terrace that's heated in chilly weather. *9am-1am Sun-Thu, to 3am Fri & Sat*	**Barça:** On bar-filled Marie Heinekenplein, with a 'Barcelona in Amsterdam' theme, Spanish wines and sparkling cava. *noon-midnight Sun-Tue, to 1am Wed & Thu, to 3am Fri & Sat*

Researched by Barbara Woolsey

OOSTERPARK & EAST OF THE AMSTEL

A LUSH, AIRY SIDE OF AMSTERDAM

Is this even Amsterdam? Spacious and airy, Oost (East) is worth exploring – if only to catch your breath. Greenery, rooftop bars and residential vibes abound.

The fascinating Wereldmuseum, a national museum confronting colonialism head-on, is a good reason to come to Amsterdam-Oost (East). Once you're here, the neighbourhood lures you into lingering: it's multicultural, expansive and lush, and there's much to enjoy. Oost retains a feeling of its past as countryside retreats and wetlands; grand, 19th-century buildings and wide boulevards are throwbacks to its earliest urban days. Today's Oost is one of Amsterdam's most rapidly gentrifying areas. Scout out Amsterdam's trendiest bars and set-menu restaurants – from rooftop bars with stupendous views to a park-hidden gin distillery. Surprises pop up between canals, green lungs and local life.

TOP TIP

Oosterpark plays host to a number of lively events during the summer and it's a great place to get a feel for the multicultural makeup of the neighbourhood. A highlight is the global music performed on an open-air stage as part of the weeklong Roots Festival (p191).

Distilleerderij 't Nieuwe Diep (p187), Flevopark

See p242 for places to stay in Oosterpark and east of the Amstel.

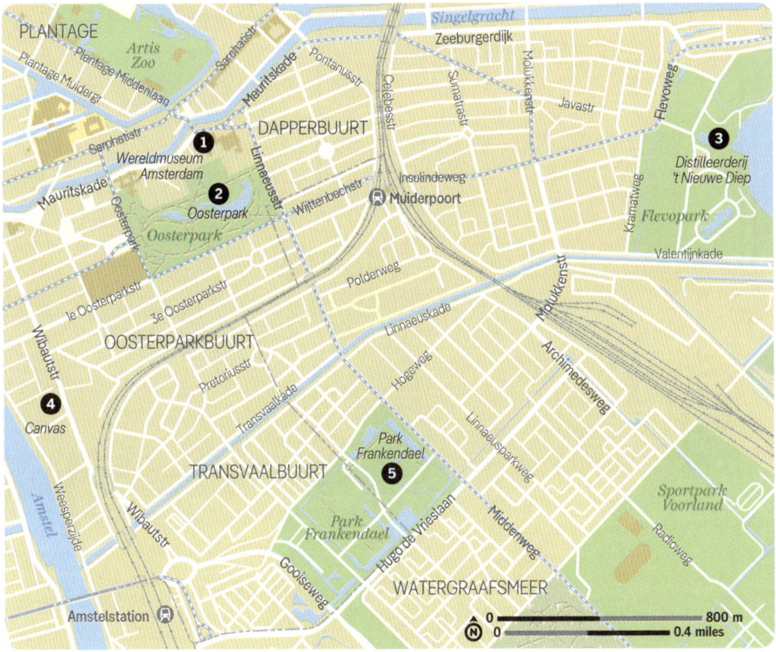

PLANTAGE

Artis Zoo

Plantage Middenlaan

Plantage Muidergr

Sarphatistr

Mauritskade

Mauritskade

Oosterpark

1 Wereldmuseum Amsterdam

2 Oosterpark

Oosterpark

DAPPERBUURT

Linnaeusstr

Wijttenbachstr

Insulindeweg

Muiderpoort

Singelgracht

Zeeburgerdijk

Pontanusstr

Celebesstr

Sumatrastr

Molukkenstr

Javastr

Flevoweg

3 Distilleerderij 't Nieuwe Diep

Kramatweg

Flevopark

Valentijnkade

1e Oosterparkstr

3e Oosterparkstr

OOSTERPARKBUURT

Pretoriusstr

Polderweg

Linnaeuskade

Hogeweg

Molukkenstr

Archimedesweg

4 Canvas

Wibautstr

Transvaalkade

Linnaeusparkweg

TRANSVAALBUURT

Park Frankendael

5

Wibautstr

Park Frankendael

Hugo de Vrieslaan

Middenweg

Sportpark Voorland

Radioweg

Amstel

Weesperzijde

Gooiseweg

WATERGRAAFSMEER

Amstelstation

0 | 800 m
0 | 0.4 miles
N

⭐ Highlights

① Wereldmuseum Amsterdam
Visit the *Our Colonial Inheritance* exhibition, which challenges Amsterdam's past. **p188**

② Oosterpark
Relax with the locals, seek out public art and watch wild parakeets and herons in this gorgeous English-style park. **p190**

③ Distilleerderij 't Nieuwe Diep
Sample the gins at this lakeside distillery hidden in lush Flevopark. **p187**

④ Canvas
Clink glasses at Amsterdam's coolest rooftop bar in Volkshotel. **p187**

◀ **⑤ Park Frankendael**
Stroll gardens full of serene spots: a market, mansion and sustainable restaurant, and more. **p194**

🚶 Getting Around

Tram
Though it feels suburban, you can reach Oost in only 15 minutes on tram 14 from Centraal Station (departing every nine minutes). Get off at Alexanderplein.

Walking
From Alexanderplein, you can walk to the Wereldmuseum, Oosterpark and find somewhere to eat along Linnaeusstraat.

Cycling
Oost is well serviced by tram lines but they aren't convenient. With two wheels, explore the area easily on your own schedule.

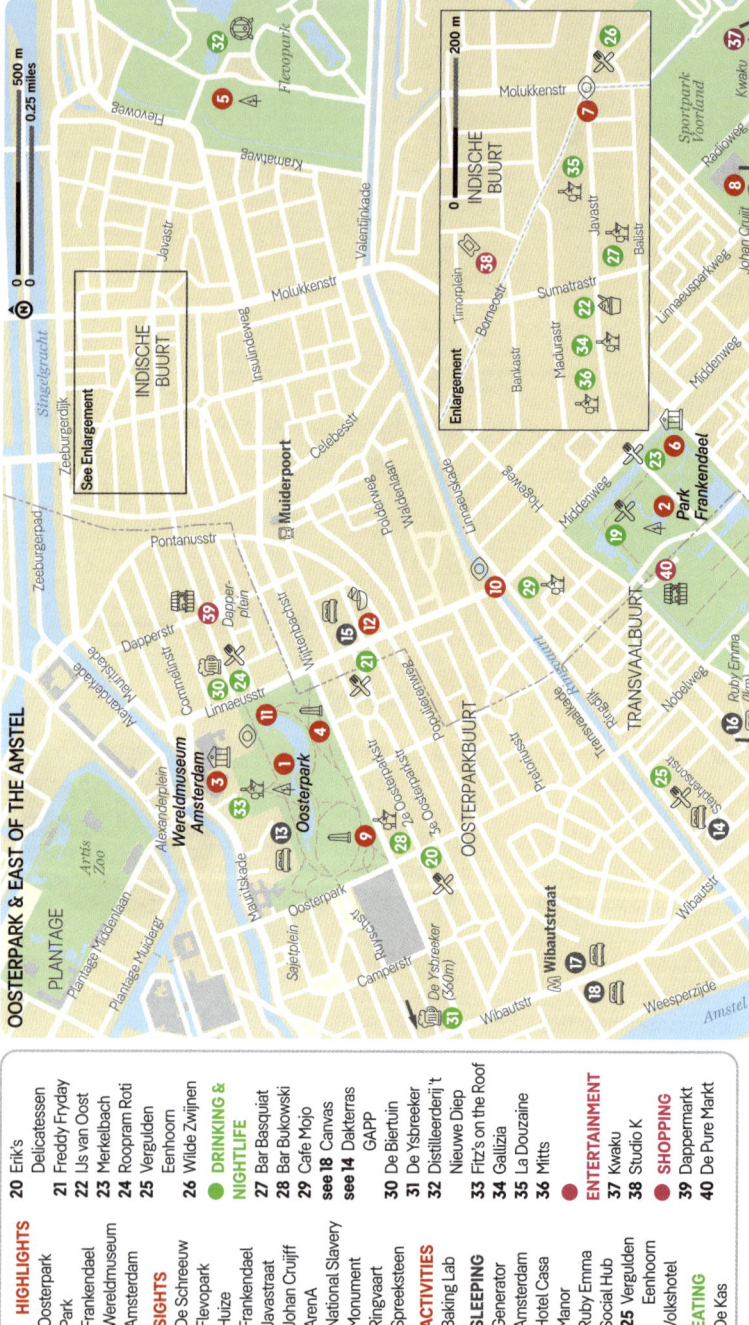

OOSTERPARK & EAST OF THE AMSTEL

See Enlargement

Enlargement

HIGHLIGHTS
1 Oosterpark
2 Park
  Frankendael
3 Wereldmuseum
  Amsterdam

SIGHTS
4 De Schreeuw
5 Flevopark
6 Huize
  Frankendael
7 Javastraat
8 Johan Cruijff
  ArenA
9 National Slavery
  Monument
10 Ringvaart
11 Spreeksteen

ACTIVITIES
12 Baking Lab

SLEEPING
13 Generator
  Amsterdam
14 Hotel Casa
15 Manor
16 Ruby Emma
17 Social Hub
  see 25 Vergulden
  Eenhoorn
18 Volkshotel

EATING
19 De Kas

20 Erik's
  Delicatessen
21 Freddy Fryday
22 IJs van Oost
23 Merkelbach
24 Roopram Roti
25 Vergulden
  Eenhoorn
26 Wilde Zwijnen

DRINKING &
NIGHTLIFE
27 Bar Basquiat
28 Bar Bukowski
29 Cafe Mojo
  see 18 Canvas
  see 14 Dakterras
  GAPP
30 De Biertuin
31 De Ysbreeker
32 Distilleerderij 't
  Nieuwe Diep
33 Fitz's on the Roof
34 Gallizia
35 La Douzaine
36 Mitts

ENTERTAINMENT
37 Kwaku
38 Studio K

SHOPPING
39 Dappermarkt
40 De Pure Markt

186

Discover a Park's Hidden Distillery

Rustic cottage

With a set of wheels, **Flevopark** *(24hr)*, about a 10-minute cycle from the Wereldmuseum, is worth exploring. Formerly a Jewish cemetery (the gravesites were relocated to a larger cemetery), Flevopark was bought by the city of Amsterdam in 1956 and turned into a park. It has a wilder, more rambling atmosphere than Amsterdam's more central green spaces – and it certainly feels more quiet and lonesome than its eastern counterparts, Oosterpark and Park Frankendael.

The main reason to come to Flevopark is to visit the gin distillery squirrelled away in its leafy foliage. Looking like a gingerbread house tucked onto the side of a pond, **Distilleerderij 't Nieuwe Diep** *(nwediep.nl; 3-8pm Tue-Fri, from 1pm Sat & Sun)* keeps the tradition of quaint Oost countryside retreats alive.

Appearing out of the woods, the Hansel and Gretel–esque cottage, an old pumping station, is a distillery making around 100 small-batch *jenevers* (Dutch gins), herbal bitters, liqueurs and fruit distillates from organic ingredients according to age-old Dutch recipes. Relax on the waterside terrace; catch the aroma of fresh fruit trees from the adjacent orchard as the wind rolls through.

Relax at Amsterdam's Best Rooftop Bar

Hot tub, anyone?

At the modern, trendy Volkshotel (p242), zoom up to the rooftop **Canvas** *(volkshotel.nl; 7am-1am Mon-Fri, 8am-3am Sat, to 1am Sun)* for some of the most splendid views Amsterdam has to offer – either through the restaurant-bar's large windows or perched upon a cosy open terrace. DJs spin on Friday and Saturday nights year-round. On summer evenings, there are sometimes open-air cinema screenings, and on Sunday afternoons non-guests can go for a dip in one of the rooftop hot tubs *(noon-6pm; first come, first served)*.

Stroll the Dappermarkt

Multicultural market

The untouristy **Dappermarkt** *(dappermarkt.nl; 10am-5pm Mon-Sat)* is a swirl of local life with around 250 stalls turning Dapperstraat into a bustling pedestrian theatre.

Continued on p192

AMSTERDAM-OOST'S EVENTFUL PAST

Today, stately boulevards and elegant architecture with candy-striped awnings are firm reminders of Oost's 1921 annexation into Amsterdam proper. Amsterdam's expansion eastward from the 19th century reflected the pressures of city industrialisation and population growth, as newly redeveloped neighbourhoods – once country estates for wealthy city folks – sprouted a wave of modest housing blocks catering to the middle class.

In the 20th century, migration reshaped Oost into one of the city's most multicultural enclaves. Communities from Suriname, Türkiye and Morocco saw new cultural expressions and cuisines become part of Oost's working-class fabric. Today, hangovers of a countryside past – meadows and marshland – intermingle with lush, residential canals and gritty (and quickly gentrifying) metropolitan streets.

🍸 DRINKING ON JAVASTRAAT: OUR PICKS

Bar Basquiat: Outside tables and a lively buzz. Local beers, well-made cocktails and excellent Indonesian street food. *11am-1am Mon-Thu, to 2am Fri & Sat, to 11pm Sun*

La Douzaine: Oysters and bubbles in elegant surrounds. Sip champers (or a *pet-nat*) on the outdoor barrel-table and take in the action. *hours vary*

Gallizia: Italian bar-resto for a dreamy antipasti adventure (bruschetta with toppings) and a long wine list. *5pm-midnight Wed & Thu, 4pm-1am Fri & Sat, to midnight Sun*

Mitts: Modern evening joint for twists on classic cocktails (rose margaritas, cardamom espresso martinis) and mezze share plates. *5-11pm Sun-Thu, to midnight Fri & Sat*

WIRESTOCK COLLECTION/SHUTTERSTOCK

Garden setting at the Wereldmuseum

Wereldmuseum

The Dutch slave trade, understanding cultural appropriation, and returning stolen artefacts to Indonesia: at the Wereldmuseum Amsterdam, themes around race, ethnicity and identity are explored from multiple perspectives. These exhibits are part of the ethnographic museum's greater vision to examine and undo colonial practices of its past. It's the perfect time to see how the museum is leading the future.

An Existential Reckoning

DON'T MISS

Things That Matter

Our Colonial Inheritance

Digital Names Monument

Temporary exhibitions

Neo-Renaissance architecture

Gift shop

In 2023, the Tropenmuseum (Royal Tropics Museum), one of Europe's leading ethnographic museums, changed its name – a symbolic break from over 150 years' of tradition.

Today, the Wereldmuseum, like many European museums that acquired collections through exploitation of power, is aiming for a better future. A sweeping decolonising mission is seeing the museum confront how its colonial past might still be shaping modern institutional practices; from rethinking how objects are displayed to whether they should be repatriated (returned), and, overall, how history can become more inclusive.

Deeply immersive, modern multimedia exhibitions are staged within the museum's grand neo-Renaissance architecture.

PRACTICALITIES

● amsterdam.wereldmuseum.nl ● adult/child €18/7.50 ● 10am-5pm Tue-Sat

Spiral staircases, cathedral-like arcaded galleries and intricate detailing are testaments to the museum's past; meanwhile, upper balconies wrapping around the atrium provide all-encompassing perspectives echoing an open, transparent future.

Koloniaal Museum

The Wereldmuseum's origins go back to 1871 when it was established as the Koloniaal Museum (Colonial Museum). Like many 19th-century European museums, the museum's collections grew out of colonial expansion and scientific research. A menagerie of possessions from colonised lands and peoples were displayed as symbols of Dutch colonial wealth. After the Dutch colonial empire ended, the institution became the Royal Tropics Museum in 1950, shifting its focus to foreign 'tropical' and not-so-tropical regions from Africa to the Middle East and beyond.

Things That Matter

The 2018-installed *Things That Matter* permanent exhibition showcases how the Wereldmuseum aims to explore global cultures, histories and identities today. The museum rebels against the standard museum experience by shifting the focus of exhibitions from inanimate objects to human storytellers. The Wereldmuseum also emphasises interactive experiences through touchable displays, games and even augmented reality.

On the ground floor, *Things That Matter* contrasts the atrium's old-world elegance with brightly lit, modern displays. The exhibition's 10 pavilions each explore a universal cultural theme such as language, belief, climate and activism. Stepping inside the custom-built structure drops you into thematic 'worlds', each honing in on a different question: 'When do you feel at home?' (belonging and identity) and 'When is culture yours?' (exploring cultural appropriation and cultural ownership), as examples. The museum's human-centred approach relies heavily on audio-visual content to bring discussions to life, mixing personal interviews with short documentary-style videos – even podcast clips and social media threads.

Our Colonial Inheritance

The exhibition *Our Colonial Inheritance* is a profound, comprehensive inspection of Dutch colonial history. Spanning 1200 sq metres, the exhibition delves into colonialism through wide-ranging access points ranging from chilling (blueprints for maximising the number of bodies on slave trading ports) to artistic (Susan Stockwell's *Territory Dress*, intricately folding Dutch colonial maps into a period frock).

Through textual displays, the museum also outlines its decolonising project, including principles and processes on returning cultural objects to their places of provenance (p266). Among the most moving is the **Digital Names Monument**, inscribed with the names of nearly 200,000 individuals who were enslaved during the colonial period in Suriname, Curaçao and Indonesia.

SHIFTING PARADIGMS

The Wereldmuseum Amsterdam's mission is a collaborative effort with three other national museums (Leiden's Museum Volkenkunde, Berg en Dal's Afrika Museum and the Wereldmuseum Rotterdam), which are all now a Wereldmuseum ('World Museum').

Each institution maintains its original collection and acts independently within the greater shared vision to 'explore what it means to be human, what our connection is with the world around us and how we relate to each other'.

TOP TIPS

● Plan at least half of your day here to see everything.

● Temporary exhibitions are included in the admission price and always excellent.

● Dark windows make the museum more immersive but disconnected from the outside world; seek out open air after your visit at Oosterpark (p190).

● The Wereldmuseum is located in Amsterdam's most multicultural neighbourhood; on the other side of the Linnaeusstraat boulevard, you'll find Surinamese cuisine at Roopram Roti (p193) and geography-spanning street foods at the Dappermarkt (p187).

FRANK CORNELISSEN/SHUTTERSTOCK

Central pond and fountain

TOP EXPERIENCE

Oosterpark

English-style gardens meet marshy flora and tropical fauna: the urban nature oasis of Oosterpark is as eclectic as the Oost locals who find relaxation here. Don't let her well-groomed flower beds fool you – from whistling parakeets to tango practice, Oosterpark also rocks a wild streak. It's a miracle she stays under most visitors' radars.

DON'T MISS

English garden–style landscaping

Walking paths

Central pond & fountain

Picnicking

Anti-colonial monuments

Tango nights

Children's playground

First things first – you can't come to Oosterpark without packing something to eat. Oost abounds with excellent snackshops and delicatessens; there's a wide range of budget-friendly cuisines reflecting the neighbourhood's working-class, immigrant roots.

Do your due diligence and get a smorgasbord together. Erik's Delicatessen (p193) is perfect for gourmet feasting on cheeses, charcuterie, fresh bread, tapenades – you can even grab a nice bottle of wine.

Baking Lab (p196) serves Oost's best pastries by far, or go for the 'refined junk food' at Freddy Fryday's (p193), where fries are piled high with pulled chicken, pepperoni and homemade sauces.

PRACTICALITIES

● amsterdam.nl ● free ● 24hr

Urban Oasis

The minute you step off Oost's bustling main boulevard, Lineausstrat, and into Oosterpark's leafy shade, modern city life instantly melts away. The pleasure park has been easing the pressures of Amsterdam hustle since 1891.

Over a century later, Oosterpark still cultivates nostalgia and appreciation for the simpler things in life. The park maintains an elegant, rambling feel across paths that meander around flower beds, chestnut trees and tranquil ponds. A noble fountain presiding over the central pond and cutesy wooden bridges are further giveaways of how the park's architect was inspired by the English countryside.

Once part of a polder (low-lying drained land), the park is a place where wild nature still mucks about. Slightly uneven terrain and marshy patches pop up on the manicured landscapes. It is even home to wild parakeets and you can usually see herons prancing around in the water.

Multicultural Monuments

For decades, the park has been a meeting ground for dynamic, diverse communities. People-watching here reveals the Oost's multicultural makeup, and rising gentrification too.

On the south side, look for two monuments revealing local history. The **National Slavery Monument** commemorates the abolition of slavery in the Dutch colonies in 1863. Surinamese sculptor Erwin de Vries was commissioned to create this monument depicting both the oppression of slaves and hope for the future; the sculpture is an enduring tribute to the Oost's large Surinamese population.

The other, **De Schreeuw**, is a metal profile shouting into the sky, celebrating free speech and, more specifically, the late Dutch filmmaker Theo van Gogh (the great-grandson of Vincent's brother Theo). A wavy profile shouting into the sky, this tall stainless-steel sculpture in the Oosterpark honours free speech.

Another (living) monument to Van Gogh is the **Spreeksteen**, a rock podium marking a 'speakers' corner' established in 2005. Organised debates occur here and people come to voice their opinion on all sorts of topics.

REMEMBERING THEO VAN GOGH

The outspoken Dutch filmmaker Theo van Gogh met an untimely end outside of Oosterpark. While cycling along Linnaeusstraat from his Oost residence, Van Gogh was shot multiple times by a Dutch-Moroccan Islamist extremist. His murderer attempted to decapitate him and left a note pinned to his body with a knife.

The killing shocked the Netherlands, sparking intense debates about freedom of speech and, in Oosterpark, memorials in his honour.

TOP TIPS

● Tango sessions take place on alternate summer Sundays in the wrought-iron bandstand. Check the website tangoalma.nl for timings.

● Families will enjoy the playground (with a summer wading pool) on the park's north side.

● Oosterpark plays host to a number of lively events during the summer. One highlight is the free global-music performances held on an open-air stage as part of the weeklong **Roots Festival** (amsterdamroots. nl), usually held in late June to early July.

● On the southern edge of Oosterpark, dive bar **Bar Bukowski** is the perfect place to escape when rain sets in.

WHY I LOVE AMSTERDAM-OOST

Barbara Woolsey,
Lonely Planet writer

It's astonishing how delightfully untouristy Amsterdam-Oost is despite being easily reached from downtown. Just a 15-minute tram ride from Centraal to Amsterdam-Oost, and the landscape changes to uncrowded canals, wide boulevards and long, leafy stretches. Head just a bit deeper – around Park Frankendael, or following the canal, and you'll have to *ask* for English restaurant menus. *Gasp.* For a popular destination where overtourism challenges the fun of residents and travellers alike, Oost's laid-back vibes are a welcome breeze. Come here for the best afternoon the capital has to offer: cycling and strolling through green parks with a little bar and *café*-hopping.

DUTCHMEN PHOTOGRAPHY/SHUTTERSTOCK

Dappermarkt (p187)

Continued from p187

Dappermarkt reflects the Oost's diverse immigrant population, with a mixed bag of local shoppers milling about. Vendors sell foods (apricots and other piled-high dried fruit, olives, fish, Turkish kebabs) and goods from costume jewellery to cheap clothes, toys (these days, lots of Lafufus and other knockoff goods) and electronics all along the street. Knickers and bras for sale flap in the breeze, women in headscarves do their daily shopping, and you can feast on fried fish and *gambas* (prawns) served with tiny mayo troughs. As the day progresses, Dappermarkt gets a little dumpy as pigeons and seagulls rummage into vendors' trash. Come for a quick snack and a little atmosphere (preferably in the morning).

Uncover Javastraat's Hotspots

Residential strip

Cutting a swath directly through densely housed neighbourhoods – between the leafy green expanses of Oosterpark (p190) and Flevopark (p187) – the lively main strip of Oost, **Javastraat**, a fantastic mix of multicultural shops and food stands,

Try a martini with house-crafted vermouth and leftover Champagne

 DRINKING IN OOST: BEST OUTDOOR TERRACES

Dakterras GAPP: On Hotel Casa's rooftop terrace, sip creative cocktails among an aromatic herb garden. *noon-10pm Fri & Sat, 9am-5pm Sun*

De Biertuin: Covered terrace and heaters for chillier weather, plus a lengthy beer list and pub grub. *3pm-1am Mon-Thu, to 2am Fri, noon-2am Sat, to 1am Sun*

Cafe Mojo: Lovely open-fronted bar right by the canal. Superb terrace perfect for summer drinks. *noon-midnight Mon-Wed, to 1am Thu, to 3am Fri, to 2am Sat, 11am-11pm Sun*

Fitz's on the Roof: Umbrella-shaded, 4th-floor rooftop terrace overlooking Oosterpark. *5pm-midnight Sun-Thu, 4pm-1am Fri & Sat*

reflects the area's melting-pot makeup of migrant (mostly Moroccan, Surinamese and Turkish) enclaves.

Take a walk along Javastraat and you'll spot everything from roti shops and Turkish bakeries to kebab stands and African grocers; it's a great spot for a cheap, round-the-world snack tour. Gastronomy and boutiques have sprouted up along the street and around it, too. It's become one of the best streets for proper bar-hopping with a cosy, less-raucous atmosphere.

Picnic on Ringvaart

Charming canal

Winding through Amsterdam-Oost, the Lisserdijk is a lasting legacy of Watergraafsmeer's wet, marshy former life. When the polder was drained in 1629 to make way for farmland and country estates, the **Ringvaart** (literally, 'ring canal') and a ring dyke were constructed to hold back surrounding water. Today, the Ringvaart, flowing from the Amstel to Flevopark (p187), retains a wild feel with lush grassy areas overlooking reed banks and birdlife. The canal is the perfect spot for a picnic – do like Oost locals and pick up snacks along Linnaeusstraat or (the area around Dappermarkt and Javastraat) and venture out.

Dine in a Historic Farmhouse

Countryside vibes

Follow the Ringvaart canal until the scenery becomes concrete pavement, canal promenades and the odd cyclist. Once you've given up hope on finding anywhere to eat at all, one of the best restaurants in Amsterdam-Oost pops up inside a cowshed.

The **Vergulden Eenhoorn** (*Gilded Unicorn; verguldeneen hoorn.nl; 10am-midnight*) is a true hidden treasure. The dining establishment's official address is on Ringdijk, but you'll find the real entrance opposite on Stephensonstraat.

In a beautifully restored, 1702-built farmhouse, relax in a lounger on the charming lawn or a summer terrace nestled between flower beds and potted plants. A rustic seasonal menu spans dishes like whole grilled chicken and steak with *frites*; plus plentiful craft beers and homemade lemonades. In the winter, leather sofas and an indoor fireplace stir up *gezellig* (cosy) feelings. Catering to a very local crowd, menus are only in Dutch – how's that for authentic in Amsterdam?

MULTICULTURAL FESTIVAL

Held on summer weekends, typically from mid-July to early August, the massive food-and-football fair **Kwaku** *(kwakufestival.nl)* is a prime reason to head to the southern part of Amsterdam-Oost (Zuidoost).

What started in 1975 as a small football tournament is now the Netherlands' largest multicultural festival, boasting 300,000 participants every year. Come for spicy Surinamese cuisine and cocktail stalls, performances from Afro-Caribbean singers and bands and more.

Kwaku is held in Nelson Mandelapark, renamed in 2014 from Bijlmerpark, shortly after the South African leader's passing (Mandela visited Amsterdam, once a vocal hub for anti-apartheid activism, multiple times).

The festival's name, 'Kwaku', comes from a statue commemorating the abolition of slavery in Suriname's capital, Paramaribo.

 EATING IN OOST: PERFECT PARK SNACKS

Erik's Delicatessen: Put together an Oosterpark picnic with cheeses, charcuterie, bread, tapenades, olives, salads and preserves. *8am-6pm* €

Freddy Fryday: Homemade fries with toppings: pulled pork, parmesan truffle or cheesy mushroom, plus 14 sauces. *noon-10pm Wed-Sat, from 1pm Sun, from 2pm Mon & Tue* €

Roopram Roti: Spot this simple canteen-style Surinamese cafe by the queue. Flaky lamb roti 'extra' (with egg) and *barra* (lentil doughnut) are winners. *2-9pm Tue-Sun* €

IJs van Oost: This popular shop makes its own ice cream in tantalising flavours from *stroopwafel* to forest berries with chocolate. *1-8pm Mon-Thu, from noon Sat & Sun* €

De Kas

TOP EXPERIENCE

Park Frankendael

Sprawling over 7 hectares, the lovely, landscaped scenery of Park Frankendael is peppered with surprises. Watery features are a reminder of the park's marshland origins; while a stately mansion and gardens hark back to the land's former life as a country estate. A stork's nest, organic market and sustainable restaurant are just a few of the park's most wild and whimsical wonders.

DON'T MISS

- Frankendael House
- De Kas
- De Pure Markt
- Stork's nest
- Marshy nature
- Walking paths
- Public benches & scenery

Thriving Wetlands

Amsterdam's urban canal expansion never left much room for backyard greenery. Enter the polder area of Watergraafsmeer; drained in 1629, the reclaimed wetlands made way for landscaped country estates, farmlands and pleasure gardens. Today, Oost's last surviving country estate *(buitenplaats)* is Park Frankendael.

Once a summer retreat for wealthy city folks (including modern science founding father Christiaan Huygens), Watergraafsmeer kept up its rural aesthetic until it was officially annexed in 1921 and became part of Amsterdam-Oost.

PRACTICALITIES
- amsterdam.nl ● free ● 7am-10pm May-Oct, to 6pm Oct-May

Along the park's walking path, plentiful watery features recollect when Watergraafsmeer was more marsh and meadows than metropolis. Strolling over decorative bridges, you'll see plenty of springy reed beds emerging from shallow, muddy banks. Centuries after the lake's draining, ecological landscaping is returning fertile wetlands back to life.

Park Wildlife

Waterbirds, frogs and endless insects are among the wildlife calling Park Frankendael's ponds and marshy areas home. From the children's playground area, look for an old chimney topped with a spindly pile of twigs: a storks' nest. It was placed here as part of an Amsterdam-wide conservation effort encouraging stork breeding, and young storks have been successfully raised here over the years. You'll notice that many of the benches are adorned with little storks in honour of the migratory birds.

Modern Art & Top Gastronomy

The elegant, restored Louis XIV–style mansion **Huize Frankendael** (*Frankendael House; huizefrankendael.nl; free; hours vary*) is Amsterdam's last remaining country estate – one out of 40 that once ruled the Frankendael roost. The building's refined, restored interiors include drippy chandeliers and classical portraiture; they play home to contemporary art exhibitions and other cultural events.

Meanwhile, visit the elegant restaurant **Merkelbach** (*9am-6pm*) for lunch in Frankendael House's former coach house. Its terrace is perfect for summer alfresco dining overlooking Frankendael's formal gardens. A small but stellar lunch menu spans Jerusalem artichoke and cockles, *panzanella* (Tuscan tomato and bread salad) with burrata cheese, and pasta embellished with unusual ingredients such as pointed cabbage and celeriac.

On the opposite end of Park Frankendael lies one more restaurant – and it is one of Amsterdam's finest. In a stately 1926 greenhouses, **De Kas** (*noon-4pm & 6pm-midnight Mon-Sat*) has an organic attitude to match its chic glass setting. It grows most of its own produce right here and the result is incredibly pure flavours and innovative combinations. The daily menus (three, four or five courses at lunch, five or six at dinner) are based on whatever has been freshly harvested. In the outdoor garden, directly behind the greenhouse, you might see kitchen staff throughout the day, picking everything from fresh herbs to edible flowers for the rotating seasonal menu. A tour of the restaurant's greenhouse is included in the dining experience.

STORK SEASON

In Park Frankendael, you can usually see the storks *(ooievaars)* during their breeding season (March to July). Early mornings or late afternoons are often when the birds are most active in such nests, for example, feeding or building. Fledging season typically goes from June to July. After breeding season (around August), most storks migrate south to warmer climes.

TOP TIPS

● Frankendael House has a free open house on the last Sunday of every month *(noon-5pm)*. Check the website for contemporary art shows and more events.

● Barbecuing is allowed.

● The gates on Nobelweg are opened and closed daily according to operating hours.

● On the last Sunday of the month, visit **De Pure Markt** *(puremarkt.nl)* and make a picnic of artisanal and organic bites.

● There is a public flower garden on the path that cuts through the park past De Kas (away from Middenweg). It leads to the children's playground where the chimney and stork's nest are located.

OOST ON TWEE WHEELS

Exploring Oost on a *twee* (two) wheeler reveals a more laid-back, local side of Amsterdam.

START	END	LENGTH
Wereldmuseum Amsterdam	Brouwerij Poesiat & Kater	11km; 1hr (not including stops)

Begin your Oost adventure at the ❶ **Wereldmuseum** (p188), one of Europe's best ethnographic museums. Its exhibition on Dutch colonialism provides historical insight into Oost's multicultural landscape. Ride (or walk your bike over to) ❷ **Oosterpark** (p190) – gorgeous greenery abounds. Take the full 2km loop around the urban park to see preening herons and relaxed locals doing their thing.

Your next stop, the bustling ❸ **Dappermarkt** (p187), couldn't be more different to Oosterpark. It's loud, and the smell of grilling hangs in the air. Park on Dapperplein (or walk your bike through the market) and snack on multicultural street food.

Get back onto the main boulevard, Linnaeusstraat, to hit ❹ **Baking Lab**. This sustainable bakery churns out fresh treats all day (the savoury danishes are divine). Proceed over the canal to ❺ **Park Frankendael** (p194), where a 5km cycling loop reveals wild nature, landscaped gardens and marshy remnants of its former polder (drained land) life. If you don't fancy taking the scenic route, a handy path also cuts through the middle.

The final stretch takes you along a scenic canal route to one of Amsterdam's best experimental breweries, ❻ **Brouwerij Poesiat & Kater**. Sip something crazy like a passionfruit *Gose* and unwind on the big waterside terrace.

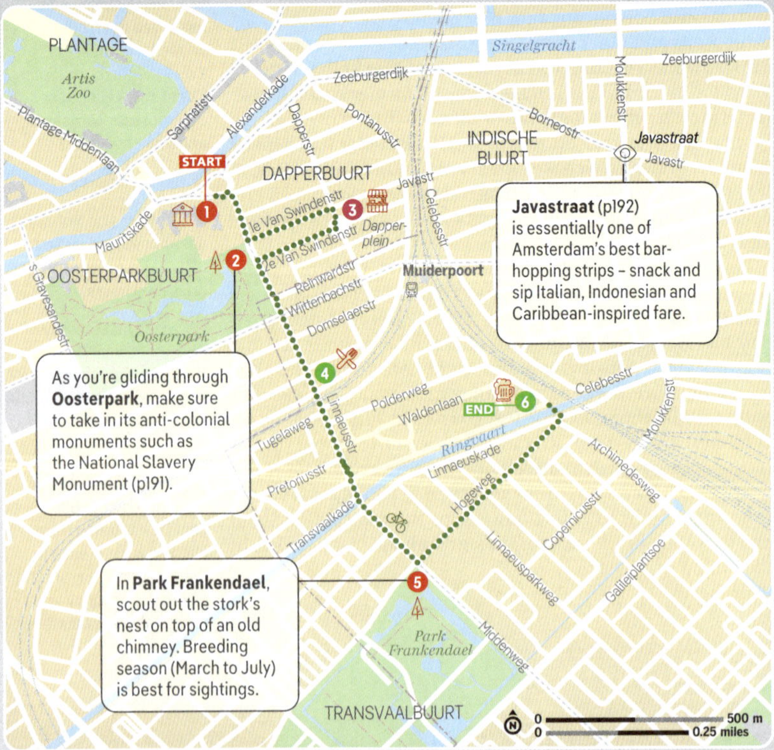

Javastraat (p192) is essentially one of Amsterdam's best bar-hopping strips – snack and sip Italian, Indonesian and Caribbean-inspired fare.

As you're gliding through **Oosterpark**, make sure to take in its anti-colonial monuments such as the National Slavery Monument (p191).

In **Park Frankendael**, scout out the stork's nest on top of an old chimney. Breeding season (March to July) is best for sightings.

Feast on Game at the 'Wild Boar'

Locavore dining

Wilde Zwijnen *(wildezwijnenwinkel.nl; 6pm-midnight Mon-Fri except Wed, from noon Sat & Sun),* meaning 'wild boar' in Dutch, is a fitting name for this hip restaurant where there's usually seasonal game on the menu (think venison and boar stew, rabbit or pheasant terrine). With cream-coloured walls and reservations scrawled in chalk on wood tables, the restaurant has a rustic-industrial feel, and serves locally sourced, seasonal dishes with a creative twist. Its daily three- to five-course menus (no à la carte) are either meat, fish or vegetarian (not vegan).

Tour AFC Ajax' Home Turf

Football stadium

The Netherlands' most famous football team, four-time European champions AFC Ajax, plays all of its home games at Amsterdam's **Johan Cruijff ArenA** (renamed in 2018 after the legendary Dutch footballer). Match tickets are sold on the stadium's website *(johancruijffarena.nl; from €80).* The retractable roof promises that poor weather never compromises play.

When no games are on, fans can tour the 68,000-capacity stadium on a self-guided **tour** *(adult/child €27.50/19.25).* Take in the dressing room and saunter through the 'Players Tunnel' emerging right onto the pitch (though just the edge of it).

Drink in a Modern Bruin Café

Traditional Dutch pub

The gloriously historic but updated *bruin café* (traditional Dutch pub) **De Ysbreeker** *(deysbreeker.nl; 8am-midnight)* first opened its doors in 1702. Antique stained-glass and quaint arches aside, De Ysbreeker's bar menu couldn't be more modern: organic and local beers and not-your-usual *borrelhapjes* (bar snacks) – homemade meatballs with local pickles and croquettes with shrimp or truffles and mushrooms. Inside, stylish drinkers hoist beverages in the plush booths and along the marble bar.

The historic establishment's name ('Icebreaker') comes from a vessel that used to dock in front to break ice on the river during winter months (stained-glass windows illustrate the scene).

Enjoy Dinner & a Movie at Studio K

Creative hub

Join local creative types catching independent flicks, local bands and theatre performances or just stopping by for vegetarian fare at the awesome **Studio K** *(studio-k.nu; hours vary).* This hip Oost arts centre always has something going on, with cinema halls, a nightclub, a stage for bands and even a theatre. There's also an eclectic restaurant *(6-9.30pm)* serving international dishes for dinner, plus a huge terrace at the back of the building. For dinner, it's best to book ahead – go for the 'Film + Dinner' *(per person €25),* which includes a main course or two small dishes and an independent film screening.

ORANGE OBSESSION

If you've ever attended a sporting event where the Dutch national team are playing, you'll already be familiar with *oranjegekte* (orange craze), or *oranjekoorts* (orange fever). The custom of wearing the traditional colour of the Dutch royal family, the House of Orange-Nassau, was originally limited to celebration days for the monarchy, such as King's Day (Koningsdag). But particularly since the 1974 FIFA World Cup, when tens of thousands of orange-clad football supporters cheered on every game, wearing outlandish orange getups – clothes, scarves, wigs, fake-fur top hats, face paint, feather boas, you name it – has become a cultural phenomenon.

Researched by Barbara Woolsey

AMSTERDAM NOORD

EVER-CHANGING CREATIVE DISTRICT

Amsterdam's shapeshifting Noord is not to be missed. Once disused maritime warehouses now anchor artists' studios and awesome street art – though commercialism's becoming a tempest.

The fun of Noord starts right on the ferry leaving Amsterdam Centraal Station. The free, five-minute cruise across the IJ River is a sightseeing experience in its own right; when you reach land again, you're in for a treat. The neighbourhood, once a neglected area (and controversially, not even considered Amsterdam at all) has trendy landmarks around open spaces. It encompasses ex-industrial areas, cutting-edge architecture and hangars turned hipster hangouts with walls covered in street art, all minutes away from fields, horses and the odd windmill.

More recently, changing winds see shiny condominiums and commercial spaces edge out obscure, alternative venues and some once-treasured haunts. Now's a great time to drift about.

TOP TIP

The best way to explore Noord is by bike. Places are spread out, there isn't much traffic and there are lots of cycle routes. You can take bikes on the free ferries.

IJ River ferry

See p243 for places to stay in Amsterdam Noord.

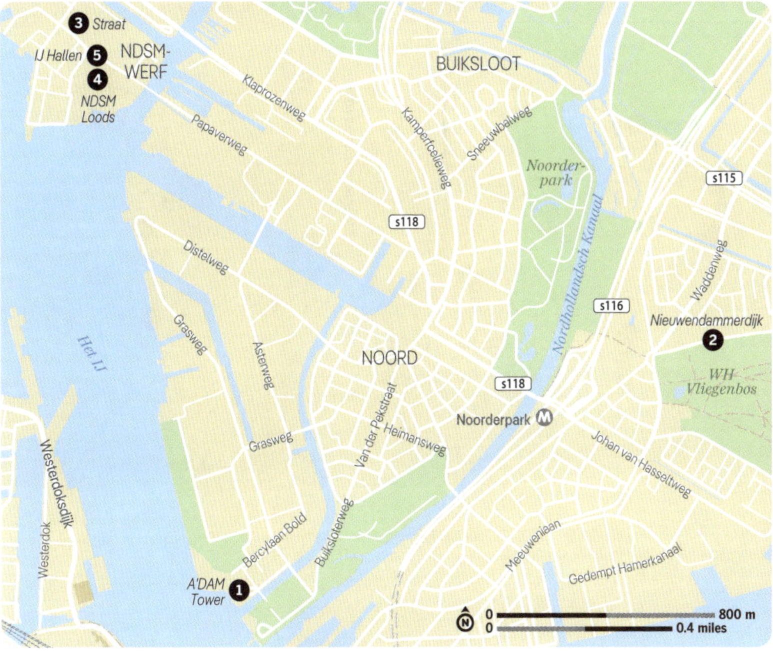

FROM LEFT: MAESTROBOOKS/GETTY IMAGES; INGEHOGENBIJL//SHUTTERSTOCK

3 Straat

IJ Hallen **5** NDSM-WERF

4

NDSM Loods

Klaprozenweg

Papaverweg

BUIKSLOOT

Kamperfoelieweg

Sneeuwbalweg

Noorder-park

s115

s118

Distelweg

Grasweg

Het IJ

Asterweg

Grasweg

Westerdoksdijk

Westerdokskade

Bercylaan Bold

Buiksloterweg

Van der Pekstraat

Heimansweg

Waddenweg

s116

Nieuwendammerdijk

2

WH Vliegenbos

NOORD

s118

Noorderpark Ⓜ

Johan van Hasseltweg

Meeuwenlaan

Gedempt Hamerkanaal

Nieuwe Hamerkanaal

A'DAM Tower **1**

Ⓝ 0 — 800 m
0 — 0.4 miles

⭐ Highlights

❶ A'DAM Tower
Strap into a skyscraper's daredevil swings or get lost in a subterranean nightclub at Amsterdam's lighthouse of cool. **p201**

❷ Nieuwendammerdijk
Cycle or meander a pretty dyke sporting wooden houses and chirpy birds. **p211**

❸ Straat
Ogle graffiti and artists toiling over monster installations at the world's largest museum dedicated to street art. **p207**

❹ NDSM Loods
In a massive former shipping warehouse, explore artists' studios and installations dangled from rafters. **p203**

▲ ❺ IJ Hallen
Shop bric-a-brac from Delftware to retro duds and snack at food trucks during the hype days of Europe's largest flea market. **p203**

🚶 Getting Around

Ferry
Free 24-hour ferries run from Centraal Station to Buiksloterweg, NDSM and IJplein. The F4 takes you to NDSM's main sightseeing.

Metro
The north–south line 52 links Amsterdam Zuid with Noord via Centraal Station. Noorderpark is the key stop for sightseeing – ferries from Centraal are faster.

Cycling
A bike is essential for exploring Noord. Places are spread out; cycle routes abound. Bikes are allowed onboard ferries.

AMSTERDAM NOORD

See Enlargement

NDSM-WERF

Enlargement

NDSM-WERF

Straat

NDSM-plein

NDSM-plein

NDSM-plein

NDSM Ferry Terminal

NDSM

Ms van Riemsdijkweg

Klaprozenweg

Papaverweg

Distelweg

Asterweg

Graveg

Mosplein

Kamperfoelieweg

NOORD

Noorderpark

Noorderpark

Buiksloterweg

WESTELIJKE EILANDEN (WESTERN ISLANDS)

Het IJ

Eye Filmmuseum

A'DAM Tower

Westerdoksdijk

IJpromenade

Graswegdam

Gedempt Hamerkanaal

Nieuwendammerdijk

WH Vliegenbos

Landmark (2.3km)

Het IJ

A'DAM Tower

The imposing A'DAM Tower on the waterfront was built in 1971 and named the 'Overhoeks' (Diagonal) because of its angle to the rest of the building. Used as the Royal Dutch Shell oil-company offices, it's now a multivenue extravaganza, with a 360-degree viewing platform on its 100m-high rooftop, complete with telescopes, where you can lounge on super-sized cushions in fine weather.

Swing High, Sweet Skyscraper

The 22-storey A'DAM Tower (1971) provides quite the contrast to Amsterdam's relatively low-rise cityscape. Once the Royal Dutch Shell oil-company offices, it's had a makeover to become a major attraction. Take the trippy lift to the sky deck for sweeping views in all directions – some of Amsterdam's best. Admission includes a free audio guide and the 'Amsterdam VR Ride' taking you on a wild simulated roller-coaster ride through the historic city. A giant six-person swing *(per person €7.50)* – Europe's highest – kicks out over the edge at a lofty 100m. Don't worry, you're strapped in.

Gastronomic Heights & Underground Clubbing

A'DAM's lift whisks you up with a mesmerising light show overhead. As well as the rooftop panorama, on the 20th floor there's the swish bar and nightclub **Madam** boasting stunning, floor-to-ceiling windows. A floor below, the revolving restaurant **Moon** pairs 360-degree panoramas (at a stomachable, one-revolution-an-hour pace) with modern Dutch, seasonally influenced gourmet tasting menus.

In the basement, **Shelter** goes deep as one of Europe's best nightclubs for underground house and techno. A raw, industrial, 700-person-capacity space runs to 7am on weekends thanks to a 24/7 licence.

TOP TIPS

● The tower has wheelchair access.

● Purchase lookout tickets online for a €2 discount.

● Lookout admission includes the bar but not Moon restaurant. For dining at Moon, you'll need to book well ahead.

PRACTICALITIES

● adamlookout.com
● lookout adult/child €16.50/10.50 ● 10am-10pm; business hours vary

WOLF PHOTOGRAPHY/SHUTTERSTOCK

TOP EXPERIENCE

NDSM

The NDSM-werf, a former shipbuilding yard, was an important industrial area that fell into disuse from the 1980s, before being taken over by squatters who filled the void. Today the NDSM neighbourhood has numerous cool waterside restaurants, striking architecture, a hangar full of artists' studios and the huge monthly IJ Hallen flea market.

Seafaring Goes Swank

DON'T MISS

Incredible street art

IJ Hallen flea market

Artists' studios

Cool restaurants

Named for the Nederlandsche Dok en Scheepsbouw Maatsch-appij (the Netherlands Dock & Shipbuilding Company, which operated here from 1946 to 1979), the derelict shipyard turned edgy arts community has a post-apocalyptic aura. Abandoned trams rust by the water's edge, and street art is splashed on most surfaces. Creatives hang out at cool cafes, bars and restaurants – many crafted out of shipping containers – and cultural businesses such as MTV are headquartered here. The area is also a hotspot for underground cultural events, including 'Art Battles' (live painting competitions) and guided tours.

PRACTICALITIES

● ndsm.nl ● free ● 24hr; business hours vary

Art City

NDSM Loods comprises a shipbuilding warehouse filled with over 80 studios, with some 250 artists working in the NDSM *broedplaats* (breeding ground). It's a big enough space that you can cycle or walk around the area, with huge artworks around hangar rafters. Up scaffolding-like stairs inside the warehouse, you'll also find an exhibition space, **NDSM Fuse** *(ndsm-fuse.eu; free; noon-6pm Thu-Sun)*, where expos and events regularly take place.

Street Art Destination

The highlight of NDSM is wandering around and discovering graffiti walls. Brick warehouse façades, containers and cranes are adorned with murals and smaller 'throw-ups' (or 'throw-ies') – smaller, simple shapes and stencilled pieces, which change quickly – from top to bottom.

Forget haphazard tagging. From murals to billboards, the eye candy here is incredible and equates to an open-air art museum. Graffiti around here is legally regulated and tolerated, so new stuff appears regularly.

Creativity reaches climax inside the world's largest museum for graffiti and street art, **Straat** (p207). Some highlights include *Let Me Be Myself* – a colourful, geometrically intricate mural of Anne Frank by Eduardo Kobra adorning Straat – as well as the eastern part of NDSM where much of the smaller art and 'throwies' abound (look out for COVID-19 era graffiti, including the *Super Nurse* depicting a care worker with a Superman-styled mask).

Between Straat and NDSM, there are changing large-scale murals and installations. 'Make Art Not War' is inscribed onto the eastern side of Straat and the works here are often political, for example a 2024-unveiled tractor towing a Russian tank against a Ukrainian flag by the Dutch artist NILS.

All of the graffiti art you see around here could very well be gone by the next time you come, creating an art experience that can always be discovered anew.

Europe's Largest Flea Market

The whopping **IJ Hallen** *(adult/child €5/2.50)* outdoor flea market – Europe's largest – takes place one weekend a month (Saturdays and Sundays), with hundreds of stalls selling vintage clothes, antiques, vinyl, art and much, much more. It moves indoors into two NDSM warehouses from October to March. The market has an entrance cost, but it's a small price to pay for serious treasure hunting across everything from dusty antiques to bikes. Numerous food trucks park up here. Check the website for the schedule.

TOP TIPS

● From NDSM, it's a five- to 10-minute bike ride to the A'DAM Tower (p201) and the Eye Filmmuseum (p205). Further along the riverbank to the east are more waterside bars and restaurants.

● In July, huge performing-arts events (dance, theatre, music) take place for 10 days around the NDSM-werf former shipyards during the **Over het IJ Festival**.

● On Easter weekend, techno and house reverberate off warehouse walls during the three-day festival **DGTL**. DGTL also hosts a programme during October's Amsterdam Dance Event (p134).

● The nearest ferry stop for this area from Centraal is IJplein.

Vintage Shop of Wonders

Giant secondhand boutique

For those who love styling up vintage wear but find jam-packed clothing racks trigger anxiety, **Figo Vintage** *(figovintage. com; 11am-6pm Thu-Sun)* is perusing paradise. Amsterdam's biggest vintage store, situated in a 1000-sq-metre former factory warehouse, offers a unique shopping experience: the huge selection you might find in a flea market, yet with a curated, well-arranged 'department store' setup.

Highly organised clothing sections are spread across a uniquely breezy pre-loved shopping area. Unique pieces abound and you don't have to look hard for them, especially when it comes to designer duds such as Italian, Japanese and American brands. Special threads don't come cheap but there are sales and accessories racks for budget browsing. Particularly attractive is a secondhand footwear area (a former oven turned into a walk-in closet) and an excellent selection for men's thrifting, including lots of sports jerseys and band shirts (although, for some reason, a high concentration of them are Kiss tees).

A spacious changing-room area and even public washrooms (a rarity across long stretches of Noord) secure comfortable, effective perusal. At the time of research, kids' clothing was the only area where diverse sizing was a little thinner.

Figo will keep this location until at least June 2026 and potentially longer depending on redevelopment plans; after this, the future is unclear.

Enter the Ballpit

Play-and-party space

An interactive art experience and pink-lacquered play space, **Wondr** *(wondrexperience.com; adult/child €26/18; 10am-7pm Mon-Fri, from 9.30am Sat & Sun)* won't be everyone's brand of bubblegum. But for kids and any millennial who's ever googled bouncy castles and ball pits for their adult birthday party, art therapy doesn't get more fun than this.

Wondr is an Instagram post brought to life. There are pits for swimming in Styrofoam 'marshmallows' and coloured balls, a pink bouncy castle, confetti room and art installations packed with teddies. Immersive pop-up exhibitions plop you right into Barbie Land and hanging with SpongeBob in Bikini Bottom. Outside, a 'beach' with pink sand has a cocktail bar and cafe. Scope out the gigantic pastel-pink building on Meeuwenlaan.

DRINKING IN NOORD: CAFE-BARS & CLUB VIBES

Skatecafe: Expansive, warehouse-like cafe-restaurant with an indoor skate ramp and DJ lineups. *3pm-1am Thu, to 3am Fri & Sat*

Café 't Sluisje: Historic *bruin café* (traditional Dutch pub) overlooking a *sluis* (lock). Very pretty spot; inviting terrace. *11am-midnight Tue-Thu & Sun, to 1am Fri & Sat*

Garage Noord: Laid-back venue with a gritty feel. Casual cafe-bar-restaurant that shifts into club mode around 11.30pm with DJs. *8pm-late Thu-Sun*

Pllek: Uber-cool Noord magnet that does it all – come for afternoon beer on the waterfront, stay for live DJs and dance parties pumping late. *9.30am-1am, to 3am Fri & Sat*

Eye Filmmuseum

A modernist architectural triumph on the banks of the IJ (also pronounced 'eye') River, Eye Filmmuseum peers over the city. Its permanent exhibition, *What is Film?*, takes cinephiles deep into the heart of motion-picture-making technology. Catch a vintage classic or current blockbuster in its cinemas, or pop into the bar-restaurant for cinematic river views and a fabulously sunny waterfront terrace.

Science Fiction, Endless Features

What started out as a one-room exhibit decades ago is now one of the Netherlands' most exciting museums. The Eye's bright-white, sci-fi inspired 'space ship' rockets you from cinema's early history into the great beyond.

Eye's permanent exhibition, *What is Film?*, lets you see how the earliest cameras worked, insert yourself into a film using green-screen technology, or make your own animated movie. Virtual reality puts focus on the future; and all these eras come together in an installation called **Film Catcher**, where an AI-powered, image-based search allows you to call up film clips from a collection of over 60,000 in mere seconds.

Cutting-Edge Movie Nights

Eye's four movie screens delivers the Oscars of cinema-going experiences. State-of-the-art cinemas screen everything from Tinsel Town's latest blockbusters to experimental arthouse; one has an organ for live sound effects, another boasts retractable seating. Analogue films twinkle anew with digital restoration.

TOP TIPS

● Buy tickets for screenings well ahead of time.

● Tickets for certain screenings (over 150 minutes, or with live musical accompaniment) are subject to supplementary charges.

● Eye's gift shop sells vintage film posters and books (card payment only).

PRACTICALITIES

● eyefilm.nl ● adult/child film €13.50/8, exhibition €21/free ● box office 10am-10pm Sun-Thu, to 11pm Fri & Sat; exhibitions 10am-7pm

SEARCH & RESCUE MISSION

Separated from Amsterdam by the IJ River, Noord can feel a world away from downtown's canals and crooked buildings. Gone are the days of geographic divide, when Noord was a largely industrial, detached entity for maritime workers. Today it's shoring up urban growth as Amsterdam's fastest-growing neighbourhood, with housing and construction expected to double its residential landscape by 2050.

Noord's maritime heritage dates back to the 1600s. When shipbuilding declined in the 1980s, industrial landscapes were marooned. Squatters and artists salvaged derelict warehouses; fast forward 20 years and Noord's the 'place to be'. What the neighbourhood continues to lose in quaint waterfront, it makes up for in edgy excitement.

WOLF PHOTOGRAPHY/SHUTTERSTOCK

Straat

The Beauty of Algorithms

Technological art powerhouse

The 2020-opened **NXT Museum** *(nxtmuseum.com; adult/child from €19.50/13.50; 11am-8.30pm Sun-Tue & Thu, to 10.30pm Fri & Sat)* is a media-art nirvana where technology channels all kinds of creative expression. Across the 1400-sq-metre warehouse space, immersive exhibitions are co-created by artists, scientists, sound engineers, coders and designers. Cutting-edge tech such as robotics and facial recognition are explored in exhibits. Changing lighting and triggered sound controlled by AI, as well as VR experiences, make for an immersive, state-of-the-art museum visit. For anyone embracing the digital future, exploring themes such as virtual worlds and the emotional side of data will be a delight.

Reserve ahead to get prime seating on the sunny terrace

 EATING IN NOORD: SEASONAL FARE

Café de Ceuvel: Off-grid spot on the cutting edge of sustainability. Recycled materials, all-vegan menu. *noon-11pm Tue, Wed & Sun, to midnight Thu, to 1am Fri & Sat* €€

Cornerstore: Rustic from the rafters to the vinyl DJ booth. Asian-influenced plates, drinks from sake to agave. *6.30pm-1am Wed & Thu, from 6pm Fri & Sat, 1.30-10pm Sun* €€

Hangar: Hangar-situated (duh) restaurant on the water's edge. Dishes include Ottolenghi-style salads and charcuterie platters. *11am-midnight Wed-Sun* €€

Barracuda: A fan favourite since opening in 2024, serving decadent small seafood plates. *5-11pm Mon-Thu, to 1am Fri, 12.30pm-1am Sat, to 10pm Sun* €€€

Explore a Living Canvas

Become one with contemporary art

Follow the smell of paint drying into **Straat** *(straatmuseum. com; adult/child €19.50/free; 10am-5pm, from noon Mon)*, where art becomes more than a spectator sport (see also p203).

The former warehouse is a living canvas where you can see artists spray and string up their murals and art installations before your eyes. Beyond watching contemporary artists at work, dive in deeper and pick up a spray can or a stencil yourself during a graffiti workshop. Dates are listed on the website.

Rustic Waterfront Market

'Remote' Noord shores

Landmarkt *(landmarkt.nl; 10am-5pm Mon & Tue, to 10pm Wed-Sat, 11am-10pm Sun)*, a large covered food market on the quieter eastern side of the waterfront, is where Noord stays true to its bucolic roots.

Here you'll find fresh fruit, vegetables, an on-site bakery, gourmet foodstuffs and a fine selection of cheese, wine and beers. There's also an in-house restaurant with well-priced snacks and dishes. It's a great place to go with kids on a sunny day, as there's a field and swings, as well as outdoor seating that feels immersed in countryside.

Landmarkt is about a 30-minute journey by metro and tram from Centraal; or a 20-minute cycle from the Buiksloterweg ferry station.

Garage Dining

Budget or high-end?

Dinner in a trendily tuned-up mechanics workshop steers across high(-end) and low(-priced) gastronomy.

With a name taken from the lyrics of the Jacques Brel song *Les Bourgeois*, the extraordinary gourmet hipster restaurant **Hotel de Goudfazant** *(hoteldegoudfazant.nl; 6pm-midnight Tue-Sun)* spreads through a cavernous former garage, still raw and industrial, and sticking to the theme by having cars parked inside. Rockstar-looking chefs cook up a French-influenced storm in the open kitchen. When warm weather revs up, staff roll up the garage's big doors and you can watch the passing barge traffic while you eat. There is no hotel, just FYI, except in name.

Continued on p210

A PERFECT EVENING IN NOORD

Jurriaan Teulings is a Dutch travel writer and photographer based in Amsterdam. He has visited over 110 countries (also, every continent and ocean). At home, he prefers to keep distances short. @jurrpix

Catching up with friends is the antidote to my untethered life. In Noord, three places within a few steps of each other form a triangle of happiness: **Kuuma**, a small sauna cabin on the water for private use; across the street, **FC Hyena**, an arthouse cinema; and **Hangar**, an industrial-chic restaurant. I try to hit all three with friends. It's a short bike ride from the ferry or metro – so most of us are home within half an hour.

The Netherlands' first urban winery

DRINKING IN AMSTERDAM NOORD: ARTISANAL ALCOHOL

Lowlander: Plant-filled former warehouse with a sun-soaked, south-facing terrace. Brews botanical beers and serves local, seasonal food. *11am-midnight, to 1am Thu-Sat*

Oedipus Brewery & Tap Room: Converted warehouse with experimental brews. *4-10.30pm Wed & Thu, to 12.30am Fri & Sat, 2-10pm Sun*

Walhalla Taproom: Relaxed microbrewery for delicious pours. Between Buiksloterweg ferry station and NDSM. *4pm-midnight Thu & Fri, from 2pm Sat, 2-9pm Sun*

Chateau Amsterdam: Grapes from around Europe become vino. Hit the terrace; tour the solar-powered production facility. *5pm-midnight Wed-Fri, from 2pm Sat, to 7pm Sun*

Cycling Amsterdam Noord

As an old Dutch saying goes, 'Cycling is freedom' – and nowhere does this ring truer than in far-reaching Noord. It's a spread-out neighbourhood with distances between attractions measuring kilometres. Cycling is perfect for feeling at ease along this route spanning food, shopping, art and Noord's most significant landmarks.

❶ Pont Neuf

When you get off the free ferry shuttle from Centraal Station to Amsterdam Noord's Buiksloterweg terminal, make your first stop this unexpected **snack bar**. Fuel up on some of Amsterdam's best *frites* (fries), hand-cut from organic potatoes and baked in soybean oil (not deep-fried) for a lighter, more digestible outcome.

The Ride: Pedal along Ranonkelkade and cross the canal to join Docklandsweg heading north.

❷ Figo Vintage

In an old factory warehouse, Amsterdam's largest **vintage retailer** (p204) is where the scenery becomes more quintessentially gritty and 'Noord'. The building is set for removal in mid-2026 to build housing.

The Ride: On the 1km ride to NDSM, water's always with you. Cross two bridges over sprawling canals with greenery between.

❸ NDSM

Welcome to where Noord's transformation all started. The NDSM-werf was a booming shipbuilding area from 1870 until bankruptcy beckoned in 1984. Now NDSM (p202) is a centre for counterculture and street art (though milling crowds prove the underground days are over).

IAN DAGNALL / ALAMY

Nieuwendammerdijk

The Ride: Park your bike and stroll around the former shipping yard.

❹ Straat

At Straat (p207), the world's largest museum dedicated to street art, more than 150 works – many large scale and all created on site – sprawl around the 8000-sq-metre converted warehouse.

The Ride: Cycling in the opposite direction you came from, Noord scenery unfolds that's much closer to countryside than the developing shoreline area. Residential areas abounding in greenery are a reminder of the polder (drained land) here.

❺ WH Vliegenbos

Dating back over a century, this 20-hectare **forest** (p211) is Amsterdam's oldest, with elm, ash and black alder trees.

The Ride: Along Nieuwendammerdijk, check out the wooden houses on your right – they're some of Amsterdam's oldest.

❻ Nieuwendammerdijk

Enchanting chocolate-box prettiness characterises this **long, narrow street** (p211) of wooden Dutch houses is prime real estate. Scenery such as this, so close to the waterfront, is becoming a rarity.

The Ride: Follow the dyke eastward for about a kilometre; the road becomes lonely with sparse houses and low-lying greenery.

❼ Café 't Sluisje

This historic *bruin café* (traditional pub; p204) feels worlds away from the graffitied up harbour area. Relax on the terrace, overlooking a *sluis* (lock) and quaint scenery – spots like these are part of Noord's identity too. Afterwards, cycle back to Buiksloterweg and ferry back to Centraal.

209

MAKING ART IN STRAAT

Emmanuel Jarus is a Canadian-born street artist who lives around the world. In 2022, he painted *Meeting in Breda* in Straat (p207). @youngjarus

Meeting in Breda was inspired by my time in Amsterdam visiting the Ukrainian photographer Emilia Kulieva. After visiting Straat and other Amsterdam museums such as the Rijksmuseum, I wanted to create a large-scale Dutch still life with the same techniques I use for murals. At a grocery store near Straat, I bought random items and arranged them against a dark background, similar to what I'd seen in museums. Emilia took a photo reference; we painted by day and explored Amsterdam at night over one week. Creating alongside other artists at work inside Straat, and having breakfast with legendary artist Hera of Herakut, were inspirational highlights.

FRANS LEMMENS/ALAMY

Continued from p207

Switching gears, **Euro Pizza** *(europizza.rest; 6-11pm, from 1pm Fri & Sat, 1-10pm Sun)* is a cult favourite for a filling meal that's less souped up. Also situated in a former garage, the sourdough pizza menu here spans straightforward toppings sourced locally and paired with lovely natural wines.

Crush-Worthy Container Spots

Shipping good vibes

Shipping containers are permanent fixtures on the NDSM waterfront. Perhaps counterintuitively, they also boast some of the cosiest hangouts you'll find across Noord.

Trendy **Pllek** *(pllek.nl; 9.30am-1am Sun-Thu, to 3am Fri & Sat)* is a Noord magnet, with people of all ages streaming over to hang out in its interior made of shipping containers and, when the weather allows, lounge on its artificial sandy beachfront. It's a terrific spot for a waterside beer or glass of wine, or something from the sustainable, mostly vegetarian menu. Look out for live music, DJs and outdoor films. In colder weather, the indoor fireplace couldn't be more inviting.

Meanwhile, Pllek's next-door neighbour, **Noorderlicht** *(noorderlichtcafe.nl; 10am-midnight)* is a soaring greenhouse-like structure built from salvaged materials. Grassy waterside lawns and a mini stage flaunt a pub-garden-meets-festival ambiance. A big play area outside makes it great for families. Its 100% circular ethos of reuse and recycling extends to its organic coffee, craft beers, natural wines, botanical cocktails and predominantly vegan food.

Don't let the sweet summer atmosphere fool you; in colder, rainy climes Noorderlicht is equally wonderful. Candlelit, communal tables indulge in 'living room' vibes.

Pllek

Camping Up Noord

Green, leafy gem

Dating back over a century, the 20-hectare **WH Vliegenbos** *(Fly Forest; vliegenbosamsterdam.nl; free 24hr)* is an unexpected emerald treasure less than 2km (15 minutes on foot) from the IJplein ferry stop.

Camping out here is truly the most unique overnighter in Amsterdam. The **campground** in the woodland is small and gets busy, but it's very leafy and feels rural considering it's so close to the city. There are some basic cabins with bunks and minimal furnishings, and tipis if you don't have your own tent (book well ahead). Staff are helpful and friendly and there's a cafe-bar and bike hire (€13 per day). A two-night minimum stay is required. There is free wi-fi on the campgrounds.

Cycle Noord's Prettiest Dyke

Idyllic countryside

There are plenty of cycle routes into the countryside from Amsterdam Noord, and from here you can explore the lakes and polder (area of drained land) that lie to the north.

Without venturing too far upstream, you can still get a feel for the countryside by cycling along **Nieuwendammerdijk**. Just a 15-minute ride from the Buiksloterweg ferry terminal, this long, narrow dyke is where Noord's waterfront is enduringly cute and quaint. A street of wooden Dutch houses is characterised by enchanting chocolate-box prettiness (now prime real estate), with hollyhocks nodding beside every porch. Many houses date from the 1500s, and numbers 202 to 204 were where the shipbuilding family De Vries Lentsch lived. Numbers 301 to 309 were once captains' houses.

AMSTERDAM'S OLDEST FOREST

Vliegenbos is named for Willem Hubert (WH) Vliegen, a municipal city planner who insisted that a large green space be created for residents arriving in the area; planting began in 1912.

Vliegenbos is Amsterdam's oldest forest, with elm, ash and black alder trees and birdlife including woodpeckers, kingfishers, falcons and blackbirds. Walking and cycling trails weave through the greenery, past ponds and waterways.

Day Trips
from Amsterdam

Researched by
Catherine Le Nevez

Amsterdam is on the doorstep of historic canal-laced cities, windmills, windswept beaches, and bulb fields blooming with tulips.

Places

One of Amsterdam's greatest treasures is its proximity to a trove of day trips. In a country that takes just a handful of hours to cross in its entirety, the Netherlands' efficient public transport and fantastic cycle paths make it quick and easy to reach destinations surrounding the capital, from Muiden's medieval castle and fort (part of the UNESCO-listed Dutch Water Defence Lines) to splendid cities like Haarlem, Utrecht, Leiden, Delft, Den Haag (the seat of the Dutch government and royalty) and Rotterdam (a veritable outdoor gallery of contemporary architecture). Beyond Amsterdam you can also escape into nature in glorious forests, watery green polders, spring-blooming tulip fields and show gardens, and invigorating dune-backed strands along the coast.

Muiden

TIME FROM AMSTERDAM: **45MIN**

Explore a Medieval Castle & Island Fortress

Stretching over 200km, the UNESCO World Heritage Site of the Dutch Water Defence Lines takes in the fortifications of the New Dutch Waterline and the Defence Line of Amsterdam, including Muiden's fairy-tale red-brick castle, the Muiderslot, and offshore island fort, Pampus. Both sites open from April to October.

Built in 1280 by Count Floris V, son of Willem II, the exceptionally preserved moated fortress **Muiderslot** (*muiderslot. nl; adult/child €19.50/7.50*) is equipped with round towers, a French innovation. The count was a champion of the poor and a French sympathiser, two factors that were bound to spell trouble; Floris was imprisoned in the castle in 1296 and murdered while trying to flee.

Muiderslot's fortifications were added in the 17th century, ensconcing its lush gardens, with a beech alley, kitchen and herb gardens and plum orchard commissioned by its then-owner, the historian, poet and playwright PC Hooft. Hooft hosted leading writers, artists and scientists here. Following its renovation by architect Pierre Cuypers (who designed Amsterdam's Rijksmuseum and Centraal Station), it has been a national museum since 1878. Themed audio tours

GETTING TO MUIDERSLOT & PAMPUS

Muiden is an easy bike ride from IJburg along a 7km cycle route.

There are seasonal ferry trips from IJburg with **Rederij Navigo** (*navigoamsterdam.nl; adult/child Muiderslot €34/24.50, Pampus €25/20*) to Muiderslot or Pampus, including admission, with around 2½ hours at either site (you can't visit both from IJburg on the same day).

You can also get to Muiden by bus from Amsterdam's Amstel Station.

From Muiden's port, ferries to Pampus (included in its admission) depart in season.

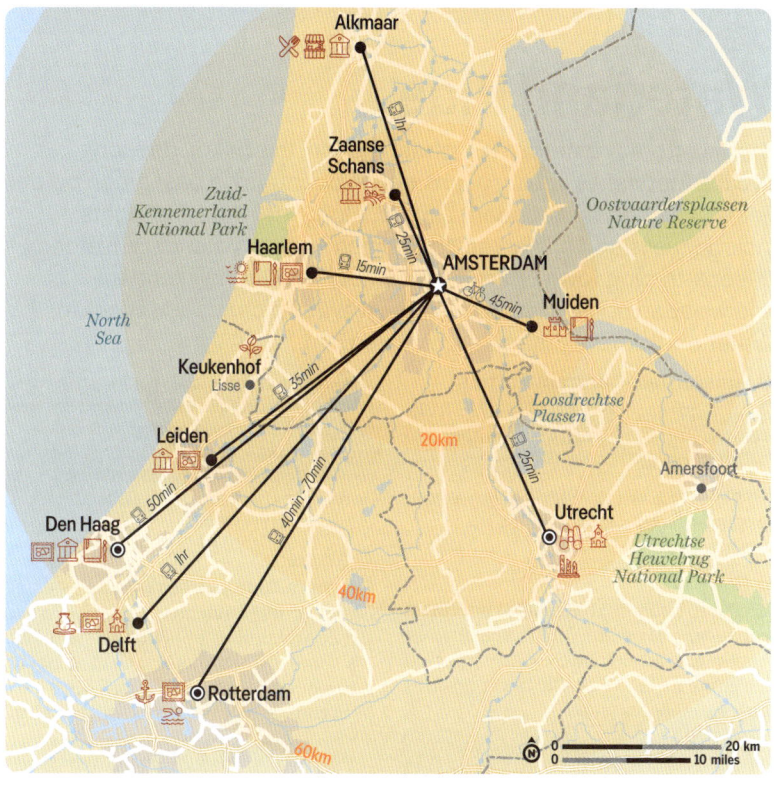

bring its centuries of history to life. I amsterdam cardholders get free entry. Beyond the ramparts, boats fill the pretty pleasure port of Muiden, lined with waterside cafes.

Off the coast lies the fortress island of **Pampus** *(pampus. nl; adult/child incl ferry from Muiden €19.50/15.50)*. This massive 19th-century bunker was a key member of a ring of 42 fortresses built to defend Amsterdam and is great fun to explore. The huge defences were designed to be flooded if the city came under attack. Unfortunately, aeroplanes came into the picture and the fortifications were never used. As the only hydraulic fortification of its kind in the world, it was rescued from disrepair by UNESCO. There's discounted entry for I amsterdam cardholders.

The island's beach-pavilion-style cafe-restaurant **Pampus Paviljoen** is entirely off-grid, powered by solar and wind, with ingredients grown on-site in vegetable and herb gardens, or sailed here from small local producers. Book ahead online for candlelit dinners (€95 including boat transfers from IJburg or Muiden).

☑ **TOP TIP**

You can buy a *fietskaart dal* (off-peak bicycle ticket) for **NS trains** *(ns.nl/en/tickets/ bicycle-ticket-off-peak; €7.95)*. Otherwise you'll find bike-hire outlets across the country.

Waterland Ride

Starting from Amsterdam Centraal Station, this 54km, day-long cycling loop takes you through bucolic countryside past green polder fields, watched by abundant birdlife. Along the route, highlights include the island of Marken, former fishing port Volendam, historic cheese-trading town Edam, 14th-century port Monnickendam, and wooden houses lining the waterways of picturesque Broek in Waterland, before returning to Amsterdam.

❶ Amsterdam Centraal Station

From Centraal, take your bicycle on the free, five-minute F3 ferry across the IJ to Buiksloterweg.

The Ride: Cycle east along Nieuwendammerdijk. Pass under the A10 ring road into Waterland; from here it's 2km to Ransdorp.

❷ Ransdorp

Ransdorp's 32m-high **Ransdorpertoren** *(ransdorpertoren.nl; €0.50)*, sketched by Rembrandt, dates from the 16th century. If you climb its 155 steps, the tower rewards with spectacular views.

The Ride: From the village's northwestern edge, take the cycle path alongside Nieuwe Gouw west to Poppendammergouw and follow it northeast to quaint drawbridge Aandammerbrug. Ride southeast on Rijperweg to Uitdam on the banks of the IJsselmeer, and cross the Zeedijk causeway north to Marken.

❸ Marken

Frozen-in-time Marken was an isolated island in the Zuiderzee until 1957 when the Zeedijk linked up with the mainland. It's home to a lighthouse and clog maker. A row of wooden eel-smoking houses have been converted into a historical **museum**.

THOMAS ROELL/SHUTTERSTOCK

Marken lighthouse

The Ride: From Marken's harbour, take the **ferry** (*markenexpress.nl; passenger & bicycle €20; 30min*) to Volendam.

❹ Volendam

Cute, touristy former fishing port Volendam is one of the most popular places in the Netherlands for fresh eel and herring. Just inland, the charming little **Volendam Museum** has displays of traditional dress.

The Ride: Cycle northwest past 1670 windmill Zuidpoldermolen to Kettingbrug, then west along Voorhaven to Edam.

❺ Edam

Synonymous with its eponymous, wax-covered rounds of cheese, Edam was once a renowned whaling port. With old shipping warehouses, hand-operated drawbridges and window boxes reflected in idyllic canals, it's a lovely place to wander.

The Ride: Follow the IJe River south, then take Hoogedijk southwest to Monnickendam.

❻ Monnickendam

Monnickendam traces its roots back to 1356. Since the demise of its fishing industry, its beautiful old trawlers mainly operate pleasure cruises. The 15th-century Speeltoren clock tower and former town hall has the world's oldest glockenspiel (carillon), dating from the 17th century.

The Ride: Head west on Monnickenmeer to Broek in Waterland.

❼ Broek in Waterland

Storybook-pretty Broek in Waterland has a restored 16th-century church dedicated to Sint Nicolaas. Hard to imagine today, but it once rivalled Amsterdam in shipping.

The Ride: Cycle southwest to Het Schouw, take the Veerpont Ilpendam–Landsmeer **ferry** (*veerpontilpendamlandsmeer.com; passenger & bicycle €1; 2min*) across the Noordhollandsch Kanaal, then follow it south to the IJ and return by ferry to Centraal.

FRANS HALS

Frans Hals was born in Antwerp in 1582, but his family fled troubled Flanders when he was a toddler – the northern provinces of the Habsburg Netherlands were fighting for independence from the Spanish Empire. The Hals family ended up in Haarlem, and Hals lived here until his 80s.

Hals painted with an almost impressionistic looseness, as if painting fast to capture a momentary expression. His paintings burst with life. Van Gogh was a great admirer, writing to his brother, Theo, 'Frans Hals is a colourist among the colourists, a colourist like Veronese, like Rubens, like Delacroix, like Velázquez.'

Haarlem

TIME FROM AMSTERDAM: **15MIN**

Explore Haarlem's Historic Heart

Charm-packed Haarlem, capital of the province of Noord-Holland (North Holland), has it all: flower-fronted gabled houses, canals and fine museums (many covered by the I amsterdam card).

Dominating the centre of town is the **Grote Kerk van St Bavo** *(bavo.nl)*, closed Sunday, topped by a 50m-high steeple. Dating from the 13th century, the building was rebuilt in the 15th, retaining its Gothic looks. It's topped by a lantern tower. It was once the city's Catholic cathedral, but was stripped of much of the interior decoration and turned into a Protestant place of worship during the Reformation. Look at the beautiful 16th-century choir screen, beyond which is Frans Hals' grave. Several times weekly there's an opportunity to hear classical musicians play on Grote Kerk's splendid Müller organ – Handel came here twice to play it, and it was also tinkled by a 10-year-old Mozart.

On the adjacent **Grote Markt** is the florid, crenellated 14th-century Stadhuis, fronted by a balcony from where the high court would announce their judgements. The neighbouring Hoofdwacht or 'head watch', which dates to the 13th century, once served as the town jail.

Off Grote Houtstraat, around 10 minutes' walk southwest of Grote Markt, is the pretty **Proveniershuis**, three residences around an inner courtyard. It started life as a *hofje* (almshouse) and for a time became the headquarters of St Joris Doelen (the Civic Guard of St George).

Take a right along charming Korte Houtstraat and turn right again to find the 17th-century red-brick **Nieuwe Kerk** (new church); the ornate tower by Lieven de Key is supported by a boxy design by Jacob van Campen.

Admire Frans Hals' Genius

Reason alone to visit Haarlem is the **Hof** branch of the superb **Frans Hals Museum** *(franshalsmuseum.nl; adult/child €17.50/free)*, closed Monday. Here you'll see firsthand what led painters such as Cezanne, Van Gogh and Courbet to revere his work.

Hals' work fizzes with life, the faces as vivid as the people you pass in the streets outside. You'll also see other great artists' work as well, from Pieter Brughel to Sarah Lucas. There's the 18th-century Dutch favourite: a monumental dolls' house that's a miniature museum rather than plaything.

EATING IN HAARLEM: BEST CASUAL DINING

DeDakkas: A fabulous rooftop cafe-restaurant in a greenhouse on top of a multistorey car park. *10am-10pm Tue, Wed & Sun, to 11pm Thu, to midnight Fri-Sat* €€

Native: Artsy small central cafe in the district filled by appealing small shops, serving brunch dishes, soups and salads. *8am-5pm Mon-Fri, from 9am Sat & Sun* €

Mogador Cafe: Small place with excellent cakes, brownies and coffees. *8am-5pm Mon-Sat, from 9am Sun* €

Stadsstrand de Oerkap: Beach bar with street-food-style food and beers on tap. *10am-11pm Tue & Wed, to 11.30pm Thu & Fri, 11am-11.30pm Sat, to 11pm Sun* €€

Grote Kerk van St Bavo, Haarlem

The museum was founded in 1913, before which these handsome buildings were an almshouse and orphanage, and one of the works here shows the stern four female administrators of the old people's home, painted when Hals himself was 80.

The Frans Hals Museum's **'Hal'** is its contemporary-art branch, only open when there is an exhibition on. It occupies two 17th-century butcher and fish 'halls' a short walk away.

Visit a WWII Hiding Place

Like the Anne Frank Huis (p100), a visit to the **Corrie ten Boom House** *(corrietenboom.com; free),* takes you into viscerally painful WWII history, as you visit the secret compartments used to hide Jews and Dutch resistors from the Nazis. Corrie ten Boom and her family risked their lives to save those persecuted. In 1944 they were betrayed and sent to concentration camps, where three died. Visit via free, guided hour-long tours (in English or Dutch): reserve at least five days ahead. English tours run at 10am and 2pm Tuesday to Saturday.

Be Enchanted by the Teylers Museum

With polished wood atriums and glass cases, the **Teylers Museum** *(teylersmuseum.nl/en; adult/child €17.50/free),* closed Monday, was founded after wealthy cloth merchant and philanthropist Pieter Teyler died without an heir and specified in his will that he wanted his collections preserved for posterity. The museum contains well-labelled fossils (including fascinating fake fossils with a great back story), early inventions, and facsimiles of drawings by Michelangelo, Rembrandt and Piranesi.

BEST HAARLEM MARKETS

Grote Markt
Haarlem's 'Big Market' is on Monday and Saturday with stalls selling fresh produce, cheese, preserves, spices, snacks, clothes (vintage and new) and antiques.

Vintage Market (Botermarkt) On a small city square, the 'Butter Market' has vintage stalls on Monday and Wednesday.

Food & Produce Market (Botermarkt) Also on the Butter Market, this market is piled high with food and produce on Friday and Saturday.

Antique Market Held every second Saturday from April to October, with stalls along the Dreef selling vintage items.

Christmas Market For a weekend in mid-December, the historic centre is filled by traditional stalls selling arts, crafts and *bischopswijn* ('bishop's wine' – mulled wine).

**HEADING
BEYOND HAARLEM**

Martin Lloyd is the author of children's role-playing game Amazing Tales. He lives in Haarlem with his wife and two children. *amazing-tales.net*

Start your day by cycling out to the beach to enjoy the sea views at Bloemendaal aan Zee. Lunch in one of the beach cafes or take a short bike ride into the dunes to cafe **Parnassia aan Zee**. Make your way back through the Nationaal Park Zuid-Kennemerland, following signs for the Vogelmeer lake, which is great for bird-watching, and Het Wed, for swimming and sunbathing. Once back in town, sample the local beers at the **Jopenkerk** or **Uiltje Bar** and finish off with dinner on the roof terrace at **DeDakkas** (p216), with views over the Grote Kerk.

Climb a Windmill

The windmill that dominates a bend on the Spaare River is **De Molen Adriaan** (*molenadriaan.nl; adult/child €7.50/3.50*), built in the 18th century to help produce cement. During the 45-minute visit, guided by volunteers, you get to climb its narrow stairs and get a great view across Haarlem. The much-loved windmill burned down in 1932 and Haarlemmers then collected money to rebuild it.

Hit the Beach

Less than 5km west of Haarlem are the dunes, lakes, lagoons and Corsican firs of **Nationaal Park Zuid-Kennemerland**. It's a fantastic place to walk, cycle or swim. A good starting point is **De Zandwaaier Visitor Centre**, which has bike hire, maps and Het Duincafé (a good cafe). Only a five-minute cycle from here is Het Wed, a lake ideal for swimming.

Ten minutes' further by bike is Strand Oosterpas swimming lake, also hugely popular for a swim on sunny days. At 50m, the Kopje van Bloemendaal is the highest dune in the country, just outside the eastern border of the park, with views of the sea and Amsterdam. Members of the Dutch Resistance are laid to rest at the Erebegraafplaats Bloemendaal cemetery. To reach the park, take bus 81 from Haarlem train station, drive the N200 towards Bloemendaal aan Zee, or cycle out of Haarlem along Brouwersvaart.

Around 7.5km west of central Haarlem is a long, gleaming beach, **Bloemendaal aan Zee**. On a warm day, it feels glorious, though the North Sea is distinctly less Caribbean than the soft white sands. Various outfits offers water sports such as kite-surfing. It's backed by laid-back restaurants and cafes, hotting up on summer evenings, with pop-up DJ events. Take bus 81 here from Haarlem (every 15 minutes) or it's a half-hour bike ride.

Zaanse Schans

TIME FROM AMSTERDAM: **25MIN**

See Zaanse Schans' Working Windmills

The Zaan region unfolds in flat, fertile fields sliced by canals and dotted with farmhouses, windmills, cows and woolly white sheep. At its heart lies Zaanse Schans. As one of the Netherlands' most popular destinations, it's fantastically touristy but retains its rustic charm and is much less busy outside the summer months.

Gloriously pretty, resembling a fantasy of Dutch early industrial life, Zaanse Schans' windmills are mostly still functioning, with enthusiastic volunteers on hand to explain the processes as you explore and a chance to get up close with the vast and complex moving parts in their interiors. They had many different purposes: **De Huisman** was a former spice mill, which used to produce the famous mustard sold from the mill shop. **De Kat** is the most-visited mill, and still produces paint and pigment; you can climb the windmill for an excellent view. **De Zoeker** and **De Bonte Hen** are both oil mills, with peanut and seed oils available in their shops.

Zaanse Schans' windmills

HISTORY OF THE ZAAN REGION

The Zaan region was home to the world's largest timber port in the 16th and 17th centuries, dotted by hundreds of windmills. In the early 20th century, they began to be demolished, and Frans Mars, a painter and educator, founded an association to try to protect them. Local mayor Joris in 't Veld suggested moving historic buildings to an area for their preservation. Architect Jaap Schipper found the location and created the layout. Mars suggested the name 'Zaanse Schans' from 'Kalverschans', which reflects the fortified area where Zaan residents held off the Spanish in the 16th century during the Eighty Years' War.

Het Klaverblad is a sawmill, only open by appointment. The **Bleeke Dood** flour mill (currently closed) is the oldest windmill in the country.

As well as windmills, the area has various small shop-museums: the supermarket **Albert Heijn** has an early incarnation here that's especially charming, a gabled, green-painted house with the original shop fittings inside. A clog factory turns out wooden shoes as if grinding keys. The **Zaans Museum** tells the history of the area with some interactive exhibits. **Catharina Hoeve Cheese Farm** has vintage interiors constructed using antique beams, doors and so on, and hosts cheese-making demonstrations and tastings.

With 2.6 million visitors in 2024 and just 100 inhabitants, from 2026 Zaanse Schans is charging an admission fee *(per person €17.50)* to the entire village; prices include the Zaans Museum and windmill entry. Remember that people live here and to respect their homes and privacy.

From the Zaandijk Zaanse Schans train station, it's a 1km walk across the Zaan river to the village. Alternatively, it's a lovely 18km cycle ride from Amsterdam Centraal via Landsmeer and De Stootersplas in western Waterland.

Alkmaar

TIME FROM AMSTERDAM: **1HR**

Catch the Cheese Market

Alkmaar is a handsome small medieval town, most famous for the flourishing tourist spectacle of its colourful **Kaasmarkt** (cheese market), on Fridays between April and September. This is photo-op heaven, full of porters in colourful cheese-guild hats, pulling cheese piled on wooden sledges, and dealers in white smocks, who insert a hollow rod to extract a cheese sample, and sniff and crumble to check fat and moisture content.

BEST ALKMAAR ACTIVITIES

Grachtenrondvaart Alkmaar Runs 45-minute canal tours every hour, passing under some 22 bridges, departing from its Mient jetty.

El Kombi SUP Has lessons, SUP hire (€20 per 1½hr) or guided tours from its base close to the city centre.

De Kraak Offers self-drive boat rental (€15 per hr), as well as kayak and SUP hire.

Alkmaar Cruises Go further afield with this outfit, with tours to Zaanse Schans or Fort Marken.

Pesie Rent a Bike Rent a bike/e-bike/ tandem/cargo bike (€13/28/23/50 per day).

The town centres on the pin-striped Gothic **Stadhuis**, Alkmaar's City Hall, built between 1509 and 1520, with a Dutch Classicist wing added in 1694. A few hundred metres on is the **Waaggebouw** ('weigh house'), a 14th-century chapel that two centuries later became the town's cheese weighing centre; the crenellated gable was added after the town withstood the 16th-century Spanish siege. It now contains more cheese at the **Hollands Kaasmuseum**, the cheese museum.

Close by is brewery **De Boom**, housing the **Nationaal Biermuseum**, a deep dive into the amber nectar, featuring beer-making equipment. Admission includes a drink in its sociable bar, and there's also the historic De Boom downstairs, a lovely old pub on the canal.

Art lovers should make a stop at the **Stedelijk Museum**, which includes Charley Toorop's fiercely realistic painting of the town cheese porters.

Visit a Sail-Through Former Auction House

The marshland area north of Alkmaar was once home to 15,000 tiny, yet productive, farms, each one an island, whose farmers tended their crops by rowboat. A 9km bike ride north of Alkmaar, Broek op Langedijk is home to the fascinating **Museum BroekerVeiling**. It centres on the extraordinary auction house that was built in 1877 on 1900 piles with canals running through it, which closed in 1973. Take a seat on the wooden benches in the auction room where buyers used to bid on produce as farmers paddled it through on boats.

Your ticket includes another amazing experience: a boat tour around the scenic floating fields, with around 200 surviving island plots like lozenges in the water. You can also hire an **electric barge/canoe** (€27.50/7.50 per hour) to explore the waterways yourself.

SEAN PAVONE/SHUTTERSTOCK

Utrecht

Utrecht

TIME FROM AMSTERDAM: **25MIN**

Discover Roman Utrecht

Utrecht's Roman origins make it one of the country's three oldest towns. With its pretty tree-lined canals, it's a cultural hub packed with entertainment, great museums and throngs of young people – this is the Netherlands' top university city with some 70,000 students in term time and a plethora of fun bars and cafes to match.

Built on the site of Roman military fort Castellum Trajectum, constructed around 45–47 CE to protect the northern Roman border, the **Domtoren** *(domtoren.nl)* is the city's iconic belfry tower and at 112m, the Netherlands' tallest. Finally revealed after years of being hidden in restorers' scaffolding, it forms a visual axis for the city seen from any direction, especially given cunning lighting effects that accentuate its features at night. Hour-long guided **belfry tours** *(adult/student €14.50/8.50)* climb steps to the highest accessible point (95m), stopping at 11m, 25m, 49m and 70m, after which the stairs get a little narrow.

Across the square is the **Domkerk** *(St Martin's Cathedral; domkerk.nl; by donation)*. If you think its shape seems odd, that's because it's only half the original size. A once-giant nave was destroyed by a freak summer hurricane in 1674. Catholics

UTRECHT HISTORY

Utrecht started life two millennia ago as Trajectum, a *castrum* (fort) on the Roman Empire's northern border. Also called 'the Limes', it guarded the Rhine, which flowed this way at that time. Northumbrian monk-bishop St Willibrord founded a cathedral here around 695 CE, with Utrecht growing into a major spiritual centre.

However, politico-religious turmoil in the 16th century proved especially severe in Utrecht. The bishops lost their secular powers and 1579's Union of Utrecht formed the core alliance of the Protestant, anti-Spanish states that would lead eventually to the formation of the modern Netherlands. Soon Amsterdam was outshining Utrecht economically. Nonetheless Utrecht's important university (founded in 1636) was developing fast and today the city is the 'Cambridge of the Netherlands'.

 EATING IN UTRECHT: OUR PICKS

VandeStreek: Steak *frites*, vegan burgers and sharing plates with canal-side seating and craft beers on tap. *3-11pm Mon-Thu, noon-2am Fri-Sat, noon-10pm Sun* €€

Stadskasteel Oudaen: Part restaurant, part *grand café*, part microbrewery, housed in a gentrified canal-side 'troubadour's castle', dating from 1280. *11am-late* €€

Olivier: Numerous Belgian beers and good-value pub fare to enjoy in a super-characterful reworking of a large former church, complete with organ. *noon-late* €

Vegitalian: Two very different rooms for delicious small-plate vegetarian dishes. Designed to share; fine alone for small appetites. *8.30am-10pm* €

saw the disaster as God's retribution for the reformation. Protestants saw it as a miracle that the belfry survived intact. The nave was never rebuilt, but if you look closely, you'll notice that the square (Domplein) is tiled in places with grey octagons. These mark where the nave's soaring pillars once stood.

Beneath is a fascinating archaeological site that unlocks more than former cathedral foundations. The site goes back to the Roman period, as you'll see if you take one of the **DOMunder Experiences** (domunder.nl), sold online or through the nearby tourist office. The standard **Discovery Tour** (adult/student €14.50/10) reveals 2000 years of history with artefacts left lying where they were found. Use your lantern to unlock information as you go. Another option explores the remains of **Paleis Lofen** (paleislofen.nl; adult/student €12.50/10). That was a 12th-century residence of the Holy Roman Emperors, partly built by recycling Roman wallstone for its floors. For a quick taster you could spot some of that site's pillars by having a drink at **Walden** and asking to see its cellar bar (usually reserved for party groups). The **Domplein Highlights Tour** (adult/child €25/12.50) gives condensed versions of both DOMunder and Paleis Lofen tours plus a climb up the first 25m of the belfry. Unsuitable for children under 8 years old.

Wander Utrecht's Double-Decker Canals

The city's two most charming canals – buzzy **Oudegracht** and idyllically peaceful **Nieuwegracht** – cut right through the historic quarter. Both are unusual for their double-decker towpaths. Before Amsterdam was of any importance, Utrecht was a major river-trading hub and merchants offloaded goods into *kelders* (storerooms) at water level. Meanwhile roadways were built above, creating the canals' special appearance, with cats protected in Utrecht as a way to reduce rodents. Today many of the Oudegracht *kelders* are used as cafes and restaurants, while some on Nieuwegracht are rented out as tourist accommodation, notably through the Court Hotel.

To take to the water you can rent 12-seater electric **'party boats'** (sloepdelen.nl or sloephurenutrecht.nl), kayaks and canoes (several providers), and **pedal boats** (stromma.com/en -nl/utrecht). For a tour experience, **Schuttevaer** (schuttevaer .com) runs two loop-routes several times daily with commentary in up to three languages. Both go down Oudegracht; then the one-hour tour loops clockwise under Hoog Catharijne while the 90-minute version takes the prettier anticlockwise route past parkland water bastions.

Rotterdam

TIME FROM AMSTERDAM: **40–70MIN** 🚆

Get a Cultural Fix at Museumpark

A greenery-filled 'city living room' with interconnected open-air spaces with shady trees, paths, terraces, water features and sculptures, Museumpark is flanked by cultural institutions. It's anchored by the **Museum Boijmans Van Beuningen** (under renovation until 2029). The museum's entire collection is

BUILDING UP ROTTERDAM

On this architectural stroll, you'll take in some of Rotterdam's most iconic examples of the city's visionary and adventurous structures.

START	END	LENGTH
Markthal	FENIX	3.7km; 2–3 hours

Eye-popping ❶ **Markthal** opened in 2014. Designed by Winy Maas, its horseshoe-shaped arch incorporates 228 apartments; inside, a giant mural soars above food stalls and restaurants.

Across Rotterdam's largest square, Binnenrotte, the ❷ **Blaakse Bos**, a yellow-and-white-coloured, crazily tilting 'forest' of 38 cube-shaped apartments perched on hexagonal pylons, was designed by Piet Blom and completed in 1984. South on Oudehaven, Europe's first 'skyscraper', the 45m-high art-nouveau ❸ **Witte Huis**, completed in 1898, is a rare survivor of Rotterdam's prewar architecture.

Cross the Nieuwe Maas via the 1996-built ❹ **Erasmusbrug** – an all-white cable-stayed bridge locally dubbed *de zwaan* (the swan). Rising on the river's southern side at Holland Amerikakade is ❺ **De Rotterdam**, a 2013-completed 'vertical city' of three interconnected towers designed by Rem Koolhaas. Southwest, the ❻ **Hotel New York** occupies the Holland America Line's former headquarters on the Wilhelminapier. Built from red brick in Jugendstil (art nouveau) style in 1901, the second of its two copper-domed clock towers was completed in 1917. Directly south on Katendrecht (De Kaap; the Cape), 2025-opened migration museum and cultural hub ❼ **FENIX** is topped with a double-helix stainless-steel-and-timber 'tornado' staircase leading to a 24m-high platform with spectacular 360-degree views.

Artists Arno Coenen and Iris Roskam's Markthal mural *Cornucopia* (Horn of Plenty) was inspired by 17th-century Dutch still-life paintings.

One Blaakse Bos apartment (with furniture custom-built to fit the odd angles), the **Kijk-Kubus Museumwoning**, is now a museum open daily to the public.

The Holland America Line's grand steam liner, the **SS Rotterdam**, now permanently moored across from its former headquarters, has tours above and below deck.

223

THE WWII BLITZ

Rotterdam changed forever on 14 May 1940, when 90 Luftwaffe planes dropped over 1000 bombs on the city, levelling the medieval centre and many neighbourhoods. The Blitz killed more than 900 people, and destroyed at least 24,000 homes, 24 churches, 2000 shops, 775 warehouses and 62 schools. Some 80,000 Rotterdam-mers were made homeless.

Reconstruction architect Cornelis van Traa devised a completely new spatial layout. New residential areas were built on the outskirts and the centre gained high-rise commercial buildings and innovations like the Lijnbaan strip-mall. The era of experimentation in urban design and architecture had arrived, and continues here today.

Het Nieuwe Instituut, Rotterdam

contained in the **Depot Boijmans Van Beuningen** *(boijmans. nl; adult/child €20/free)*, a world-first open-access storage facility in an extraordinary mirrored disco-ball-like structure covered by 1,664 glass panels, designed by Winy Maas, with a panoramic rooftop home to a garden and restaurant.

Also in Museumpark are design hub **Het Nieuwe Instituut** *(nieuweinstituut.nl; adult/child incl Huis Sonneveld €18/ free)*, containing the Dutch Architecture and Urban Planning National Collection; preserved 1933 villa **Huis Sonneveld** *(adult/child €12/free)*; the 1938 villa-housed International Expressionism **Chabot Museum** *(chabotmuseum.nl; adult/ child €12/free)*; dynamic gallery the **Kunsthal** *(kunsthal.nl; adult/child €18/free)*; and kid-friendly **Het Natuurhistorisch Museum** *(hetnatuurhistorisch.nl; adult/child €13.50/7.50)*, in what was the original estate's family home before the museum's – and park's – foundation in 1927.

Cruise Rotterdam's Harbour & Port with Royal Spido

Setting sail since 1919, **Koninklijke Spido** *(Royal Spido; spido. nl)* runs 75-minute **harbour tours** *(adult/child €17.50/9.80)* departing from Willemsplein, with awesome views of the skyscraper-filled skyline and ship-filled harbour, accompanied

Award-winning fries

EATING IN ROTTERDAM: OUR PICKS

Bas Bakt: Handcrafted sourdough and buttery croissants are used in sandwiches and toasties to eat at its sociable tables or sunny terrace. *8am-4pm Mon-Sat* €

Teds: All-day brunches using herbs, vegetables and honey harvested here on the rooftop of the 1950s Schieblock. *10am-5pm Mon-Wed, 10am-7pm Thu-Sat, 9am-5pm Sun* €€

Ter Marsch & Co: Former butcher's with multiaward-winning burgers like the Gojira (dry-aged ribeye, bulgogi pulled pork, kimchi and yuzu-ginger sauce). *noon-10pm* €€

Celest: On top of the Netherlands' tallest building, Zalmhaventoren, with panoramic skyline views. *restaurant noon-11pm Wed-Sat, Sky Bar to 11.30 Wed-Sun* €€€

by multilingual commentary. There are up to 10 departures daily in July and August, fewer during the rest of the year.

At least one Saturday a month, you can book a 2½-hour **extended tour** *(adult/child €29.50/17.75)* for closer views of the cranes, containers and precision shipping operations of Europe's biggest port.

Hit the Surf in Downtown Rotterdam

For a wild one-of-a-kind ride, you can surf year-round right beside the city centre's landmark Markthal at **RiF010 Urban Surf Rotterdam** *(rif010.nl; surf session/lesson from €45/50).* In the works for over a decade before launching in 2024, this open-air wave pool surrounded by skyscrapers has an energy-efficient design and 100% sustainably generated wave pool with perfect broken and unbroken waves from 1m up to 1.6m (settings are adjusted for experience levels) every seven seconds.

For surfers who know the fundamentals, sessions start with a safety briefing before you get in on the beach side (De Baai) and paddle to the Rif and wait in the takeoff zone lineup – even at peak capacity you can catch upwards of 10 waves a session. Lessons are available for all levels. Boards are provided, with wetsuits and other rentals available. Bring swimwear and sunscreen and arrive around 45 minutes beforehand. Kids must be aged eight and over, and be able to swim. Its surfbar-restaurant has a terrace overlooking the waves.

View the Nederlands Fotomuseum

The nation's premier platform for visual storytelling, the **Nederlands Fotomuseum** *(Netherlands National Museum of Photography; nederlandsfotomuseum.nl; adult/child €16/ free),* closed Mondays, curates diverse exhibitions from its exceptional collection of over six million images that reflect Dutch photography from 1842 on, and mounts topical temporary exhibitions.

From early 2026, its spectacular new home is the Pakhuis Santos on the Rijnhaven in Katendrecht. Built between 1901 and 1903 to store coffee, this bluestone-based red-brick warehouse has been redesigned by Rotterdam's WDJArchitecten and Hamburg's Renner Hainke Wirth Zirn Architekten, and topped with a two-storey glass-and-lacy-aluminium 'crown'. Along with exhibition space, the building's eight open-plan floors incorporates archives, studios, a photography bookshop, ground-floor cafe and panoramic restaurant overlooking Rotterdam's skyline.

DUTCH DISTILLERS DISTRICT, SCHIEDAM

Infused with history (like Amsterdam, Schiedam turned 750 in 2025), this municipality on the Schie, a quick metro ride away on Rotterdam's western edge, became an 18th-century hub for the production of *jenever* (Dutch gin). At the industry's height, Schiedam had over 30 windmills and 392 businesses distilling malt wine and adding juniper to produce the liquor, which was shipped all over the world. Schiedam is still home to seven central windmills (the world's tallest) and around a dozen active distilleries. They're listed on sdam.nl, along with *jenever* public artworks including a 50m fire-iron-branded, clay-tiled walkway and vintage advertising murals on and around Hoogstraat, plus festivals, gin-making workshops and guided district tours.

Den Haag

TIME FROM AMSTERDAM: **50MIN**

Stroll Den Haag's Historic Centre

Stately Den Haag (The Hague; locally known as 's-Gravenhage, 'The Counts' Hedge') is the Dutch royal residence and seat of government (despite Amsterdam being the country's capital). It's home to the under-renovation Binnenhof parliament on the Hofvijver lake and institutions including the UN at the **Vredespaleis** (Peace Palace).

RENOVATING THE BINNENHOF

In autumn 2021, work began on renovating one of the world's oldest parliaments and the country's oldest monumental structure. Home to both houses of the Dutch government, the 4000-room, 90,000-sq-metre Binnenhof (Inner Court) complex by the Hofvijver lake ranges around a central courtyard once used for executions; its ceremonial Ridderzaal (Knights' Hall) dates from the 13th century. The buildings' condition is proving to be worse than foreseen, and spiralling costs and heightened security requirements (including a fortified bunker for logistics operations) have so far quadrupled the budget to €2 billion and prolonged completion until at least 2030. Parliament meanwhile meets in a temporary building on Bezuiden-houtseweg.

King Willem-Alexander's official offices are at **Paleis Noordeinde** (he and his family live at Huis ten Bosch, northeast of Den Haag's city centre). Originally a medieval farmhouse, it was enlarged by Frederik Hendrik, Prince of Orange, Count of Nassau between 1640 and 1645, creating its current 'H' form. It's mostly closed to the public but you can picnic amid the lawns, hedgerows, flower beds, fountains and ponds of the Paleistuin (palace gardens).

At Plaats, the former forecourt of the **Binnenhof**, the **Informatiecentrum Binnenhof Renovatie** *(binnenhofrenovatie. nl; free)* has details of the Binnenhof's multiyear renovation and archaeological finds unearthed during the process. By the reflective **Hofvijver** lake, the 28m-high viewing platform **Kijksteiger Uitzichtpunt** overlooks the Binnenhof's renovation works: climb its 149 steps to see the mirrored construction shed with a coastal-dune roof garden.

On the Groenmarkt, **Het Oude Stadhuis**, built in 1664–65 and extended in 1733, is a splendid example of Dutch Renaissance architecture with stepped gables, pediments, and brick and natural stone. Opposite is Den Haag's magnificent **Grote Kerk** *(Great Church; grote-kerk.nl; adult/child €3/free),* one of the city's oldest buildings, also known as Grote of Sint-Jacobskerk (St James' Church). A wood chapel was built in 1256 and construction of the stone church began in 1335, expanding to its current size during the 15th century, with a 16th-century carved wooden pulpit. Its hexagonal tower, **De Haagse Toren** *(dehaagse toren.nl; adult/child €8.50/6.50),* was completed in 1424; the city carillonneur plays its 80m-high, 51-bell carillon from noon to 1pm on Monday, Wednesday and Friday. Climbing the tower's 288 steps (book ahead) provides spectacular views.

Puzzle Over MC Escher's Complex Works

The wonderful **Escher in Het Paleis** *(escherinhetpaleis.nl; adult/child €13.50/10.50),* closed Mondays, celebrates Dutch graphic artist MC (Maurits Cornelis) Escher (1898–1972), displaying over 120 of his woodcuts and lithographs, including many of his best-known works. Fascinated by mathematical patterns, Escher investigated themes of repetition, circularity, infinity and symmetry throughout his career. In 2002, the museum moved into the 18th-century Lange Voorhout Palace, perhaps attracted by its beautiful staircase, which appears to

Continued on p230

Going strong since 1861

EATING IN DEN HAAG: OUR PICKS

Botanica: Locally grown fruit and vegetables served from an open kitchen. Butterflies on the ceiling and courtyard-garden tables outside. *7am-5pm* €€

Simonis in de Stad: Take away pickled herring, smoked eel, shrimp and battered whitefish. Restaurant upstairs. *10am-6.30pm Mon-Sat, noon-6.30pm Sun* €

Zebedeüs: Daytime dishes include open sandwiches, soups and toasties, with more elaborate mains at night. *noon-4pm & 5.30-9.30pm* €€

Dungelmann: Famous *kroketten* (croquettes) and *gehaktballen* (meatballs). *9.30am-6pm Tue, Wed, Fri & Sat, to 9pm Thu, 11.30am-6pm Sun & Mon* €

TOP EXPERIENCE

Mauritshuis

One of the world's great art museums, the Mauritshuis is the repository of 17th-century Dutch and Flemish masterpieces by Vermeer, Rembrandt, Rubens, Hals and many others. Situated on the reflective Hofvijver, it has housed the Royal Cabinet of Paintings since 1822. It was privatised in 1995 and expanded in 2014. Its predecessor, the silk- and chandelier-adorned Galerij Prins Willem V, can be visited on the same ticket.

Jewels of the Collection

Vermeer's *Girl with a Pearl Earring* (c 1665) is the pride of the museum's collection. It hangs alongside Vermeer's *View of Delft* (c 1660–61) with its interplay of light and shade.

Other exquisite masterpieces include Carel Fabritius' lifelike *The Goldfinch* (1654), and *Ice Scene* (c 1610) by Amsterdam-born Hendrick Avercamp, depicting skaters on a frozen river, with windmills and thatched houses in the background.

The collection is rich in portraits, including Rembrandt's *The Anatomy Lesson of Dr Nicolaes Tulp* (1632), painted in Amsterdam when he was only 25, and Hals' portraits of Aletta Hanemans (1625) and her husband Jacob Olycan (1625).

Re-Examining the Past

The Mauritshuis occupies the 1641-built mansion by architect Jacob van Campen for Count Johan Maurits van Nassau-Siegen (1604–1679), governor of the colony of Dutch Brazil, captured from the Portuguese by the Dutch West India Company. In recent years, the museum has addressed Maurits' role in the transatlantic slave trade. A permanent exhibition features works such as *Brazilian Landscape with a House under Construction* (c 1655–60) by Frans Post, among the artists and scientists who travelled with Maurits to Brazil.

● Tickets are by time-slot entry only. The museum is quietest after 3pm. Download the free multimedia smart tour app.

● Mauritshuis admission includes entry to the **Galerij Prins Willem V** (otherwise adult/child €5.50/free; no time slots required).

● **Brasserie Mauritshuis** serves dishes made from local ingredients inspired by the museum's paintings.

PRACTICALITIES
● mauritshuis.nl
● adult/child €20/free
● Mauritshuis 1-6pm Mon, 10am-6pm Tue-Sun; Galerij Prins Willem V noon-5pm Tue-Sun

Den Haag City to Sea

Den Haag's history is intertwined with its fishing port and harbour, and long, sandy strand. An extraordinary cylindrical painting of Scheveningen – the oldest 19th-century panorama still displayed in its purpose-built original location – is the ideal place to set off on this 6.3km-long cycling trip to the coast it depicts, via avenues, forest and rose gardens. It's also possible to walk this route and return to central Den Haag by tram.

❶ Panorama Mesdag

Begin at the Panorama Mesdag. This immense, 14m-high, 360-degree painting of the sea, dunes and fishing village of Scheveningen, 120m in circumference, was created in 1881 by Hendrik Willem Mesdag of the Impressionist-influenced Hague School. (Closed Mondays.)

The Ride: Cycle northwest along Zeestraat then Scheveningseweg, passing the Vredespaleis (Peace Palace), to reach the leafy Scheveningse Bosjes.

❷ Scheveningse Bosjes

A bronze bust of poet Constantijn Huygens marks the entrance to the forested, squirrel-filled Scheveningse Bosjes: a dune area planted with oaks, elms and poplars in the 17th century, with snowdrops, foxgloves and wild hyacinths in spring.

The Ride: Exiting the Scheveningse Bosjes on the northern side at the Cremerbrug, you'll pass the 1953 monument to Social Democratic Workers Party leader Pieter Jelles Troelstra (1860–1930), where Labour Day is commemorated on 1 May.

Rode Havenlicht and sailboat near the harbour

❸ Westbroekpark

Crossing the wooden foot/cycle bridge brings you to the 1920s-created, English-style Westbroekpark, located on a small island. From June to November, 20,000 roses in 300 varieties bloom in its rosarium. Sculptures include the charming bronze *De Gelaarsde Kat* (Puss in Boots; c 1943) by Den Haag artist Johan Keller (1863–1944).

The Ride: Take Nieuwe Duinweg to the charming paved shopping street of Keizerstraat, and ride towards the tower of the red-brick Oude Kerk Scheveningen.

❹ Oude Kerk Scheveningen

Appearing in the Panorama Mesdag, the former fishing village's oldest remaining building is the Oude Kerk Scheveningen (1466). Its ceiling represents an upturned ship's hull; look too for the stained-glass window featuring a ship with red sails, and 17th-century whale jawbone.

The Ride: Continue northwest past the church to the beachside promenade where you'll see the Vissersvrouw van Scheveningen.

❺ Vissersvrouw van Scheveningen

Follow Keizerstraat to the beachside promenade, where Gerard Bakker's 1982 bronze sculpture the *Vissersvrouw van Scheveningen* (Fisherman's Wife) stares out to sea. Footsteps north, Marcel van Zijp's 2013 Vissersnamenmonument records 1366 fishermen who have drowned offshore.

The Ride: Cycle southwest along the promenade past the red-painted lighthouse Vuurtoren van Scheveningen to Noordelijk Havenhoofd. Follow the breakwater.

❻ Rode Havenlicht

Guarding the entrance to the harbour, the red-and-white-striped beacon Rode Havenlicht gives you sweeping views of the 4.5km-long Scheveningen Strand's kite-surfers, board riders and beach bars.

Continued from p226

go up to the second floor but doesn't – a very Escher-like optical illusion. Collection highlights include the *Tower of Babel* (1928) and the 7m-long circular work *Metamorphosis III* (1967–68), inspired by the interlinked concepts of eternity and infinity.

Constructed between 1760 and 1764, the palace was designed by Pieter de Swart for Anthony Patras, mayor of Sloten and the States General representative. Later owned by the Hope family, financers of European nobility (Napoleon stayed briefly in 1811), it was purchased in 1896 by Queen Emma (great-great grandmother of current king, Willem-Alexander), who used it as a winter residence until her death in 1934. Queen Emma's former kitchen, with beautiful floor and wall tiling, now houses the MC Café.

Brave a Medieval Prison

A remnant of the 13th-century city fortifications, the Gevangenpoort functioned as a prison from 1428 to 1825. Now the **Rijksmuseum de Gevangenpoort** *(gevangenpoort.nl; adult/ child €15/7.50, guided tour extra €5)*, it vividly evokes the experiences of both prisoners and their jailers. The museum's displays (branding irons, flogging benches and frightening torture devices) mean it's not suitable for kids aged under eight. Capacity is limited; book time-slot tickets ahead online.

Delft

TIME FROM AMSTERDAM: **1HR**

Ascend the Tower of Delft's Nieuwe Kerk

Gracing Delft's skyline with the Netherlands' second-highest tower (after Utrecht's Domtoren; p221), the **Nieuwe Kerk** *(oudeennieuwekerkdelft.nl; adult/child with Oude Kerk €9.50/4.50, tower only €7/4, churches & tower €14.50/6)* is only 'new' in relation to the city's Oude Kerk (Old Church). In 1351, a beggar and shopkeeper both saw a vision of a golden church dedicated to Mary, an apparition that recurred for the next 30 years. Eventually, the city was persuaded to begin construction in 1381 on a temporary wooden church, with the stone basilica built around it from 1384; it was finally completed in 1655.

The Nieuwe Kerk has been the final resting place of almost every member of the House of Orange since 1584, including William of Orange (Willem the Silent), who lies in an over-the-top marble mausoleum designed by Hendrick de Keyser. Statesman Hugo de Groot is also buried here. Other interior highlights include its 1839-built organ with over 3000 pipes; see kerkconcertendelft.nl for concert programmes.

Climbing 376 narrow, spiralling steps in its 109m-high tower rewards with views to Rotterdam and Den Haag on a clear day (kids must be over six).

Pay Your Respects to Vermeer at the Oude Kerk

Willem II granted Delft city rights in 1246, the church's official founding date, though it actually dates from an earlier wooden

---

THE DUTCH ROYALS

A constitutional monarchy since 1814, the Kingdom of the Netherlands' ruling House of Orange-Nassau *(royal-house.nl)* has roots in the 16th century when Spain's Philip II appointed William of Orange (William the Silent) *stadtholder* (governor and commander in chief). Dutch royals have no substantive power within the government, performing a largely ceremonial role.

After exiling in WWII, Queen Wilhelmina abdicated for her daughter, Queen Juliana, who abdicated in 1980 for her daughter Queen Beatrix; her own abdication in 2013 ended more than a century of female reign, when her son King Willem-Alexander acceded the throne with his wife, Máxima. The eldest of their three daughters, Catharina-Amalia, is heir apparent.

Nieuwe Kerk, Delft

VERMEER'S DELFT

The great Dutch Master Johannes Vermeer (1632–75) lived his entire life in Delft, fathering 11 children and leaving behind fewer than 40 paintings. (The actual number is disputed as the authorship of some canvases attributed to him has been questioned by modern-day Vermeer experts.) Vermeer's subjects were drawn from everyday life in Delft, his interiors depicting domestic scenes and his portraits remarkably lifelike. Vermeer's best-known exterior work, *View of Delft* (c 1660–61) captures the light and shadow of a partly cloudy day. It's possible to visit the location where he painted it, across the canal at Hooikade, southeast of the train station.

church here in 1240. Originally known as Sint Bartholomeusas, its 75m-high, 1350-completed tower leans nearly 2m from the vertical due to subsidence caused by its canal location, giving it its nickname Scheve Jan ('Leaning John'). Halfway up in its oak belfry, one of its two bells rings every half hour.

From 1396, the church was known as Sint Hippolytuskerk until the Nieuwe Kerk's construction, when it became the **Oude Kerk** *(oudeennieuwekerkdelft.nl; adult/child with Nieuwe Kerk €9.50/4.50)*. Its older section features an austere barrel vault; the newer, early 16th-century northern transept has a Gothic vaulted ceiling. Its beautiful carved main pulpit dates from 1548, surviving fires and Reformation ransacking. Its 2832-pipe organ is played during services and concerts ; see kerkconcertendelft.nl for programmes.

Look for Johannes Vermeer's memorial stone, upgraded in 2007.

Understand Vermeer's Art

The great painter Johannes Vermeer was born in Delft in 1632 and lived here until his death in 1675. While none of his works remain in the town, the **Vermeer Centrum Delft** *(vermeerdelft.nl; adult/child €12/free)*, in a reconstructed building on the historic site of the former St Lucas Guild, where Vermeer was Dean of Painters for four years, fills the gap with 37 actual-size, high-quality digital reproductions, video presentations and displays about 17th-century painting techniques and materials.

Cubes throughout Delft's historic centre mark significant places for Vermeer; the centre sells a booklet *(€3; English available)* for the Vermeer cube walk, illustrating the artist's life in the city.

RENOVATING THE MUSEUM PRINSENHOF DELFT

The former convent where William of Orange (William the Silent) was assassinated in 1584, becoming the world's first political leader to be murdered by a handgun (the bullet hole in the wall is preserved), now houses the **Museum Prinsenhof Delft** *(museumprinsen-hofdelft.nl)*. In early 2025, it closed for renovations that will enhance accessibility with a lift, and create a new entrance and allow natural light to stream through the building, with a cafe, shop and hands-on studio, in addition to exhibitions centred on William the Silent, the Delft Masters and Delftware, bringing Delft's stories to life. It's scheduled to reopen in 2027.

Marvel at Delft's Monumental Markt

One of Europe's largest historic market squares, the rectangular **Markt** has had a market here since the 13th century and was first paved in the late 15th century. The Nieuwe Kerk looms over its northeast end, with the **Stadhuis**, Delft's town hall, at the southeastern end, with its combination of Renaissance construction surrounding an early 14th-century tower. Behind it, the **Waag**, Delft's 16th-century weighing house, remained in use until 1960. It now houses the cafe-restaurant **De Waag**.

Markets still set up here on Thursdays, with around 150 stalls selling fresh fruit, vegetables, cheeses, spices, flowers, homewares and plenty of blue-and-white Delft souvenirs.

Delve into the History & Production of Delftware Pottery

In the 17th century, Delft had 32 factories producing Delft Blue earthenware but today only one remains. Koninklijke Porceleyne Fles, trading as **Royal Delft** *(royaldelft.com; adult/child €17/7.50)*, 1.5km south of the Markt, has been handcrafting its blue-and-white-painted porcelain since 1653.

Allow around an hour for an audio-guided tour of its museum's collections and a painting demonstration and the factory's production process. Book ahead for hands-on painting **workshops** *(adult/child from €45.50/35.50)*.

For a real treat, reserve ahead for **high tea** *(€31.50; minimum two people)*, served on Delft Blue tableware at its **Brasserie1653** (it also serves lunch). Delft Blue Line tickets include a **canal cruise** *(adult/child from €27.50/12)*.

Leiden

TIME FROM AMSTERDAM: **35MIN**

Visit Leiden's Foremost Museum

Threaded by canals lined by 17th-century buildings, Leiden is renowned as Rembrandt's birthplace, home to the Netherlands'

DMITRY RUKHLENKO/SHUTTERSTOCK

Markt, Delft

oldest, most prestigious university and a cache of museums within walking distance of each other. It's a grand gateway to the bulb fields and dunes of the Bollenstreek.

Leiden's foremost museum for fine art, history and crafts, the **Museum De Lakenhal** (*lakenhal.nl; adult/child €16/ free*), closed Monday, occupies a 1640-built premises (a former cloth warehouse) where it displays its exceptional permanent collection. Masterpieces include *The Spectacles Pedlar* by the city's native son Rembrandt, *The Astronomer* by Gerrit Dou (Rembrandt's first student), *Wrestling Couple* by Jan Steen, and *The Last Judgement* by Lucas van Leyden. Adjoining it, a striking contemporary building hosts temporary exhibitions.

Learn About Illuminating Subjects

The Netherlands' oldest university, **Universiteit Leiden** (*uni versiteitleiden.nl*) was a gift to Leiden from William the Silent in 1575 for withstanding two Spanish sieges in 1573 and 1574. The campus is a mix of modern and historic buildings that are scattered around town. Illustrious professors who have taught here include Einstein, and scientists' collections have enriched the city's dense concentration of museums.

Named in honour of physician, botanist, chemist and University of Leiden teacher Herman Boerhaave (1668–1738), the impressive museum of science and medicine **Rijksmuseum Boerhaave** (*rijksmuseumboerhaave.nl; adult/child €16.50/6*) has exhibits profiling major scientific discoveries in the Netherlands, and the doctors and scientists behind them. The museum is housed in a 15th-century convent that later became the first academic hospital in Northern Europe, with a multimedia introduction presented in a recreated anatomical theatre.

The **Rijksmuseum van Oudheden** (*National Museum of Antiquities; rmo.nl; adult/child €14/free*), with Greek,

Etruscan, Roman and Egyptian artefacts, is especially renowned for its Egyptian halls, which include the reconstructed Temple of Taffeh, mastabas from Saqqara and a room of mummy cases.

National research institute for biodiversity, **Naturalis Biodiversity Centre** *(naturalis.nl; adult/child €18/free)*, houses Europe's first T-Rex skeleton, named Trix. Sections span botany, geology, entomology (insects), invertebrates, vertebrates and palaeontology (fossils and more) collected by Dutch explorers, archaeologists and scientists all over the globe.

Founded by the university in 1590, the 'living museum' **Hortus Botanicus Leiden** *(hortusleiden.nl; adult/child €16.50/4.50)* is one of Europe's oldest botanical gardens; the majority of its collections originate from Southeast and East Asia, including steamy, orchid-filled tropical greenhouses. Admission often includes exhibitions at its 1633-founded **Oude Sterrewacht** (Old Observatory).

Follow in Rembrandt's Footsteps

The ninth child of a local miller, Rembrandt van Rijn was born in Leiden in 1606. The Dutch Master is celebrated at the **Young Rembrandt Studio** *(visitleiden.nl; adult/child €2.50/free)*, closed Mondays. It's set in the 17th-century house at Langebrug 89 where Rembrandt learned his craft between 1606 and 1630, studying in the studio of Jacob van Swanenburgh. A seven-minute video offers an introduction to his artistic development. Tech wizardry lets you create your own portrait in Rembrandt's distinctive style by holding your face in front of the camera and choosing from its six options (printing €10).

The studio is along the 4.5km **Rembrandt Route** walk (brochure €6.95), downloadable at visitleiden.nl or available from the tourist office opposite Centraal Station. The route passes significant locations in the artist's early life, including the gabled 1600-built **Latin School**, which Rembrandt attended from 1616 to 1620.

Trace the Pilgrims' History

Commemorating the city's Pilgrim history, Leiden's **Pilgrim Museum** moved to Kloksteeg 16a next to Pieterskerk in late 2025. It co-created Leiden's **Pilgrim Route** walking tour, with a route brochure *(€6.95)* downloadable at visitleiden.nl or available from the tourist office.

Cruise Leiden's Waterways

Leiden has 28km of city-centre canals spanned by 88 bridges that are idyllic for exploring by boat for a unique perspective of its historic architecture. Numerous companies rent boats typically accommodating six people (no boat licence required). Rates start at around €100 for two hours. Try **Bootjes en Broodjes** *(bootjesenbroodjes.nl)*.

If you'd rather sit back with someone else at the helm, Bootjes en Broodjes is also among Leiden operators offering guided **canal cruises** *(50min cruise adult/child €12.50/7.50)* in open-topped electric boats that are covered and heated in winter.

Keukenhof

Millions of multicoloured flowers bursting into bloom is a magical sight each spring at Keukenhof, in the Bollenstreek town of Lisse. Starting with daffodils, hyacinths, crocuses and early-blooming tulips from mid-March, with larger tulips and fritillaria from early April, and azaleas, rhododendrons and irises from early May, the 'most beautiful spring garden in the world' is a must in season.

Background

Originally 15th-century castle kitchen hunting grounds, Keukenhof's English-style gardens were laid out in 1857 by landscape architects Jan David Zocher and his son Louis Paul Zocher. Bulb growers debuted their spring-flower exhibition here in 1950. Today, upwards of 7 million bulbs incorporating over 800 varieties of tulips are planted by hand every autumn to bloom during Keukenhof's two-month-long opening season.

Activities & Facilities

Meandering the wooded paths winding through Keukenhof's themed gardens is the highlight but there are many other activities, including flower shows in Keukenhof's pavilions, climbing its 19th-century windmill, and taking a 45-minute cruise alongside bulb fields on open-topped electric whisper boats *(adult/child €11/5.50)*. Bike hire *(3hr/all day €11/16)* is also available for cycling in the surrounding flower fields.

Restaurants are located throughout the park. If the weather's fine, bring a picnic to designated areas beside the blooms.

Getting to Keukenhof

Keukenhof is a 35km bicycle ride southwest of Amsterdam Centraal; cycling one-way takes around two hours. 'Keukenhof-Buzz' shuttle buses from RAI Amsterdam, Haarlem, Schiphol Airport or Leiden, with round-trip public transport, are included in combitickets with Keukenhof admission.

TOP TIPS

● Prebook tickets with time-slot entry; tickets are valid until the park closes.

● Tickets are available online from mid-November.

● Bring extra layers in case it turns chilly (spring weather can be fickle), as well as waterproof shoes for muddy ground, and a rain jacket or umbrella.

PRACTICALITIES

● keukenhof.nl ● adult/child €21/9; combiticket from RAI €37/17.50; from Haarlem, Schiphol or Leiden €32/15 ● 8am-7pm mid-Mar–mid-May

Bollenstreek By Bike

Bring your bike from Amsterdam (or hire one nearby) for a beautiful 26km loop from Sassenheim through fragrant bulb fields that are ablaze with colourful tulips, jonquils, daffodils and hyacinths in spring (around mid-March to mid-May), and blooms such as dahlias, asters and sunflowers in late summer (mid-August to mid-October) in the heart of the Bollenstreek.

❶ Sassenheim

At the southern edge of the bulb fields, the charming red-brick town of Sassenheim is on the route of mid-April's 42km-long Bloemencorso (Flower Parade). Its **train station**, with direct services (25 minutes) from Amsterdam Zuid, makes the perfect *grand départ*.

The Ride: Skirt Sassenheim's southwest edge via Zandslootkade and follow the canal into the bulb fields. Head northwest on Frank van Borselenlaan; just north is De Tulperij.

❷ De Tulperij

Flower farm De Tulperij grows spring and summer blooms. You can take a farm tour, visit its show gardens, and pick your own flowers in season.

The Ride: Cycle northeast through the colour-filled bulb fields to the town of Lisse.

❸ Lisse

Lisse's 1900-built church **Sint Agathakerk**, co-financed by local bulb growers and featuring flower motifs, is known as the 'Cathedral of the Bollenstreek'. Ahead in Lisse's town centre, in a former bulb shed, the small

IPICS/SHUTTERSTOCK

Windmills, Bollenstreek

but fascinating **Museum de Zwarte Tulp** (Museum of the Black Tulip) has displays detailing mythical black tulips that helped fuel Tulipmania (p108) in 1636–37.

The Ride: Cycle northwest on Stationsweg past Kasteel Keukenhof (you can visit the forest and gardens but not the castle) on your left, and Keukenhof (p235) on your right, before cycling through bulb fields. Ahead on your left is the Tulip Barn.

4 Tulip Barn

The Tulip Barn grows upwards of 1.5 million tulips in 200 varieties and has flower-garden photo props, a cafe and flower stand.

The Ride: Cycle northwest to De Zilk and take Zilkerbinnenweg southwest to the Tulip Experience.

5 Tulip Experience

To visit the show garden of the Tulip Experience, you'll need a prebooked time slot. Alongside its colourful tulip fields, it has a small museum and an indoor picking barn.

The Ride: Head south on Delfweg and northwest on Houtvesterslaan to reach the Uitkijkpunt Tespelduyn.

6 Uitkijkpunt Tespelduyn

Climb the wooden boardwalk-like staircase to the 14m-high Uitkijkpunt Tespelduyn, a lookout tower for rare elevated views of the colour-streaked fields below.

The Ride: Return to Delfweg and take Leidsevaart southwest along the Trekvaart Haarlem–Leiden canal through polder and bulb fields.

7 I Love Dahlia

An organic farm with a show garden and pick-your-own flowers, I Love Dahlia has over 20,000 blooms in 500 varieties over 10,000 sq metres. It's a wonderful stop for organic homemade fruit ice cream.

The Ride: Continue southwest along the Trekvaart Haarlem–Leiden canal and turn southeast, passing the town of Voorhout, then swing northeast to return to Sassenheim.

237

Where to Stay

Amsterdam's charming accommodation includes wonderful spaces where architects have breathed new life into old buildings. But charm doesn't come cheap and space is at a premium – reserve as far ahead as possible all year round.

Where to Stay If You Love...

Centuries-old canal houses, bars & entertainment

Medieval Centre & the Red Light District (p42) At the beating heart of sights, nightlife, theatres and transport; parts can be noisy, touristy and seedy.

History, green spaces & family attractions

Nieuwmarkt, Plantage & the Eastern Islands (p68) Lower-key Nieuwmarkt is near the action. Plantage properties sit amid peaceful greenery. Eastern Islands addresses can be further flung.

Atmospheric streetscapes & markets

Western Canal Ring, Jordaan & the West (p96) Charming canals, boutiques, *bruin cafés* (traditional pubs) and markets are close to popular sights; West's creative spaces are easily reached.

Famous nightlife venues & unique museums

Southern Canal Ring (p118) Central location handy for canal-house museums and restaurants. Can be crowded and touristy, especially around nightlife hubs Leidseplein and Rembrandtplein.

Blockbuster museums, parks & neighbourhood strolls

Vondelpark, Oud-West & Oud-Zuid (p144) Oud-Zuid's genteel, leafy streets around the Vondelpark are walking distance to Museumplein; increasingly happening Oud-West's backstreets are liveliest around cultural centre De Hallen.

Epicurean adventures & parklands

De Pijp & Zuid (p168) With fast metro access, De Pijp has fantastic drinking, dining and markets; further south in Zuid are sprawling parklands and striking modern developments.

Lush parks, multicultural dining & markets

Oosterpark & East of the Amstel (p184) Quiet residential streets surrounding parks with a local atmosphere just a short tram/metro ride to the action.

Street art & reimagined industrial spaces

Amsterdam Noord (p198) Just across the IJ, Noord has a burgeoning drinking, dining and creative scene, and some unique places to stay. Transport is limited in some areas.

Medieval Centre & the Red Light District

ARTSY & DESIGN

St Christopher's at the Winston €
MAP P44

Rock 'n' roll rooms, a busy nightclub with live bands nightly, a bar and restaurant, a beer garden and a smoking deck downstairs. En-suite dorms designed by artists (some are kinda 'out there').

Hotel The Exchange €€
MAP P44

Eye-popping rooms designed by students from the Amsterdam Fashion Institute. Rooms range from one- to five-star (with concept-driven designs). All have en-suite bathrooms.

art'otel amsterdam €€€
MAP P44

Rooms have original artwork and there's a basement public gallery with changing exhibitions; the lobby boasts a fireplace and library. Located directly opposite Centraal Station.

OH-SO LUXURY

Die Port van Cleve €€€
MAP P44

Opened in 1870 on the site of Heineken's first brewery, three monumental buildings give palatial vibes. Elegant design cues from blue-and-white Delftware.

Hotel de L'Europe €€€
MAP P44

Heineken family-owned, Amsterdam's 'other royal palace'. Classical elements (doorkeepers in top hats) and modern luxury rooms with canal views.

Hotel TwentySeven €€€
MAP P44

Ultra-luxury hotel in a monumental 1916 building overlooking the Royal Palace. Room sizes vary considerably but all are sumptuously decorated. Suites have butlers.

Hotel V Nesplein €€€
MAP P44

Sleek, spacious rooms filled with comfy vintage and designer furniture (some bathrooms even have tubs). Its industrial-styled restaurant, the Lobby, excels at brunches.

W Amsterdam €€€
MAP P44

Design-forward and trendy hotel in converted historic buildings (Royal Dutch Post's former telephone exchange). The rooftop lap pool is amazing.

Nieuwmarkt, Plantage & the Eastern Islands

BUDGET BARGAINS

Camping Zeeburg €
MAP P80

Colourful waterside cabins (single, double, quad), tent and van pitches, plus bike, kayak and SUP hire.

Elephant Hostel €
MAP P80

Friendly hostel with a gloriously preserved common room and cafe in an 1884 mansion. Dorms have box bunks, air-con and decent lockers. Showers are small but well designed.

Stayokay Stadsdoelen €
MAP P70

HI hostel behind a canal-front 1730 façade, fully renovated in 2025. Spacious dorms with un-curtained bunk beds and narrow lockers. Lots of chilling space with kettle, microwaves and beanbag seats. Bring along your own soap, towel and padlock.

Hotel Park Plantage €
MAP P80

Modestly priced midrange rooms with air-con and kettle in a location that's ideal for the Plantage museums and zoo. Tram 14 stops nearby.

HOTELS IN HISTORIC BUILDINGS

Hendrick's Hotel €€
MAP P70

One of several good options on Prins Hendrikkade, 10 minutes' walk from Centraal Station, the 25 rooms come in 11 different categories with wide price variations but all have air-con, coffee-maker and most are elevator-accessible.

Hotel Nes €€
MAP P70

Attractive 1890 building with canal-side location that's a quick hop across the Amstel

HOW MUCH FOR A NIGHT IN A...

Top-end hotel
from €180

Midrange hotel
from €100

Budget hotel
under €100

Hostel dorm bed
€25–80

from the Rembrandtsplein nightlife zone. However, rooms are pretty small and lack air-con.

Tivoli Doelen €€€
MAP P70

Triangle of pampered luxury in a historic flat-iron building dating from 1882, retaining some features of its original grandeur. Fabulous canal-side location; Rembrandt connections but no pool.

Hoxton Lloyd Hotel €€€
MAP P80

The 1921 Lloyd Hotel is worth visiting even if you don't stay in one of the 136 rooms, restored to show off its stylishly retro sense of early art deco.

CONTEMPORARY COMFORT

Rooms25 €€
MAP P80

Contemporary designer rooms at midrange prices right on the harbour above Kanteen25 restaurant. Some guests

love the peaceful yet fairly central location, others find it a little too obscure. Bike rental available.

Hotel Jakarta €€€
MAP P80

Swish contemporary hotel on the tip of Java Eiland with floor-to-ceiling windows, Indonesian woodcarvings, soaring palms and a swimming pool.

Western Canal Ring, Jordaan & the West

UNIQUE SLEEPS

Houseboat Ms Luctor €€
MAP P111

An organic breakfast basket (included) is delivered daily at this solar-powered, mahogany-panelled 1913 houseboat, moored in a quiet waterway. Guests can borrow bikes and a canoe for canal explorations. Minimum stay is three nights.

BackStage Hotel €€
MAP P98

Music-themed hotel loved by musicians, with a band-signature-covered piano and pool table in the bar, gig posters (many signed) lining the corridors, and retro-styled rooms with drum-kit lights plus guitars, turntables and vinyl to loan.

Conscious Hotel Westerpark €€
MAP P111

Entirely wind-powered, Westergas' 89-room Conscious Hotel (there are three more near the Vondelpark) incorporates recycled materials, down to coat hangers made from radiator parts. Aquaponic walls grow the cafe's vegetables and herbs for all-organic breakfasts.

WERNER LEROOY/SHUTTERSTOCK

Conscious Hotel Westerpark

CANAL-HOUSE JEWELS

Ambassade Hotel €€€
MAP P98

Rambling across 16 Herengracht canal houses, these 56 variously sized rooms and suites have antique furniture, gilded mirrors, chandeliers and CoBrA-movement art; most have romantic canal views. There's a library, bar and French brasserie.

't Hotel €€€
MAP P98

This 17th-century canal house's eight rooms are decorated with patterned wallpapers by interior-print designer Katarina Stupavska, whose family owns the hotel. A ladder reaches the family room's loft area. Breakfast is served in the tearoom.

Dylan €€€
MAP P98

Exquisite Keizersgracht canal house set around a herringbone-paved, topiary-filled inner courtyard. Bespoke furniture like silver-leaf and mother-of-pearl drinks cabinets adorns its 40 rooms. Its two-Michelin-starred restaurant Vinkeles also hosts private chef's tables aboard its boat.

Southern Canal Ring

MODERN & GOOD VALUE

Hotel Adolesce €€
MAP P120

Canal house just across from the H'ART Museum. This little family-owned hotel has comforting, old-fashioned charm. Steep steps lead to spotless, bright rooms of all shapes and sizes.

Weber Hotel €€
MAP P120

In a prime canal-side location, these simple yet contemporary rooms are the best you will find

TOURIST TAXES

Amsterdam levies a *toeristenbelasting* (tourist tax) of 12.5% excluding VAT on all accommodation (paid directly to the property; not always included in quoted rates). From 2026, VAT for all accommodation except camping rises to 21%.

around Leidseplein. Rooms for larger groups need to be booked well ahead. Provides bike rental.

SUSTAINABLE STAYS

ClinkCoco €
MAP P120

Once a high-end brothel, this boutique hostel's doubles and dorms are light, bright and airy. There's a relaxing back garden, a well-equipped kitchen and a super-comfy lounge.

Hotel La Boheme €€
MAP P120

Small, sustainably focused hotel. Rooms are clean and simple, but the central location makes it a favourite. Book well in advance.

SCENIC ON SQUARES

Hotel V Frederiksplein €€
MAP P120

Soothing, leafy views and designer digs over a lush square. Only a quick shimmy from the bars and restaurants of Utrechtsestraat.

Clayton Hotel Amsterdam American €€€
MAP P120

Magnificent art-nouveau beast on Leidseplein. Today's hotel is an expansion of the original 1880s Viennese Renaissance–

style building. Its grand Café Americain (p135) is dubbed 'Amsterdam's living room'.

FINEST CANAL VIEWS

Seven Bridges €€
MAP P120

Beautifully set on a lovely canal, aristocratic opulence is alive and well across these sumptuous rooms with oriental rugs, polished antiques and breakfast on fine china.

Banks Mansion €€€
MAP P120

Swish, renovated hotel with plush, comfortable art-deco-style rooms and a stylish Frank Lloyd Wright–inspired lobby. Canal views cost extra; rooms on the side get glimpses for free.

Hotel Notting Hill €€€
MAP P120

Office block turned boutique beauty featuring outsized contemporary art and sleek, calm rooms with lots of feature wallpaper. Higher-priced rooms have canal views. Bull's-eye location between Utrechtsestraat and De Pijp.

Hotel 717 €€€
MAP P120

Exquisite hotel hidden along the canal. Decorated rooms here come with that all-too-rare luxury: space. It'll be hard to tear yourself away, from soaring ceilings to contemporary-meets-antique decor.

Vondelpark, Oud-West & Oud-Zuid

ON A BUDGET

Stayokay Amsterdam Vondelpark €
MAP P146

Practically in the Vondelpark, this HI-affiliated 536-bed hostel offers private rooms and fresh mixed, female- and male-only en suite dorms with well-spaced bunks sleeping four to

10. Generous breakfasts in the bar-restaurant cost extra.

Hotel Fita €€
MAP P146

One of the best-value digs near Museumplein (it books up fast!), family-owned Fita has 21 light-filled rooms in mint condition with modern bathrooms; fantastic free breakfasts of eggs, pancakes, cheeses and breads; and a lift.

REPURPOSED ARCHITECTURE

Hotel De Hallen €€
MAP P164

Housed in a former tram depot, this designer hotel has 58 industrial-chic rooms and six loft-style apartments, and cool art and sculptures in its lobby, lounge areas, restaurant, bar and wraparound terrace. Breakfast costs extra.

SWEETS Hotel Overtoomsesluis €€
MAP P146

One of 28 historic bridge houses citywide converted into suites by a team of architects, designers and builders. There's a cosy bed nook, kitchenette and local life buzzing around you (expect a bit of noise).

College Hotel €€€
MAP P146

Originally a 19th-century school, the impressive-looking College Hotel has 40 stylish rooms you'd never think were former classrooms. It's a celebrity favourite, and is well situated between Museumplein and De Pijp (about 1km from both).

De Pijp & Zuid

SUSTAINABLE STAYS

Bicycle Hotel Amsterdam €€
MAP P170

With bikes mounted on the exterior and solar roof panels providing power, this green-minded hotel has six comfy, familiar rooms (the cheapest share bathrooms), fab organic vegetarian breakfasts, and affordable bike-hire for guests. No lift.

CONTEMPORARY LUXURY

Sir Albert Hotel €€€
MAP P170

At the peaceful western end of market street Albert Cuypstraat, a 19th-century diamond factory houses 90 designer rooms (10 have balconies) with high ceilings, large windows and Illy espresso machines, and a refined fusion restaurant.

Hotel Okura Amsterdam €€€
MAP P170

Rising 23 stories with rare-for-Amsterdam panoramas, three Michelin stars (two at top-floor Ciel Bleu, one at ground-floor Japanese restaurant Yamazato), and health club with an 18m pool. The roof acts as the Netherlands' largest barometer.

Oosterpark & East of the Amstel

BUDGET STAYS

Social Hub €
MAP P186

Brutalist tower boasting slick, modern rooms ranging in sizes from student, budget options (with en suite bathrooms) to deluxe. Hangout-worthy public spaces.

Generator Amsterdam €
MAP P186

Outpost of a cool designer hostel chain. Occupies a century-old zoological university building with large windows overlooking lush Oosterpark. Great bars and restaurants nearby.

HISTORIC & CHIC

Manor €€
MAP P186

A grand 19th-century building (former hospital) brightened with contemporary artworks and striped awnings. Prices only occasionally spike to the upper range.

Vergulden Eenhoorn €€
MAP P186

Restored 1702-built farmhouse with modern, stylish rooms. Excellent on-site restaurant. Hiring a bicycle makes the stay more enjoyable.

WITH COWORKING & SOCIAL SPACES

Hotel Casa €€
MAP P186

Bright, clean modern rooms kept simple with two room categories: standard and premium. The highlight is the 8th-floor Dakterras GAPP, a wooden-decked terrace with picnic tables, a herb garden and a wide selection of beers and snacks.

Ruby Emma €€
MAP P186

Easy on the eyes, high-tech and sustainability focused. Rooms are iPad-controlled and furnishings feature recycled materials. Rooftop greenhouse and facilities use energy-saving technology. The location requires a bike.

Volkshotel €€
MAP P186

Designer eco-certified rooms and rooftop hot tub. Coworking spaces and a full cultural programme (film screenings, DJs etc) at the restaurant-bar Canvas (p187) attracts youthful, creative professionals.

Volkshotel

Amsterdam Noord

MODERN & GOOD VALUE

Doubletree Hilton €€
MAP P200

Noord's best located lodging is right on NDSM, close to super bars and restaurants, in easy (ferry) reach of the city centre, and much cheaper than Hiltons across the river.

SWEETS by Hotel Gerben Wagenaarbrug €€
MAP P200

Historic bridge house turned modern, well-equipped hotel along the Noordhollandsch Kanaal. A short walk from Noord's excellent crop of bars, restaurants and cafes.

UNIQUE & UNUSUAL

Bunk €
MAP P200

Trendy budget rooms and 'pod' rooms in a converted, neo-Gothic church. All-day dining restaurant has a neighbourhood feel from terrace to a cosy living-room-like space.

Camping Vliegenbos €
MAP P200

Secretive camping in Amsterdam's oldest forest. Unique cabin stays include wi-fi and basic furnishings. Less than 2km from the IJplein ferry stop.

ClinkNOORD €
MAP P200

In a 1920s laboratory on the IJ riverbank, hostel dorms with designer edge. By Buiksloterweg's ferry terminal (a free, five-minute ride to Centraal Station 24/7).

Faralda €€€
MAP P200

Fantasy-world suites perched at varying heights on a crane atop NDSM-werf. Rooftop hot tub with astounding views.

Sir Adam €€€
MAP P200

Cool design hotel located in the A'DAM Tower (p201). Take your pick of on-site gastronomy and visit the soaring observation deck with Europe's highest swing.

TOOLKIT

The chapters in this section cover the most important topics you'll need to know about in Amsterdam. They're full of nuts-and-bolts information and valuable insights to help you understand and navigate Amsterdam and get the most out of your trip.

Money
p246

Family Travel
p247

Food, Drink & Nightlife
p248

LGBTIQ+ Travellers
p250

Health & Safe Travel
p251

Responsible Travel
p252

Accessible Travel
p254

Nuts & Bolts
p255

Language
p256

Money

CURRENCY: EURO (€)

Cash or Cards?

Contactless or chip-and-PIN cards are the norm for the vast majority of transactions. By no means do all businesses accept cash and a 2025 survey suggested that more than 25% of the Dutch never or almost never carry any. Occasionally, however, a few small businesses do demand cash payments.

Changing Money

Should you find yourself without a credit card, debit card or other electronic means of payment, it's still possible to exchange currencies. Rates at the airport are typically dreadful, even when advertised as being 'commission free' thanks to high buy/sell rate splits. Rates are consistently better from **Pott Change** (pottchange.com) on Damrak.

Paying for Transport

Ride buses, trams and trains by tapping your contactless credit/debit card on entry. Tap again when you get off: forgetting incurs a much bigger bill.The easiest way to buy citywide GVB travel passes *(24/72hr €9.50/21.50)* and other barcoded tickets is on the GVB app (no subscription needed).

HOW MUCH FOR A...

Museum ticket
€10–25

Public transport ride
€3.40

Coffee
€3.50–5

HOW TO... Save Money on Sleeping

Amsterdam's accommodation situation is overloaded. Especially at weekends, prices can be sky-high with even dorm beds costing up to €80 some Saturday nights. Visiting midweek can reduce costs. Last-minute cancellations mean that booking sites often have new options around five days ahead of arrival. StayOkay hostels offer free cancellation until 24 hours before arrival so may have last-minute beds.

MUSEUM PASSES

For non-residents the temporary version of the **Museum Card** *(museum.nl/en/museumpass; €69)* is often worthwhile but has complications. The **I amsterdam Card** *(iamsterdam.com)* only makes sense if you plan carefully and cram several big-ticket museums into each day.

TIPPING

Tipping for drinks at a bar would be decidedly odd. In restaurants, it was common practice to round up a bill to the nearest €5 or €10. With the demise of cash, it's now normal for the credit card terminal to offer guests a choice of tip amounts: 5% is fine, 10% generous. Rounding up your taxi fare to the nearest euro is also common. On so-called 'free tours' you should offer a generous tip as that's the only way the guide earns an income.

Family Travel

Amsterdam is often seen as a place for adult art lovers and outgoing hedonists. Less well known is the plethora of attractions that will entrance toddlers, children and teenagers. Almost every museum goes out of its way to think of younger audiences.

Food for Youngsters

Some cafes have very short kids' menus *(kindermaaltijden)* while many snack options include items that children might favour anyway. Look for a *pannenkoekenhuis* serving thin, over-sized Dutch pancakes and *poffertjes* (mini doughballs): some like **Pannenkoekenhuis Upstairs** (p55) and **Café Schreierstoren** are in historic buildings. There are even harbour cruises on a **Pancake Boat** (p12). At **Kinderkookkafé**, children can prepare simple meals themselves.

Admission Prices

Most places have free entrance for babies and/or toddlers and reduced prices for children. However, the exact ages at which these cut off varies. For example, Artis Zoo (p84) is free for two-year-olds but 3–12 year olds pay only slightly less than adults. Many other places give discounts for children under 18 and are free for those under six.

Parklife

Vast **Vondelpark** (p160) has duck ponds, lawns and cool space-age slides. There are playgrounds in **Westerpark** (p115) and many lesser known suburban courtyard areas. The huge, forested **Amsterdamse Bos** (p180) has loads of activities, a tree-climbing park and goat farm.

Rainy-Day Options

OBA Oosterdok (p91), the central library, has a very thoughtfully designed children's floor. Kids' films show in many cinemas, most notably shorts at **Eye Filmmuseum** (p205), which also has a Sunday *Cinemini* for toddlers under seven.

CHILD-FRIENDLY TOP PICKS

NEMO (p88) Dazzling hands-on science museum with a whole day's worth of engrossing activities.

Artis Zoo (p84)Time a visit to include either of the 11am or 1pm child-specific planetarium shows.

Wereldmuseum (p188) The dedicated 'Junior' sub-museum sets out to help children understand each other across cultural divides.

Joods Museum (p78) Also has a very engaging 'Junior' section. Includes afternoon baking sessions.

Van Gogh Museum (p152) Treasure hunts, 'checklist' quiz, painting workshops and more.

FAMILY TRANSPORT TACTICS

Children under four ride for free, as do permanent resident children under 12 if they have a relevant OV-card. However, for non-resident tourists aged four to 11, the best deal is often a €5 GVB children's day pass. These need to be purchased physically from a GVB service point. If using a debit card to tap in and out, full fare will be charged and each individual will need their own card or at least device (even if linked to a parent's account). A family might find a GVB five-person 'Group Day Pass' (€26) cost-effective.

Food, Drink & Nightlife

When to Eat

Breakfast *(ontbijt;* 6-9am) International brunch cafes abound but a Dutch family breakfast is typically bread with cheese, peanut butter, ham or, most iconically, *hagelslag* (chocolate sprinkles).

Lunch (noon-2.30pm) Standard Dutch lunches also favour *broodjes* (sandwiches or open sandwiches) and *eieren* (eggs) along with *tosti* (toasted sandwiches), soups and salads.

Dinner (5.30-9.30pm) While some cafes serve basic snack meals all afternoon, swankier restaurants rarely start serving before 6pm. Some serve drinks earlier.

MENU DECODER

Seizoensmenu Seasonal menu

3 Gangen Three courses

Voorgerechten Appetisers

Soepen Soups

Friet [Potato] Fries

Hoofdgerechten Main courses

Vlees/vis Meat/fish

Bijgerechten Side dishes

Groenten Vegetables

Sla Abbreviation for small salad as a garnish

Nagerechten Desserts

Zoet Sweet (alternative term for dessert)

Kazen Cheeses

Brood Bread

Broodjes Sandwiches (open or otherwise)

Hapjes Light bites

Borrelhapjes Fingerfood to go with drinks (for more about *borrel,* see opposite)

Dranken Drinks

Wijnen Wines

Bieren op flees Bottled beers

Gebakken Baked

Gegrilde Grilled

Gerookte Smoked

Gevuld Filled

Krokant Crispy

Vega Vegetarian

Vegan Vegan

Where to Eat & Drink

Cafés When the Dutch say *café,* they often mean a pub. Most serve food as well as booze, ranging from snacks and sandwiches to excellent meals.

Bruin cafés (brown cafes; traditional pubs) Those with particular old-world atmosphere, originally so named because of the nicotine stains.

Eetcafés Informal bistro-like restaurants. Their cited opening times often start well before and end well after the kitchen has closed.

Restaurants Amsterdam is thoroughly international with restaurants covering virtually every conceivable cuisine.

HOW TO...

Decide on a Rijsttafel

Thanks to the Netherlands' historical links, this is a particularly great place to sample snacks from Suriname and especially the deliciously pungent, peanutty flavours of Indonesian cuisine. To enjoy that fully you'll need a whole vocabulary of terms starting with *sate* (skewered meat) and *gado-gado* (blanched-veg salad, tempeh and boiled egg), both served with tangy peanut sauces, the latter topped with *krupuk* (crispy fried crackers). To avoid a decision you might be pointed towards an extravagant multi-plate feast called a *rijsttafel* (literally 'rice table'), which allows you to taste a dozen or more beautifully presented dishes at once. It's worth knowing that the *rijsttafel* concept is not something you'll generally find in Indonesia itself: it was essentially a Dutch colonial invention so there are potentially negative overtones. Many authentic Indonesian restaurants offer a smaller selection of side dishes with your main as a matter of course.

HOW MUCH FOR A...

Supermarket
croissant
€0.49–1.30

Flat white
€4

25cL glass of
standard lager
€3.20–4

33cL glass of
craft beer
€5.50–7

Lunchtime soup
€8

Sit-down pizza
€16–22

Three courses at a
family restaurant
€59–89

Tasting menu with
wine at a Michelin-
starred restaurant
€250–400

HOW TO...

Enjoy Borrel

In Dutch the word *borrel* has three linked yet distinct meanings. Strictly translated, the term simply means 'drink' – as in a glass of booze, traditionally *jenever* (Dutch gin). However, in social parlance, to be invited to *borrel* means to take part in an informal gathering for drinks and conversation, inevitably accompanied by an array of nibbles. The concept is integral to Dutch social life.

Any occasion can be a reason for *borrel*: a birthday, a beautiful sunset that invites patio sitting, or a *networkingborrel* as a way to get to know business contacts. *Borrel* at the end of any work day is nice but Friday afternoon work drinks with colleagues are common enough to have their own name: *Vrijdag middagborrel*, usually shortened to *vrijmibo* or just *vrimibo*. When you see a group of locals spilling out of a bruin café (traditional pub) onto the street with a glass of beer in hand? That's classic *borrel*.

Meanwhile, if you look on a bar menu and see *borrel,* that refers to neither the meeting nor the drinks themselves but to a category heading for finger foods – more accurately described as *borrelhapjes* (bar snacks). These will likely include olives, *oude kaas* (cheese cubes), *borrelnootjes* (peanuts covered in a crisp, spicy outer shell) and small, deep-fried bites such as *kroketten* (croquettes), *loempia* (spring rolls), *kaastengels* (fried cheese-fingers) and especially *bitterballen* (round meat croquettes).

Why Bitter?

The name *bitterballen* (literally 'bitter balls') was originally derived from a tradition of serving them with bitters, namely *jenever* (gin). These days wine or beer are just as likely accompaniments.

NIGHTLIFE APLENTY

A typical tourist-eye view of Amsterdam at night might be escaping from the uncomfortably voyeuresque vibe of red windows on Oudezijds Voorburgwal towards the post-midnight buzz of bars on the northern ends of Warmoesstraat and Zeedijk. Or heading the other direction past the full-voiced karaoke bars on Halvemaansteeg to Rembrandtplein. Gruff bouncers there ensure that queues move slowly enough to contrive an aura of exclusivity around a gaggle of nightclubs, the best-known of which is **Escape** *(escape.nl/en/agenda)*. The further you go down adjacent Thorbeckplein, the less exclusive the bars appear to become. Or if you head west, things get friendlier and more predominantly oriented towards an LGBTIQ+ crowd.

More famous than any of the above, Leidseplein has become synonymous with Amsterdam nightlife through clubs and music venues **Paradiso** and **Melkweg** (p134).

Some of Amsterdam's top clubbing venues are in repurposed out-of-centre buildings like **Radion** (p167), in a former dentists' academy. Another very popular hub is **Shelter** (p201) beneath the A'DAM Tower. Several high-profile clubs have closed in the last couple of years but the scene is constantly evolving.

If your idea of fun is less boisterous, there is an incredible range of **bruin cafés** (p32), great **cocktail bars** (p124) and a whole raft of lower-key night spots that blur category lines. For example, try laid-back, waterside beer-garden **Hannekes Boom** (p90).

LGBTIQ+ Travellers

To call Amsterdam a queer capital doesn't fully express just how welcoming and open the scene is here. Historically tolerant, the Netherlands was the first country to legalise same-sex marriage (in 2001), and in 2025 it was rated by A3M as the third-safest place in the world for LGBTIQ+ travellers. So it's no surprise that Amsterdam's gay scene is among the world's most vibrant.

Party Areas

These days the main concentration of gay bars are towards the western end of **Reguliersdwarsstraat** (*reguliers.net*) around **Club NYX** (*clubnyx.nl*). The strip makes itself obvious with fluttering rainbow flags and there's a community hub.

Busy Warmoesstraat in the Red Light District, once a major hot spot, now hosts just a couple of infamous, kink-filled leather and fetish bars: ring doorbells to enter. There are laid-back alternatives nearby at the upper end of the Zeedijk, notably **Café 't Mandje** (*cafetmandje.amsterdam*), which first became a gay bar in 1927.

Festivals

Pride Amsterdam (*pride. amsterdam*) A big event from late July to early August, featuring the world's only waterborne Pride parade on the first Saturday of August.

Roze Filmdagen (*rozefilmdagen.nl*) LGBTIQ+ film festival that's mostly held in March though there are also some summer screenings.

Activities

Queer Storyteller (*specialamsterdamtours.nl*) Henk leads two-hour walking tours explaining Amsterdam's LGBTIQ+ history spanning 750 years. Runs most Saturdays at 11am.

Tijgertje (*tijgertje.nl*) Started as a self-defence group but is now an LGBTIQ+ sports club for fitness, swimming, basketball etc.

FIGHTING THE GOOD FIGHT

COC Nederland (*coc.nl/en/engels*), the world's oldest still-existing LGBTIQ+ organisation, was founded in 1946 with a discreet name translating as 'Centre for Culture and Leisure'. It is a lobby group for equal rights, emancipation and social acceptance, and a powerful voice in the international fight to decriminalise non-hetero sexual orientations and gender identities. The group even has special consultative status with the United Nations.

RESOURCES

Gay Amsterdam (*gayamsterdam.com*) Lists hotels, shops and clubs, and provides maps.
Pink Point (*pinkpoint.nl*) An information kiosk and souvenir shop on Westermarkt that can help with details of parties, events and social groups.
Roze in Blauw Call 088-1691234 or email rozeinblauw@politie.nl to report discrimination or assault based on sexual identity to the police. Or report more informally, even as a bystander, to ritacommunity.com.

Health & Safe Travel

PICKPOCKETS & SCAMS

Amsterdam is remarkably safe. Nonetheless, it's worth being alert for pickpockets, especially in the Red Light District and Leidseplein areas, where crowds of merrily intoxicated visitors make for easy targets. Also be mindful of your possessions around Centraal Station, Bloemenmarkt and on busy trams. Beware of very occasional 'fake police' scams where a stranger demands to look through your possessions.

TAP WATER

There's no need to pay for drinking water. City supply is excellent and there are quite a few public water fountains.

Look Twice, Think Bike

Watch out for bicycles, which can appear as if from nowhere. Never walk in bicycle lanes and always check carefully before you cross. Look both ways even on a one-way street! If you're cycling yourself, lock your bike with a very hefty chain (or two): bike theft is one of Amsterdam's most prevalent petty crimes.

Cannabis

Although marijuana is technically illegal, it's tolerated to the degree that 165 registered 'coffeeshops' in Amsterdam are allowed to sell up to 5g per person per day. Don't buy weed on the streets. Remember to finish or destroy any coffeeshop supplies before leaving town: it's all too easy to forget a stash and find yourself in trouble at customs.

CANALBOAT PILOTING SIGNS

Wait if other boat is passing

No entry to canal

No mooring

No mooring

Proceed with caution

Canal Hazards

Amsterdam's trademark canals are beautiful but most are not equipped with barriers to prevent the unwary from falling in – or driving in, when messing up a canal-side parking manoeuvre. Around 18 people drown in canals each year, a large percentage under the influence of drink or cannabis, and 80% of them men. Peeing from the bank can prove fatal!

HEALTH & EMERGENCY HELP

For emergency medical help, call 112. Website huisartsenpostenamsterdam.nl can help you decide whether to call an ambulance or seek non-critical assistance via a family doctor (huisart) or out-of-hours general practice centre (huisartsenpost). **Amsterdam Tourist Doctors** (amsterdamtouristdoctors.nl) are very familiar with foreign insurance systems. **Mondzorg Poli** (mondzorgpoli.nl) has a 24/7 emergency dental service.

Responsible Travel

Climate Change & Travel

It's impossible to ignore the impact we have when travelling; Lonely Planet urges all travellers to engage with their travel carbon footprint, which will mainly come from air travel. While there often isn't an alternative, travellers can look to minimise the number of flights they take, opt for newer aircrafts and use cleaner ground transport, such as trains. One proposed solution – purchasing carbon offsets – unfortunately does not cancel out the impact of individual flights. While most destinations will depend on air travel for the foreseeable future, for now, pursuing ground-based travel where possible is the best course of action.

The **UN Carbon Offset Calculator** shows how flying impacts a household's emissions.

The **ICAO's carbon emissions calculator** allows visitors to analyse the CO_2 generated by point-to-point journeys.

World's Most Sustainable

Amsterdam topped the 2024 Arcadis Sustainable Cities Index *(arcadis.com)* with a whole raft of plans to ensure that by 2050, greenhouse gas emissions are cut by 95% from their 1990 levels.

Rubbish Disposal

Also by 2050, the Netherlands is aiming for a waste-free circular economy. Visitors need to play a part. Consider taking your trash back to your hotel's recycling skips rather than over-filling the already overloaded city centre public bins.

Mediamatic *(mediamatic.net)* is a ground-breaking attempt to bring together elements of science, art and experience to look at issues of food production and sustainability. Check its calendar of imaginative events.

In 2016, the Dutch government set a goal of stopping all scientific testing on animals. This has been only a very limited success, due in part to COVID-19 and the lack of serious funding for finding alternatives.

HAPPY HOSTELS

stayokay

StayOkay, the Dutch HI hostel group, is making efforts at improving sustainability: it uses green energy providers and claims to have cut energy use by 35% in recent years. Its anti-plastic strategies includes use of curious '100% non plastic' keycards.

LESS FOOD WASTE

Consider buying your food supplies from **Little Plant Pantry** *(littleplantpantry.com)*, a plastic-free, zero-waste food store with a vegan cafe. Or on Saturdays take your own bags to the *boerenmarkt* (farmers market; p107) and support local producers.

Green Hothouse

Keeping tropical greenhouses warm in winter is typically an energy intense task. However, **Hortus Botanicus** (p82) uses a mixture of clever computerised management, modern materials and a 'waste heat' cycle to approach carbon neutrality.

Homegrown Vegan

TestTafel (p90) serves experimental gastronomic vegan dinners made using vegetables from Mediamatic's urban garden and scientific hydroponics greenhouse. Sandwich-maker **Gartine** (p49) and greenhouse-restaurant **De Kas** (p195) also grow their own produce.

Celebrating Diversity

Appropriately for one of the world's most multicultural cities, **Wereldmuseum** (p188) looks at diverse cultures and colonial legacies. **Rederij Lampedusa** (p91) runs canal tours conducted by recent immigrants who share their astonishing life stories.

Fishing for Waste

Plastic Whale *(plasticwhale.com)* runs cleanup events and boat trips fishing waste plastic out of the canals (aimed at schools and corporate groups rather than individuals). **Vepa** *(vepa.nl)* turns the plastic into furniture.

Clean Transport

Walking or cycling is best of all but it's great to know that trains and all new buses use green electricity and that by 2030 all buses are required to be emission-free.

Carry a reusable bottle and fill up from drinking water fountains around the city.

Driving further afield? Check greenwheels.nl, a car-sharing set-up to reduce a journey's carbon footprint.

28,000

The number of sensors employed by **The Edge**, the 2014 'smart' office tower block that's Deloitte's Amsterdam HQ and which, for years, has been cited as the world's 'greenest building'.

RESOURCES

conscioushotels.com
Small boutique hotel chain stressing 'eco-sexy' approach.

degezondestad.org
'Healthy City' foundation making Amsterdam more sustainable (in Dutch).

breeam.nl
Certifies a building's green credentials.

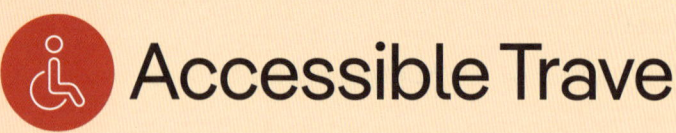

Accessible Travel

While there are plenty of old buildings and uneven canal sides to negotiate, Amsterdam has made great strides in improving access for visitors with limited mobility and other specific requirements.

Top Sights

Most of Amsterdam's big-hitter attractions are well equipped, but wheelchair users can't fully explore antique houses like Rembrandthuis. Anne Frank's 'secret annexe' is similarly inaccessible but a VR alternative is available.

Airport

Schiphol Airport *(schiphol .nl/en/assistance)* offers extensive advice and potential help for a range of needs, but it's necessary to reserve most assistance at least 48 hours ahead.

Accommodation

Newer hotels typically have accessible rooms. However, many smaller hotels and guesthouses in older buildings either lack elevators or require guests to negotiate some steps.

RESOURCES

iamsterdam.com
Listings come with icon-based 'general accessibility provisions' for each attraction.

accessibletravel.nl
Full tour packages and organises equipment.

amsterdamobile.com
Very personal agency with specialist tours for those with reduced mobility plus short-term mobility-device rentals.

ableamsterdam.com/ practical-information-1
Provides a roundup of observations on the realities of transport practicalities.

TRISTANJ / SHUTTERSTOCK

MUSIC VENUES

Amsterdam's foremost concert halls are fully accessible with dedicated spaces for wheelchair users. These include the Opera-Ballet, the Concertgebouw (orchestral classics), Muziekgebouw aan 't IJ (contemporary classical music) and Bimhuis (jazz).

Audio Guides

Blind users are likely to struggle with 'podcatchers', audio guides designed to work by pointing them at a target box. At the Rembrandthuis, the soundtrack relies on the user matching a track to an image.

Transport

While many accessibility provisions exist in principle, public transport can still prove problematic thanks to crowding, faults (such as broken metro-station lifts), variable slopes on ramps into trams etc.

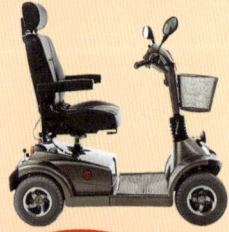

TAXIS

Brouwer *(taxibrouwer.nl/en/taxi-services/ wheelchair-taxi)* has a few mini-van taxis that are equipped with either ramps or lifts to allow two wheelchairs to be ridden aboard plus room for at least four additional passengers. Pre-booking is strongly recommended.

If you're staying in Amsterdam longer term, consider joining **Test Team Toegankelijk Amsterdam** *(toegankelijkamsterdam.nl/test -team-toegankelijk-amsterdam)*. They aim to thoroughly test the accessibility of city facilities and need people with specific restrictions to join the team.

# Nuts & Bolts

OPENING HOURS

Museums 10am-5pm; some close Mondays, especially outside the summer months.

Bruin cafés (pubs), bars & coffeeshops
Open around noon and generally close by midnight or 1am Sunday to Thursday, but possibly 3am Friday and Saturday.

Restaurants 11.30am-2.30pm and 6-9.30pm. Between 2.30pm and 6pm, and after 9.30pm, you might find the kitchen closed.

Shops 9am or 10am to 6pm is typical, maybe closing Sundays and Monday mornings. Later opening is common in tourist areas and on Thursdays.

Supermarkets Open 7am or 8am. Close between 8pm and 10pm.

Internet Access

Mobile 4G and 5G signal is widespread and generally strong. Decent wi-fi is free in most accommodations and many other businesses.

Weights & Measures
The Netherlands uses the metric system.

Smoking
Smoking tobacco indoors is prohibited. In coffeeshops, marijuana consumption is tolerated with tobacco substitutes.

GOOD TO KNOW

Time zone
CET (UTC+1) winter
CEST (UTC+2) summer

Country calling code +31

Emergency number 112

Population
934,000 (metro area 2.5 million)

Electricity

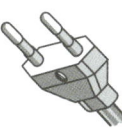

Type C
230V/50Hz

Type F
230V/50Hz

PUBLIC HOLIDAYS

Nieuwjaarsdag (New Year's Day) 1 January

Goede Vrijdag (Good Friday) March/April

Eerste Paasdag (Easter Sunday) March/April

Tweede Paasdag (Easter Monday) March/April

Koningsdag (King's Day) 27 April, or 26 April if the 27th falls on a Sunday

Dodenherdenking (Remembrance Day) 4 May (unofficial) followed next day by Bevrijdingsdag (Liberation Day), officially a holiday every 5th year

Hemelvaartsdag (Ascension Day) 40th day after Easter Sunday; May

Eerste Pinksterdag (Whit Sunday; Pentecost) Seven weeks after Easter Sunday; May/June

Tweede Pinksterdag (Whit Monday); May/June

Eerste Kerstdag (Christmas Day) 25 December

Tweede Kerstdag (Boxing Day) 26 December

Language

As a member of the Germanic language family, Dutch has many similarities with English. If you read our pronunciation guides as if they were English, you'll be understood just fine. It's a rarity for foreigners to make the effort to speak Dutch so if you do, you'll win friends quicker than you can say 'Nederlands' (Dutch).

Basics

Hello. Dag./Hallo. dakh/ha·*loh*
Goodbye. Dag. dakh
Yes. Ja. *yaa*
No. Nee. *ney*
Please. Alstublieft. (pol) al·stew·*bleeft*
Please. Alsjeblieft. (inf) a·shuh·*bleeft*
Thank you. Dank u/je. (pol/inf) dangk ew/yuh
Excuse me. Excuseer mij. eks·kew·*zeyr* mey
Sorry. Sorry. *so·ree*
What's your name? Hoe heet u/je? (pol/inf) *hoo heyt ew/yuh*
My name is ... Ik heet ... ik heyt ...
Do you speak English? Spreekt u Engels? spreykt ew *eng*·uhls
I don't understand. Ik begrijp het niet. ik buh·*khreyp* het neet

Directions

Where's ...? Waar is ...? waar is ...
What's the address? Wat is het adres? wat is het a·*dres*
Can you please write it down? Kunt u dat alstublieft opschrijven? kunt ew dat al·stew·*bleeft op*·skhrey·vuhn
Can you show me (on the map)? Kunt u het mij tonen (op de kaart)? kunt ew het mey *toh*·nuhn (op duh kaart)

Signs

Ingang Entrance
Gesloten Closed
Open Open
Uitgang Exit
Toiletten Toilets

Time

What time is it? Hoe laat is het? hoo laat is het
It's (10) o'clock. Het is (tien) uur. het is (teen) ewr
Half past (10). Half (elf). half (elf) (literally: half eleven)
am (morning) 's ochtends *sokh*·tuhns
pm (afternoon) 's middags *smi*·dakhs
pm (evening) 's avonds *saa*·vonts
yesterday gisteren *khis*·tuh·ruhn
today vandaag *van*·daakh
tomorrow morgen *mor*·khuhn

Emergencies

Help! Help! help
Leave me alone! Laat me met rust! laat muh met rust
I'm sick. Ik ben ziek. ik ben zeek
Call a doctor! Bel een dokter! bel uhn *dok*·tuhr
Call the police! Bel de politie! bel duh poh·*leet*·see

Eating & Drinking

What would you recommend? Wat kan u aanbevelen? wat kan ew *aan*·buh·vey·luhn
Cheers! Proost! prohst
Delicious! Heerlijk/Lekker! *heyr*·luhk/*le*·kuhr

NUMBERS

1	**één** eyn
2	**twee** twey
3	**drie** dree
4	**vier** veer
5	**vijf** veyf
6	**zes** zes
7	**zeven** *zey*·vuhn
8	**acht** akht
9	**negen** *ney*·khuhn
10	**tien** teen

TOOLKIT

LANGUAGE

256

DONATIONS TO ENGLISH

buoy, cookie, cruise, dock, landscape (among many others)

WIDESPREAD ENGLISH

Some 90% to 97% of Dutch citizens speak conversational English.

Distinctive Sounds

The pronunciation of Dutch is fairly straightforward. Some vowel sounds are a bit trickier for English speakers as they have no equivalent in English. Most common are *eu* (nasal eu, similar to the French vowel sound in *heur*) and *ui* (oey, similar to the French vowel sound in *oeil*). For consonants, note that kh is a throaty sound, similar to the 'ch' in the Scottish loch, r is trilled and zh is pronounced as the 's' in 'pleasure'.

Local Talk

Hey! He daar! hey daar
Great! Fantastisch! fan·*tas*·tis
Sure. Natuurlijk. na·*tewr*·luhk
Maybe. Misschien. mi·*skheen*
No way! Geen sprake van! kheyn *spraa*·kuh van
Go ahead! Doe maar! doo maar
Just a minute. Een minuutje. uhn mee·*new*·chuh
Just joking! Grapje! *khrap*·yuh
It's OK. In orde. in *or*·duh
No problem. Geen probleem. kheyn proh·*bleym*
All's OK! Alles kits! *a*·luhs kits

Hold Your Vowels

Most vowels have a long and a short version, which simply means that you hold vowels for a greater or lesser length of time. It's important to make the distinction between long and short versions, as they can distinguish meaning – eg *maan* means 'moon' but *man* means 'man'.

What's in a Name?

Dutch words in street names and on signs are often combined into a single long place name, which can be tricky for a foreigner to decipher (eg *Derde Leliedwarsstraat* means 'third lily-cross-street').

WHO SPEAKS DUTCH?

Dutch, along with its variants including Flemish (Vlaams) in Belgium and Arrikaans (in South Africa), is spoken by between 20 and 25 million people worldwide.

Flanders (Belgium) has the same written language but spoken dialects of Flemish (Vlaams) have considerable differences.

Netherlands

Belgium

Spoken Afrikaans is a somewhat simpler, mutually intelligible form of Dutch. Written forms look more different.

Aruba

Suriname

South Africa

STORYBOOK

Our writers delve deep into different aspects of Amsterdam life.

A History of Amsterdam in 15 places

The extraordinarily rich history of the Dutch capital.

Catherine Le Nevez

p260

Meet the Amsterdammers

Blunt truths, endearing insults: a crash course in Amsterdam manners.

Jurriaan Teulings

p264

Dark Heirlooms

Amsterdam's major museums are navigating their colonial legacies.

Barbara Woolsey

p266

Meet the Havermelkelite

In the last decade, Amsterdam has been transformed by a new e-bike-peddling, natural-wine-drinking urban elite.

Sara van Geloven

p270

The VOC Reassessed

Global pioneers, 'Golden Age' heroes or evil colonialists?

Mark Elliott

p273

Zeedijk street, Chinatown (p52)
FRANCIS CRISOSTOMO/SHUTTERSTOCK

A HISTORY OF AMSTERDAM IN
15 PLACES

Amsterdam has an extraordinarily rich history and outsize influence on Europe and the world. Water has been its lifeblood since its inception: lying at or below sea level, its swamps, lakes and rivers were repeatedly reshaped by storms and floods. This fluid landscape presented challenges yet opportunities that still define it today. By Catherine Le Nevez

IN 2025 AMSTERDAM celebrated its 750th birthday, but evidence of human activity goes back much further. Excavations during the 2005–12 tunnelling of the Noord/Zuidlijn (north–south metro line; M52) unearthed artefacts from the Amstel's depths that show humans have lived here (at least transiently) since c 2600 BCE.

It was around the 13th century that the city's story began in earnest with the construction of dams retaining the IJ River between the Zuiderzee and Haarlem. In 1275, inhabitants were granted toll-free status, and Amsterdam gained direct ocean access via the Zuiderzee (now the IJsselmeer), then free access to the Baltic to become a global player.

The 1600s saw major advances in engineering (especially the canal ring) and trade (Amsterdam was the site of the world's first stock exchange when the Dutch East India Company's offices traded its own shares). In recent years, the nation has confronted the era's dark colonial history; King Willem-Alexander formally apologised for the Netherlands' involvement in slavery and its ongoing effects on 1 July 2023, the 160th anniversary of its legal abolition.

Today, the multifaceted Dutch capital, with a population of 934,374, is home to 174 nationalities, making it one of the most multicultural cities in the world.

1. Dam
EARLY BEGINNINGS

The IJ River formed the Roman Empire's northern border but the mighty Romans – who had conquered the lands now known as the Netherlands in the 1st century – left practically no evidence, much less any grand gestures, of settlement. The swampy topography made construction problematic and they had more important lands south of the Low Countries to inhabit and rule.

Following the catastrophic Allerheiligenvloed (All Saints' Flood) of 1170, which channelled an open connection to the North Sea, around 1200, a fishing community known as Aemstelredamme emerged at what is now the Dam – today the city's main square.

For more on the Dam, see p54.

2. Oudezijds Voorburgwal
SETTING SAIL

The marshland was unsuitable for farming but with the sea on the doorstep, commercial trade flourished. Amsterdam was granted a bridge toll exemption by Count Floris V in 1275, making it lucrative for international merchants. Amsterdam set its sights on the maritime routes, especially the prized North and Baltic Seas – in the backyard of the powerful Hanseatic League, a group of German trading cities. Amsterdam's *vrijbuiters* (buccaneers) sailed in with cloth and salt to exchange for grain and timber. To guard the city, the canals of the present-day Medieval Centre were dug; the oldest, the Oudezijds Voorburgwal, dates from 1385.

For more on the Medieval Centre, see p42.

3. Waag

TAKING SHAPE

Devastating fires in 1421 and 1452 burned down much of Amsterdam's centre, and building with wood was outlawed (only two historic wooden buildings, at Begijnhof 34 and Zeedijk 1, remain). While there was plenty of clay, it was too heavy, as was stone. Engineers innovated by driving piles into the peat, and thatched roofs were replaced by tiles. Eventually brick and sandstone became standard. The castle-like Waag, fronted by a moat-like canal, was built as a gate in the city walls in 1488. In 1601 the walls were demolished as the city expanded and the building became Amsterdam's main weigh house.

For more on the Waag, see p74.

4. Oude Kerk

RELIGIOUS CONFLICTS, INDEPENDENT REPUBLIC

Following the Protestant Reformation in the Low Countries, the Calvinists stood for local decision-making rather than Catholicism's top-down hierarchy. The 13th-century, formerly Catholic Oude Kerk survived the fire of 1452. Staunchly Catholic Philip II of Spain, who ruled the Low Countries in the mid-16th century and supported the Inquisition, cracked down on Protestants. In 1566 Calvinists stripped bare Catholic churches in response, hence the stark appearance of Dutch church interiors like this one. In 1579 the seven northern provinces, including mighty Amsterdam, became an independent republic, led by William of Orange (William the Silent): the Netherlands' founder and forefather of today's Dutch royal family.

For more on the Oude Kerk, see p50.

5. Grachtenmuseum Amsterdam

CREATING THE CANAL RING

Designed at the end of the 16th century and constructed in the 17th century, Amsterdam's *grachtengordel* (canal ring) came to life after the population grew beyond its medieval walls and city planners devised an expansion west and south of the old town and medieval port. The concentric waterways they built remain today – in 2010, UNESCO designated them a World Heritage Site. The canals were crucial to drain and reclaim the waterlogged land. On the Herengracht, the Grachtenmuseum Amsterdam details this epic feat of engineering.

For more on the Grachtenmuseum Amsterdam, see p103.

6. West-Indisch Huis

GOING GLOBAL

By the 17th century, shipbuilding boomed, Dutch ships controlled sea trade between England, France, Spain and the Baltic, and mariners embarked on trade routes, giving rise to the powerful 1602-founded Dutch East India Company (Verenigde Oost-Indische Compagnie; VOC) and 1621-founded Dutch West India Company (Geoctroyeerde West-Indische Compagnie; GWC). However, the VOC enslaved people in Asia, and through the GWC, the Dutch Empire colonised in South America and the Caribbean, and trafficked enslaved people from Africa to work on its sugar, cotton and coffee plantations. At the GWC's Herenmarkt HQ West-Indisch Huis, its governors signed off on constructing a Manhattan fort in 1625, establishing Nieuw Amsterdam (now New York City).

For more on the West-Indisch Huis, see p104.

Oudezijds Voorburgwal

MATT MUNRO/LONELY PLANET

7. Museum Rembrandthuis
'GOLDEN AGE' PROSPERITY

Although the 17th century has been referred to as a Gouden Eeuw ('Golden Age') of wealth accumulation, today it's a contentious term, given it ignores the era's rampant poverty, trafficking and slavery. The flow of money extended to the inflated prices paid for tulips (peaking in 1636–37's Tulipmania investment bubble) and art. With no Church or court to buy artworks, painters became entrepreneurs, churning out works in factory-like studios. Rembrandt set up his own studio (each influential subject paid 100 guilders to feature in 1642's *The Night Watch*), living during his most successful years from 1639 to 1656 at what's now the Museum Rembrandthuis.

For more on the museum, see p72.

8. Royal Palace
PATH TO A MONARCHY

Amsterdam's grandiose 1665 city hall would – eventually – become the Royal Palace. Following the British capture of Nieuw Nederland, the 1667 Treaty of Breda saw the Dutch colonisers retain Suriname (until 1954) and claim the Indonesian spice island of Run (until 1949). France's Louis XIV invaded the Netherlands in 1672. He was repelled in 1688 by William III of Orange, who in turn invaded England, becoming Britain's monarch.

French troops occupied the Netherlands in 1795, and in 1806, Napoleon installed his brother Louis Napoleon as king of the Dutch Republic. The French were overthrown in 1813–14 and William VI of Orange crowned as Dutch King William I.

For more on the Royal Palace, see p46.

9. Centraal Station
INDUSTRIALISATION AND EXPANSION

Domination of the seas now belonged to the British but the country's first railway, between Amsterdam and Haarlem, was a game-changer when it opened in 1839. Trade with the East Indies was the backbone of Amsterdam's economy, and the 1865–76 construction of the North Sea Canal, later extended to the Rhine, helped it benefit from the Industrial Revolution underway in Europe. Amsterdam again attracted immigrants, and its population doubled in the second half of the 19th century. In 1889, the Pierre Cuypers–designed Centraal Station made its grand debut, and Amsterdam was connected by rail to the rest of Europe.

For more on Centraal Station, see p53.

10. Olympisch Stadion Amsterdam
BOOM AND DEPRESSION

After WWI, in which the Netherlands remained neutral, Amsterdam was a shipbuilding and manufacturing powerhouse. In 1920 KLM began the world's first regular passenger air service between Amsterdam and London. The Olympic flame was lit for the first time since ancient Greece at the Olympisch Stadion when the city hosted the 1928 Olympic Games.

The 1930s Depression hit hard. Employment projects didn't defuse the mounting tensions between socialists, communists and a small, vocal fascist party. Amsterdam took in 25,000 Jewish refugees fleeing Germany; many were turned back because of the country's neutrality policy.

For more on the stadium, see p174.

11. Anne Frank Huis
WWII OCCUPATION

Although the Netherlands attempted to remain neutral during WWII, Germany invaded in May 1940. For the first time in almost 400 years, Amsterdammers experienced war firsthand. The Dutch Resistance became large-scale when the occupiers rounded up able-bodied men to work in Germany. The Nazis' devastation of Amsterdam's Jewish community was near-total: scarcely one in 16 people survived. Among the victims was Anne Frank, who hid with her family in a secret annexe of her father's business for nearly two years until their betrayal and deportation to concentration camps. Her father, the sole survivor, published her diary and requested the annexe remain unfurnished.

For more on Anne Frank Huis, see p100.

12. Vondelpark
CULTURAL REVOLUTION

During the 1960s and '70s, hippies flocked to Amsterdam, while a housing shortage saw speculators leave buildings empty and rebellious *kraken* (squatting) become widespread, with the Vondelpark becoming a temporary open-air dormitory. The country's 'blind-eye' principle of *gedogen* stemmed from the influx making the polic-

Olympisch Stadion Amsterdam (p174)

ing of drug laws impracticable. Squatting was subsequently made a criminal offence in response to 1980's Vondelstraat riots, when military tanks rolled onto Amsterdam's streets for the first time since WWII.

Official government policy was long supportive of same-sex relationships, and in 2001 the Netherlands became the first country to introduce marriage equality.

For more on the Vondelpark, see p160.

13. Oosterpark

POLITICAL QUESTIONS, NATIONAL RECKONING

In recent years, the Netherlands' tolerant sense of self has been challenged. In peaceful Oosterpark, the 2005 free-speech Spreeksteen ('speakers' corner') and 2007-installed sculpture *De Schreeuw* (The Scream) are dedicated to filmmaker Theo van Gogh, murdered in 2004 by a Moroccan-Dutch terrorist. This came two years after the murder of anti-immigration politician Pim Fortuyn by an environmental activist. In 2007, the government passed stricter integration laws requiring non-EU/EEA newcomers to pass tests before being granted residency. King Willem-Alexander's 1 July 2023 apology for the Netherlands' role in slavery took place at Oosterpark's 2002-installed National Slavery Monument commemorating the Dutch colonies' 1863 abolition of slavery.

For more on Oosterpark, see p190.

14. Red Light District

AMSTERDAM'S CHANGING IMAGE

As early as the 1300s, women carrying red lanterns greeted sailors near the port, and the Red Light District's sex-worker windows, coffeeshops (cannabis-smoking cafes) and copious bars have lured hedonistic visitors. Aiming to curb antisocial behaviour and crime, authorities set a cleanup agenda in 2007 and has since outlawed guided tours, instituted earlier bar closing hours, and banned cannabis smoking in the streets (coffeeshop restrictions for visitors remain under discussion). At the time of writing, a decision on whether to relocate the district's brothels by building a purpose-built, multistorey 'erotic centre' on Europaboulevard in Zuid (widely opposed by both residents and sex workers) was due to be made by the end of 2026.

For more on the Red Light District, see p58.

15. Houthaven

SUSTAINABLE FUTURE

Low-lying landscapes have kept climate awareness at the fore. In 2024, Amsterdam was ranked the world's most sustainable city in the Arcadis Sustainable Cities Index. By 2030, only emission-free vehicles will be allowed within the A10 ring road, and 80% of household energy generated from solar and wind, and by 2040, all buildings will be natural-gas-free. By 2050, the city plans to be completely climate-proof, and to have a fully circular economy. Transformed from former lumber ports from 2010, Houthaven, with a thermal-energy heating/cooling system using water pumped from the IJ, is Amsterdam's first climate-neutral neighbourhood.

For more on Houthaven, see p116.

MEET THE AMSTERDAMMERS

Blunt truths, endearing insults: a crash course in Amsterdam manners. JURRIAAN TEULINGS introduces his people.

EVERYONE IS AN expert at home. Mine is in De Pijp neighbourhood, just outside Amsterdam's canal belt – one train and two metro stops from Schiphol Airport. Here I never have to guess where the light switches are or figure out how the shower works. I know exactly what's considered polite (being brutally honest), what's rude (white lies), and how much an appropriate tip should be (10%, but only if an effort was made). I know which baristas won't burn my espresso (you'll find them at De Wasserette) and where to buy cheap tulips that last a full week (Albert Cuypmarkt; p172).

I share this city with roughly 900,000 people, each using it in their own expert way. That leaves 899,999 opinions – this is a city where people speak their mind. Amsterdammers, especially those born and raised, value openness, resist hierarchy and despise pretence. You'll find this often results in impertinent questions and unsolicited opinions. Though English is confidently spoken, the typically Dutch good humour behind it is often lost in translation. But those who dole out what I'll call insults of endearment will be delighted if you respond in kind.

To learn from the masters, spend some time in the Jordaan neighbourhood (p96), famous for its quintessential, no-nonsense working-class Amsterdammers whose colourful insults capture much of the city's insolent soul. These range from *pannenkoek* ('pancake', meaning 'idiot') when you

park your bike in front of someone's window, to *krijg de tering* – literally 'get tuberculosis' – shouted when you accidentally block a bike lane (which you will). Rest assured, all of this is nowhere near as harsh as it sounds. That same Jordanees will be the first to strike up a conversation over a *vaasje* of Amstel beer in a local *bruin café* (Dutch pub) and teach you how to deliver their slang with perfect timbre (look up 'Robbie Williams speaks Dutch' on YouTube to see how this delights people).

That said, don't stay in Jordaan too long. Soaring real-estate prices and the monoculture driven by overtourism, influencers and transient expats have changed the character of the historic city centre to such an extent that Amsterdam & Partners, the city's marketing organisation, has shifted its strategy from promotion to visitor management, starting with the removal of a much-hated 'IAMsterdam' monument that had been installed on Museumplein since 2004 and many argued reduced Amsterdam's identity to a marketing slogan and a backdrop for selfies.

Nowadays, visitors are encouraged to explore lesser-known areas such as Noord (p198), Oost (p184) and Nieuw-West (p167). I couldn't agree more. I always have to resist the urge to shout at the long lines waiting outside the Heineken Experience to stop wasting their precious time at that tourist trap and explore those neighbourhoods further afield. It's just my opinion: don't be a *pannenkoek*.

A Young City

Amsterdam is a relatively young city dominated by twenty- and thirtysomethings: 87% of its population is below the age of 65, and almost half (48%) is between the ages of 18 and 45.

AN AMSTERDAMMER ABOVE ALL

I was born in the Hague, with mostly French and German, a dash of British and Irish, and a dollop of Scandinavian DNA. My family tree, however, suggests I am as Dutch as cheese and *nasi rames*. At 16, I moved to the US to spend a high-school year in Savannah, Georgia, and at 19, I moved to Amsterdam to study law. I've never really left the city since, but I've moved around quite a bit between neighbourhoods (16 times) and, working as a travel writer and photographer, I accumulated many years abroad, reporting from some 110 countries. Today, I consider myself an Amsterdammer more than anything else, part of the largest (and most vanilla) cohort of Dutch-born nationals that make up 60% of the city's denizens. I won't say I am a citizen of the world – I've travelled enough to know that is a ridiculous thing to assert – but life in Amsterdam, a small town of 180 nationalities, has certainly has given me a cosmopolitan mindset.

DARK HEIRLOOMS

Across Amsterdam's most famous museums, confronting the colonial past is a pervasive, highly nuanced and intensive affair. By Barbara Woolsey

IN AMSTERDAM, MAJOR historical and cultural institutions are learning to navigate their colonial legacies. By examining their collections, museums are hoping to reframe national history with a more inclusive, honest and ethical approach. Returning stolen artefacts, correcting historical inaccuracies and diversifying documented viewpoints represent some of the most significant undertakings.

Colonial Shadows

Amsterdam's world-class museums hold esteemed repositories spanning hundreds of thousands of artefacts, including countless rarities. Digging into these collections unearths the uncomfortable truths of the colonial past. Investigations by the Nationaal Museum van Wereldculturen (NMVW), a national body overseeing ethnographic museums in Amsterdam, Rotterdam and Leiden, found that some 450,000 items, or around 40% of its collections, have been dubiously acquired under a self-proclaimed 'colonial context'.

Through archival work, questions are emerging regarding artefacts and how they were acquired: were items obtained under coercion, exploitation or looting? And, if so, how does displaying, or simply holding, such objects perpetuate colonialism in the present day?

Empire Artefacts

During the Dutch Empire's controversially labelled 'Golden Age', colonial expansion played an insurmountable role in garnering affluence and power (p273). The extraction of resources from colonies wasn't only an economic endeavour, but also a symbolic one. Amassing artefacts through archaeological digs, confiscation and ethnographic missions was framed as necessary to gaining knowledge on colonies and better civilising them.

After the 'Golden Age', artefacts became propaganda tools stirring up national pride. In 1871, the Koloniaal (Colonial) Museum (today's Wereldmuseum Amsterdam; p188) was established to display colonial artefacts and portray colonialist exploits as firmly linked to Dutch prestige and worldly wisdom. In 2022, the museum installed the permanent exhibition, *Our Colonial Inheritance,* to drive a new understanding of colonialism as a bygone era still deeply affecting of Dutch society today across 500-some displays.

Our Colonial Inheritance represents a new form of exhibition narration bringing diverse, once-excluded historical accounts to the forefront. Similarly, the Rijksmuseum's landmark 2021 exhibition *Ten True Stories of Dutch Colonial Slavery* documented deeply personal,

firsthand accounts from enslaved peoples and dissenters.

Colonial slavery history 'can be considered divisive, but it is also history that can be told to make connections,' said Valika Smeulders, the Rijksmuseum's head of history, as reported in the *Dutch Times*. The historian, born on the Dutch Caribbean island of Curaçao, told Dutch media in October 2025 that decolonising museums is not a journey of making apologies, but rather, taking accountability. 'Colonial slavery is behind us and modern-day society has no responsibility for it any more. But what we can take responsibility for is what we do with it.'

Acknowledging the Colonial Past

The Netherlands' acknowledgment of its colonial past has been a gradual and evolving process, influenced by activism, scholarship and public debate. For much of the 20th century, colonialism, and particularly, the transatlantic slave trade, remained glaringly absent from public memory. Finally, during the late 1990s and into the early 2000s, calls for the recognition of slavery's legacy by Afro-Dutch and Suri-

namese activists prompted a national dialogue so resounding it could no longer be ignored.

The 2002 establishment of the National Institute for the Study of Dutch Slavery and Its Legacy (NiNsee), followed by the 2006 unveiling of the National Slavery Monument in Amsterdam's Oosterpark, initiated national acknowledgment. Sculpted by the Surinamese artist Erwin de Vries, the monument commemorated the 1863 abolition of slavery in Dutch colonies. The bronze depiction of enslaved peoples breaking free set an important tone for a dialogue defined not by dwelling upon oppression but celebrating resistance. In De Vries' own words on publicart.amsterdam, the national monument was created in an artistic journey exploring 'the pain of the slaves, including my ancestors. But I also felt their enormous strength.'

In 2013, a ceremony commemorating the 150th anniversary of slavery's abolition was perceived as a blatant disregard for a reconciliation based upon such recognition and respect. Addressing an audience of Dutch monarchy and Black activists, the Dutch social minister expressed 'deep regret' in a

Wereldmuseum is home to the permanent exhibition *Our Colonial Inheritance* (p189)

ceremonial speech, though not the explicit apology activists had hoped for. Furthermore, a lack of symbolic gesture from the Dutch monarchy at the gathering, for example laying a wreath on the monument, added insult to injury. It was not until 2022 when a formal, unequivocal apology finally came from former Prime Minister Mark Rutte. Responding to the Slavery History Dialoguke Group's *Chains of the Past* report, Rutte acknowledged the Netherlands' role in colonial slavery on the nation's behalf and promised to 'find a way forward together'. Regarding future engagement with the colonial past, he said that 'with this apology we are writing not a full stop, but a comma.'

Finally, in 2023, King Willem-Alexander offered a royal apology on the 160th anniversary of abolition, which was largely considered heartfelt and sincere. 'Today, I am asking for forgiveness for the crystal-clear lack of action,' he said, emphasising an ongoing commitment to 'healing, reconciliation and restoration'.

Woman at Keti Koti (p155), an annual festival to mark the abolition of slavery in Dutch colonies

Moving Forward, Looking Back

The global reckoning with racial injustice, spurred on by the Black Lives Matter movement, has also provided impetus. In 2020, the Advisory Committee on the National Policy Framework for Colonial Collections and Restitution formalised guidelines for the repatriation of artefacts and the right of former colonies to reclaim cultural objects without proving illegitimate acquisition. The framework calls upon museums and institutions to identify and return looted items as part of a broader national effort to address colonialism via bindingly legal and transparent frameworks. Meanwhile, in 2022, the Dutch government approved a €200 million fund to support public awareness initiatives on slavery and colonialism and committed to contributing to developing a National Slavery Museum in Amsterdam. In 2024 and 2025, the Netherlands began working closely with government and museum officials in Indonesia and Nigeria to return artefacts to rightful ownership. Ongoing collaboration, including inviting specialists from both nations to visit Dutch museums to examine artefacts and contribute to cataloguing and conservation, is meaningful. It represents a clear example that other countries should be compelled to follow.

Though museums and cultural institutions are walking their talk, revisiting history through ethical stewardship, activists are highly critical of such efforts. The national debate on reconciliation is rife with calls for officials to act faster, asserting that the last 20-some years of accountability remains, overwhelmingly, defined by actions that are too little, too late. Decolonisation is a process ultimately defined not by singular acts, but rather, the sum of many actions shifting national consciousness. These actions, including the renaming of institutions and removal of statues upholding colonial legacies, is work that is slow and dogged by red tape.

Still, there is no denying the transformation taking place across public awareness. As more institutions, in the Netherlands and beyond, join this reckoning, the challenge ahead will likely be in sustaining momentum even when outcomes are not always substantial and observable. Turning acknowledgment into action, and remembrance into reform, will require national unity and unwavering determination.

MEET THE HAVERMELKELITE

In the last decade, Amsterdam has been transformed by a new e-bike-peddling, natural-wine-drinking urban elite. But is it change for the better? By Sara van Geloven

GO ON A people safari along Amsterdam's canals and you'll spot them within minutes – whizzing past on designer e-bikes, lounging on a terrace with tiny tables precariously balancing sharing plates, or chatting away while queuing for a loaf of sourdough bread at a minimalist bakery. Meet Amsterdam's new young urban professionals.

Got Oat Milk?

The term *havermelkelite* – literally 'oat milk elite' – was coined by journalist Jonas Kooyman in 2019. As a born-and-bred Amsterdammer, Kooyman had a front-row seat to the city's boom years after the economic malaise of the early 2010s, and the new urban elite that started to take shape during it.

Kooyman's Instagram account @haver melkelite took off, drawing in thousands of views with its weekly submitted confessions such as: 'Don't drink cow's milk, but love a cheese platter'. By 2024, Kooyman had quit his job, written a bestselling book about the *havermelkelite*, and happily admits he himself belongs to this new elite just as much as the people he loves to mock.

All in Good Taste

So, who exactly is the *havermelkelite*? Unlike the yups that came before them, they're elite not necessarily in wealth, but in taste.

They signal their identity to others by displaying specific consumption behaviours. One of which, unsurprisingly, is that they order matcha and flat whites made exclusively with oat milk.

They know exactly where to find the latest natural wine bar or ramen spot, which means that the city has seen a rise of amazing food spots, even in neighbourhoods that used to be a bit of a culinary wasteland. Their wardrobes skew towards minimalist brands and vintage streetwear – they wear Salomon sneakers or Birkenstock sandals, depending on the season. They might live in small apartments, but they still manage to carefully style their interiors, with design lamps, monstera houseplants and Aesop soap in their bathrooms.

It's a lifestyle built as much on curation as consumption. Posting the experience on social media is part of it: the perfectly baked bread, the expensive bottles of orange wine, the club-style spin class. They all strive to be in the know, and to be seen as in the know. In the process the city has, as Kooyman calls it, gone through quite the vibe shift.

A City Transformed

Amsterdam has always had a progressive identity. That of a squatters' stronghold, a free haven home to eccentric characters, with

affordable housing and plenty of rowdy bars. But in the past decade, following the economic recovery after the crisis years, gentrification has swept in.

Nowhere is this more apparent than in De Pijp (p168). Once a working-class neighbourhood known for its mix of immigrants, students and artists, its streets are now lined with brunch cafes and designer boutiques. The food scene has also undergone a transformation: third-wave coffeeshops and fusion kitchens have pushed out traditional *bruin cafés* (brown cafes; Dutch pubs) and Turkish bakeries. What was once rough around the edges, has become increasingly polished.

Global Trends, Global Crises

Of course, it's a change echoing similar trends in other metropolises, like New York, London and Lisbon. Part of an increasingly global and connected culture, the *havermelkelite* both shape and embody the transformation. As once-affordable neighbourhoods like the Jordaan (p96) and Oost (p184) become hot spots for locals and visitors alike, rents soar and long-time residents are priced out.

In Amsterdam the housing issue is especially acute. For decades the city was famous for its radical squatters' movement – *krakers* – who in the housing crises of the 1970s and '80s reclaimed empty buildings and demand-

ed affordable living. Those same areas are now among the priciest in the Netherlands, as a new housing crisis has swept across the country and Amsterdam grows increasingly unaffordable.

Admired or Mocked?

Meanwhile, the *havermelkelite* still vote progressively and read left-leaning newspapers (digitally, of course, but on paper at the weekends – another subtle identity signal). But their lives are full of contradictions: they take part in climate protests but overwinter in Cape Town, eat healthily during the week but do designer drugs on the weekend.

This has made them a bit of a punchline, especially outside the Randstad, the narrow stretch of land home to the country's four biggest cities. Provincials see them as urban snobs who rarely venture beyond Amsterdam's ring road, except for status-elevating trips outside of the country. The *havermelkelite* gladly join in on taking the mickey out of each other – Kooyman never lacks for new inspiration.

Substituting Security

Of course, on a more serious note, they might project a life of abundance, yet they struggle with sky-high rents just the same. Prices in Amsterdam have risen faster than in most European cities, with even dual-income households now struggling to buy.

So they spend on what they can: experiences. A €6 oat-milk matcha is affordable in a way a €600,000 two-bedroom flat will never be. A weekend retreat offers just enough relaxation to be able to keep up with their demanding jobs in tech or the creative industry. Food, fashion and travel have become the stages where their identity plays out, substitutes for a security that, due to global crises, seem to be out of reach for this generation.

As for the city, what happens when unchecked gentrification pushes out the very people who gave Amsterdam its edge? The future will tell, but of course, trends are fleeting – and at some point the *havermelkelite* will give way to another tribe of tastemakers. Perhaps quite soon...apparently, whole milk is making a comeback. From swamp settlement to progressive metropolis, Amsterdam has reinvented itself countless times in its 750 years. One constant remains: change.

Oat-milk matcha

IRYNA POSPIKH/SHUTTERSTOCK

THE VOC REASSESSED

Global pioneers, 'Golden Age' heroes or evil colonialists?
By Mark Elliott

DURING THE EARLY 17th century, Amsterdam went from marshy backwater to global trade entrepot with incredible speed. This era of stunning growth, long known as the Dutch 'Golden Age', was powered by innovations in financing global trade networks led by the Vereenigde Oostindische Compagnie (VOC; Dutch East India Company), which dominated the Asian markets for almost 200 years. Inevitably many an Amsterdam museum includes elements related to the legacy of the VOC and other major trading companies. However, such coverage is steadily changing from celebration to apology, as awareness grows of the darker sides of the nation's colonial history, including significant involvement in the slave trade – for which the Dutch king made an official apology in 2023. There's now a serious question as to whether it's appropriate to call the era a 'Golden Age' at all.

Birth of the VOC

Founded in 1602, the VOC's meteoric rise was intimately interwoven with that of Amsterdam itself. Indeed, in *Amsterdam: A History of the World's Most Liberal City* (2013) historian Russell Shorto claims that 'it's by no means a stretch to say that the VOC remade the world'. Though a private corporation, within a few years it projected as much power as a nation

state with its own army and colonial bureaucrats which – most notably – came to administer the city of Batavia (today's Jakarta) and much of what's now Indonesia. The particular innovation that stoked the company's initial expansion was financial: the VOC pioneered re-sellable share certificates, unleashing the first modern securities market. Money poured in, allowing the Dutch to quickly eclipse the Portuguese in the 'spice islands' of the Moluccas (now the Maluku provinces of Indonesia) in the highly profitable pepper and clove businesses. As share prices soared, future funding ballooned and Amsterdam became a financial centre as well as one of the world's most multicultural and liberal cities. At least, that's a positive reading of the history.

Underbelly of Cruelty

But of course the VOC was not only sending out neutral merchant fleets. It was also setting up trading posts, which developed into colonial settlements complete with military and judicial powers. Corruption and abuse was common, and trade deals could be forced at the barrel of a musket. Most infamously in the Banda Islands, the VOC 'governor-general' Jan Pieterszoon Coen essentially instigated the first modern genocide – depopulating the islands and killing or enslaving a large percentage

273

of the islanders in 1621 after they refused to produce mace and nutmeg at prices that suited the VOC. For centuries such horrors were largely air-brushed from Dutch history. When the VOC went bankrupt in 1799, its main overseas territories passed to the Dutch state: they would remain Dutch colonies right up until the Japanese occupation of WWII and Indonesian independence in 1947.

Slightly younger and arguably even more rapacious than the VOC was the Geoctrooieerde Westindische Compagnie (GWC; Dutch West India Company; 1621–1792). It's best known for building a fort on the then-obscure North American island of Manhattan. However, it played a similar role to the VOC in the western hemisphere and its involvement in the slave trade was far more pronounced. Some of its colonies (Suriname, Aruba etc) retain close Dutch links to this day. It's not by chance that you find so many Indonesian and Surinamese restaurants in Amsterdam.

Reevaluation & 21st-Century Framing for Visitors

In the fabulous Rijksmuseum (p148), gallery 2.9 is full of paintings celebrating the sailing expeditions of the Dutch 'Golden Age'. Above the door is *View of Ambon* c 1617, showing the major Indonesian spice island that the VOC seized in 1605. The associated text says that the company 'mounted ruthless "punitive expeditions" to counter the sale of cloves to its rivals'. That's a considerable understatement. In fact, to ensure its monopoly, the VOC committed the torture and murder campaign now known as the Ambonya massacre, which reverberated for decades afterwards.

Many other Amsterdam museums take a far more stridently critical approach to the VOC's colonial legacy. The Scheepvaartmuseum (National Maritime Museum; p85) leads the charge questioning whether these days, it would be at all appropriate to build a full-size reconstruction of a VOC tall-ship as happened in 1990. Moored behind the museum, the eye-catching wooden vessel is a major draw but now comes with ample signage addressing issues of slavery and colonial contexts, and it no longer flies the VOC flag. The museum's hardest-hitting exhibition is the very self-critical *Shadows on the Atlantic,* looking at the human suffering upon which colonial wealth was actually built and the realities of slavery having dislocated so many lives in creating the Dutch possessions in the Caribbean and South America.

The Verzetsmuseum (Dutch Resistance Museum; p78) primarily focuses on Dutch suffering and responses during WWII, but it now incorporates a very significant section looking at the wartime context in Indonesia, Suriname and the Dutch Caribbean. This is addressed with carefully nuanced personal stories and we learn some terrible statistics: that Indonesia suffered over 2 million victims of wartime and post-war famine, and 12,000 were executed by the Japanese.

VOC's Restored Boardroom: Should it be Seen?

Particularly intriguing is Oost Indische Huis itself, the VOC's 1606 former headquarters, at which the very first share transactions were validated. It is now part of Amsterdam University's faculty but visitors are welcome to look inside and peep inside the *bewindhebberszaal,* the VOC's former boardroom. This was reconstructed in all its period grandeur in 1997. However, in 2022 the university had second thoughts, recoiling from the apparent expression of pride in power and wealth that the room exudes while the 'suffering of exploited, enslaved Asians is invisible'. However, after closing it for a while, the room reopened as a part of a public programme of *Decolonial Dialogues.* A video narrative now includes the voices of descendants of those exploited, calling for more visitors to be given a fuller appreciation of the building's true historical implications...a common thread that is developing traction more widely as Amsterdam grapples more than ever with the demons of its past.

VOC tall-ship replica of *Amsterdam* at Het Scheepvaartmuseum (p85)
SUNFREEZ/SHUTTERSTOCK

INDEX

INDEX

N–T

279

Witness millions of bulbs burst into bloom at Keukenhof (p235) in spring.

Sarphatipark (p173) is a lush sanctuary of lawns, statues and fountains.

Mapping data sources:
© Lonely Planet
© OpenStreetMap http://openstreetmap.org/copyright

THIS BOOK

The 14th edition of Lonely Planet's *Amsterdam* guidebook was written and researched by Catherine Le Nevez, Mark Elliott and Barbara Woolsey. The previous edition was written and researched by Catherine, Barbara and Kate Morgan.

This guidebook was produced by the following:

Destination Editor
Daniel Bolger

Production Editor
Sasha Drew

Image Researcher
Jo-anne Riddell

Cartographer
Jennifer Johnston

Coordinating Editor
Anita Isalska

Assisting Editors
Charlotte Orr, Gabbi Stefanos

Cover Researcher
Beatriz Atunes

Thanks Ronan Abayawickrema, Sandie Kestell, Jenna Myers, Darren O'Connell

Paper in this book is certified against the Forest Stewardship Council™ standards. FSC™ promotes environmentally responsible, socially beneficial and economically viable management of the world's forests.

Published by Lonely Planet Global Limited
CRN 554153
14th edition – Jun 2026
ISBN 978 1 83758 428 4
© Lonely Planet 2026 Photographs © as indicated 2026
10 9 8 7 6 5 4 3 2 1
Printed in China